Fighting the Greater Jihad

NEW AFRICAN HISTORIES SERIES

Series editors: Jean Allman and Allen Isaacman

David William Cohen and E. S. Atieno Odhiambo, *The Risks of Knowledge: Investigations into the Death of the Hon. Minister John Robert Ouko in Kenya, 1990*

Belinda Bozzoli, *Theatres of Struggle and the End of Apartheid*

Gary Kynoch, *We Are Fighting the World: A History of Marashea Gangs in South Africa, 1947–1999*

Stephanie Newell, *The Forger's Tale: The Search for Odeziaku*

Jacob A. Tropp, *Natures of Colonial Change: Environmental Relations in the Making of the Transkei*

Jan Bender Shetler, *Imagining Serengeti: A History of Landscape Memory in Tanzania from Earliest Times to the Present*

Cheikh Anta Babou, *Fighting the Greater Jihad: Amadu Bamba and the Founding of the Muridiyya in Senegal, 1853–1913*

Fighting the Greater Jihad

Amadu Bamba and the Founding of the Muridiyya of Senegal, 1853–1913

∽

Cheikh Anta Babou

OHIO UNIVERSITY PRESS
ATHENS

Ohio University Press, Athens, Ohio 45701
www.ohio.edu/oupress
© 2007 by Ohio University Press

Printed in the United States of America
All rights reserved

Ohio University Press books are printed on acid-free paper ∞ ™

14 13 12 11 10 09 08 07   5 4 3 2 1

An earlier version of one section of chapter 4 appeared as "Educating the Murid: Theory and Practices of Education in Amadu Bamba's Thought," *Journal of Religion in Africa* 33, no. 3 (2003): 310–27. An earlier version of chapter 7 appeared as "Contesting Space, Shaping Places: Making Room for the Muridiyya in Colonial Senegal, 1912–1945," *Journal of African History* 46, no. 3 (2005): 405–26.

Library of Congress Cataloging-in-Publication Data

Babou, Cheikh Anta Mbacké.
 Fighting the greater jihad : Amadu Bamba and the founding of the Muridiyya of Senegal, 1853–1913 / Cheikh Anta Babou.
   p. cm.
 Includes bibliographical references and index.
 ISBN-13: 978-0-8214-1765-2 (hc : alk. paper)
 ISBN-10: 0-8214-1765-7 (hc : alk. paper)
 ISBN-13: 978-0-8214-1766-9 (pb : alk. paper)
 ISBN-10: 0-8214-1766-5 (pb : alk. paper)
 1. Bamba, Ahmadu, 1852–1927. 2. Muridiyah—Senegal—Biography. 3. Islam and politics—Senegal—History. 4. Islamic sects—Senegal. I. Title.
 BP80.B238B33 2007
 297.4'8—dc22

2007023162

Contents

List of Illustrations		vii
Preface		ix
Abbreviations		xi
Note on Orthography		xiii
Introduction		1
Chapter 1	Islam, Society, and Power in the Wolof States	20
Chapter 2	The Mbakke: The Foundations of Family Traditions	33
Chapter 3	The Emergence of Amadu Bamba, 1853–95	51
Chapter 4	The Founding of the Muridiyya	77
Chapter 5	Murid Conflict with the French Colonial Administration, 1889–1902	115
Chapter 6	Slow Path toward Accommodation I *The Time of Rapprochement*	141
Chapter 7	Slow Path toward Accommodation II *Making Murid Space in Colonial Bawol*	162
Conclusion		175
Appendix 1	*Ijaaza* Delivered to Momar A. Sali by Samba Tukuloor Ka	185
Appendix 2	Sharifian Genealogy of Amadu Bamba from His Mother's Side	187

Appendix 3	Amadu Bamba's Sons and Daughters and Their Mothers	189
Appendix 4	List of the Transmitters of the *Qadiriyya wird* Whom Amadu Praises in His Poem "Silsilat ul Qadiriyya"	191

Notes	193
Bibliography	263
Index	285

Illustrations

MAP

Important places in Amadu Bamba's life   xiv

FIGURES

2.1	Maaram's sons and daughters	35
2.2	The Mbakke and Sy families	37
2.3	The Mbakke and Jakhate families	38
2.4	Momar Anta Sali's sons and their mothers	46
3.1	Amadu Bamba's paternal and maternal lineages	53

PLATES

Following page 140

1. Amadu Bamba's arrival in the port of Dakar on his return from exile in Gabon
2. Amadu Bamba teaching disciples in front of his house
3. The trial of Amadu Bamba
4. Homecoming celebration in Daaru Salaam
5. Sokhna Njakhat Sylla, a wife of Amadu Bamba
6. Cell in the basement of the governor-general's palace where Amadu Bamba was kept in custody while awaiting trial
7. Mausoleum of Jaara Buso, Amadu Bamba's mother, in Porokhaan
8. Gigis tree in Porokhaan where Amadu Bamba's father, Momar Anta Sali, taught his disciples

9. Mosque of Diourbel
10. Mosque of Tuubaa
11. Murid businesses in "Little Senegal," Harlem, New York City
12. Murids marching during the annual celebration of Amadu Bamba Day (July 28) in New York City
13. The late Cheikh Murtala Mbakke, youngest son of Amadu Bamba, and Mayor David Dinkins at New York City Hall
14. William Ponty, governor-general of French West Africa (1908–15)
15. Amadu Bamba
16. One of the four small minarets of the great mosque of Tuubaa
17. The well of mercy, dug at the instruction of Amadu Bamba in Tuubaa
18. *Mihrab*, or prayer niche, of the mosque of Tuubaa

Preface

This book concerns the genesis and development of the Muridiyya of Senegal, and especially the role of education in its founding. Previous works have shed light on the political and economic dimensions of the Murid *tariqa*, and scholars have expounded on its remarkable capacity to adapt Islam to the local cultural context. This research draws on the abundant but largely untapped Murid internal oral, written, and iconographic sources, as well as archival data, to offer a comprehensive reconstruction of the history of the Muridiyya that pays special attention to the impact of the often overlooked Murid sheikhs' and disciples' voices. The book focuses on the early years of the tariqa's founding, but the discussion of issues such as ethics, educational practices, sacred space, and memory provides clues for understanding the unusual ability of the Murid order to maintain cohesion and continuity across space and time.

I wish to acknowledge the assistance and support provided by several institutions. A fellowship from the Rockefeller Foundation's African Dissertation Internship Awards funded one year of field and archival research in Senegal. A merit fellowship from the College of Arts and Letters at Michigan State University made possible a semester of leave devoted to writing. I have benefited from the support of the West African Research Center in Dakar, which graciously offered office and computer facilities during my fieldwork in Senegal. I am also grateful to Saliou Mbaye, Mamadou Ndiaye, Babacar Ndiaye and all of the staff of the National Archives in Senegal. For their help, I would like to thank Al Hajj Mbakke, former head of the library Sheikh ul Khadim in Tuubaa; Serigne Mustafa Jatara, his successor; and their assistants. Gora Dia and his colleagues at the library of Institut Fondamental d'Afrique Noire (IFAN) have aided greatly. I thank Jean Pierre Diouf and Abou Moussa Ndongo at the documentation center of the Council for the Development of Social Science Research in Africa (CODESRIA) for their assistance.

I am particularly grateful to my hosts, colleagues, and informants in Senegal. My friends Aida and Grégoire Lawson welcomed me into their beautiful house and made my stays in Dakar both pleasant and fruitful. I thank Ibrahima Thioub and Charles Becker for sharing references and useful comments on my work. I have also benefited from the support of numerous Murid sheikhs, disciples, and teachers who opened their private libraries to me and graciously gave their time to respond to my questions. Omitting the names of some of them here does not in any way diminish my gratitude to them. I particularly wish to thank Afia Niang, Serigne Modu Maamun Niang, my late mentor, Serigne Mbakke Astu, the late Sawru Mbay, Sheikh Bass Anta Niang Mbakke, the late Sheikh Mustafa Ceytu, Mustapha Ley, Mustafa Njaate Mbakke, Sheikh Maam Balla Mbakke, the late Sheikh Khadime Mbakke, and Al Hajj Jakhate. My childhood friend Ahmadu Fall has long followed my work and has been a constant support in the pursuit of my research on the Muridiyya.

Several colleagues have read and commented on earlier drafts, in whole or in part. I would like to give special recognition to my friend and mentor, David Robinson, whose unwavering backing and encouragement have been a constant source of inspiration. I have benefited greatly from the close reading and suggestions of Ellen Foley, Steve Feierman, Louis Brenner, Allen Roberts, Lee Cassanelli, and Jonathan Steinberg. I would also like to thank Boubacar Barry, Khadim Mbakke, and Marty Klein for discussions and feedback. These colleagues' observations and suggestions have immensely contributed to the quality of this work.

I must also express my thanks to the two anonymous external reviewers and to Jean Allman and Allen Isaacman, editors of the New African Histories series, for their insightful suggestions. The recommendations of Gill Berchowitz, my principal editor at Ohio University Press, John Morris, my project editor, and Joan Sherman, who copyedited the manuscript, have considerably enhanced the value of this work.

My warmest gratitude belongs to my wife, Faatim Joob, and to Jaara. I am eternally indebted to them for their love and support. Just as I was putting the last touches on this work, Faatim and I were graced with a baby boy, Bamba Idrissa Babou. Bamba's joyful companionship has made the task of finishing this book most enjoyable.

Cheikh Anta Babou
Philadelphia, January 2007

Abbreviations

ANFOM	Archives Nationales de la France Section Outre-Mer (French National Archives [Overseas Section])
ANS	Archives Nationales du Sénégal (National Archives of Senegal)
AOF	Afrique Occidentale Française (French West Africa)
BCAF/RC	*Bulletin du Comité d'Études Françaises/Renseignements Coloniaux*
BCEHSAOF	*Bulletin des Comités des Études Historiques and Scientifiques de l'Afrique Occidentale Française*
BIFAN	*Bulletin de l'Institut Fondamental d'Afrique Noire*
CEA	*Cahiers d'Études Africaines*
CNRS	Centre National de Recherches Scientifiques, Paris
CRA	Centre de Recherches Africaines, Paris
DEA	Diplôme d'Étude Approfondie
DOSSAB	Dossier Amadou Bamba
EHESS	École des Hautes Études en Sciences Sociales
IBLA	Institut des Belles Lettres Arabes
IJAHS	*International Journal of African Historical Studies*
JAH	*Journal of African History*
JRA	*Journal of Religion in Africa*
ORSTOM	Organisation pour la Recherche Scientifique et Technique Outre-Mer, now Institut pour la Recherche et le Développement (IRD)
UCAD	Université Cheikh Anta Diop de Dakar

Note on Orthography

This book makes extensive reference to written documents and oral testimonies in several languages, most notably Wolof, French, and Arabic. I have opted for a simplified orthography in transcribing foreign languages into English. I omit all diacritics except in book and article titles and in French words, and I use the double vowel to express the elongated Arabic and Wolof sounds. I also have chosen not to adopt special symbols for consonants that have no equivalents in roman script, such as the *ng* and *gn* in Wolof. I use the consonant *j* to render the Wolof sound *dj* and the consonant *c* to render the sound *thie*, but I retain *kh* as in *khidma* and *q* as in *qadi*. Plurals of nouns are marked by adding *s* to the singular. I have kept Wolofized Arab words in their Wolof spelling, unless in titles of Arabic books or names of Arabs and Mauritanians. Proper names of African actors and places, except for authors of widely known published works, are spelled following the preceding rules.

Important places in Amadu Bamba's life (map made with the the technical contribution of Eric Ross)

Introduction

IN 1913, the influential French administrator and specialist of Islam Paul Marty delivered his assessment of the Muridiyya to the colonial administration of Senegal. He wrote: "It [the Muridiyya] subsists today without growing by the sole virtue of the presence and charisma of its founder. But Amadou Bamba is now sixty years old and his death from natural or violent causes could occur any time.... It is highly probable that [his] demise will lead to the disintegration of the Murid order."[1]

Marty's statement carried significant weight. Born in the village of Boufarik in the district of Algiers, he had garnered much experience about what the French viewed as "real" Islam, working as a colonial interpreter in his native land of Algeria, in Morocco, and in Tunisia.[2] He arrived in West Africa in 1912 as an expert to fill an important slot as head of the Office of Muslim Affairs in the administration of Governor-General William Ponty. He spoke Arabic, he knew Islam, and over his career he authored numerous articles and books that established the colonial orthodoxy about Islamic beliefs and politics in sub-Saharan Africa. He popularized the concept of "Islam noir," which became central to the orientalist construction of the identities of sub-Saharan Muslims.[3]

Today, some eight decades after Amadu Bamba's death in 1927, the population of Murids in and outside Senegal is estimated at roughly 4 million.[4] The annual pilgrimage (*maggal*) to his tomb in Tuubaa, the holy city of the Murids, attracts hundreds of thousands of people and constitutes one of the largest religious gatherings in the world.[5] In fact, it has recently been featured in the pages of the *New York Times* and on the BBC Web site.[6]

History has clearly proven Marty wrong. But the ability of the Muridiyya to maintain cohesion and continuity across space and time is unusual for this type of organization. *Tariqas* (Muslim mystical orders) are notoriously fissiparous, and they are often prone to fragmentation, especially after the death of the founder.[7] The continuing relevance of the Muridiyya despite the changing economic, political, and social circumstances in Senegal remains intriguing to scholars of Islam.[8] The history and contemporary development of the Muridiyya raise the question of how an organization founded on the values of communality, religious spirituality, and solidarity, primarily associated with "traditional ways of life," was able to adapt and even prosper in the modern era, shaped by individualism, rationalism, and secularity. Murid resilience is even more intriguing because the structural factors that Western scholars believed to have contributed to the emergence of the tariqa (colonization and peanut cultivation) were no longer operative during the order's expansion in more recent times.

In this study, I do not pretend to offer a definitive answer to the questions raised by the atypical trajectory of Murid history. Rather, my intent is to open new avenues for our understanding of the historical dynamics of the Muridiyya by locating the sources of its longevity, at least partly, in the long-range vision of its founder. I aim to provide a view of the tariqa from within, during a critical period of its founding, by asking new questions about the Murids' religiosity and conception of education, by examining their relations with African chiefs and French colonial administrators, and by rendering Murid voices more audible through the exploration of sources hitherto inaccessible to scholars of the organization. I am particularly interested in investigating the persona and role of Amadu Bamba, the founder of the Murid order. It is my contention that his thought, practices, and teachings and the memories, whether real or imagined, of his life are among the principal contributing factors to the cohesion and continuity of the tariqa.

The literature on the Muridiyya is rich by the standards of African history. By the late 1970s, when the study of Islam in sub-Saharan Africa (outside northern Nigeria) was still in its infancy, substantial works were already devoted to the organization.[9] However, although the scholarship on the Muridiyya has increased considerably, particularly since the mid-1980s, this work has mostly focused on the political and economic dimensions of the organization. Three major trends can be discerned in the literature on the Murids.

Some scholars have concerned themselves with explaining the role of the Muridiyya as an instrument used by the Wolof ethnic group (the majority of the Senegalese population) to adapt to French colonial rule.[10] These same scholars also have strived to demonstrate how, in the postcolonial era, the Murid order continued to perform its political function by helping foster a "social contract" that mitigated the new rulers' lack of legitimacy in the eyes of rural masses and provided stability to the state.[11] Under this contract, the Murid leaders, among other Muslim political brokers, assured the loyalty of the citizens and in return received recognition and material support from the state.

A second trend has concentrated on the economy and particularly on Murid contributions to the expansion of the colonial cash crop of peanuts. Jean Copans gave his book on the Muridiyya the suggestive title *Les marabouts de l'arachide* (Marabouts of Peanuts), before recognizing, in the late 1980s, the "death" of the Murid peanut economy. Other scholars looked at the ways in which the Murid work ethic and values helped rural disciples shift from agriculture to trading and international migration.[12] For these authors, the Muridiyya was an interesting topic of scholarly investigation insofar as it provided the ideological basis and cultural flexibility that allowed Senegal's integration into the world market economy and the adjustment of disciples to varying socioeconomic situations.

The religious dimension of the Muridiyya has attracted some scholarly interest, especially among Senegalese and French specialists of Islam. These scholars have examined some of Amadu Bamba's writings to verify the orthodoxy or heterodoxy of Murid beliefs and the ability of the Muridiyya to adapt Islamic concepts and values to the local cultures.[13]

Despite the relatively abundant body of literature on the Muridiyya, there is a real dearth of historical scholarship on Amadu Bamba and the early formation of the Murid tariqa. The broad outlines of Bamba's life and of the development of the Muridiyya are fairly well known. But the observation made by Donal Cruise O'Brien in the early 1970s that little was known about the thinking, actions, and role of the founder of the Muridiyya is still largely valid.[14] One might add that most of what is known has been reconstructed from colonial sources and focuses on the post-1912 era, which is considered a period of accommodation or intense collaboration between the Muridiyya and the French administration of Senegal.[15]

Scholarly interpretations of the Muridiyya reflect a general trend that, until recently, has marked the literature on religion in general and on religion in the former European colonies in South Asia and Africa in particular. One defining characteristic of this trend is the importance ascribed to economic and political aspirations spurred by colonization as the major causative and explanatory factors of religious social movements. Referring to the case of Islam in Bengal, Richard Eaton, for example, deplored the tendency among scholars to explain religious change as simply a cultural dimension of political or economic transformation.[16] In an important article on traditional and Christian religious organizations in Africa in the colonial and postcolonial eras, Terence Ranger observed that "all religious movements . . . have been treated as new and as explicable in terms of special pressures and transformations of colonialism."[17]

The same can be said about the scholarship on Muslim social movements. With the exception of a small number of writers, students of Islam in Africa have been fascinated by jihad, resistance, collaboration, and Muslim efforts at state building and have not paid as much attention to the religious thought and motivations of the Muslim leaders and their followers.[18] More often than not, religion has been conceived as a dependent variable subordinated to the perceived political and economic ambitions of the Muslim leadership at particular moments in time. Although students of other religions have recognized the crucial influence of "cultural and psychological tensions" in the emergence of religious movements,[19] most scholars of Islam in colonial Africa continue to emphasize the centrality of political antagonism.

This book offers a different approach. Without neglecting the role of politics and the economy, it emphasizes the cultural and the religious. It proposes an interpretation of the Murid tariqa from the perspective of the Murids. Rather than seeing the Muridiyya as simply a response to the stimuli of external structural factors (colonization, peanut production, the postcolonial state), I view its emergence as part of the internal dynamics of the expansion of Islam in Senegal in the nineteenth century. I underscore the motivations of Amadu Bamba and his earliest followers and stress the centrality of the theme of education in the founding and development of the order. By emphasizing Murid educational practices and values as enduring goals and strategies with far-reaching influence, this study departs from the existing literature even as it seeks to renew and broaden scholarly knowledge of the history and development of the Muridiyya.

Such an approach requires a serious examination of Murid religious beliefs and spirituality. Islam is no longer perceived as a mere interstitial force whose significance is transitory and secondary in the history of the Muridiyya but rather as a central element. Following Louis Brenner, I consider that "the emergence of *turuuq* [plural of *tariqa*] in West Africa . . . was not an accident but the result of conscious decisions by Sufi leaders who saw in them a potential not only for religious change, but also for social and political transformation."[20] Brenner's view, indeed, resonated well with that of Amadu Bamba, who conceived of the Muridiyya as a major weapon in the *jihad al-akbar* (greater jihad) he waged against the detrimental political and social forces of his time. This greater jihad was the jihad of *nafs* (the ego or carnal soul), which aimed at using *tarbiyya* (the education of the soul) as a tool to instill Islamic values and shield people against the corrupting effects of negative traditional and French influences. In a much-quoted verse, Bamba wrote, "The warrior in the path of God is not who takes his enemies' life, but the one who combats his nafs to achieve spiritual perfection."[21]

UNDERSTANDING ISLAMIC MYSTICISM IN AFRICA: SUFISM, *MARABOUT,* AND *BARAKA*

Sufism

Amadu Bamba's rejection of violence and his espousal of mystical means to confront adversity are not unusual among followers of Sufism or Islamic mysticism. To be sure, Sufi beliefs do not always translate to quietism and pacifism. As shown by Richard Eaton in his study of the Sufis of Bijapur and the examples of the West African Sufi jihadists Uthman dan Fodio and Al-Hajj Umar Tal, Sufism can also lead to militancy.[22] But Sufis have always considered that keeping a safe distance from rulers and politics is the best way to maintain moral and spiritual integrity. It was, in effect, dissatisfaction with the extravagant use of wealth and power by the Ummayad and Abbasid dynasties, in contradiction to the stern and sober rule of the Prophet Muhammad and the Four Rightly Guided Caliphs, that fueled the development of Sufism in the first four centuries of Islam.

Sufism may be defined as a system of thought and a method for understanding and learning to control the nafs. This method is based on teachings and practices developed by generations of Sufi thinkers and practitioners.[23] The Sufi system is shaped by actions and behaviors that aim at freeing the human body from the grip of worldly preoccupations in order to gradually lift the spirit toward the neighborhood of God's kingdom; the ultimate goal is to become a *wali Allah* (friend of God).

Most studies of Sufism deal with philosophical issues and hermeneutics and do not offer an approach that examines the actual development of Sufi organizations. J. S. Trimingham's *The Sufi Orders in Islam,* although somewhat dated, is still the most comprehensive study of the historical development of institutional Sufism.[24] Trimingham distinguished three phases in the development of Sufism as an institution: the *khanaqah* (place for Sufi teaching), *tariqa,* and *taifa* stages.

The first, or khanaqah, stage of Sufism, which spanned the period between the eighth and twelfth centuries, witnessed the flourishing of ideas and an exceptional intellectual creativity and productivity among Sufi thinkers. It was also a period of loose and rather unstructured social organization, in which masters and disciples mingled in an informal setting without formal bonds between them. Sufi thought formed an evolving but undifferentiated body of knowledge.

In the tariqa stage, which started around the thirteenth century and ended in the fifteenth, the Sufi movement became further institutionalized. Disciples or aspirants organized themselves in different mystical orders, or tariqas, each shaped by a specific set of structured spiritual exercises and led by sheikhs linked through saintly lineages, or *silsilas*. These lineages connected Sufi masters belonging to the same school of thought and sharing the same method of training and could be traced back to the ultimate founders. Thus, the silsila of the Qadiriyya order is traced back to its founder, Abd al-Qadir al-Jilani (d. 1166); the Shadiliyya order to Abu Hassan al-Shadili (1196–1258); and the Tijaniyya order to Muhammad al-Tijani (1738–1815).

The *wird* and *dhikr* became basic communal practices of Sufi orders. Wirds are excerpts from the Quran and special prayers communicated mystically to the founder of a Sufi order by the Prophet Muhammad. The *dhikr* is the continuous remembrance of God through the recitation of His names (Allah has ninety-nine names, some of which are secret and confer special spiritual power). The *khalwa*, or spiritual retreat, and the *fikr*, or meditation on God's works, are other techniques used by Sufis to purify the spirit and soul.

In the final, or taifa, stage, from the fifteenth century onward, the authority of the sheikh was further emphasized, but its nature was fundamentally transformed. The spiritual power, or *baraka*,[25] of the master now took precedence over his mastery of the Islamic sciences and Sufi mysticism that was central during the two previous stages of khanaqah and tariqa. Moreover, the belief that baraka was hereditary put blood over merit as the principal criterion for the succession of a sheikh. Spiritual and biological genealogies became entangled, giving birth to powerful saintly dynasties that claimed special spiritual status based on descent. The taifa stage inaugurated a shift of Sufism from a mystical movement confined to a selected elite to a devotional movement appealing to the larger populace.[26] Trimingham aptly summed up this transformation when he observed, "If we characterize the first stage [khanaqah] as affecting the individual, as surrender to God, and the second [tariqa] as surrender to a rule, then this stage [taifa] may be described as surrender to a person."[27]

Trimingham's model is useful in understanding the changes that affected the Sufi movement over time, but its artificial tertiary configuration is less helpful in grasping the complexity, continuity, and fluidity of Sufi beliefs and practices. If one had to follow Trimingham's lead, it would appear that the role of the Sufi master became important only during the tariqa stage that started around the thirteenth century, whereas already in the ninth century, Sahl al-Tustari (818–96) was stressing the need to surrender to the sheikh like a cadaver to the mortician. In addition, an application of Trimingham's chronology to sub-Saharan Africa, where Sufism entered in the sixteenth century, would suggest that this part of the world only experienced the taifa phase. But the cult of saints, which is the most salient characteristic of this stage in the development of Sufism, did not become significant in sub-Saharan Africa until the eighteenth century.[28] Moreover, most leaders of Sufi orders in sub-Saharan Africa were also thinkers and sages who did not have the intellectual credentials of their counterparts in Muslim Spain and the Middle East but made important contributions to the interpretation and dissemination of Sufi ideas, like masters of the khanaqah and tariqa stages.[29] This was the case with the Kunta of Timbuktu, the Moorish Sufi masters, Uthman dan Fodio, and al-Hajj Umar Tal, who was one of the major theoreticians of the Tijani doctrine.[30] More recently, Amadu Bamba and Malick Sy, to refer to the case of Senegal, are known for their baraka but also for their writings and mystical orientation.[31] It seems to me that in sub-Saharan Africa, particularly in the case of the Muridiyya and Tijaniyya of Senegal, characteristics typical of Trimingham's three stages are found simultaneously in Sufi movements. Sufi masters are at once thinkers, masters, and baraka-laden sheikhs. In fact, in most places where Sufism exits today, it continues to display elements consistent with the three stages.

Marabout

In the taifa stage, Trimingham particularly insisted on the role of baraka and sainthood. His description of the sheikh taifa echoes the ubiquitous marabout of French orientalist literature. The term *marabout* is a francophone corruption of the Arabic word *murabit* (from the Arabic words *rabata*, meaning "to tie," and *ribat*, a border fort and also a Sufi monastery or lodge in North Africa). This term was used in Algeria to designate a rural holy man.[32] In the context of Senegal, *marabout* has become the substitute for *waliyu*, *serigne*, *cerno*, and *yaaram*, used in the local Sufi lexicon and languages to refer to saints and men of religion.

According to French orientalists, the marabout was the key figure in the development of popular Islam in North and sub-Saharan Africa. Paul Marty opened the first chapter of his book on Islam in Senegal with this statement: "The black Muslims of Senegal align themselves, without exception, behind the banner of marabouts. They do not conceive of Islam outside the affiliation to a Sufi order, or more exactly, without allegiance to a 'serigne' or 'Tierno.'"³³ Closely associated with rural life, the marabout performed important religious and social functions. Superficially educated, he was seen as "human fetish," miracle worker, intercessor, and teacher, often engaged in heterodox magical practices to satisfy the superstitions and spiritual needs of his illiterate clients. Socially, he mediated conflicts and used his prayers and most feared curse to protect his flock from the abuses of rulers.

Vincent Cornell convincingly exposed the political agenda behind the French paradigm of maraboutism. As he observed, French colonial writers (he specifically referred to the work of Alfred Bel in Morocco, but his observations were also valid for most French writers of the colonial era) created an artificial dichotomy between the so-called natural religious syncretism of the Berbers, who were said to be prone to beliefs in miracles, sainthood, and marabouts, and the supposedly "sober, authoritarian, and culturally alien ethos of classical Islam of the Arabs."³⁴ This scholarship was produced at a time when French colonial officials were most concerned with countering the influence of Islamic reformists in Algeria, and it served well the policy of divide and rule. Ironically, in sub-Saharan Africa, as implied in Marty's statement referred to earlier, it was the "Berbers" who became the uncompromising holders of sober Islamic orthodoxy, whereas their black neighbors to the south inherited the stereotype of syncretism and superstition.

Baraka

When discussing the role of marabouts in the development of Islam in Senegal, scholars especially underscore the importance of the concept of baraka (*barke* or *barka* in local Senegalese parlance). The word *baraka* is found in the Quran but only in its plural form (*barakat*). Its meaning runs the gamut from "divine gift of grace," "blessing," or "beneficient force" to "magic" or "supernatural power." ³⁵ Although people often differ about the meaning of the word, there is a consensus that baraka is a power that emanates from God, which He confers as He wishes but often on uncommonly pious people, on the family of the Prophet Muhammad, and on his words enshrined in the Quran. Although Allah is recognized as the ultimate source and giver of baraka, it is also accepted that there are special circumstances that can single a person out as its recipient. Exceptional learning, piety, and descent from certain families reputed for their integrity and moral qualities are sometimes signs for election. Therefore, unlike the charismatic authority of Weberian sociology, baraka has a history, and the wali Allah may be accorded some agency in the achievement of sainthood.³⁶ In the Senegalese context, the role of the mother is particularly important. Amadu Bamba's mother, Maam Jaara Buso, for example, receives much of the credit for her son's election as a saint. She is portrayed in the hagiographic literature as an erudite Muslim woman and an exemplary wife and mother, endowed with much spiritual power.[37] This power continued to be effective even after her death, when she mystically intervened many times to succor and reassure her son, then under French custody. Her tomb in the village of Porokhaan in east-central Senegal is the object of a cult of men and women (but mostly women) whose devotion culminates each year in the only pilgrimage dedicated to a female Muslim saint in Senegal.[38]

Human beings who are blessed with baraka also have the power of transmitting it through their bodily fluids (blood, sweat, saliva), their feelings and speech, their clothes, anything they are in contact with, and even their tombs after they are dead. As Islam and particularly Sufi beliefs expanded, baraka became central in the social construction of holiness, and one of the most visible manifestations of baraka, although not a necessary one, was the ability to work miracles, or *karamas*.[39] But Sufis differentiate between the karamas of the saints and the *Mudjizas* of the prophets. Both are considered miracles, understood as the suspension of the natural order of things through divine intervention, but they are of different natures. The miracles of the prophets are considered necessary to convince the skeptics and doubters of the truth and divine origin of their messages, whereas the karamas of the saints are contingent and meant to confirm the validity of prophecy. In other words, the *wilaaya* (sainthood) of the saints, which is manifested in their ability to perform miracles, proceeds from their role as inheritors of the prophetic mission.[40] Amadu Bamba discussed the relations between sainthood, prophecy, and miracles in his major work, *Massalik Al-Jinan* (Paths to Paradise). He observed that like prophets, saints may also work miracles, for they are successors of the prophets. The saints are proofs of the authenticity and eternal truth of the prophetic message. Prophets are perfect and impeccable, whereas saints are protected and honored by God.[41]

THE QUESTION OF SOURCES: ORAL TRADITION AND HAGIOGRAPHY

Oral Tradition and Murid History

Most Murid writers and bearers of oral traditions strive to make the case for Amadu Bamba's sainthood and closeness to God. They are members of a community of believers for whom God's intervention in human history is a matter of faith. At the same time, these sources are critical in reconstructing a history of the Muridiyya from within, as I endeavor to do in this book. The use of previously untapped Murid sources in several languages (Arabic, Wolof, and French) and different media (oral, written, and iconographic) has been instrumental in my own work.[42]

Since the publication of Jan Vansina's *Oral Tradition* (in 1965), which dealt both with oral history (the remembered recent past) and oral tradition (orally transmitted history over generations), scholars have produced more extensive guides for the collection and interpretation of oral data. They have recognized the special conditions and limitations of oral testimonies and traditions. But more significantly, beyond the issues of historical truth, objectivity, and authenticity that preoccupied earlier generations, historians have discovered the value of oral testimony as a means of comprehending how Africans saw and understood their lives and places in history.[43]

Murid oral traditions embody the strengths and weaknesses of all oral testimonies. They differ in their nature and quality, and there is a constant readjustment of the oral narratives to smooth conflicts, erase contradictions, and adjust information to later developments and changing power structures within the organization. They have what Jack Goody termed a rationalizing and transforming power.[44] The history of Amadu Bamba and the Muridiyya told by bearers of oral traditions or written by faithful disciples is therefore subject to editing and refashioning; it remains a living history of a cultural hero and guide, whose life and deeds still constitute an inspiration for millions of people.

However, the Murid tariqa is not a homogeneous organization with a linear and conflict-free history in which everybody has agreed about everything, as most of the literature on the Murids would lead us to believe. To be sure, there is a hegemonic and apparently consensual master narrative of the history of the Muridiyya, but alongside this narrative, there are also muted but important dissonant, undercurrent historiographies that have developed in the interstices and fault lines of Murid history. From the tariqa's inception, Amadu Bamba faced the hostility of some members of his family and his fellow Muslim teachers, and the organization he founded was riddled by conflicts between competing factions that struggled to earn his confidence and build their own power bases in hopes of taking control after his death.

The conflicts that marked the early development of the Muridiyya and generated differing historiographies were rooted in a competition for power and authority among agnates within the Mbakke family, as well as rivalries among Murid sheikhs in a later period. Lineages in the Mbakke clan that opposed Amadu Bamba's grandfather were, in retrospect, denied baraka and excluded from the saintly genealogy.[45] However, it was among members of these agnate branches that I have found the best information on the history of the Mbakke.[46] In effect, for members of these downgraded lineages, documenting their blood relations with Amadu Bamba still constitutes a means to maintain some measure of social prestige. Ironically but not surprisingly, the direct descendants of Bamba did not know much about the history of the family beyond their fathers and grandfathers.[47]

Another fault line that produced contrasting historiographies exists among the different lineages of Murid sheikhs. From the founding of the Muridiyya, there have been tensions between disciples and sheikhs of different cultural backgrounds. Those who originated from historically learned families put much emphasis on knowledge and piety in their allegiance to Amadu Bamba, whereas those who were his blood relatives or from less learned families stressed sainthood and baraka.[48] The types of loyalties to the Muridiyya that these two groups developed were different. Although both honored Amadu Bamba as a saint, the former was more inclined to look critically at the history of the organization, to question the motivations and practices of certain sheikhs and disciples, and to use Islam and Sufi idioms to rationalize Amadu Bamba's life. Most of what I have learned about the conflicts, tensions, and contradictions in the development of the Muridiyya as well as the ethical practices of Amadu Bamba comes from descendants of these sheikhs from learned families.

During the Diourbel era (1912–27), when the Muridiyya was becoming stronger and Amadu Bamba was starting to age, a rift developed in the Murid community between the leaders of two opposing groups, which some bearers of oral traditions called the *penku-penku* (people from the east) and the *ajoor* (people from the precolonial kingdom of Kajoor).[49] The penku-penku were mostly blood relatives of Amadu Bamba and originated from eastern Bawol, the heartland of the Mbakke; the ajoor were the sons of Amadu Bamba whose mothers originated from the kingdom of Kajoor. After Amadu Bamba's death, the latter allied with their maternal uncles from Kajoor and formed a determined resistance to Amadu Bamba's half brothers who were suspected of attempting to take control of the Muridiyya and deny them their inheritance.[50] The history of this rift may be older and more complex than suggested here, but it was in Diourbel that the division started to affect the organization in a visible and important way. The differing narratives stemming from this conflict are more relevant to understanding the dispute sparked by Amadu Bamba's succession, but they are also useful in interpreting local historiographies of the Muridiyya generated by competing lineages of Murid sheikhs.

Murid oral traditions are supplemented by an abundant but understudied written literature in Arabic and Wolofal (the Wolof language written with Arabic script). Some of these documents were contemporaneous with the events they described; others were transcribed oral histories or biographies composed by disciples or members of Bamba's family. Dating these written documents is the main challenge to the historian. However, they contain clues such as names of places and administrators, outbreaks of epidemics, ecological phenomena, and allusions to historically dated events that can help place the stories in a historical time line. Moreover, many of the writers used the Muslim calendar, and they were able to correlate the events they narrated with their own ages, the ages of their parents, or the ages of the historical actors involved in the stories.

The historical value of these written sources is uneven. Some constitute what Pierre Nora has called the "unwilling witnesses to history" that often convey some of the most reliable information.[51] This is the case, for instance, with Amadu Bamba's correspondence, sermons, and advice to disciples as compiled in the *Majmuha* or collected by some disciples.[52] Bamba's written account of his first arrest and exile and the two known extensive biographies by his son Bachir Mbacké and his disciple Muhammad Lamine Diop are also important historical sources. Other writings, including most of Amadu Bamba's own works, deal with abstract and esoteric religious and spiritual subjects that, at first glance, may seem of not much use to the historian seeking to document historical events. But buried in this sacred literature is precious information that is useful in unearthing what proponents of the Annales school would call an *histoire des mentalités* (history of mentalities or states of mind). Because of their ethical nature, some of Bamba's religious writings reveal as much about his Sufi orientation and beliefs as about his perception of the mores and social practices of his time.[53] His postexile writings are also replete with allusions to his conflict with the French, and they teach us much about his conception of the relations between rulers and clerics. These writings, along with the memory of Bamba's teachings and practices, were instrumental in producing the ethic that helped sustain his movement after his death.

Hagiography

The history of the Muridiyya told by oral traditions or Murid written sources develops at the intersection of hagiography and local historical evidence. The challenges that hagiographic sources present to the historian are well known. They raise questions regarding historicity and the believability and trustworthiness of the informants and writers. Most Muslim hagiographies are oral traditions that, at some point in history, were put in writing by disciples or family members of the saint whose history is told. They were often written centuries after the events they described, with the intention of silencing skeptics and strengthening the brethren's faith and their bonds with the saints' descendants. Hagiographers seek to expose in the open (*zaahir*) the tangibility of sainthood by making manifest the hidden *(baatin)* power of their favorite sheikhs through the description of their karamas. Through the life and words of the saint, they aim to revive the sheikhs' mystical doctrines primarily for affective and didactic purposes. Therefore, an author's goal was not to trace the everyday stories of the saint's life as a historical being but to transmit the aspects of the saint's teachings that he deemed useful to the disciples at a specific moment in history.[54] What most mattered to the author was not what really happened but what was exemplary.[55] Hagiography may be seen as an invention or reinvention of the saint's life to respond to the perceived spiritual needs of an epoch. In the words of Edith Wyschogrod, it does not merely exist in history: it is constructed and reconstructed in endless refabulation.[56] Hagiography may, then, tell us more about its audience than about the object of its study.

But in the age of postmodernism and deconstruction, when positivistic approaches have lost their attraction and when the relativity and possible plurality of "historical truth" is increasingly acknowledged, scholars have become more tolerant of nonconventional historical sources such as hagiography. Nonetheless, the difficulty of using hagiographies as historical evidence is still recognized. Trimingham expressed these difficulties when he wrote, "Hagiographia is simply biography designed, and consequently distorted, to serve the cult of the saints. It forms an essential aspect of any study of the orders since these qualities, deeds, and manifestations are real to the believer, but they obscure the historical personality."[57] To the defense of hagiographers, Michel de Certeau observed that it would be unfair to consider hagiography exclusively from the angle of authenticity or empirical value; this would subject one literary genre to the rule of another, historiography.[58] If one agrees with de Certeau, then a question remains: of what use can hagiographic sources be to the historian if he or she does not subject this information to rigorous historical criticism?

It is important first to note that, contrary to Trimingham's statement, not all hagiographies are distorted biographies crafted to serve a saint's cult. There are many hagiographies that refer to saints without any known existing cult and that are therefore less prone to manipulation. Furthermore, as noted by Eric Geoffroy, one should distinguish between hagiography as a literary genre that proposes a first-degree reading of sainthood based on miracles and hagiography as a "science of sainthood" that focuses on expounding doctrinal questions and elaborating on the thinking of a saint founder.[59] Hagiography as a science of sainthood can be a rich source for a history of ideas. Bachir Mbacké's biography of Amadu Bamba, for example, belongs to this last genre and offers an interesting analysis of the development of Bamba's thinking as a Sufi.

Even hagiographies that were designed to serve a cult can be valuable assets to the historian. These saintly biographies do not recount the lives of the

Sufis as if they had lived in a historical vacuum. In effect, unlike the Christian hermit, the Sufi lives in society and is, most of the time, an active participant in cultural, political, and economic transactions in his community. He is involved with rulers and commoners. He intervenes in times of peace, war, outbreak of epidemics, natural disasters, and economic stress. Hagiographers therefore make reference to events, persons, or places that also impact the lives of other historical actors whose stories can be used to check the accuracy of hagiographic sources. Thus, by comparing the time line of the life of the last king of Kajoor produced by royal court historians and French archival sources with the time line of Amadu Bamba provided by hagiographers, I was able to correct some mistakes in the historiography of the Muridiyya and reconstruct a complete chronology of the life of the founder of the Murid tariqa.

Stories of miracles may even prove to be useful sources of information for the historian if, as suggested by Eaton, one ignores questions about the veracity of those miracles and instead concentrates on the intent behind them.[60] Miracles have a purpose, and the type of miracles and the ways in which they are performed can tell us much about historical circumstances. The first miracles attributed to Amadu Bamba, in the early years of the founding of the Muridiyya, were, for the most part, related to knowledge and erudition. The savant Maniaaw Sylla, who was among the most vociferous critics of the Muridiyya, found himself, in the presence of Amadu Bamba, unable to translate and comment on the first verse of the Quran (the *basmala*), something he was used to performing routinely. He acknowledged the superior spiritual power of his nemesis and finally submitted to him. The imam of Mbakke, also a known Murid opponent who insisted on leading Bamba in prayer, forgot key verses of the sura (chapter of the Quran) that he tried to recite and renounced his position. These miracles reflected the struggle for intellectual legitimacy that Amadu Bamba waged in the beginning of his calling and tell us much about the responses he received from the clerical establishment. They differ greatly from those miracles he performed later when confronted by the French colonial administration.[61]

THE QUESTIONS OF METHODOLOGY
THE USE OF MURID INTERNAL SOURCES

Murid Oral and Written Sources

The hagiographic literature used in composing this book shares many similarities with classical Muslim and Christian hagiography, but there are differences, as well. In the tradition of Muslim hagiography, the portrait of

Amadu Bamba painted by Murid hagiographers tends to replicate the life of the Prophet Muhammad. The descriptions of his everyday life, trials, and tribulations reproduce the prophetic experience in Mecca and Medina and fit well with what Annemarie Schimmel has called the "imitatio Muhammadi" model.[62] Murid writers also drew extensively from Sufi eschatology to tell the epic story of the confrontation of their sheikh with the French. Bamba's miraculous deeds as told by hagiographers, such as praying on the sea, taming a hungry lion, fast traveling, or surviving exposure to a raging fire or a firing squad, are also found in the repertoire of the miracles of Sufi masters in South and Southeast Asia, the Middle East, and North Africa.[63]

Despite the similarities, Murid hagiography presents significant particularities. First, Amadu Bamba was a historical personality who was mentioned in many parallel contemporary sources. So one is spared the task of establishing the historicity of his persona, which, according to Father Hippolyte Delehaye's method, constitutes the first step in the study of a saint's life.[64] Second, unlike in traditional Muslim and Christian hagiography, the time elapsed between the occurrence of events and their recording was very short. Amadu Bamba's biography in Arabic by his son Bachir Mbacké, which is the largest hagiographic work on the Muridiyya, was completed in 1932, just five years after Bamba's death.[65] The author was born in 1895 and had a close relationship with the subject of his study, and he was an eyewitness to, or consulted eyewitnesses to, most of the stories he told. Muhammad Lamine Diop, the author of the other well-known Arabic biography of Amadu Bamba, was a close aide to the founder of the Muridiyya, whom he had joined in the first decade of the twentieth century. His book was published in 1963.[66]

The content of these biographies represents another area of difference. The motivations of the writers were not distinct from those of other Muslim authors of saintly biographies. They aimed to demonstrate the superior spiritual and moral qualities of their sheikhs, and they expected godly rewards from their works.[67] But the approach was different. Both mentioned some miracles of Amadu Bamba but did not dwell extensively on this topic as a classical hagiographer would. Bachir Mbacké, for example, noted in the preface of his book that he had decided not to devote a chapter to Bamba's miracles because they were numerous and because other Murid writers had dealt with them.[68] M. L. Diop concluded his work by stating that he had refrained from writing everything he had learned from his fellow disciples because this would have led him to recount extraordinary deeds that would prove false.[69] The two authors instead reported many stories related to the everyday life of Amadu Bamba. Nine of the ten chapters of Diop's book are reconstructions of important episodes of Bamba's life as a historical being: his life from birth to his father's death, his life after the death of his father, his arrest and exile in Gabon and then Mauritania, and so forth. Although mostly concerned with documenting the spiritual journey of his father, Bachir Mbacké also found it necessary to deal with current historical events. He observed that even though the political history of the precolonial Wolof kingdoms was not particularly relevant to his study, he nevertheless needed to touch on it in order to better explain the different attitudes that Bamba harbored regarding temporal and spiritual power holders.[70]

The time and circumstances in which these biographies were written and the types of audience they targeted explain the orientation taken. Both authors tried to demonstrate the orthodox credentials and sound Islamic bases of Murid doctrine and practices through the life of the saint founder by downplaying controversial miracles. They also wanted to offer a narrative of Bamba's life that would contrast with the historiography produced by French administrators.[71] Moreover, they wished to sway their potential readers among the small literati community of Senegal who belonged to rival Muslim orders and who were most critical of certain Murid religious practices and skeptical of Bamba's claim to sainthood. These works appeared, then, as responses to competing historiographies and offered alternative interpretations of the Muridiyya. Because of these exceptional circumstances, the two hagiographies constitute useful sources for understanding the history of the Muridiyya from a Murid perspective.

Writing a History of the Muridiyya from Within

I developed an interest in the study of the Muridiyya in my third year in the History Department at University Cheikh Anta Diop of Dakar (Senegal), where I was first exposed to scholarship on the history of Islam in West Africa. The reading list on the Murids included works by sociologists, political scientists, and anthropologists. There were some articles and books by specialists of Islam and colonial administrators but nothing by historians. I was struck by the absence of historical works on such an important social, economic, and cultural phenomenon in the past and present of Senegal. I was further struck by the difference between scholarly reconstructions of the history and development of the Muridiyya and the way that the Murids themselves understood and interpreted their history. I decided to devote my master's and diplôme d'étude approfondie (DEA) theses to the Muridiyya in order to bring a historical and internal perspective to the study of the tariqa.[72]

I grew up in Mbakke Bawol, the historical village of the Mbakke family, just 7 kilometers away from Tuubaa, the holy city of the Murids. My father was introduced to Amadu Bamba at a young age and was raised by the latter's half brother and close aide, Sheikh Anta Mbakke; he also personally knew and frequented most of the leading sheikhs of the Muridiyya. He had a sharp memory and could be considered a historian of the Muridiyya in his own right. Since I was the youngest child in our family, growing up at a time when my father was living a less active life, I was closest to him and benefited the most from his knowledge of the history of the Murid order. Being his traveling companion, I had also benefited from his networks of fellow disciples and friends.

Therefore, when I sat in that class on the history of the Muridiyya in the fall of 1990, I brought with me much background knowledge. It soon struck me that there seemed to be two parallel versions of the history of the Muridiyya. Each of these versions was based on specific premises and sources. The scholarly version, which was, for the most part, produced by social scientists, was built on ideas, perceptions, and evidence primarily influenced by French colonial sources and interpretations; the Murid version was inspired by the abundant but largely unexploited collection of oral reports and written documents generated within the tariqa. One goal of the present work is to bring into conversation these two versions of the history of the Muridiyya by bridging the clearly perceptible gap in Murid literature between precolonial and colonial history, archival and internal Murid sources, and secular and religiously sensitive approaches.

But to initiate this conversation, one must first assess the playing field. The dominant interpretation of the history of the Muridiyya was established by Paul Marty's study of the order in 1913. This interpretation was articulated around three basic assumptions: first, that Bamba was influenced by the precolonial Wolof aristocracy and that the founding of the Muridiyya was an attempt to re-create the old political order destroyed by the French occupation of Senegal; second, that the Muridiyya was merely a response of distraught Wolof farmers to colonization and had no major historical significance; and third, that the driving force behind the founding of the Muridiyya was not Amadu himself, but the social forces that coalesced behind him.[73] Despite its obvious flaws, Marty's interpretation has enjoyed an unusually enduring influence.[74] Some scholars have sought to distance themselves from the Marty paradigm by proposing new interpretations of aspects of the history and development of the Murid tariqa, inspired by Murid sources. Some of those scholars have put an emphasis on religiosity and culture by looking at Murid visual piety and sacred geography.[75] More recently, the ongoing debate between David Robinson and James Searing, both historians of Senegal, has called attention to the critical importance of internal sources in developing alternative perspectives on the history of the Muridiyya.

In his book on Wolof state politics, colonization, and Islam in Senegal, Searing proposed a major revision of Murid history that challenged the conventional historiography of the organization.[76] He criticized students of the Muridiyya for their heavy reliance on French archival sources and interpretations and for their failure to appreciate Murid internal sources. To correct the perceived distortions in the scholarship, Searing relied on Murid written and oral data to reconstruct a Murid-centered history (or history of commemoration), which he opposed to the history of the academy and to that produced by traditional royal court historians. He drew the bulk of his material from Bachir Mbacké's biography of Amadu Bamba and the lineage oral tradition of Daaru Muhti, the stronghold of Amadu Bamba's half brother and companion Ibra Faati, better known as Maam Cerno.

Searing's bold, revisionist stance has come under heavy criticism. Richard Roberts and David Robinson, both noted historians of West Africa, appreciated the great lengths Searing went to in collecting internal sources, and they applauded his attempt to present a Murid-sensitive interpretation.[77] However, they also identified substantial weaknesses in his approach. They faulted Searing for his uncritical use of Murid sources that ignored dissonant voices. Searing was also criticized for generalizing from an analysis based on a very limited body of material collected mainly from a single lineage source. More seriously, the work was suspected of merely substituting a Murid-centered master narrative to the so-called archive-driven master narrative, without an effort at synthesis.[78]

In this debate, both sides recognized the critical importance of internal sources in reinterpreting the history of the Muridiyya. What was in contention was not the scientific validity and usefulness of Murid oral or written sources but rather the appropriate methodology with which to approach these sources. Searing's provocative thesis represented an interesting alternative to the Marty paradigm, but to fulfill its potential, it needed to be backed by a larger, more diverse, and stronger body of evidence. Any attempt at developing a credible alternative to the dominant scholarly interpretation of the Muridiyya would also have to be based on a dialogue between the archival and Murid internal sources.

This book contributes to the debate, but it goes further by proposing, for the first time, a comprehensive reconstruction of the complex internal stories of the Muridiyya. This reconstruction is based on a careful analysis of a variety of sources, mainly Murid oral reports and written documents, that are integrated with substantial archival materials and other data. My connections within the tariqa have been vital in helping reconstruct the internal stories. They have given me access to sources that have until now eluded scholars of the Muridiyya and Islam in Senegal. Because of my familiarity with these sources and the internal politics of the order, I was able to disentangle the layers of information and to fill some of the gaps and silences by interrogating specific families and lineages. By comparing and contrasting a variety of sources from various provenances and by applying a rigorous internal and external critique to Murid oral reports and written documents, I hope to minimize some of the adverse effects of this material.

However, the critique leveled against Searing clearly highlights the difficulties of dealing with an organization with a living history and whose past is constantly being reinterpreted to adjust to changing circumstances. These difficulties are even greater when one is committed to writing a history of the Muridiyya from within. The advantage of a view from the inside is recognized, since, as Victor Turner observed, the inside view of an alien culture might well make comprehensible many of its seemingly bizarre components and interrelations.[79] But one should also be aware of the drawbacks of the insider's position. In effect, the empathy and open collaboration of informants who feel a bond with the researcher do not come without cost, as the researcher may be subject to manipulations or subconsciously indulge in self-censorship to avoid social sanction or preserve ties with the community.

However, as the Searing debate has shown, outsiders writing about the history of the Muridiyya face equally daunting challenges. The nature of the challenges may be different, but the struggle to untangle and objectively analyze and interpret a large body of written and oral materials produced by faithful disciples in unfamiliar and esoteric religious languages—or by biased colonial administrators—is the same. In reality, any historian writing about his or her own culture or society will, in one way or the other, have to confront the insider's challenge. When scholars write about people whose values they share or cherish, they tend to be less skeptical and suspicious and more willing to listen and convey the stories they are told. But as noted by Paul Ricoeur, "To confess that one is a listener is from the very beginning to break with the project dear to many, and even perhaps all, philosophers [one may add historians]: to begin a discourse without any presuppositions." Yet, as Ricoeur confessed, the presupposition that "Christian speaking is meaningful, that it is worthy of consideration" has been a guiding principle of his work on Christianity.[80] Like Ricoeur, I claim the position of the listener vis-à-vis the Muridiyya. And as Ricoeur might agree, I believe that to adopt the sympathetic attitude of the listener does not necessary disable one's ability to write critically and objectively. In other words, the historian's ability to write a critical history of a people does not hinge on his or her position but rather on his or her capacity to effectively apply the historical method of inquiry and criticism to the sources.

1 ∽ Islam, Society, and Power in the Wolof States

MANY OF THE MUSLIM militant and mystical movements that emerged in the western Sudan in the nineteenth century have been studied in the narrow context of the end of the Atlantic trade and European colonization. The Muridiyya is no exception. This approach has shed light on the ways in which these two momentous events in the history of Africa influenced the spread of Islam in Senegal, but it has also obscured the deeper trends that framed the expansion of Islamic religious practices among the Senegalese. Therefore, a reconstruction of these deeper trends is crucial for grasping the profound ideological and empirical underpinnings that explain people's adherence to Islam beyond the crises of the nineteenth century. The transformations that occurred in that century are better understood when analyzed in the broader context of the development of Islam in Senegal. Moreover, it is difficult to comprehend the history of Amadu Bamba's life and the organization he founded without an awareness of the cultural and political context that shaped the core values and traditions of his family.

This chapter provides background information for understanding the establishment and expansion of Islam in the precolonial Wolof states of Senegal, where the Muridiyya was founded in the second half of the nineteenth century. It stresses the role of Islam as an agent of cultural and social change and documents the variety of ways in which it affected different segments of Wolof society. In contrast to the conventional wisdom that sees the jihadist and the ruler as the principal agents of Islamization in Africa, I contend that both the village Quranic teacher and the Muslim holy man played the critical role in the expansion of Islam among the Wolof. They played this role by offering the populace continuing access to Islamic knowledge and practices and by inscribing Islam in the landscape of the Wolof states through the founding of a network of schools and Muslim villages.

PRESENCE OF ISLAM AMONG THE WOLOF

The beginning of continuous contacts between the Wolof and Islam could be dated from the first half of the eleventh century.[1] We learn from Abu Abdallah al-Bakri (1014-94) that by 1040 CE, Islam had spread to the Senegal River valley due to the efforts of Waar Jaabi, the first ruler of Tekrur (in northern Senegal), to become Muslim.[2] Waar Jaabi was a supporter of the Almoravid movement, which originated in present-day Mauritania and then established its politico-religious domination over Morocco and southern Spain.

Little is known about the development of Islam among the Wolof in the following four centuries. From the fifteenth century on, reports by European travelers and writers give us a better understanding of the pattern of Islamic practices in the Wolof states. Accounts by early Portuguese visitors to Senegal indicated that Islamization was superficial and primarily confined to the ruling class. Alvise da Mosto noted that Islam was practiced among the Wolof, especially by the rulers and their entourage.[3] Valentim Fernandes made similar remarks. He observed that the king and the nobility of Jolof (the first historically known Wolof state) were followers of Muhammad, but only a minority of the lay population was Muslim.[4] Both writers emphasized the religious influence of Moorish clerics from Mauritania and Morocco on the Wolof kings, but neither referred to Muslim ceremonies or Quranic schools. Fernandes instead stressed the Wolof habit of drinking alcohol and the practice of "pagan" rituals. Wolof society, as described by Portuguese travelers, was mostly characterized by religious mixing, whereby Islamic rituals were observed alongside elements of traditional religions. Similar practices can still be observed among some Wolof Muslims.

The information provided by Portuguese writers is fragmented and selective. Moreover, these Europeans were not good observers of Wolof society. They were not primarily interested in culture; their main preoccupation was with economic order. Their accounts were more reflective of the religious practices of rulers and their retinues rather than the commoners. And their testimonies about the lay population, with whom they had neither prolonged contact nor significant communication due to their lack of language skills, are less reliable.

From the sixteenth century, changing political circumstances gave an impetus to the development of Islam. In this century, Islam started to gradually expand from the circles of power. This development was partly due to the emergence of new polities. The Jolof Empire, which had dominated the political landscape of Senegal for over two centuries, had collapsed.[5] Its demise gave birth to a number of smaller states, among which were the Wolof kingdoms of Jolof, Waalo, Kajoor, and Bawol and the state of Saalum, dominated by Wolof and Sereer ruling dynasties. These Wolof states shared similar social and political structures, characterized by a division in endogamous occupational groups, sometimes called castes, and the presence of classes of slaves, rulers, and freemen.[6] The head of each kingdom bore a specific title—*dammeel* in Kajoor, *teigne* in Bawol, *buurba* in Jolof, *buur* in Saalum—and were tied together by diplomatic relations and marital alliances. Rulers of these new states were more open to the influence of Muslim traders and clerics who supplied them with material goods and ideas about statecraft.

MUSLIM CLERICS AND STATE POWER IN KAJOOR AND BAWOL

Until the French colonial takeover in the second half of the nineteenth century, the social perception of the Muslim clerics in the Wolof and Fulbe states of Senegal was primarily shaped by their attitudes toward royal courts. In fact, Jean Schmitz has even developed a model correlating the location of clerics' villages to the degree of their involvement with rulers.[7] As we shall see in the following chapter, issues of space and proper relations with rulers were also important features of Amadu Bamba's ancestral heritage.

The involvement of Muslim clerics in the politics of Kajoor and Bawol dated back to the founding of these states in the second half of the sixteenth century. The first ruler (dammeel) of Kajoor, Amary Ngoone Sobel Faal (1549?–93), counted among his advisers Moor and Fulbe Muslims who took an active part in the founding of this kingdom.[8] They advised and prayed for the king during the struggle against the Jolof Empire and helped organize the new state after it seceded. The king granted land and recognized a measure of administrative and cultural autonomy to some influential Muslim learned men, who in return provided him with mystical protection and political support. This policy of exchanging services became an enduring trait of the relationships between rulers and clerics in the Wolof states, which the French colonial administration would try to replicate centuries later.[9]

The association of Muslim clerics with the business of government helped enhance the prestige of Islam and its expansion among the commoners. The Portuguese traveler André de Almada, writing in 1594 about events that took place at an earlier date, gave us an idea of Islamic practices in the Wolof states during the reign of Amary Ngoone Sobel. He mentioned that the Wolof did not eat pork or drink wine and that they had in their midst many religious leaders.[10] De Almada's remarks contrasted with the observations made by Da Mosto and Fernandes less than a century earlier.[11] His description suggests that Islam was expanding among the lay population of the Wolof country and that Islamic learning was sufficiently developed to produce a relatively large body of indigenous clerics.

Because of its increasing influence on the wider population, Islam gradually became an important political force. It was a refuge for oppressed commoners and members of the lower nobility who were excluded from power, and beyond that, conversion to Islam became a means of political protest for dissenting members of royal families.[12] Some of the clerics, mostly those originating from ruling lineages, turned into vociferous critics of the Wolof aristocracy and its allies, whom they portrayed as unbelievers, and began presenting themselves as the only legitimate leaders of the growing Muslim community.

When Nasir al-Din declared his jihad in southwestern Mauritania in the second half of the seventeenth century, his calling was welcomed in the Wolof states; there, the situation was ripe for Muslim clerics to challenge the power of the ruling aristocracy, which was nominally Muslim but increasingly perceived as illegitimate. In his letter to the rulers of Fuuta and the Wolof states, al-Din urged the kings to change their way of life and abide by the teachings of Islam. He also warned them that Allah did not permit rulers to pillage or enslave their subjects and that, to the contrary, kings were required to support their people and protect them against their enemies.[13]

The reformist movement of Nasir al-Din (also called the Toubenan movement) swept the Wolof states between 1673 and 1677.[14] According to the French chroniclers Father Jean B. Labat and Jean Louis Chambonneau, the party of jihad initially enjoyed a rapid success. In less than two years, partisans of the jihad had taken over in Fuuta and in the Wolof kingdoms as *buur jullit* (Muslim kings). But this success was short-lived. By 1677, the reformers were defeated by a coalition of Moorish dissenters, French traders, and the local aristocracies in the Wolof states.

Historians agree about the enduring influence of this movement on the relations between Muslim commoners and so-called pagan rulers in the Wolof and Fulbe states, but they diverge about the interpretation of its meaning. This divergence echoes the larger debate about the political significance of religious movements that I explored in the Introduction. Boubacar Barry perceives the jihad as a reaction of the trans-Saharan trade, which was controlled by Muslim traders, against the growing Atlantic trade, which was dominated by Europeans. As he metaphorically has put it, it was a confrontation between the Muslim caravan and the Portuguese caravel.[15] Philip Curtin emphasizes the religious dimension of the movement. He links the tradition of religious revolt and the struggles of Muslim state builders, which marked the history of Senegambia in the eighteenth and nineteenth centuries, to Nasir al-Din's reform.[16] James Webb stresses the influence of ecological factors, suggesting that the continuing desiccation of the Sahara caused a southward migration of "Berber" and Arab nomads whose continuous pressure led to violent confrontations with black African farming communities farther south.[17] There is some truth in all of these interpretations, for, as noted by John Hanson in the case of the Umarian movement, Muslim jihadists are not always motivated by one clearly articulated agenda; their commitments might be based on different expectations in different circumstances.[18] The Muslim warriors of Nasir al-Din may have been motivated by religious grievances, social and economic discontent, and perhaps environmental degradation or by some combination of these factors. But for the common people who joined the reformers in Wolof country, what mattered most was the realization of social change and the establishment of less oppressive and peaceful rule, as promised by the ideology of the jihad.[19] For the Muslim leadership on both banks of the Senegal River, the triumph of the movement would mean the imposition of their cultural and political dominance and control of the economy of the river.

THE REFORM OF KING LAT SUKAABE IN KAJOOR AND BAWOL

Whatever might have been the true intentions and motives of the leaders of the Nasir al-Din jihad, this movement laid the foundations of a new political culture that greatly affected the relations between rulers and clerics in the Wolof states and transformed the nature of Muslim leadership. I share Barry's view that the hostility of the Wolof aristocracy to Muslims, who had enjoyed the support of Wolof kings up to that point, dated from this period.[20] The jihad also hardened the variations that differentiated the Muslim militant, the court cleric, and the pietistic teacher and turned their superficial differences into more rigid, distinctive features. The politics of King Lat Sukaabe played an even greater role in solidifying the distinctions among the Muslim leaders of the Wolof states.

The rule of Lat Sukaabe Faal (1697–1719), who rose to power in Kajoor and Bawol two decades after the al-Din jihad, illustrated the transformation in the relationship between clerics and rulers. Lat Sukaabe initiated an important reform primarily designed to contain and control the increasingly powerful and restless Muslim clerics of his kingdom.[21] His strategy consisted, on the one hand, of drawing cultural and ethical boundaries between the Muslim leadership and temporal power holders and, on the other, of co-opting some Muslim learned men into the camp of rulers.

Lat Sukaabe rejected the policy of accommodation inaugurated by Amary Ngoone Sobel, founder of the kingdom of Kajoor, which seemed to have more or less guided the relations between clerics and rulers in Kajoor and Bawol since the sixteenth century. He agreed to respect the immunity of the Muslim leaders from state violence only if the latter refrained from becoming involved in politics and remained faithful to their professions as teachers and men of religion. He also built alliances between the *geej* matrilineage (one of the seven ruling dynasties of Kajoor) he brought to power and certain dominant Muslim families.[22] His most important initiative in regard to the Muslim clerics was the creation of the position of *serigne lamb* (drum). The serigne lamb was a clerical head of a territorial jurisdiction. The *lamb*, which was used to sound the alert in times of war or to announce major events, symbolized the secular nature of the power that the king bestowed on this cleric. The serigne lamb had the same prerogatives as the traditional *kangam* (holder of public office), the only difference between them being that the former was the leader of a Muslim community and partly owed his appointment to this status. The serigne lamb participated in wars and pillages and collected taxes and other dues on behalf of the king. Through this policy, Lat Sukaabe brought some of the semiautonomous Muslim villages at the borders between Kajoor and neighboring kingdoms back into the fold of the central power.[23]

In contrast to the serigne lamb, some Muslim learned men kept their distance from the rulers. This group, called *serigne fakk taal*, maintained the tradition of Islamic scholarship and teaching and stressed their identity as Muslim clerics.[24] Some of them were very learned in the profane and Islamic sciences; many others had modest intellectual credentials, often limited to rote knowledge of the Quran or portions of it. Numerous villages founded and led by this category of clerics were located in northern Kajoor. But serigne fakk taal were found everywhere in the Wolof states. They were welcomed in all communities, where they presided over naming ceremonies and funerals, taught the youth, healed the sick, and educated people about the basics of Islam.

The serigne fakk taal were peace-loving farmers who primarily relied on their disciples' labor and the support they received from local communities. They were generally members of the lower classes or demoted junior lineages of ruling dynasties, and some were assimilated immigrants belonging to minority ethnic groups (Mandinka, Fulbe), which perhaps explains their tendency to adopt political neutrality. The serigne fakk taal benefited from the respect given them by the rulers, and they enjoyed political immunity. They were the only ordinary subjects allowed to speak to the king with their headwear on and without prostrating themselves.[25] Because they were thought to have supernatural power, they were feared and honored, and they often officiated as peace brokers and mediators in times of conflict.

Although many serigne fakk taal shunned any direct involvement with the ruling class, some members of this community were close collaborators of the rulers. They lived within or near the king's compound and worked as advisers, scribes, or judges but more often as diviners and providers of talismans for the magical protection of the kingdom and its leadership. The serigne fakk taal were, to paraphrase Searing, the true agents of the "quiet revolution" that ingrained Islam in the cultural fabric of Wolof society.[26] Amadu Bamba's family belonged to this category of Muslim clerics.

Lat Sukaabe's reform established a modus vivendi between the leaders of the Muslim community in the Wolof states and the rulers. This tacit agreement was based on some simple principles.[27] The king agreed to appoint judges from trusted Muslim learned families, and he also recognized their power and authority to decide judicial matters regarding the Muslim population of the kingdom. Descendants of these clerics were given the right to inherit the functions and estates granted to their families. The rulers affirmed the immunity of Muslim villages against raids and pillages as long as their clerical chiefs remained respectful of their authority. They also agreed to send some of the children of the ruling elite to Quranic schools. The Muslim clerics, in return, recognized the historical rights of the reigning dynasties to rule the country and assented to confining their actions strictly to the religious domain and ministering to their flock.

But the interpretation of the terms of this unwritten agreement depended largely on the political context in the kingdoms and the parties' changing perceptions of their power. With the expansion of Islam in the Wolof states, some clerics, especially those who belonged to royal lineages, started to view themselves as the legitimate rulers of the growing Muslim population of Kajoor and Bawol and became resentful of the rule of the *ceddo* (slave warriors and courtiers resistant to Islam).[28] The frustration and discontent of these clerics grew into an open revolt during the reign of the *dammeel-teigne* (title of the king holding the dual crowns of Kajoor and Bawol) Amary Ngoone Ndeela.

KING AMARY NGOONE NDEELA AND THE MUSLIM CLERICS (1790–1809)

Like the rule of Lat Sukaabe, the reign of Amary Ngoone Ndeela was a defining moment in the development of Islam in the Wolof states. For the first time, Islam became a potent threat to the power of the geej ruling dynasty because of combined pressure from the Muslim rulers of Fuuta Tooro and mounting tension with local Muslim clerics. The king's response to the crisis fostered a new paradigm that governed the relations between rulers and clerics in Kajoor and Bawol until the second half of the nineteenth century, when French irruption on the political scene imposed a new shift. Maaram Mbakke, Amadu Bamba's great-grandfather, moved to Bawol during the rule of Amary Ngoone Ndeela, and the attitude of the Mbakke family toward temporal power holders was profoundly influenced by the political environment they found in the kingdom.

Since the triumph of the Tooroodo Revolution in the second half of the eighteenth century, the clerical rulers of Fuuta Tooro, led by *Almaamy* (from *imam*, or Muslim leader) Abdul Kader, had not hidden their ambition to extend their influence over neighboring states.[29] After a series of confrontations, they compelled the king of Waalo to grant autonomy to the Muslims of his kingdom and to pay an annual tax as token of submission to Islam.[30] They also imposed a military alliance on the sovereign of Jolof.[31] To the more powerful and distant kingdoms of Kajoor and Bawol, they sent proselytizers to win Muslims to the cause of the Islamic revolution.

The aggressive proselytism of the Fuuta rulers in the Wolof states negatively affected the relationships between the Muslim leadership and the ruling class in Kajoor and Bawol. The continuous deterioration of relations between the two groups erupted in open confrontation in the last decade of the eighteenth century. The killing of Malaamin Saar, a prestigious teacher in Bawol, by the king's warriors was the immediate cause of the Muslims' revolt, which ended with their defeat in 1795. Almaamy Abdul Kader, who marched with his army in Kajoor in response to their appeal, was also defeated by Amary Ngoone Ndeela. Louis Faidherbe, the writer and influential French governor of Senegal, found some connection between Saar and the clerical rulers of Fuuta. Following the tradition conveyed by Wolof court bards, he argued that Malaamin Saar was the leader of a conspiracy inspired by the Fuuta clerics that aimed at overthrowing Amary Ngoone Ndeela and establishing a Muslim theocracy in Kajoor and Bawol.[32]

Local Muslim sources give a different but seemingly more accurate account of the conflict.[33] These sources tell us that Saar was a successful Muslim teacher in the village of Caareen in central Bawol. He angered the rulers of Bawol when he opposed the raiding of his herd and refused a request by the head of the army to supply a large amount of food and cattle to feed his men. Caareen was located near Kaba, headquarters of the army of Bawol, and just a few kilometers away from Lambaay, the king's residence. The vulnerable location of Saar's village close to a major army garrison and the kingdom's capital certainly would have dissuaded him from fomenting an open rebellion against the king, as Faidherbe stated.[34] However, it is probable that, like his fellow Muslim clerics in the Wolof states, Saar bore some resentment against the ceddo, and perhaps he was a passive (if secret) supporter of the reformist regime in Fuuta. The slaying of Saar was the king's warning to the Muslims of Kajoor and Bawol not to emulate their colleagues in Fuuta.

The Saar incident and the harsh repression that followed the clerics' revolt set a new precedent in the relations between rulers and the Muslim leadership in the Wolof country.[35] The kings adopted a carrot-and-stick policy, rewarding those clerics who supported them or embraced political neutrality and holding a hard line against Muslims suspected of rebellious behavior. Clerical families continued to administer their fiefdom, but the granting of immunity from state violence increasingly depended on loyalty to the rulers and less on the prestige and recognized spiritual power of the cleric.

LAT JOOR AND ISLAM

The reign of Lat Joor Joob (from 1862 to 1864 and again from 1871 to 1886) marked one of the most significant episodes in the history of Islam in the Wolof states of Kajoor and Bawol. His rule also profoundly marked the history of the Mbakke family, for Lat Joor was a close friend to Amadu Bamba's father, Momar Anta Sali Mbakke. As will be shown in the following chapters, the development and implications of this friendship were key milestones that greatly influenced the life of the founder of the Muridiyya.

Lat Joor rose to power at a time when divergent opinions about the role of Islam in the state were dividing the ruling class, whose unity had until then prevented the Muslim establishment from defeating the traditional rulers. This divergence developed in the context of the weakening of the geej dynasty that had dominated Kajoorian and Bawol politics for over a century. The ruling elite was plagued by internal divisions and was confronted by the rising power of the slaves of the crown as well as aggressive French interference in local politics.[36] Lat Joor's rule also coincided with major changes in the leadership of the Muslim community, marked by a power shift from militants to teachers, who were more committed to the peaceful expansion of Islam. As a result of these changes, the Islamization of the Wolof was intensified, spearheaded by Sufi organizations such as those led by Sad Buh, Sidiyya Baba, Bu Kunta, Amadu Bamba, Malick Sy, and Abdulaay Niass, in the late nineteenth century. Lat Joor's attitude toward Islam reflected the instability of his rule and the shifting basis of political power in Kajoor and Bawol.

Lat Joor's great-grandfather and grandfather were Muslims devoted to study and worship.[37] They renounced their ancestral inheritance as chiefs of the province of Geet and settled in the village of Ker Amadu Yala, which they founded in the predominantly Muslim northern Kajoor, away from the center of power.[38] It was under Lat Joor's father that the Joob returned to Kajoorian politics and reclaimed their fiefdom. Following his father's example, Lat Joor did not show an interest in Islam until he was overthrown by the French and was compelled to seek refuge with Almaamy Maba Jakhu Ba (also sometimes spelled MA BA or Mabba), the Muslim ruler of Saalum in 1864.

After Maba's death in 1867, Lat Joor returned to Kajoor under pressure from his mother, the remnants of his army that followed him into exile, and probably his Muslim advisers. He entered Kajoor in February 1869 to petition the French for his return to the throne. After failing in this endeavor, he accepted the less prestigious position of chief of the province of Geet and established his headquarters in his ancestral village of Ker Amadu Yala. Lat Joor remained in Geet until 1869 or 1870, when the jihad of Amadu Sheikhu Ba transformed the geopolitics of the Wolof states.

Amadu Sheikhu, the Madiyanke, started his campaign in the wake of a cholera epidemic in Fuuta Tooro in 1868–69.[39] He viewed the epidemic as a punishment that God sent to Muslims for their sins and for tolerating the occupation of their land by infidels. He called for atonement, the imposition of Muslim rule, and a war to drive the French out of Muslim territory. Unsuccessful in his native land, he turned his attention southward, toward the Wolof states. By 1870, he was able to overrun Jolof, forcing its king to surrender.

Lat Joor abandoned his position of chief of the province of Geet and joined the jihad. But from 1871 on, a set of circumstances in Senegal and in France imposed a shift in colonial policy. The new policy was dictated by pressure from the French trading companies of Bordeaux, whose businesses were hard hit because of the war, and the institution of the Third Republic. The emphasis shifted from political domination at all costs to creating conditions favorable to trade.[40] The treaty of January 1871 allowed Lat Joor, for the second time, to return to the throne of Kajoor as dammeel, recognized by the French authority of Saint-Louis.[41]

The momentum of the Madiyanke movement was cut short when Lat Joor, reinstated as king, turned against the jihad. Unable to defeat Amadu Sheikhu on his own, he eagerly joined Governor François X. Valière, who, fearing the political consequence of the creation of a powerful Muslim regime in the Wolof states, agreed to join the war against the jihadist. The jihad's army was defeated, and Amadu Sheikhu was killed by Lat Joor's warriors at the battle of Bundu in 1875. The controversies about the treatment of prisoners from this war propelled Amadu Bamba, for the first time, to the forefront of the political scene in the Wolof states.[42]

The Madiyanke defeat, however, did not end Lat Joor's political woes. It divided his Muslim supporters. Moreover, the tension between the dammeel, his clerical advisers, and the ceddo that had been muted because of the bigger threat that Amadu Sheikhu represented escalated after the latter's demise. In a report on the political situation in Kajoor in 1879, the French administrator Valière (not to be confused with the governor of the same name) gave a description of the crisis.[43] He indicated that after the second coronation of Lat Joor as dammeel, Kajoor experienced a grave political crisis over the location of the king's residence.[44] The heavily Islamized northern territories of the kingdom supported Lat Joor's decision to remain in Ker Amadu Yala, where he had had his headquarters since returning to the kingdom in 1869, but the population living farther south opposed the king's choice and insisted that the dammeel relocate to Mbul and Ngigis, the traditional capitals, in central Kajoor.

The dispute was as much about respecting tradition as it was about political influence and power. In Ker Amadu Yala, Lat Joor was surrounded by Moorish and Wolof Muslim learned men, the most prominent of them being Bekaye, a cleric of Mauritanian origin; Momar Anta Sali, Amadu Bamba's father; and Khaali Majakhate Kala, an influential judge. These Muslim clerics tried to keep the dammeel under their control and to isolate the ceddo, whose influence on the king they deemed detrimental to the people of Kajoor.

Demba Waar Sall, Lat Joor's former mentor and head of the army, and Ibra Fatim Saar, his nephew, led the camp of the ceddo. These two leaders of the slaves of the crown were among the most powerful people of Kajoor. They criticized Lat Joor for installing his headquarters away from the center and the legitimate dignitaries of the kingdom. They also accused the king of favoring an entourage of unworthy people who were not motivated to serve the public good but only their selfish interests.[45]

The tension between the two camps was compounded by the issue of the Dakar-Saint-Louis railroad. In 1879, with the blessing of his Muslim advisers, Lat Joor had signed a treaty with the governor of Saint-Louis allowing the building of a railroad across his kingdom, provided that land previously annexed by the French would be returned to him.[46] However, he soon changed his mind when he learned of the full economic and political implications of the railroad, and he vowed to fight the project to death. From 1882 on, he threatened to boycott the cultivation of peanuts, which were becoming the principal export of the colony, and he sent his warriors to harass the French posts and the workers engaged in the construction of the railroad.

But by taking up arms against the French, Lat Joor further alienated himself from the ceddo faction, which, since 1879, had seemed to have reconciled to the idea of sacrificing the sovereignty of Kajoor for a power sharing with the French. The warlike ceddo may have realized that dynastic rule was doomed and that their interests resided in an alliance with Saint-Louis. The dammeel also alienated the Muslim clerics in the northern province, who were angry with him because of his alliance with the French against the Madiyanke or were reluctant to support him because of their vulnerability to French retaliation.[47] Abandoned by the bulk of his army and unable to count on his Muslim allies, Lat Joor preferred death in battle to falling into French hands or returning to the life of a commoner. He was killed in October 1886 in an engagement with the combined forces of the ceddo led by Demba Waar and the French. Lat Joor's death spelled the end of Kajoor's independence.

CONCLUSION

As revealed by the preceding discussion, Islam has a long tradition among the Wolof. Its influence on the state and society varied over time, depending on the scope and nature of its constituency and on changes in what it meant to be a Muslim. Islam has sometimes served as an ideology for the legitimization of local rule; at other times, it has functioned as an instrument of contestation and opposition to rulers. From the seventeen century on, it gradually became a refuge for the powerless, who were the primary victims of the violence and insecurity spurred by the slave trade, dynastic wars, and French encroachment. Some Muslim clerics responded to the deleterious economic and political situations in the Wolof states by waging jihads and seeking political autonomy. Some remained involved with the rulers in various capacities. And many others pursued their laborious work as educators at the grassroots levels and away from the centers of power, contributing to a gradual but steady implantation of the Islamic religious culture among the Wolof.

However, when seen from a long-term perspective, the actions of Muslim jihadists and teachers were neither contradictory nor disjointed; they were, rather, complementary and parts of the same continuum that James Searing termed the quiet (Islamic) revolution in West Africa.[48] "Holy warriors" certainly contributed, sometimes in a dramatic fashion, to a rapid geographic expansion of Islam, as proponents of social change and examples of an alternative political leadership; they were less successful in establishing enduring Islamic influence among the communities they conquered. But they paved the way for the teachers and holy men who often marched with, or followed, their armies. These pietistic Muslim clerics, through their patient and day-to-day work and interactions with grassroots people, gradually helped realize the cultural compromise that made possible the hegemony of Islam over local beliefs. They created the conditions for the founding of the Muslim Sufi orders of the late nineteenth century that consecrated the triumph of Islam among the Wolof. The following chapter examines the history of a family of Muslim learned men that played an vital role in the expansion of Sufi Islam in Senegal, the Mbakke.

2 ⤳ The Mbakke

The Foundations of Family Traditions

THE PREVIOUS CHAPTER discussed the expansion of Islam among the Wolof and the gradual differentiation of the Muslim leadership after the rule of King Lat Sukaabe in the early eighteenth century. It was argued that along with rulers and Muslim warriors, Quranic teachers and holy men played a crucial role in the spread of Islam in the Wolof states. This chapter examines how some of the transformations analyzed earlier affected Amadu Bamba's forebears and ultimately helped, along with other factors, to foster a Mbakke family ethos. The history of Amadu Bamba, especially after the encounter with the French in the late nineteenth century, is broadly known. However, not much is known about his ancestral heritage; the historical context in which he grew up; and the ideas and practices (political and religious) he was exposed to, which, in my view, were a major influence on his character and personality. This chapter aims to provide critical biographical information that is indispensable in illuminating the past and understanding current relationships. It explores the tradition of education among the Mbakke, their marital alliances and internal conflicts, and their relations with Muslim learned families and the royal courts.

In this chapter, I contend that during their peregrinations across the Wolof states of Jolof, Bawol, Saalum, and Kajoor, the Mbakke were guided by a single purpose—the accumulation of the credentials of scholarship, wisdom, and *baraka* that would earn them a legitimate place among the prominent families of Muslim learned men, or *doomi sokhna*, in the Wolof states.[1] An examination of the family's genealogical and intellectual trajectories reveals a strategy consciously elaborated to this end, at least since Maaram Mbakke,

Amadu Bamba's great-grandfather. This strategy consisted of two things: first, the acquisition of religious knowledge by frequenting the most renowned schools and teachers in the Wolof and Fulbe countries and, second, the investment of the social, cultural, and symbolic capital conferred by this knowledge to marry into prestigious Muslim families.[2] The ultimate goal was to acquire religious authority and prestige through learning and by tapping recognized sources of baraka.

FROM FUUTA TO JOLOF

The Mbakke originated in Fuuta Tooro in northern Senegal, but they migrated to Jolof, in Wolof country, sometime in the second half of the seventeenth century. It was after their settlement among the Wolof that they earned the reputation of a distinguished family of Muslim learned men and teachers. Sources addressing their life in Fuuta and the causes of their migration are scarce and fragmentary. The scanty information gleaned from oral traditions, however, allows for a partial reconstruction of the family's history in northern Senegal.[3] We learn from historians of the Mbakke family that the village of Abdallah in the Lao province of Fuuta was the cradle of Amadu Bamba's ancestors. Gollera, another village in the same area, is also often cited as the birthplace of the Mbakke, but this village is actually associated with the ancestors of Maam Jaara Buso, Amadu Bamba's mother.[4]

There are varying traditions about the circumstances and motives of the Mbakke migration to Jolof.[5] Some sources indicated that they left Fuuta to join family members who were already living in Jolof. Others suggested that the migration was precipitated by a conflict with the "pagan" rulers of Lao, who were hostile to the Muslims. The move to Jolof may also have been prompted by a prolonged drought or a protracted period of unrest in Fuuta. But it is more plausible to assume that the Mbakke were a family of nomad pastoralists in the process of adopting a sedentary lifestyle. Whatever might have happened in Fuuta was an additional incentive to join relatives already installed in Jolof as farmers.

Although sources disagree about the causes of the migration, they concur that Usmaan Ba was the first member of the Mbakke clan to move to Jolof with his cattle and family.[6] He was welcomed and accommodated by the *bergel* (the title of the province chief of Mbelekhe).[7] The relationship between Usmaan and the bergel's family were gradually strengthened by marital alliances. In Jolof, the Mbakke adopted a new identity over time, characterized by an abandonment of the nomadic lifestyle, an increasing inclination toward Islamic learning, and assimilation to Wolof culture. (See fig. 2.1.)

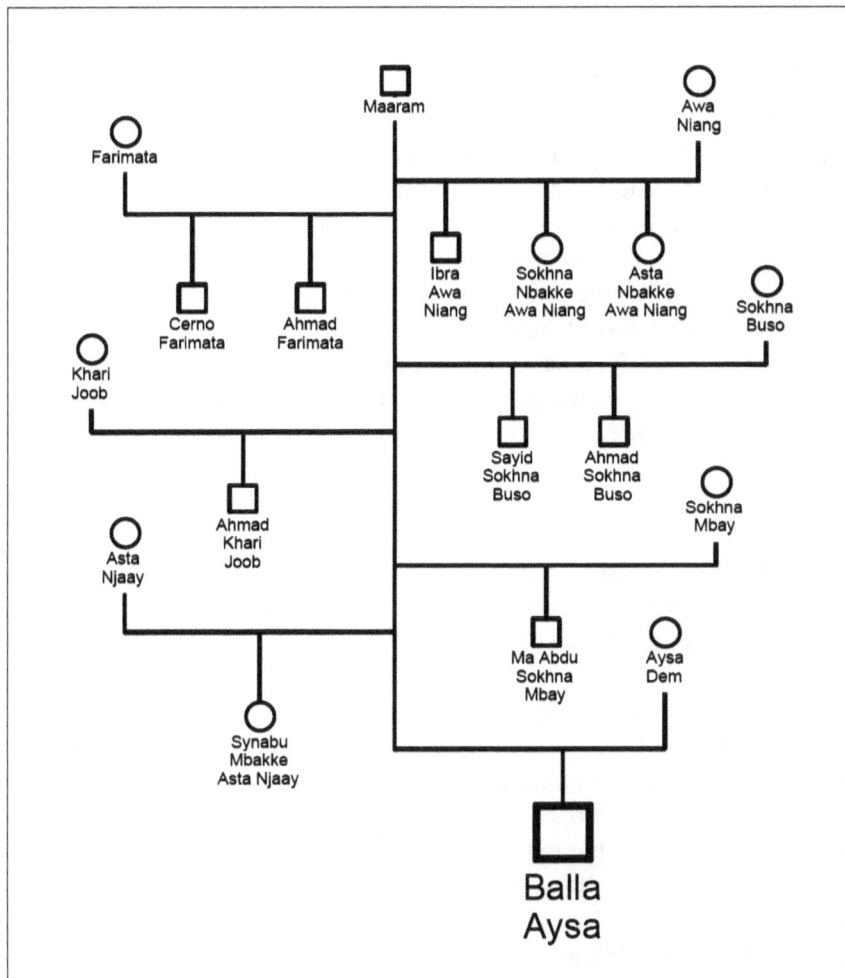

Fig. 2.1. Maaram's sons and daughters

For the next four generations, the Mbakke continued to live in Jolof as modest teachers and clients of the bergel's family. Yet they maintained the ancestral tradition of pursuing Muslim scholarship and moral virtue. Murid oral traditions portray Usmaan's heirs as lacking the prestige and baraka that their ancestor possessed.[8] This judgment could be understood as the result of a lack of information about this episode in the history of the Mbakke family or simply as a device to highlight the importance of the period that followed, which was marked by the emergence of Maaram Mbakke, Amadu Bamba's great-grandfather.

MAARAM: THE FOUNDING FATHER

The history of the Mbakke family in eastern Bawol began with Maaram Mbakke. He was the founder of the village of Mbakke Bawol, which is the heartland of the family, and the first member of the Mbakke clan to earn fame and prestige in Wolof country. Maaram was born in AH 1111 (1700–1703 CE) in Jolof.[9] He devoted a great part of his lifetime to acquiring knowledge.[10] He studied at the famous school of Kokki, where *dammeel* Lat Joor's great-grandfather and the cleric Malaamin Saar were his schoolmates. He also frequented the school of Samba Caam, a teacher from Fuuta and an ancestor of Ibrahima Niass, founder of a powerful branch of the Tijaniyya order in West Africa. Maaram probably attended other schools in the Wolof states and in Fuuta. One source even indicates that he had sojourned among the clerics of Mauritania.[11]

Maaram's effort to acquire advanced education reflected the high value that the Mbakke family placed on Islamic learning since moving to Wolof country. Higher learning became a central feature of family traditions and a means to accumulate social and cultural capital. And as we shall see, the example set by Maaram was duplicated by his sons, his grandsons, and his great-grandson Amadu Bamba.

Through education, Maaram garnered many credentials as a Muslim learned man, and he used these credentials to bolster the prestige of his family. When he returned to Jolof after completing his training, he left the family compound and founded his own village-school, which he called Mbakke Jolof. For the Wolof, the founding of a village is the manifestation of independence and a means to assert one's authority and power. After establishing himself as a teacher, Maaram sought wives in the most respected Muslim families of the Wolof states.[12] He had a large number of offspring, and his numerous male descendants were seen as a sign of baraka and considered an asset in the Mbakke family, where women outnumbered men.[13]

Besides his own marriages, Maaram also used his daughters and granddaughters to build alliances with famous Muslim clerical families and further anchor the Mbakke in the Islamic religious culture of the Wolof states. These women were married among the Jakhate, Sy, Joob, and Faal clans, which were among the most esteemed Muslim families in Kajoor, Bawol, and Jolof. Many of the Muslim leaders in Senegal today are descendants of Maaram or of his allies.[14] (See fig. 2.2.)

The high quality of Maaram's education and his marriage ties earned him a prominent social status. He was among the respected notables of Jolof, and his networks of friends and colleagues spanned the Wolof country. His name

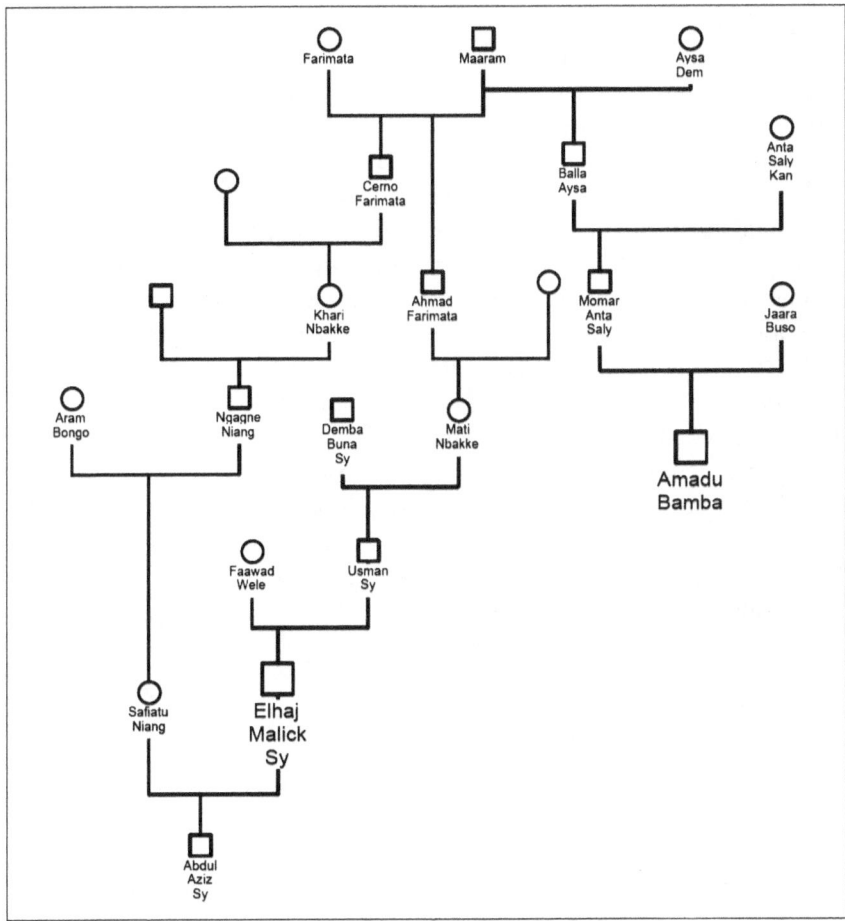

Fig. 2.2. The Mbakke and Sy families

appeared for the first time in the political history of Bawol on the death of his colleague and schoolmate Malaamin Saar. Saar's death, as noted in the previous chapter, occurred during the Muslim revolt against dammeel Amary Ngoone Ndeela (in 1796) and the jihad of *Almaamy* Abdul Kader of Fuuta Tooro. Maaram was aware of the deteriorating relations between the clerics and rulers in Kajoor and Bawol, where some of his wives originated and where some of his former schoolmates taught. However, he did not take part in the conflict and even disapproved of the political stance of his colleagues. Maraam's prestige was not based on association with kings or contestation of their rule but rather on Islamic knowledge and wisdom. He maintained a position of political neutrality and kept his distance from rulers.[15] This tradition of regarding temporal leaders with suspicion became a key trait of the family and would be shared by Amadu Bamba.

Maaram undertook the trip to Bawol to present his condolences to the family of his deceased friend during a period of heightened tension between the clerics and rulers of this kingdom.[16] He sent a letter to the dammeel to seek his approval, and although he traveled with a large following because of the volatile security situation, he chose to pay homage to the local administration.[17] For example, after entering the territory of Bawol, he camped seven kilometers from the border and sent one of his disciples to inform *ber siin laa* (the title of the administrator of the province of eastern Bawol) about the trip and his good intentions. The latter, who had already collected some information about the cleric, was reassured by Maaram's responses to his questions, and he cleared the way for him to pursue his trip. Maaram's respectful attitude was appreciated by the king, who extended an invitation for him to settle in Bawol. Maaram declined the offer but gave his blessings for the founding of a village that would be headed by his elder son, Amadu Farimata.[18] He chose the land at the border between Jolof, Bawol, and Kajoor in the eastern region of the kingdom and named the village Mbakke Bawol. (See fig. 2.3.)

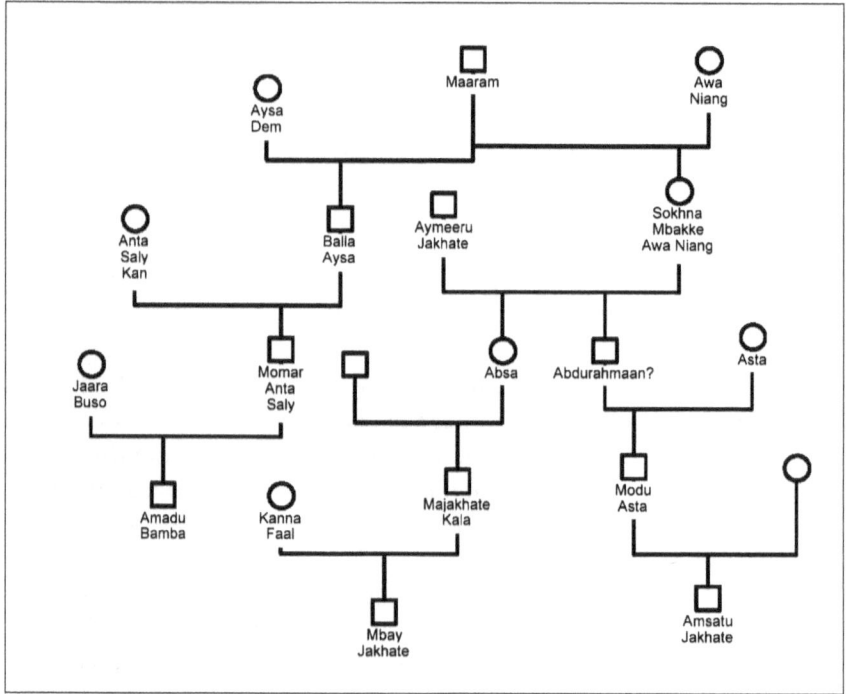

Fig. 2.3. The Mbakke and Jakhate families

The king's proposal to Maaram was not without political motive. The last quarter of the eighteenth century was a period of conflict between clerics and rulers in the Wolof states. By inviting Maaram to settle in Bawol, Amary Ngoone Ndeela had certain political aims in mind. First, he wanted to show the Muslim community of Bawol and Kajoor that he was not hostile to Islam and that it was the clerics who bore the responsibility for the conflicts that had marred their relationships with the court since the second half of the seventeenth century. Second, the king wanted to present Maaram as a model for the Muslim leadership of his kingdom to emulate. Maaram's decision not to migrate to Bawol and to choose land away from the central authority and along the borders of the kingdom also was politically significant. We have seen that in the western Sudan, the location of a cleric's residence was usually indicative of his political orientation. The choice of a remote location, away from the center of power, often expressed political neutrality and an unwillingness to be implicated in the business of rulers.[19] Maaram's preference to remain away from the king and his entourage reflected the inclination of the Mbakke family to pursue high Islamic knowledge and political independence.

AFTER MAARAM

Maaram's heirs strove to maintain and expand the family traditions of pursuing Islamic learning and maintaining political neutrality. However, the development of the village of Mbakke Bawol and the accumulation of the prestige, material wealth, and power it generated introduced a new challenge to the maintenance of family cohesion. Competition for control of the village divided the family. The position of village chief was coveted because it was associated with honor and authority. Since Mbakke Bawol was a Muslim village, the chief was also the imam (that is, the leader of prayer and of the community). He collected the *zakaat* (the annual Muslim income tax), managed the land, settled disputes, and mediated the relationships between the population and the king's representatives.

As noted, Maaram's elder son was the first chief of Mbakke Bawol. After his death, his younger brother, Ibra Awa Niang, took over as head of the village.[20] The succession of this young brother, which occurred between 1834 and 1835, created a rift in the Mbakke family.[21] The tension stemmed from the competition between Ibra's sons and their uncle Balla Aysa Mbakke (Amadu Bamba's grandfather) for the leadership of the village. After Ibra's death, Balla Aysa was the only living son of Maaram and therefore the legitimate successor to his elder brother as head of the village. Succession among the Mbakke followed a collateral line.[22] But Balla was very young when his father died, and

Ibra acted as surrogate father to him. Ibra taught him the Quran, oversaw his training in the Islamic sciences, and helped him found a family. In addition, some of Ibra's children, such as his elder son Modu Jee, were older than their uncle Balla. Ibra's sons saw Balla as a cousin and not as an uncle who should have authority over them. They insisted that the leadership of the village should remain within their lineage and that Modu Jee should become head of Mbakke Bawol. The majority of the population of the village sided with Modu Jee, who became the de facto chief of Mbakke. Realizing that the village was against him, Balla sought help from his maternal clan. With the backing of his uncles and the king's representative, he was reinstated as chief. Thereafter, the Modu Jee faction left Mbakke Bawol to found the villages of Mbakke Dimb and Mbakke Baari.

This conflict and the memories it generated have loomed large in the history of the Mbakke family. The conflict had an enduring effect on the relations between Balla Aysa and the people of Mbakke Bawol, and it undermined the unity of the Mbakke clan. In addition, the rift with Modu Jee affected relations between Balla Aysa's son Momar Anta Sali (Amadu Bamba's father) and his relatives in Mbakke. It also explains why branches affiliated with Modu Jee were ignored when, in the late nineteenth century, Murid hagiographers started to build a sacred genealogy for their sheikh and his family.

Under Balla Aysa's leadership, Mbakke Bawol continued to grow. New communities were founded around the village, and Balla continued the tradition of cooperation and interaction with the clerical families of the Wolof states. His eldest son, Momar Anta Sali, was sent to Kokki and Saalum for his education. Balla also upheld the family tradition of maintaining political neutrality and respect for the king of Bawol and his administration. But he still faced lingering resentment from some of his constituents who favored Modu Jee and only reluctantly submitted to his authority.

The tension between Balla Aysa and the village of Mbakke culminated with the death of his second but most cherished son, Abdul Khaadir, which occurred in 1863 or 1864.[23] Younger than Momar Anta Sali, he was probably in his late twenties when he was killed by a group of slave warriors who were avenging the slaying of one of their colleagues during a foiled raid in Mbakke. Balla Aysa was so affected by the loss of his beloved son that he refused to see the body and ordered that the burial occur at a location out of his sight.[24] Finally, he decided to leave Mbakke and migrate to Ngay in the Signi province of Saalum, arguing that he could no longer live and walk on the land sullied by the unjust shedding of his son's blood. Balla's stay in Saalum was, however, short: he lost his life one or two years after migrating to Ngay, killed by a robber.[25]

THE JIHAD OF MABA AND
THE MIGRATION OF THE MBAKKE TO SAALUM

The jihad of Maba Jakhu Ba marked a critical moment in the history of the Mbakke clan. It created a situation that challenged the family's traditional political neutrality and mistrust of rulers. For the first time, the Mbakke were thrust into the thick of Wolof politics and were forced to take side in a conflict that divided the Muslim leadership in the Wolof states and imposed on many the necessity to rethink the purpose of jihad.

Maba began his jihad in the kingdom of Saalum in 1861.[26] By the summer of 1863, he had swept away the traditional rulers and established his authority over the area between the Saalum and Gambia rivers. The struggle between the French and the kingdom of Kajoor helped his cause. Makodu Faal, the former king of Kajoor, who had been driven into exile by the French, joined the jihad. Soon after, Lat Joor Joob, another dammeel also forced out of power by the French, moved to Saalum.

By 1864, Maba had turned his attention away from Saalum. By the end of the year, he was able to create a base of operations in Mbakke Bawol, where the forces of Lat Joor, which would henceforth be the strong arm of the jihad, unleashed relentless raids against Kajoor.[27] By May 1865, the jihadist Maba was able to occupy his native land of Jolof. From there, he contacted the Moor rulers of the state of Trarza in southwestern Mauritania and the almaamy of Fuuta to build a strong coalition against the French.[28]

However, Maba was not successful in his bid to mobilize the Muslim population of the Western Sudan for his cause, and he was compelled to retreat to Saalum, taking with him many of the clerics of the areas he occupied. The French military presence at the mouth of the Senegal River deterred the emir of Trarza and the chief of Fuuta from making any substantial contribution to the jihad. The Wolof rulers also ignored his appeal. With the exclusion of the Muslim chief of Kokki, whose support was primarily motivated by the involvement of his cousin Lat Joor, the Muslim leadership of Bawol and Kajoor grew critical of Maba and his movement.[29]

Maba's controversial decision to deport the clerics of Jolof, Bawol, and Kajoor to Saalum after he withdrew from these kingdoms fueled the hostility of many Muslims toward his movement. Bachir Mbacké, son and biographer of Amadu Bamba, reported that this initiative was judged unfortunate by the clerics, although they understood that Maba might have acted to protect them against the retaliation of the local kings and their warriors.[30] Mbacké mentioned that despite his good intentions, Maba made many mistakes due to his authoritarianism and impatience. He also objected to the almaamy's method of government and questioned the legitimacy of his political ambitions.[31] Majakhate Kala, another respected Muslim cleric from Kajoor, also doubted Maba's competence. He criticized him for forcing new converts to shave, arguing that it was only during the rituals of pilgrimage that a Muslim should be instructed to shave his head.[32] A smoker himself, he also challenged Maba to provide the doctrinal basis for his interdiction of tobacco. Maba is said to have responded to the cleric that he did not care about doctrine and that his guns gave him the power and authority to enforce his will.[33]

Bachir Mbacké's unfavorable assessment of Maba's actions reflected the Mbakke tradition of political moderation and the detrimental effect that the jihad had on the family. The Mbakke were profoundly affected by the violence associated with the jihad.[34] We know that from the end of 1864, their village served as the rear base for the army of the jihad. The village of Mbakke was a populous and relatively wealthy settlement where millet and other food crops were grown, and Maba's army certainly benefited from the generosity of the village's predominantly Muslim population. Yet oral traditions, as well as archival documents, report many instances of raids and conflicts that opposed the inhabitants of Mbakke to bands of warriors affiliated with or against the jihad. These warriors were part of Lat Joor and Maba's army or members of punitive forces sent against them by the king of Bawol. As already noted, Balla Aysa's son Abdul Khaadir was killed during one of these raids. It was also in this same period that slave raiders abducted Momar Anta Sali's daughter and the little sister of Amadu Bamba, Faati Mbakke, then nine or ten years old.[35] The Mbakke were not happy to see their village transformed into a battlefield, their children killed or abducted, and their harvest pillaged. They also certainly resented the forced migration to Saalum to participate in a jihad, given that their family tradition had always promoted peaceful interactions with rulers regardless of their religion. Further, Amadu Bamba's mother died not long after the arrival in Saalum.[36] The jihad and the events it precipitated shook up the Mbakke family and impressed the young Bamba, who was between twelve and fourteen years old at the time, and also helped fashion his philosophy of nonviolence and his suspicious attitude toward temporal rulers, whether secular or religiously inspired.[37] Within a short period of time, he had lost his younger sister, an uncle, his grandfather, and his mother, and he himself was forced to leave the land of his ancestors.

MOMAR ANTA SALI IN SAALUM AND KAJOOR

The stay in Saalum and Kajoor was a watershed in the history of the Mbakke family. In these two states, Momar Anta Sali occupied positions and had encounters that dramatically changed the direction of his life and that of his family. It was also in Saalum where the young Bamba learned about Islamic mysticism and started to form his ideas about religion and politics.

Before the migration to Saalum, Momar Anta Sali was a successful teacher in the village of Khuru Mbakke, in eastern Bawol. Momar was born in Mbakke Bawol in the early 1820s, but he grew up in Njah Kan under the protection of his uncle Gammu Kan.[38] He read the Quran with Kan and his father, then pursued the study of the Islamic sciences and Arabic literature at the school in Kokki and in Saalum, where he studied with the cleric Amadu Sall in the village of Bamba: he named his third son, Amadu Bamba, after Sall. Like his grandfather Maaram, Momar spent a good part of his life seeking knowledge; he was a lifelong student.[39]

Momar Anta Sali returned to Mbakke Bawol in his early twenties after completing his education. He soon left the village again to join his uncle at Njah Kan. Some sources reported that tensions with his father's family caused him to leave Mbakke Bawol.[40] It may have been, however, that Momar was uncomfortable in Mbakke because of the conflict that pitted his father against the population of the village. Or he may simply have been following tradition, for among the Wolof, it is customary for a young man at the age of marriage to seek his maternal uncle's support to found a family.

Momar first sought a wife among his maternal clan but without success. He then turned to his paternal family and was offered his cousin Astu Mbakke, better known as Anta Njaay Mbakke. After his marriage, Momar left Njah Kan and founded the village-school of Khuru Mbakke, the birthplace of Amadu Bamba, which was a short distance from Njah. This move might have been prompted by the antagonism of his uncle's sons, as some sources indicated, but it also might have been that Momar Anta wanted to establish his own authority as a teacher and scholar, out of the shadow of his uncle and mentor.[41] His grandfather Maaram had done the same after he completed his education. And one day, his own son, Amadu Bamba, would follow his grandfather's and father's examples and found many villages in Bawol as well.

Gradually, Momar earned the respect of the clerical families of Bawol and Kajoor. The change in his social status was evidenced by the marriages he was able to contract. He married Faati Joob from the prestigious Muslim family of Kokki and then Jaara Buso, his cousin from the Busoobe of Jolof. The Mbakke and the Buso originated from Fuuta and Jolof, and the bond sealed by this common origin had been reinforced through marriages since the time of Maaram. However, the prosperity of the school of Khuru Mbakke was affected by the tension and violence associated with the jihad of Maba. In 1865, Momar Anta Sali was forced to abandon his school and to migrate with his family to Saalum.[42]

The Mbbake: The Foundations of Family Traditions ⌇ 43

Momar's reputation as a teacher and a respected learned man preceded him to Saalum. There, Maba entrusted him with the education of his son, Saer Mati, and the children of the Muslims from Kajoor and Bawol who joined the jihad. Momar settled in the village of Porokhaan, 8 kilometers from Nioro, Maba's capital, where he opened a school and taught the Quran to the youth and Islamic sciences to the adults. In Porokhaan, Momar interacted with clerics from all over the Wolof states who had ended up in Saalum, voluntarily or by force. It was in Saalum that he built a close relationship with Khaali Majakhate Kala, who belonged to a family of Muslim teachers that had a long tradition of cooperating with the rulers of Kajoor and Bawol.[43] His ties with Majakhate Kala may have steered him away from the Mbakke family tradition of political neutrality and toward collaboration with the rulers. Momar and Khaali did not participate in the fighting; instead, they worked as teachers and advisers to the Kajoorian community in Saalum. Khaali Majakhate Kala also taught Amadu Bamba.

In Saalum, Momar for the first time established close ties between the Mbakke family and the *zawiya* (lodge) of the branch of the *qadiri* order of Butilimit, in Mauritania. We have seen that Balla Aysa, his father, named his second son after the founder of the Qadiriyya tariqa, Abd al-Qadir al-Jilani (1077–1166). This suggests that he (Balla) was a member of the Qadiriyya, but we do not have evidence that he entertained formal relations with branches of the qadiri order in Senegal or Mauritania. Momar, however, had strong connections with some of those branches. He named his son Sheikh Anta after Sheikh Sidi Mokhtar al-Kunti, the renovator of the Qadiriyya in the Western Sudan in the eighteenth century. He also renewed his initiation to the Qadiriyya order with the zawiya of Sheikh Sidiyya al-Kabir (1780–1868) in Butilimit and named his son Sheikh Coro after Sheikh Sid Muhammad Khalifa, al-Kabir's son and successor.[44] Momar traveled to Butilimit with his cousin Samba Tukuloor Ka, who was a representative of the Sidiyya order in Senegal, and later received a certificate attesting to his initiation from Ka.[45] The relations that Momar established between the Mbakke and the family of Sheikh Sidiyya would be consolidated by Amadu Bamba, who was a disciple and friend of Sheikh Sidiyya Baba, al-Kabir's grandson.

In Saalum, Momar Anta Sali had another encounter that greatly influenced his life and that of the Mbakke family. This was his encounter with Lat Joor Joob, the former dammeel of Kajoor. Bachir Mbacké noted that Lat Joor was among the many people who frequented the school of Porokhaan for the purpose of education or for advice on religious and other matters.[46] Lat Joor had a lot of affection for Momar, to whom he offered his niece, Coro Maarooso Joob, as a wife. This was not the first contact between the Joob and

Mbakke families. As mentioned earlier, Maaram, Momar Anta's grandfather, was a schoolmate of Lat Joor's great-grandfather, and some marital alliances might even have existed between branches of the two families before the encounter of the second half of the nineteenth century in Saalum. However, Momar's close collaboration with Lat Joor, especially after the latter was reinstated as king of Kajoor, was unprecedented in the Mbakke family, which was known for its reluctance to be involved with temporal power holders. Momar played an active role in the campaign Lat Joor initiated in the late 1860s to regain his throne. In 1869, he was cited in a French intelligence brief as one of the clerics encouraging the former dammeel to get rid of the ceddo.[47]

Despite his obvious political engagement, Momar displayed some ambivalence in his relations with the former dammeel. Although many of Lat Joor's clerical advisers and members of his entourage in Saalum followed the ruler when he moved back to Kajoor in 1869, Momar did not join them until three years later. His decision to delay his settlement in Kajoor could be explained by the turmoil that marked the first years of the return of Lat Joor in the kingdom. But his hesitation could also be explained by a reluctance to hold a central position in the court of the dammeel, whose declared faith to Islam was suspect in the eyes of many Muslims.[48]

When he finally decided to move to Kajoor, Momar Anta Sali settled in the village of Pataar,[49] away from Ker Amadu Yala, Lat Joor's headquarters. He remained an adviser to the dammeel, who consulted with him in the court every Thursday.[50] This arrangement may have been a compromise between Momar's desire to keep some measure of autonomy vis-à-vis the court and his willingness to continue to support Lat Joor.

Momar remained in Kajoor even after Mbakke Bawol had been reoccupied. For example, when two of his cousins called on him to return and lead the village in his capacity as the oldest living grandson of Maaram, he declined the offer.[51] Instead of returning to Mbakke, Momar preferred to follow Lat Joor to central Kajoor when the dammeel, under pressure from his army and some of the dignitaries of the kingdom, decided to leave the northern province and move his capital to the village of Sugeer.[52]

In central Kajoor, where he moved in 1880 or 1881, Momar founded the village-school of Mbakke Kajoor, some 20 kilometers from the king's capital, on the border between Kajoor and Bawol, thereby returning to the tradition established by Maaram. This decision was probably influenced by Amadu Bamba, who was becoming increasingly critical of his father's role in the court of Lat Joor. The *daara* (school) of Mbakke Kajoor was mostly devoted to the teaching of the Islamic sciences, and it accommodated primarily older

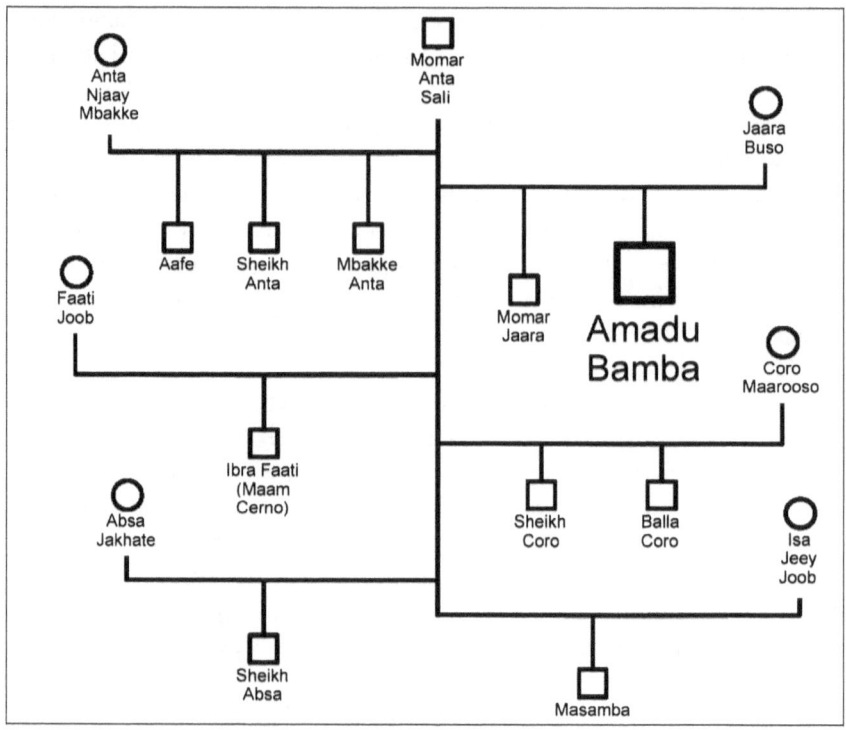

Fig. 2.4. Momar Anta Sali's sons and their mothers

students. Amadu Bamba, then in his mid-twenties, helped his father with the teaching and started to emerge as a respected cleric. (See fig. 2.4.)

In Mbakke Kajoor, Momar Anta Sali remained one of Lat Joor's most powerful Muslim advisers.[53] He enjoyed the confidence of and consideration from the court and received subsidies from the dammeel, who generously supplied his family in order to supplement the resources Momar drew from his farms; for instance, Momar was entitled to part of the cattle slaughtered in the court.[54] His prestige in Mbakke Kajoor was exemplified by his marriages with Isa Joob, a niece of the Muslim chief of Kokki and former wife of Lat Joor, and with Absa Jakhate, a sister of Khaali Majakhate Kala.[55]

The resumption of full-scale fighting between Lat Joor, the French, and the different candidates to the throne of Kajoor in 1882 rendered the situation of the cleric supporters of the dammeel precarious. The destruction of the dammeel's capital in 1883 by French troops put Lat Joor in the position of an outcast and negatively affected the situation of his maraboutic advisers.

Momar Anta Sali, then in his early sixties, continued to live in Mbakke Kajoor, but his position became uncomfortable. He was from Bawol, and the

Mbakke clan had neither the historical roots nor the credentials that the clerics of Kajoor origins, such as the Jakhate, could claim. Some ceddo also expressed their resentment against the Mbakke family. When Momar Anta Sali died in 1882 or 1883, even his burial in the village of Deqele was opposed. Moor Maam Jeey, one of the leaders of the ceddo camp in the village, protested the burial of the marabout in the village without his permission.[56]

THE DEATH OF MOMAR ANTA SALI

On his deathbed, Momar Anta Sali called Amadu Bamba to confer with him about his last wishes. Murid sources present different versions of the meeting. I recorded the most commonly told version from Sheikh Maam Balla Mbakke. The story goes that when Amadu Bamba entered the room, he sat on the bed near his father; Momar began the conversation, which went as follows:

> "Now I know that I have entered the path to the hereafter. Among my sons, you are the one I trust the most and I know that Allah has bestowed on you exceptional blessings. During my life, I have done my utmost to do and recommend the right, to avoid and forbid the wrong, as Allah recommends all Muslims. But I want you to assure me here that I will face no harm in where I am headed." Amadu Bamba responded: "I guarantee you that." Momar Anta Sali added, "I entrust you with the whole Mbakke family and I want you to assure me that none of them will ever experience any hardships and that God will bestow on them his baraka so that never will they be forced to earn their lives by the sweat of their brow." Amadu Bamba said, "I guarantee you that." He [Momar] added some more requests, and Amadu Bamba gave his assurance that all of his father's wishes would be fulfilled.[57]

Some statements in this conversation clearly conflict with principles of the Murid doctrine and practices as articulated by Amadu Bamba and his early companions.[58] This is the case, for instance, with the lines related to work. The guarantee that Amadu Bamba reportedly made to the effect that members of the Mbakke family would forever enjoy a comfortable life without sweating contradicts the well-known and much written-about Murid ethic of hard work. It is probable that the vision of work conveyed through this statement, which implicitly makes working an exclusive duty of the disciples, is a late modification aimed at justifying the privileged position that members of the Mbakke family enjoyed within the Murid tariqa. This interpretation is all the more plausible because by the time of his father's death, Amadu Bamba was an emerging cleric without disciples of his own, virtually unknown beyond a small circle of colleagues and friends in central Kajoor. He did not have the baraka and prestige that would have given him the confidence to make such promises.

Some Muridiyya specialists, influenced by ideas of the *salafists* (proponents of a return to pristine prophetic traditions), also questioned the assumption that Amadu Bamba had promised paradise to his father. They argued that a man as knowledgeable about sharia, or Islamic law, as Amadu Bamba would never have made such a commitment, for it manifestly contradicted Islamic teachings.[59] It is probable that Bamba did not promise to take his father to heaven, as inferred in the preceding extract, but one should be aware that most followers of Sufism believe not only that Islam authorizes intercession but also that they themselves have the power to intercede for their kin and disciples.

Sheikh Coro Mbakke, Amadu Bamba's younger brother, gave a much shorter version of the conversation in his interview with Robert Arnaud in 1912. He said that Momar Anta Sali had called Bamba and told him: "Among my sons, you are the one I trust the most. I entrust you with your younger brothers and sisters, take care of them."[60] The versions of the story told by Sheikh Maam Balla and Sheikh Coro omit any mention of a recommendation that Momar Anta Sali might have made to his son regarding the school of Mbakke Kajoor and the relations between the Mbakke and the zawiya of Butilimit, whereas these two matters were probably at the center of Momar Anta Sali's concerns and legacy. The account recorded by Cheikh Tidiane Sy from Falilu Mbakke, the son and second successor of Amadu Bamba, by contrast, emphasized recommendations urging Bamba to pursue education and to avoid involvement with rulers.[61] The renderings provided by Sheikh Coro and Falilu, because they were collected in writing and from older members of the family at an earlier point, are less likely to have been subject to later modifications inspired by recent developments within the Muridiyya. Momar Anta Sali was close to Amadu Bamba, and he counted on him for the perpetuation of the family's tradition of scholarship and the preservation of their relationships with the family of Sheikh Sidiyya. Drawing from the lessons of his collaboration with Maba and Lat Joor, which was not successful, he probably encouraged his son to maintain his distant and wary attitude toward temporal power holders.

The story of Amadu Bamba's ultimate conversation with his father carries great historical significance. By the time of Momar's death, Bamba had earned the trust of some of his father's disciples, and they became his first followers.[62] But his legitimacy in the Mbakke family and particularly the quality of his relationships with his brothers were enhanced by the belief that his father had entrusted him with the family. Bearers of Murid traditions inform us that Ibra Faati (best known as Maam Cerno) and Sheikh Anta, the first disciples and closest collaborators of Amadu Bamba, pledged allegiance to their brother immediately after the conversation he had with Momar.[63] Both were young men in their late teens and were urged to submit to Amadu Bamba by their mothers, who had overheard the words exchanged between the father and his son. This behavior was rather unusual in polygamous marriages, in which the death of the father often triggers competition and conflicts between brothers of different mothers and between cowives. Consequently, the story of the last conversation between Bamba and his father was crucial in legitimizing the founder of the Muridiyya as inheritor of the spiritual authority of his father and ultimate recipient of the baraka accumulated in the family since the time of Maaram, even though he was not the oldest son. This also explains why Momar Jaara Mbakke, Amadu Bamba's older brother—who seemingly was not present at the scene—was initially so critical of his younger siblings and did not join the Muridiyya until decades later when the organization became well established. The seed of baraka and spiritual authority that Bamba inherited from Momar because of his privileged position as the recipient of his last will provided the foundation on which he built his own spiritual power.

CONCLUSION

The examination of the history of the Mbakke clan between the time of its residence in Fuuta and its move to the Wolof country has highlighted some significant features of Amadu Bamba's family heritage. This heritage included the pursuit of high Islamic learning, the building of close relations with prestigious Muslim families, and the maintenance of cordial but distant relationships with rulers (Momar Anta was an exception in this regard). This tradition determined how members of the family conceived their place and role in society. Like other family members, Amadu Bamba was profoundly shaped by Mbakke traditional values.

By the time of the French conquest of the Wolof country in the late nineteenth century, Bamba had become the leader of the Mbakke family. He was over thirty years old and had lived all his adult life under his father's shadow, mingling with the religious and political elite of the Wolof states. His character and his conception of life were deeply marked by this experience. He was not a passive and disinterested observer of the changes that Wolof society was experiencing. He had a vision and ideas that were inspired by his family tradition, his education, and the lessons drawn growing up in Bawol, Kajoor, and Saalum during a period of rapid change. Therefore, the history of his life should not be read solely as a reaction against colonization, as suggested in most of the scholarship on the Muridiyya. Rather, his spiritual and political orientations should be seen as the result of the conjunction of three defining elements: his family heritage, his life experience, and the constraints of the sociopolitical environment in the Wolof states in the late nineteenth century. The following chapter investigates the ways in which these three factors conspired to shape the itineraries of Bamba's life.

3 ∽ The Emergence of Amadu Bamba, 1853–95

AMADU BAMBA is the most influential figure of contemporary Senegalese history, and the *tariqa* he founded is one of the most widely studied Muslim organizations in sub-Saharan Africa. Yet paradoxically, Bamba himself has been largely written out of the scholarship on the Muridiyya, either because of a lack of information about his life, thinking, and practices or because of methodological choice.[1] In this chapter, I endeavor to bring Bamba back to the center of Murid history by reconstructing his life and role as a historical actor. To accomplish this, I have drawn from a variety of Murid oral and written sources, royal court chronicles, and colonial archives to provide a careful description and analysis of signal events in Amadu Bamba's life.

I examine the socioeconomic and cultural context in which Bamba grew up; his interactions with relatives, teachers, disciples, and local rulers; and the progressive development of his religious and political thinking. The narrative starts with his birth in 1853 and stops at 18 Safar (the second month of the Muslim calendar) AH 1313 (10 August 1895), the date of his arrest, which was followed by his trial and deportation to Gabon, French Equatorial Africa. This historical marker is significant for the Murids and for the colonial historiography as well. The French expected the deportation to put an end to what they perceived as a real threat to the stability of the newly conquered colony of Senegal. For the Murids, 18 Safar AH 1313 was the coronation of their sheikh's spiritual quest and a turning point in his career as a saint. The commemoration of this date is the most important religious event of the Muridiyya order.

YOUTH AND EDUCATION

Amadu Bamba was born in Khuru Mbakke, the first village founded by his father near Mbakke Bawol, in the early 1850s.[2] He was the fourth child of Momar Anta Sali and the second son of his mother, Maam Jaara Buso. He grew up in his native village, where, as he told his disciple Mbay Jakhate, he "learned to crawl and walk."[3] Bachir Mbacké, his son and biographer, mentioned that as a baby, Bamba displayed behavior that clearly showed he was not an ordinary child.[4] Bamba did not cry as much as most babies do. In fact, he would cry hysterically only when he was taken to places where people were engaged in actions prohibited by Islam, such as wrestling or drumming parties, and he would calm down as soon as he was removed from those places. Mbacké also noted that the young Amadu Bamba avoided his mother's bed and preferred to play and sleep in the corner of the room reserved for prayers. His parents noticed this odd behavior and wondered about the sanity of their child.

Besides this peculiarity, Bamba grew up as an ordinary Wolof boy. When he was seven, the age when young Muslims in Senegal are usually sent to Quranic school (this is also the age when they are taught how to pray, for at ten, praying becomes compulsory), his father placed him in the care of his maternal uncle, Muhammad Buso. Buso, who at the time was living in Jolof, introduced the young Bamba to the Quran and then sent him to Mbakke Ndumbe, better known as Tafsir Mbakke Ndumbe, his granduncle. Tafsir had farms in Jolof, where he spent the rainy season with his student, and they would return to Mbakke Bawol in the dry season. During their stay in Mbakke, Amadu Bamba also frequented the school of Balla Jatara, imam of the village at the time, but he received the bulk of his Quranic education from Tafsir Mbakke Ndumbe.[5] (See fig. 3.1.)

Studying the Quran involved learning the Arabic alphabet, then memorizing each of the 114 suras, or chapters, that compose the book, starting with the shortest.[6] The lessons were written on a portable wooden board, or *aluwa* (*luah* in Arabic), with black ink made by the pupils. After a lesson was memorized, the board was erased to allow for the writing of a new lesson. Students would start studying with a book after they had reached the longer suras and had an adequate command of the alphabet. They devoted four to six years exclusively to studying the Quran, until they could recite and write the whole book from memory.[7] At this stage, they were not required to understand what they were reading.

Amadu Bamba completed his Quranic education by the time of the Mbakke family's migration to Saalum in 1865; he was then twelve years old. In Saalum, the young Bamba started the second phase of his education in earnest. He fo-

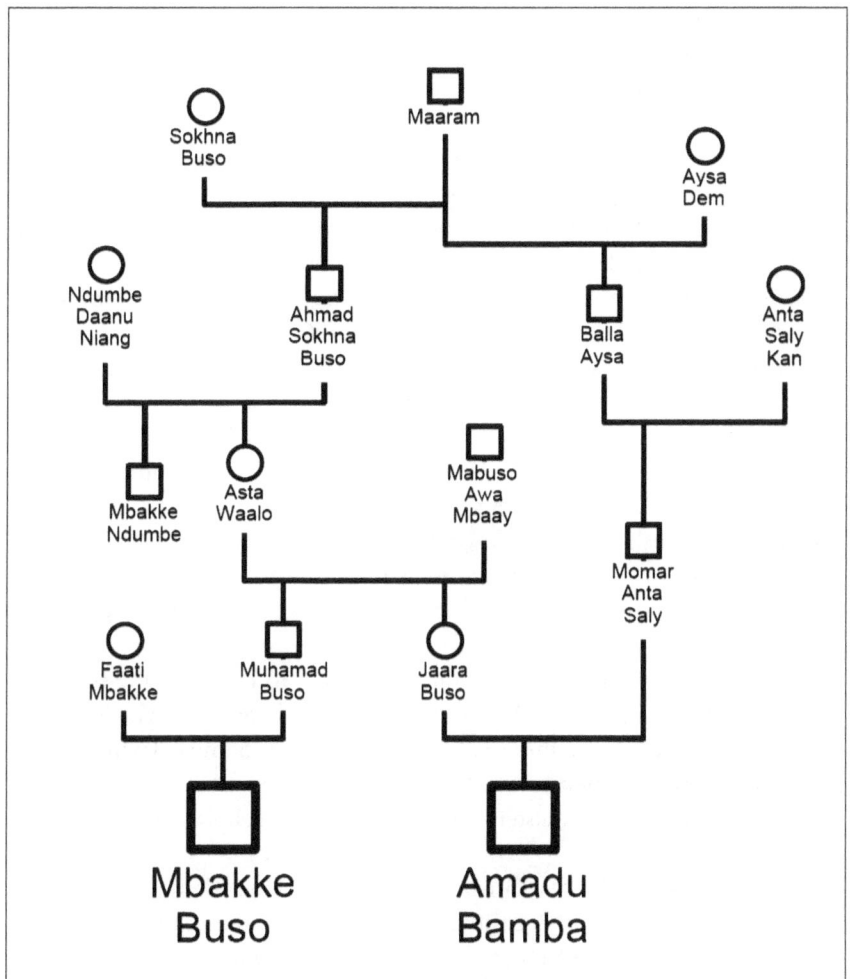

Fig. 3.1. Amadu Bamba's paternal and maternal lineages

cused on the study of the *uluum al-diin,* or Islamic sciences, which consisted of: Quranic exegesis, or *tafsir; hadiith,* or traditions of Prophet Muhammad; *fiq,* or Islamic jurisprudence; *tasawwuf,* or Islamic mysticism; *siira,* or biography and hagiography of Prophet Muhammad; and the *uluum al-arabiyya,* or sciences of the Arabic language including *nahwu* (grammar), *luqa* (lexicography), *balaqa* (use of the language), and *uruud* (poetry).[8] He did not study the *uluum al- awalii,* or sciences of the ancients, which involved logic, astrology, and traditional medicine, although he made an effort to initiate himself into those sciences at a later age.

The intellectual atmosphere in Saalum, where Maba had deported some of the best teachers of Bawol and Jolof, provided a suitable environment for Amadu Bamba's pursuit of the Islamic sciences. He was taught primarily by family members and their associates. Bamba's father introduced him to Islamic jurisprudence and to other religious sciences. Khaali Majakhate Kala, a friend of Momar Anta Sali and a gifted poet, taught him the art of writing poems; he did not teach him a specific book, but he gave him practical training in techniques and styles of Arabic poetry through composing assignments and correcting his drafts.[9] Bamba studied some elementary principles of law and *tawhiid*, or theology, with Samba Tukuloor Ka.

It is likely that it was in Saalum where Amadu Bamba was first introduced to the science of tasawwuf and to Sufi practices, probably through imitation and later through formal education. And it was in Porokhaan, his father's settlement in Saalum, where he started to show an inclination toward mysticism. He used to spend long periods of time away from his schoolmates and remain isolated in the bush during prolonged séances of meditation.[10] He may have learned about Sufism and Sufi practices from Samba Tukuloor, who, as already noted, was also a representative of the Sidiyya branch of the Qadiriyya in Senegal.

When his father moved to the village of Pataar in Kajoor at the behest of *dammeel* Lat Joor in 1871–72, Amadu Bamba stayed in Saalum, where he continued his education in the Islamic sciences with Samba Tukuloor and Muhammad Buso. When he finally joined the paternal family, he was over twenty years old and had mastered a good deal of the scholarship available in the Wolof states.

In Kajoor, Amadu Bamba pursued his training in the Islamic sciences and in Arabic on his own, with occasional masters he met in his father's school or by visiting the different venues of education in Kajoor, Bawol, and Saalum. He did not follow the Wolof tradition of *lakhas* (to travel away from one's family to seek an education).[11] The fact that he was not subject to the time-honored tradition of traveling for the sake of knowledge further intensified his thirst for an education. He studied rhetoric and was initiated in logic by Muhammad Ibn Muhammad al-Karim, better known as Muhammad al-Yadaali, a Moorish cleric who used to visit the village of Njaagne near his father's compound.[12] During his stay in Kajoor, Amadu Bamba tried to build ties with prestigious Muslim families. He used to travel to Longoor, where the Mbay family had a rich library. He also visited the schools of Kokki, Pir, and other highly learned masters in the area. He was not readily accepted in the closed circle of Kajoor's *doomi sokhna*, who did not have much respect for families of Muslims without deep Wolof roots and long dynastic tradition of Islamic learning.[13]

THE PERIOD OF MATURATION

Amadu Bamba gradually emerged as a knowledgeable teacher, and he became his father's lead assistant. Some of the disciples preferred to study with him because he was more patient and had better communication skills than Momar Anta Sali, who was busy with his duties as a judge and disliked slower students.[14] It was after he joined his father in Pataar in Kajoor that Bamba started writing.[15] In his first works, he concentrated on theology, mysticism, and Islamic rituals, three themes that loom large in his teachings. In the tradition of North and West African Islamic scholarship, most of the books that he authored were commentaries and versifications of classics produced by medieval Muslim thinkers. They consisted of titles such as *Muwayibul Quduuss* (Gift from the Holiest), which is a versification of *Umul Barahim*, a book of theology by al-Sanusi (d. 1490); *Mullayinu Suduur* (The Enlightener of the Heart), a commentary on *Bidaya al-Hidaya*, a book on mysticism by Abu Hamid al-Ghazzali (d. 1111), which he completed in AH 1294 (1877); and *Jawharu Nafiis* (The Precious Jewels), a versification of *Abderrahman al-Akhdari*, a popular book on Islamic ritual practices by Abdrahman al-Akhdari (d. Algiers, AH 983 [1575]). To show his appreciation for and pride in his son, Momar Anta Sali included some of these books in the program of his school. *Jawharu Nafiis* was, for example, used as a substitute for *al-Akhdari*.[16] Amadu Bamba also became his father's secretary, accompanying him during his visits to colleagues and writing his *fatwas* (legal opinions) and the responses to questions sent by disciples; he also handled, albeit reluctantly, some court businesses on his father's behalf.

Amadu Bamba contracted his first marriage in his mid-twenties in Pataar. He initially married the widow of his half brother, who bore him his elder daughter, Faati Jah Mbakke.[17] (The practice of levirate is common among the Wolof.) Following the tradition set by his ancestors, he sought other wives among some well-known clerical families in Kajoor and Bawol. Although unsuccessful in the beginning, he was later able to marry widely among these families when he acquired recognition as a learned man and a saint.

In Kajoor, Amadu Bamba's personality and attitudes continued to develop along the lines already perceptible in Porokhaan, marked by a rejection of deliberate involvement with rulers, an aspiration to separate the politics of Islam from the politics of kings, and an attraction to mysticism. Bamba's ideas about life and religion were forged in the course of his stay in Saalum and Kajoor. There, he experienced firsthand the devastating effect of political violence on Wolof society and the failure of the remedies proposed by the Muslim leadership, whether through alliance with rulers or violent opposition to them. He expressed his sense of dismay about the situation in the Wolof states when, decades later, he told Bachir Mbacké, "I lost the slightest interest I had in worldly and temporal matters when I saw, while living in Kajoor, the bodies of Muhammad Fati and Ale Lo, two persons from a respected Muslim family in Njambur, killed by dammeel for mere political reasons."[18] The names of these two persons suggest that they belonged to the clerical family of Ndaam or Niomre in northern Kajoor; their deaths may have been linked to the repression during the Madiyanke conflict.

Amadu Bamba's resentment about the situation in the Wolof country, especially the role of the Muslim leadership, informed his perception of the relations between his father and the rulers of Kajoor. He grew increasingly uncomfortable about the close ties between Momar Anta Sali and Lat Joor, and he used every occasion possible to let his father know that he disapproved of his position as judge in the royal court.[19] Momar justified his position by insisting on the positive impact that his involvement with Lat Joor could have on the king's administration of the Muslims of Kajoor and on the well-being of the Mbakke family, but he could not win Bamba's consent. At one point, Amadu Bamba even contemplated leaving the Wolof country altogether and migrating to Mauritania.[20] This initiative was perhaps motivated by the will to further his education with renowned masters away from his own country, in the tradition of Muslim learned families, but it also could have been caused by dissatisfaction with his father's role in the court. Momar's response to the initiative seemed to support the second hypothesis: he convinced Amadu Bamba to stay by soliciting the intervention of people in the family who had a great deal of influence on him, by arranging his first marriage, and by choosing to settle away from the dammeel's headquarters when he moved to central Kajoor some years later.[21]

By the time Momar Anta Sali founded the village-school of Mbakke Kajoor between 1880 and 1881, Amadu Bamba had started to gain some recognition as a new kind of Muslim cleric. He became the de facto head of his father's school and was increasingly drawn to Sufism. He spent a lot of time alone, reading and meditating at a place now known as *gigis* bamba.[22] He also continued to write, mostly on religious rituals and ethics, targeting the youth, as is suggested by such titles as A *Viaticum for the Children*.[23] Bamba started to attract a small group of disciples who followed his teachings and emulated his example.

It was also in Mbakke Kajoor that he began to display the physical appearance and the moral traits that shaped his image and reputation.[24] A medium-sized man, he had already adopted the legendary all-white outfit composed of a *jellabah* (Moroccan-style robe) with a cape over a frock, pants, and a turban covering the all of his face except his eyes. This impressive outfit is immortalized in the unique picture of Amadu Bamba taken by a colonial administrator after an *asr* prayer (late afternoon prayer) in front of his wooden mosque in Diourbel.[25] People would only see his slightly discolored lips when, after praying for visitors, he removed the turban from over his mouth to blow some saliva on their open hands. His favorite shoes were leather sandals, which he wore with wooden soles during the rainy season and leather soles when the weather became dry. He did not like to wear the Marrakech-style moccasin, or *Maraakiss*, that was popular with Muslims in Senegal. He was slim, but this was not due to delicate health; to the contrary, he was rarely sick. Neither oral tradition nor colonial sources report any serious illness. However, both of these sources do mention his austerity and frugality. Very early on, Bamba adopted the diet of Sufi ascetics, which meant eating little, since for ascetics of all religions, nourishment of the body is always seen as a hindrance to spiritual enlightenment. His favorite food was dry couscous made from the local small millet, softened with water and seasoned with salt. However, Bamba did not indulge in the self-mortification characteristic of extreme asceticism. To the contrary, later in his career, he enjoyed tea and coffee and even wrote poems to glorify God for making these treats available to humanity.[26] He used to shave his head, but sources do not agree about the treatment of his beard. Some indicate that he had a long beard folded into his turban; others hold that he had a short beard.[27] He was energetic, with a tendency to make swift gestures, and he used to walk quickly, looking straight to the front. He prepared his own tea and served his guests personally before he became overwhelmed by followers. He often objected to disciples who rushed to grab something for him or to lay out his prayer mat. He disliked idle talk and was quick to cut off visitors engaged in extended greetings, as is customary among the Senegalese. He spoke sparingly, but when he did speak, he expressed himself in a strong voice and in short and dense sentences full of idioms and imagery from Islamic and Wolof culture. He repeated anything he said twice or three times, and nobody dared to go ahead and do anything on his behalf without his expressed demand. He is described by some sources as an intimidating figure. Once he had made a decision, it was not easy to make him change his mind, and he did not fear adversity once he thought that he was in the right. He did not like to ask for favors, although oral traditions as well as French sources emphasize his lack of interest in material wealth.[28]

Amadu Bamba's attitude toward his wives and children is more difficult to reconstruct. He spent most of his adult life in his father's compound. In addition, in the tradition of Muslim conceptions of privacy, any information concerning his relations with his wives and offspring was and is considered taboo. However, sources offer some hints that give us a glimpse of his family life.

First, all members of his family, wives and children included, looked up to him as a master, a sheikh. This feeling is best expressed by Falilu Mbakke, his son and second successor, who, in one of his poems, asserted that he had traded the biological tie with his father for a spiritual master-disciple relation.[29] Murid historians insist that in the Muridiyya, spiritual bond and trust in Amadu Bamba trump all ties, whether biological or of another nature. Yet Bamba was well aware that his children would be expected to assume leadership roles, and he did his best to prepare them for those responsibilities: he was very selective in his marriages and was attentive to the education of his wives.[30] He commissioned some of his most learned disciples to educate his sons and daughters. In addition, when the latter behaved in a manner he considered inappropriate to their social status, he was prompt to correct them and remind them of their duties.[31]

AMADU BAMBA AND THE COURT CLERICS OF KAJOOR

Amadu Bamba's personality and temperament made the last years of his life in Kajoor particularly difficult. He was torn between loyalty to his father and an internal calling that directed him toward mysticism and distance from people of power. Bachir Mbacké described the dilemma in these terms: "At that period, he struggled between two opposite sentiments. On the one hand, he wanted to remain loyal to his father, who interacted with many scholars and secular leaders and who counted on his assistance for teaching and other duties related to his position as judge and adviser to the rulers. On the other, he aspired to wed himself with God and to stay away from people and their futile earthly preoccupations."[32]

This internal dilemma exploded into the open during a controversy that pitted Bamba against his former teacher, Majakhate Kala. The dispute stemmed from conflicting legal interpretations about the fate of prisoners captured after the defeat of Amadu Sheikhu, the jihadist. There are two versions of the circumstances that led to the dispute. Some sources indicate that Momar Anta Sali, in his capacity as judge in the dammeel's court, had received two male slaves as his part of the booty collected after the battle. When Amadu Bamba saw the two young male slaves reciting the Quran in his father's yard, he urged their release because, he argued, it was unlawful to enslave a Muslim.[33] Other sources stated that the incident occurred around 1882, on the occasion of Ibrahim Makodu Joob's submission to Amadu Bamba (pleading allegiance as a disciple).[34] Joob was a cousin of Lat Joor who also owned Muslim slaves from the Madiyanke war, and Bamba conditioned the acceptance of his allegiance to the release of those slaves.

It is likely that the incident happened in 1882 or 1883, probably after Momar's death and in a context in which Amadu Bamba was directly challenged to take a stand. In 1875, the time of Amadu Sheikhu's jihad, he was in his early twenties and had not yet earned the intellectual authority to confront the king's clerical advisers. In effect, the decision to enslave the Madiyanke prisoners was made in consultation with the dammeel's Muslim entourage. At the request of Lat Joor, Khaali Majakhate Kala had issued a fatwa establishing the lawfulness of enslaving the vanquished Muslims, arguing that their leader, whom he considered to be an imposter and an apostate, had excluded himself from Islam by proclaiming to be a prophet, whereas Islam accepts no prophets after Muhammad.

Amadu Bamba contested the ruling of the *qadi* (Muslim judge), stressing the fact that Amadu Sheikhu never actually said that he was a prophet. Rather, this claim was made for him by his enemies, who therefore could not be trusted as credible witnesses. Bamba also refused an invitation by Lat Joor to a debate with his advisers to settle the matter. Already showing the influence of al-Ghazzali on his thinking, he declared that he would be ashamed to be seen by the angels responding to the summons of any other king but Allah.[35] Summoned by the court clerics to justify his position, he sent them a letter quoting a certain Muhammad Ibn Maslama, who wrote, "A cleric who seeks the favors of a king is like a fly feeding on excrement."[36] This remark angered Lat Joor, who vowed to inflict a severe punishment on Bamba. In Bachir Mbacké's view, it was the resumption of hostilities between the French and the dammeel that eventually resulted in the latter's removal, which prevented Lat Joor from ultimately dealing with Amadu Bamba.[37]

The second major dispute between Amadu Bamba and the clerics of Kajoor occurred at his father's funeral. Mandumbe Mar Sill, a prominent Muslim notable in Kajoor who was also a close friend and schoolmate of Momar Anta Sali, led the mortuary prayer and pronounced the eulogy. After finishing his speech, he presented his condolences to Amadu Bamba and recommended that Bamba come with him so that he could be introduced to the rulers as the heir to his father. Bamba thanked Sill for his condolences and good intentions but added: "I do not have the habit of mingling with rulers, and I do not expect any help from them. I only seek honor from the Supreme Lord (God)."[38]

Amadu Bamba's response upset the crowd. His reluctance to interact with the royal court was known, but the circumstances made his attitude particularly striking. First, it was a violation of the Wolof code of conduct to express one's mind so crudely in public. Second, the incident took place in front of the entire village, between a man and someone old enough to be his father. Third, a funeral was expected to be an occasion of communion and not of dispute and disagreement. According to Murid traditions, the people present at the event reacted to the incident in two ways.[39] Some among the clerics, who clearly understood that Bamba's position was in accordance with Islamic ethics and morals, blamed the zeal of their younger colleague for his uncompromising attitude toward the rulers and their Muslim clients. Among the common people, Bamba was thought to have mental problems because they could not understand why somebody would renounce a position that would guarantee him wealth and fame.

Amadu Bamba was aware of the reactions that his attitude spurred. In a short poem he drafted soon after his father's death, he wrote, "Because I refused to follow their suggestions, they accused me of madness." In another line, he stated, "Lean towards the sultans (rulers) they told me, so that you could benefit from gifts that would solve all your material needs. I responded, I am satisfied with God, I put my trust in Him." He concluded the poem with these words, "If my only shortcoming is my renunciation of the wealth of the kings, then here is a precious shortcoming that does not dishonor me in any way."[40] This attitude of distrust and separation from temporal power holders also characterized his relations with the French colonial administrators who replaced the Wolof kings in the late nineteenth century.

We can see that by the time of his father's death, Amadu Bamba had already formed his opinions about the relationship that should exist between Muslim clerics and rulers. He was thirty years old and had certainly already endorsed the well-known Sufi saying that speaks of the desirability of neither knowing nor being known by temporal leaders.[41] He was opposed to jihad of the sword, but he also understood that the domination of the French (whom he called Christians in his writings) over local power was inevitable.[42] However, he was convinced that he had a role to play in society. Since he was dissatisfied with the models available to him, he had to devise his own way of coping with the problems of his day. The long trip he took across Senegal and Mauritania after the death of Momar Anta Sali was the first step in his quest for a vocation and a role in society.

THE SPIRITUAL QUEST

In the first months after the death of Momar Anta Sali, Amadu Bamba pursued his usual business. He continued to teach, pray, write talismans for those who requested them, and visit his father's former disciples to collect *zakaat* and other alms; these were much needed after the demise of Lat Joor, whose support was critical to the family.[43] Then, from late 1883 to early 1884, Bamba broke with the routine of the school. He undertook an eight-month-long trip across Senegal and Mauritania, leaving the task of teaching to his advanced disciples.[44] During this extended journey, he visited many clerics, read from their libraries, followed their teachings, consulted them about questions related to Islamic practices and mysticism, and received *ijaazas* (diplomas or certificates). He also made pilgrimages to the tombs of saints and holy sites. He visited al-Hajj Kamara in Saint-Louis. Kamara was the local representative of the Sidiyya branch of the Qadiriyya with which Amadu Bamba was also affiliated. Kamara retained Bamba for some time, testing his knowledge and resolve and initiating him into some secrets of the Qadiriyya. He appointed him to the position of *muqaddam* (representative with the power to initiate disciples), giving him the cane and turban that symbolized this rank.[45] Despite this consecration and against Kamara's recommendation, Amadu Bamba proceeded to Butilimit in Mauritania, the headquarters of the Sidiyya family.

Bamba had long desired this trip to Mauritania, which was seen by Muslim clerics in the Wolof country who could not travel to Mecca or North Africa as a source of Islamic knowledge and baraka. He had unsuccessfully planned such a journey before. In Mauritania, Amadu Bamba was hosted by Sidiyya Baba, who, despite his relatively young age (he was twenty-two years old), was the head of the branch of the Qadiriyya founded by his grandfather, Sheikh Sidiyya al-Kabir (1780–1868).

Amadu Bamba's voyage to Mauritania had an marked impact on his career, but sources disagree about the length of his stay.[46] Bachir Mbacké and M. Lamine Diop mentioned the visit, but they did not specify its duration. Cheikh Tidiane Sy spoke of a couple of months; Ahmadou Dramé and Khadime Silla suggested that it lasted one month. Whatever the length of time spent in Mauritania, Bamba's contact with the family of Sheikh Sidiyya affected his life in many ways. On an intellectual level, the rich library of Butilimit gave him access to books he had never had the opportunity to study.[47] Immediately after returning from Mauritania, he produced his two most influential books: *Nahju*, a work on religious ethics of conduct inspired by the Muslim thinker Muhammad al-Hajj, written in 1884–85, and his most important book on Islamic mysticism, *Massalik Al-Jinan*. This work is a commentary and versification of *Khatimat-ul tasawwuf* by al-Yadaali, and it was completed in 1885–86.[48]

Bamba received his third initiation into the Qadiriyya (after the initiation he received from his father or his uncle Muhammad Buso and from al-Hajj Kamara of Saint-Louis) in Mauritania, this time from Sheikh Sidiyya Baba, a direct descendant of the founder of the order.[49] The direct linkage with the Sidiyya family gave him access to a powerful source of baraka. After this initiation, Bamba wrote a poem entitled *Silsilatul Qadiriyya*, in which he described the chain of authority of the Qaidiriyya *wird* from the Prophet Muhammad, the ultimate inspirator, to Sheikh Abd al-Qadir al-Jilani, the founder, and on to himself through the Kunta and the Sidiyya families.[50] In Mauritania, Amadu Bamba was also exposed to the daily tasks of running a Sufi network and to the kinds of relationships that a sheikh established with different types of disciples. Sometime between 1893 and 1895, he solicited and received an ijaaza from Sheikh Sidiyya authorizing him to distribute the wird qadiriyya.[51]

Amadu Bamba most likely also experienced how fraternity between Muslims, especially Muslim clerics—so celebrated in the Quran and the prophetic traditions—could be ambiguous in practice when it involved people of different skin colors and cultures. Sidiyya Baba and his Moorish compatriots did not have much regard for their black colleagues on the other side of the Senegal River. Paul Marty, for example, quoted an excerpt from an unspecified work authored by Baba in which the latter wrote, "The Blacks think of themselves as Muslims, however the majority among them do not have the slightest correct notion of what Islam is really about, they ignore the Islamic ethic, its law and principles. But we [the Moors in our capacity as teachers and guides] have a lot of responsibility to bear in this situation."[52] On another occasion, Baba expressed his scorn for the uncivilized "little black kinglets" of Senegal who did not deserve the attention the French gave them.[53]

Amadu Bamba's experience during his first trip to Mauritania prompted him to write in the preamble of *Massalik Al-Jinan*, "Do not let my condition of a black man mislead you about the virtue of this work" because "the best of man before God, without discrimination, is the one who fears Him the most" and "skin color cannot be the cause of stupidity or ignorance."[54] If Amadu Bamba had once longed for an extended stay in the country of the Arabs where he could devote his life to the study and practice of Sufism, as suggested by Bachir Mbacké,[55] his trip to Mauritania might have convinced him once and for all that his future was in Senegal.

TARBIYYA AS A VOCATION

The access to sophisticated Sufi literature and the lessons learned from the trip across Senegal and Mauritania strengthened some of Amadu Bamba's ideas about education and the social responsibilities of a Muslim cleric, and they provided the principles and inspiration for a new pedagogy. Now that he was no longer bound by loyalty to his father, he could experiment with his own thoughts and worldview. We know that he was quite critical of the attitude of court clerics. Less apparent was his view on the education dispensed in the Wolof states. The fact that he dedicated most of his early writings to responding to what he perceived as a need among the youth for knowledge about religious practices and ethical behavior suggests that he detected some inadequacies in the education that was offered. The changes he initiated after returning from Mauritania were an attempt to address these inadequacies. Soon after he returned to the school of Mbakke Kajoor, Amadu Bamba convened all his adult disciples and let them know that he was henceforth going to focus his actions on education of the soul, or *tarbiyya*, and he invited those who were not satisfied with his new orientation to look for another master.

Tarbiyya is a holistic approach to education invented by the Sufis that goes beyond the mere transmission of knowledge and seeks to transform the whole being by touching the body, the mind, and the soul. It establishes a special relationship between the sheikh and his disciple, who is no longer a *taaleb* (student) but a *murid* (aspirant) on the path to God who surrenders his will to his master and gives him command of every aspect of his life. Tarbiyya requires from the aspirant a clear commitment to follow the sheikh's recommendations on all matters, temporal and spiritual.

Many of Amadu Bamba's disciples were disconcerted by this change. Only a small group of students stayed, mostly those who had developed a personal relationship with him since his installation in Mbakke Kajoor and knew about his Sufi inclination.[56] These disciples were adults who had already finished memorizing the Quran and were advanced in the study of the religious sciences.

The pedagogic innovations that Amadu Bamba introduced did not help his relationships with the clerics of Kajoor. His rapport with the court clerics was already strained because of the legal disputes that pitted them against one another and the incident at his father's funeral. Now, it was the clerics specializing in teaching who felt antagonized by tarbiyya. The opposition of the clerical establishment to the educational model that Bamba was propounding was rooted in disagreements about methodology and resentment about the violations of traditional status (corporate) norms. By making piety, asceticism, and faithfulness to one's sheikh legitimate sources of religious authority, tarbiyya upset the consensually validated standards that in Wolof country defined the social status of the Muslim cleric. These standards were the lengthy study of the Quran and religious sciences and marriage into the right families. The tension was compounded by the fact that the Sufi ideas on which Bamba based his approach were not widespread enough to create a broad basis for understanding his method. In addition, the material implications of the divine favor that the disciples expected to earn through the system threatened traditional hierarchies of power and the way of life of entrenched clerical dynasties. If Bamba's criticism of court Islam could be tolerated as an excess of zeal from a younger colleague, his pedagogic innovations were seen as a deviation from a tradition of teaching built by prestigious families of Muslim learned men and consecrated by centuries of practice.

Murid oral traditions have preserved a vivid memory of the hostility of the Wolof clerics toward Amadu Bamba early in his career. This memory is expressed dramatically in the story of the encounter between the cleric Maniaaw Silla and Amadu Bamba that took place after the latter's return from exile to Gabon in 1902. The story goes as follows:

> When Maniaaw Silla came to greet Amadu Bamba soon after he returned in Senegal, Amadu Bamba asked him: "Maniaaw, what was your occupation when I was in exile in Gabon?" He responded, "Every Friday we would cook a lot of food to give away in the form of alms, recite the Quran many times and pray to God so that you would never return to this land"; Amadu Bamba pursued, "Why were you doing that?" Maniaaw said, "Mbakke, we are *doomi sokhna*, we live by our schools and the labor of our disciples and you were about to take all that from us." Amadu Bamba said, "Maniaaw, you are telling me this only because you are an honest man, but you were not alone in doing this"; and he added: "but the man I am going to make of you will never need his pupils' help to earn a livelihood."[57]

The arrival of Sheikh Ibra Faal (also Ibrahima Faal), one of the most influential Murid sheikhs, at the school of Mbakke Kajoor added to the tension with the clerics. Faal is said to have been the fortieth disciple to join Amadu Bamba just at the time when he started the system of tarbiyya.[58] He belonged to a modest family of Quranic teachers in Njambur, in northern Kajoor. He received an advanced Islamic instruction and is even said to have authored a book.[59] Ibra Faal certainly had some notions of tasawwuf, or Muslim mysticism, when he met with Amadu Bamba. We learn from Murid sources that he was looking for a sheikh who could guide him in the way of the Sufis when he met Adama Gey, a disciple of Amadu Bamba. He followed Gey to the school of Mbakke Kajoor, then submitted to Amadu Bamba. What follows is, in the words of Sheikh Ibra Faal as recorded by Bachir Mbacké, an account of the first conversation between Amadu Bamba and his famous disciple:

> When I (Sheikh Ibra Faal) was first introduced to the Sheikh, I told him: "The only reason why I left my house was to seek a guide, a bearer of a beam of light that could lift me from darkness and unveils the light of truth. I think that if I had not found such a guide but just his tomb, the sincerity of my quest and my willingness to

follow his example would have helped me reach my goal. I pledge before you that I will devote all the remaining time of my life in this world to the exclusive quest of God and (salvation) in the hereafter [through your guidance]." Amadu Bamba responded with these words, "[. . .] I accept your pledge and urge you to obey God's recommendations, to avoid His interdictions, and to devote all your life to seeking His pleasure."[60]

Ibra Faal inaugurated a new ethic of behavior between master and disciples in the school of Mbakke Kajoor. This ethic required excessive veneration of the persona of Amadu Bamba. Faal knelt and removed his headwear when talking to the cleric, bowed his head when greeting him, abstained from eating out of the same bowl as Bamba, and refused to allow anybody to lead his sheikh in prayer. He devoted his life at the school to work instead of instruction and worship. He collected firewood and timber for construction during the day and fetched water for Amadu Bamba's wives during the night. He neglected praying and fasting and gradually abandoned these canonical acts of worship. Faal's behavior toward his sheikh was not uncommon among Sufi, especially at what Trimingham terms the *taifa* stage. His demeanor was consistent with that of a *majzub*—an ascetic who is so consumed by his love of God that he has lost all sense of reality, blurring the boundaries between the lawful and unlawful and putting spiritual exercises and disciplining the body over formal worship.[61] Majzub behavior was seemingly unknown in Wolof country. Amadu Bamba, who was well versed in Muslim mysticism, was in a position to understand and tolerate his disciple's odd outlook, but this was not true for his entourage.

Ibra Faal's attitude shocked the students in the school but impressed Amadu Bamba, who refused to get rid of him despite growing protestations from his followers. Faal's neglect of the fundamental Islamic rituals outraged many who considered him to be a madman.[62] Amadu Bamba's refusal to dismiss his atypical disciple prompted many families of doomi sokhna to withdraw or put pressure on their sons to abandon the school of Mbakke Kajoor.[63]

The rift with the clerics and the aristocracy of Kajoor negatively affected the economy of the school. Musa Ka, the Murid poet and specialist of Wolofal (the Wolof language written with Arabic script), recounted an instance at Mbakke Kajoor in which Amadu Bamba, accompanied by his younger brother Ibra Faati, toured areas of Kajoor and Bawol for days and failed to sell a Quran he had handwritten in order to pay a debt of three francs that he owed to a Moorish scribe named Sheriful Hassan.[64] Ka may have exaggerated the story for the sake of drawing similarities between the suffering of the

Prophet Muhammad in Mecca and that of Amadu Bamba in his earlier career, but evidence shows that the Mbakke went through a difficult situation in the years following Momar Anta Sali's death. I have come across a letter that Bamba wrote while in Mbakke Kajoor, in which he asked one of his disciples living in Mbakke Bawol to sell a horse he had entrusted to him and send him the money through a certain Njamme Saar. Amadu Bamba thought first of selling the female servant attached to his daughter Faati Jah Mbakke but then changed his mind.[65] The Mbakke also faced pressure from the Silla family, founders of a village near the compound of Mbakke Kajoor, who contested their rights to the land they were occupying.[66] The Silla were a family of Quranic teachers who were probably unhappy about Amadu Bamba's pedagogic innovations. They argued that they owned the rights of first occupants on the land of Mbakke Kajoor, where they had settled at least three centuries before Momar Anta Sali, a newcomer who had been imposed by the dammeel without historical rights to the land.[67] By the end of 1884, confronted by the critiques of the clerics of Kajoor and the deteriorating economic conditions of his family, Amadu Bamba decided to move to Mbakke Bawol. He reversed the journey that Momar Anta Sali had taken nearly twenty years earlier, and just as his father never lived in Bawol after leaving the kingdom in 1865, Amadu Bamba never again lived in Kajoor.

BACK TO THE LAND OF THE ANCESTORS

Amadu Bamba's migration from Kajoor to Bawol marked a crossroads in his life. He was now reunited with the larger Mbakke clan after decades of separation, at a time when he had started to build his own constituency on a basis that did not always conform to the family traditions. His older brother Momar Jaara, his uncle Muhammad Buso, and some other members of the lineages of Maaram, his great-grandfather, lived in Mbakke Bawol. Bamba settled with a small group of his followers and family on the western side of the village and was allotted a plot of land, which he worked with his family and disciples. He continued to write, completing *Massalik al-Jinan* (Paths to Paradise) soon after he arrived in Mbakke. He also pursued the implementation of the system of tarbiyya, which increasingly gave his school and disciples a unique identity.

Donal Cruise O'Brien has argued that it was in Mbakke where, for the first time, Sheikh Ibra Faal experimented with the idea of the working *daara*, or school, which he perceives as the most important innovation of the Muridiyya.[68] But it seems that the school of Mbakke did not have the characteristics of this type of daara, which would develop later in Daaru Salaam and Tuubaa when adult disciples began to join Amadu Bamba in greater numbers and when he enjoyed greater latitude in translating his thoughts into practice. In fact, contrary to some Murid traditions relayed by secondary sources that attribute a large following to the founder of the Muridiyya when he returned to Bawol, Bamba's school in Mbakke was rather modest. Bamba indirectly acknowledged this when he wrote in *Massalik al-Jinan*, "My lack of renown in this generation should not lead you to reject this pious work."[69]

Amadu Bamba's method of teaching and the kind of relationships he established with his disciples soon became sources of friction between the newcomers and the people of Mbakke Bawol. Like their counterparts in Kajoor, clerics in the area and members of Bamba's own family criticized him for the way he was managing his daara. They were particularly critical of the emphasis he put on spiritual education and the way he was treated by his disciples. Sheikh Ibra Faal was the major target of this criticism.[70] In effect, Ibra Faal continued to behave the same way he had in Mbakke Kajoor, refusing to follow the canonical Islamic rituals and devoting most of his time to working for his sheikh. He also objected to anybody trying to stand in front of his master in the mosque, arguing that he was the most qualified to lead the community in prayer.

The claim of saintliness and scholarly authority that Murid disciples made for Amadu Bamba fueled the resentment. Khadim Mbacké noted that many members of the Mbakke clan considered the veneration given the cleric by his disciples was excessive and unjustified.[71] The situation was only aggravated by the fact that the criticism directed at Bamba and his followers seemed to have no effect. In these circumstances, Muhammad Buso (Bamba's former teacher and uncle) and Momar Jaara (his older brother) wrote a letter to the cleric asking him to justify his method of teaching on the grounds of Islamic jurisprudence and his family traditions. Bamba is reported to have responded to the letter by stating that there was no difference between his intentions and objectives and the precepts of Islam and his family traditions. He added that his single preoccupation was to spread Islamic teachings among his people.[72] The tensions between Bamba and the Mbakke clan was evidenced by another letter he addressed to Momar Jaara, probably while in Mbakke Bawol or Daaru Salaam, in which he said, "I ask you not to feel insulted by what may seem to be lack of respect or misbehavior on my part. Just know that I am engaged in spiritual retreat [*khalwa*] and nothing else [keeps me from interacting with you], I will come out as soon as I receive the permission [from God] to do so."[73] Some sources also referred to an incident that took place in the same period and that was triggered by Amadu Bamba's changing of the name of his elder son, Mustafa Mbakke; his brother Momar Jaara had named the child after himself while Bamba was away.[74]

The disagreement between Amadu Bamba and the clerics of Mbakke about how to promote Islam was profound. The dispute was not only about teaching practices; it was philosophical as well. In *Massalik*, Amadu Bamba deplored the fact that many clerics of his generation ignored Sufism and that by doing so, they were also losing the benefit of mastering the mystical sciences. He regretted that this same group hated the Sufis and condemned their mystical practices and methods of education without trying to understand them. He wrote, "The fact that the blind cannot see the sun does not mean that it is not shining; the eminence of the men of wisdom cannot be hurt either by the jealousy of some men of sciences or by the ignorance of the idiots."[75] Conflicts between Sufis and more juridically minded *ulamas* (learned Muslims) have marked the development of institutional Sufism.[76] Ulamas have often faulted followers of tasawwuf for not rigorously complying with normative Islam as defined in the Quran and the Sunna of the Prophet Muhammad. Similar considerations may have played a role in the controversies between the Murids and the clerics of Mbakke, but what was even more vexing for these clerics was the introduction of teaching practices that conflicted with long-established educational customs.

The quarrel that resulted from the diverging perspectives on education and the attitude of Ibra Faal forced Amadu Bamba to abandon the central mosque of Mbakke Bawol and build his own mosque in his compound.[77] But isolation did not solve the conflict. The persistent discord caused the village's leaders to ask him to choose between conforming to their will or leaving the town. Eventually, in Safar AH 1304 (November 1885), about two years after his arrival in Mbakke Bawol, Amadu Bamba moved to found the village of Daaru Salaam, 2 kilometers northeast of Mbakke Bawol.[78]

Daaru Salaam was the first village founded by Amadu Bamba. Murid accounts of the founding of this town give us a measure of the tense relations that existed between the nascent Murid community and the inhabitants of Mbakke Bawol. They indicate that Bamba moved to the new location with his wives and disciples, but when they called on people in Mbakke to help them haul the roof of the first hut they built there, those residents refused and threatened to punish anybody who dared to help.[79] Sheikh Anta Mbakke, whose family on his mother's side was from Mbakke, was mocked and jeered by his relatives; they blamed him for being subservient to his brother, who was, after all, his equal.[80]

In Daaru Salaam, Amadu Bamba was able to further assert his authority and attract disciples. The site offered a suitable environment for his séances of *khalwa*, when he spent days and nights alone, praying and meditating to seek spiritual purity.[81] The retreat was located in the *jatti* (wasteland) near the borders of Jolof and Bawol and was covered by a forest roamed only by migrating Fulbe cattle herders.

The founding of a village is an important step in establishing the authority of a Muslim teacher. In Wolof country, specific families of clerics are associated with typical village names. Thus, villages founded by the Lo clerical family are always called Ndaam; for the Sy, it is Suyuuma; and for the Njaay, it is Njare. Amadu Bamba's ancestors liked to derive the names of their villages from their patronym (as in Mbakke Bawol, Mbakke Jolof, Mbakke Baari, and Mbakke Kajoor). Bamba, however, did not follow this tradition; instead, he often used one of the ninety-nine names of Allah—such as *Salaam* (Peace), *Halimul Khabir* (the Supreme Savant), and *Rahman* (the Merciful)—or Quranic references such as *Tuubaa* to name his villages. He was conscious of his role as founder of a new organization that he wished to separate from his ancestral heritage, and the names of God and Quranic idioms better expressed this ideal.

It was in Daaru Salaam that Amadu Bamba's following started to grow. The separation from the Mbakke family and the creation of his own community enhanced his reputation as a teacher and scholar. People certainly learned the details of his life in Kajoor, his conflicts with the rulers and clerics of this kingdom, and his political stances. Some among those who joined him at Daaru Salaam were probably attracted by the aura that had begun to surround the cleric. The communitarian life that the Murids were practicing may have also appealed to former slaves who had regained their freedom after the demise of the traditional rulers and their clients.[82] Others wanted to experiment with the education that Bamba proposed to inculcate in his disciples.

After Lat Joor's defeat in October 1886, it is possible that some of the warriors and notables who had sided with him joined Daaru Salaam, perhaps in hopes of rebuilding another coalition against the French, as argued by colonial sources and some scholars.[83] But this group could not have been significant in number. By the time of Lat Joor's death, the bulk of the army of Kajoor had been disbanded or had been taken by Demba Waar Sall, their general, to the camp of the French.

In Daaru Salaam, Amadu Bamba enjoyed some stability. His two sons and first two successors, Mamadu Mustafa and Falilu, were born in the village. The community built a school and a mosque and cleared large tracts of land for the cultivation of millet, corn, and other food crops.[84] They did not grow peanuts. This cash crop was mostly produced in northern Kajoor and in the provinces of Waalo that were connected to the colonial economy. Firmly in control of his village, Amadu Bamba could, for the first time, implement his conception of education without many obstacles. But he soon faced the difficulty of handling disciples with differing profiles and varying expectations.

The Emergence of Amadu Bamba, 1853–95

Many of the disciples who flocked to Daaru Salaam were atypical. They were adults who had passed the age for attending the classic Quranic schools, and they joined the sheikh at a time when he was still thinking and working on the implementation of his system of tarbiyya. He was also continuing his spiritual quest, often spending extended amounts of time in meditation alone. In other words, he was not yet ready to play the role of spiritual guide that the disciples sought in him, and the organization and education of the growing number of adult disciples remained a challenge. The *daara tarbiyya* (working school) started to take form as a way of managing the followers that streamed into Daaru Salaam.[85] Between 1888 and 1889, the number of these followers was estimated at about two hundred.[86]

Decentralization and mobility constituted other forms of response to the situation. In 1888 and 1889, Amadu Bamba formally gave the order to Sheikh Anta, Sheikh Ibra Faal, Adama Gey, Ibra Saar, and Massamba Joob, some of his earliest disciples, to separate from him and found their own communities as independent sheikhs. Sheikh Ibra Faal was ordered to settle in Saint-Louis, then the capital of the colony of Senegal. Sheikh Anta was given Daaru Salaam and half of the disciples living in that village.[87]

The newly consecrated sheikhs returned to their provinces of origin, founded their own villages, and started to proselytize. Each of these men had been following Amadu Bamba for many years. Sheikh Ibra Faal, the last to join him among this group, had been with him for four to five years. For Bamba, these disciples had the skills and capacity to propagate his message or at least to check the flow of people toward Daaru Salaam by founding new centers of tarbiyya throughout Kajoor and Bawol. For some reason, Sheikh Ibra Faal was sent to Saint-Louis and not to his native land of Njambur. Perhaps Amadu Bamba thought that life in the highly Islamicized city of northern Senegal would compel his disciple to change his behavior and become more observant of Islamic orthodoxy.[88] He also might have seen him as a suitable intermediary with the political and trading African elite of Saint-Louis, whose services he might need in the future. By AH 1306 (1888), after dispatching most of his senior disciples, Amadu Bamba decided to leave Daaru Salaam to found the village of Tuubaa 4 kilometers to the northeast, hoping to start a new school under more manageable circumstances.

FINDING AND SETTLING TUUBAA

Amadu Bamba did not choose the site of Tuubaa at random.[89] He was probably aware of the strategic location of the village, as the colonial administration would notice later. Tuubaa was located at the intersection of the precolonial states of Bawol, Kajoor, and Saalum and on the main road linking Bawol to Jolof and Fuuta, in northern Senegal. The African chiefs appointed by the French loosely controlled the area, which by and large served as grazing land. It was an area covered by a thin forest and bereft of water for most of the dry season.[90] During the rainy season, the pond of Mbal supplied water to people and animals alike.

For Amadu Bamba, Tuubaa was the ideal place to train his disciples in the way of tarbiyya. Its remoteness protected the Murids, or aspirants, from the distraction and disturbances of life in the big villages of Kajoor and Bawol and facilitated their concentration on meditation, study, and work. The tasks of clearing the forest, building and maintaining houses, and growing food for the community made for a workload that left little time for amusement after the disciples had completed their religious duties. The harsh living conditions in Tuubaa were also a test of the commitment and faith of the novices. In addition, Amadu Bamba certainly appreciated the distance from the colonial administration and its representatives, as well as the relative administrative autonomy that the remote site of Tuubaa offered.[91]

The founding of Tuubaa marked a key stage in the building of Amadu Bamba's status as a saint and a guide. Settlement in this village was part of his effort to construct the spiritual capital, which, together with the cultural and intellectual capital he had amassed, would provide the basis for his religious authority. Hassan El Boudrari has argued that the first action of a saint who succeeds in gaining recognition for his charisma is to found a town in an attempt to engrave in a territory (people and things included) the power he has earned in the rather abstract religious field.[92] In the case of Bamba, the founding of villages was not a consecration but part of the very process of constructing his spiritual authority and power.

For the Murids, the holy site of Tuubaa is considered among the secrets of God that he reveals only to those who are dear to him. According to Murid historians, Amadu Bamba was not the first *wali Allah* (friend of God) to have had a hint about the site and to have tried to locate it. Even Al-Hajj Umar Tal, the famous jihadist, had researched the holy site, but after failing to find it, he realized that it was not destined for him.[93]

Stories of the founding of Tuubaa emphasize the challenges Amadu Bamba had to overcome to discover the holy land. We are told that while living in Daaru Salaam, he made many attempts but failed to locate the sacred site. He spent countless days and nights in spiritual retreats and prayers in the forest of eastern Bawol to seek God's help in his endeavor. One day, his fortune changed when he heard a voice telling him where the place was situated.[94] The voice would become louder and then it would fade. Bamba walked back and forth until he got tired, and then he sat in the shade of a *bepp* tree (*platane du Sénégal*, or *Sterculea setigera*) and fell asleep. In his sleep, he dreamed that he was sitting right in the place he had been looking for for all this time. Another version tells us that Amadu Bamba was taking a nap not far from the pond of Mbal when he was told in a dream that the site he was searching for was located where he had performed the *takusaan* (afternoon prayer, or *asr* in Arabic) the day before, and this site happened to be located under a bepp tree. This story is reminiscent of the experience of Sufi masters and holy men in other parts of the Muslim world. The tenth-century North African Sufi saint Abu Ibrahim Ismail, for instance, left Jeddah in the current kingdom of Saudi Arabia guided by a voice that instructed him to follow a light; this light led him across the Arabian Desert and the Sinai Peninsula and eventually took him to the Atlantic coast of Morocco, where he founded the *ribat* of Tit and became the spiritual guide and saint of the Sanhaja Berber.[95]

Like Ismail, who settled near the pure water spring where the light that guided him stopped, Amadu Bamba built his village near the bepp tree. He designated the place where he would be buried after his death and also the area for a central mosque, a school, and a library. All these projects and ideas were enshrined in "Matlabul Fawzayn" (Quest for Happiness in the Two Worlds [meaning this world and the hereafter]), a short poem of supplications he composed soon after discovering the land of Tuubaa; the Murids see this work as a sort of constitution for the holy city. In the poem, Bamba prayed, "[God] make of Tuubaa a place of knowledge, faith and mercy." He also wrote, "[Lord] make of my home . . . a crucible for the flourishing of [Islamic] ideas and thinking,"[96] and he begged that God would pour wealth and blessings on the village and protect its inhabitants against evil.

Soon after the discovery of the sacred site, Amadu Bamba asked some of his disciples to clear the area and to construct a house, which he named Tuubaa. This house gave its name to the village. The origin of the name *Tuubaa* is the subject of many conflicting interpretations.[97] Some suggest that the word was derived from *tawba*, an Arabic term widely used in Sufi literature that means "repentance." *Tuubaa* means "mercy" as well; it is also the name of a tree that grows in heaven, and some Murid sources indicate that one branch from that tree hovers over the village of Tuubaa. Others associate the name with the Wolofized Arabic word *tuub*, which means both "conversion" and "regret." Tuubaa is also another name for Medina, the city that welcomed Prophet Muhammad after he fled Mecca and one of the three holiest sites of Islam. Perhaps by naming his house Tuubaa, Bamba intended all of these meanings, but his use of the word in his writings suggests that he conceived the site as a place of felicity and happiness.

Amadu Bamba moved to Tuubaa with several dozen disciples in 1888, leaving part of his family in Daaru Salaam. A short time after the settlement, he ordered his followers to build four houses, which he named Daaru Khudoos, Daaru Rahman (also Daaru Naar), Daaru Mannaan, and Daaru Halimul Khabiir (also Ndaam). Each of these houses had a mosque and a school except for Daaru Rahman, which was a guesthouse reserved for Moorish visitors.[98] Daaru Khudoos served as a place of retreat where Amadu Bamba spent time in meditation and spiritual exercises.

The disciples were distributed between the different schools according to their interests. The younger disciples frequented the daara where the Quran was taught. The adults were divided into two groups, those who were pursuing the study of the religious sciences and those who were disciples in the daara tarbiyya, dividing their time between work, worship, and meditation. Amadu Bamba, his cousin Mbacké Bousso, his disciple Ndaam Abdrahman Lo, and some other older disciples assumed the tasks of supervising the teaching.[99] Families were discouraged from settling in the village, which was functioning as a sort of ribat. Tuubaa at that time was not very different from the village Paul Marty visited over three decades later. Marty described Tuubaa as an Islamic *zawiya*, or lodge, composed of a school where students were taught religious and profane disciplines, a convent where Murid sheikhs trained disciples in the way of the Sufi, and a busy pilgrimage site.[100] The practice of commissioning the senior sheikhs that Amadu Bamba started in Daaru Salaam was maintained. He continued to release disciples who endeavored to start their own communities, and by 1889, a growing number of Murid villages were being founded in northern Kajoor.[101]

The growth of the Muridiyya in Kajoor increasingly became an object of concern to the local African chiefs representing the French colonial administration.[102] And because of complaints lodged by the chiefs, the Murids began attracting the attention of French administrators. In March 1889, Tautain, the director of political affairs for the colony of Senegal, filed the first report on Amadu Bamba. He did not know the cleric or the exact location of his village of Tuubaa, but he deemed that the forest of Mbafar where Bamba was building his house was strategically situated. He instructed the French administrator of Kajoor to keep a discreet but watchful eye on the cleric and his disciples.[103]

In late April 1889, the administrator Angot was sent to Njambur and Bawol to settle some political disputes in the area, but he felt it necessary to inquire about Amadu Bamba and the Murids. He observed that the information he collected about the cleric was positive but that Murid disciples were causing some troubles in the area.[104] The positive tone of Angot's report, however, did not have an impact on the governor's office, which was growing ever more suspicious of the Murids. Followers of Ibra Saar, one of the early disciples of Amadu Bamba, were expelled from Kajoor and Njambur.[105] Demba Joob, the chief of Gania and a disciple of Amadu Bamba, was also dismissed. In 1892, Amadu Bamba made a goodwill trip to Saint-Louis, where he met with the governor to try to improve the situation, reaffirming that he was not interested in this terrestrial world and that he had devoted his life to seeking God. He may have continued to Mauritania to visit Sheikh Sidiyya Baba, who was his spiritual guide and soon to become a close ally of the French colonial administration.[106]

Amadu Bamba's reputation as a scholar and a Sufi sheikh continued to expand as more people submitted to him and joined his village. The rise of his prestige was exemplified by his marriage with Fatu Madu Maam Joob of Kokki, mother of Bachir Mbacké, in 1895. The Joob of Kokki were a prestigious and powerful lineage of clerics in northern Kajoor. There was even a saying that went, "If a dammeel loses the support of the Joob and the Lo, he had better resign."[107] Prior to this marriage, Amadu Bamba had wed two widows and his cousin Awa Buso. The marriage with Fatu Madu Maam was a sort of recognition of his status as a respected Muslim cleric, and it helped to augment his symbolic and spiritual capital.

THE MOVE TO JOLOF

Despite his increasing popularity, the mounting tension between the Murids and the colonial administration remained a subject of concern to Amadu Bamba. The meeting with the governor had helped calm the situation temporarily. But Bamba had lived and interacted with the notables of Kajoor, who were now back in charge as African chiefs under the authority the French, and he understood that cohabitation would not be easy. In the past, he had criticized their style of government, and there may have been lingering resentment against him among some of these people. To make matters worse, some defeated factions of the Wolof aristocracy that continued to oppose colonial rule joined the Muridiyya, perhaps as a way of expressing dissent.

By the beginning of 1895, Amadu Bamba had begun to ponder the idea of moving his school to Jolof. We know that his great-grandfather originated from this area and that the rulers of Jolof had a reputation for being tolerant of and kind toward Muslim clerics.[108] According to Mbacké Bousso, Amadu Bamba's cousin and close disciple, with whom he consulted about this initiative, the main reason for the relocation was that Tuubaa was no longer suitable for educating disciples in the way of tarbiyya.[109] The village had become too crowded because many former disciples had married and brought their families there, and it had grown impossible to maintain the separation between disciples and daaras engaged in different types of training. In addition, many people who were not interested in education were living in the village. Bousso may have been right in pointing out the difficulties of managing the large number of disciples that flocked to Tuubaa; this was one of the reasons why Amadu Bamba had left Daaru Salaam seven years earlier. However, it seems that fear of a new crisis with the colonial administration was also an important incentive for the cleric to relocate away from Bawol and Kajoor, where the French and their African allies had more direct and tighter control.

In Shawal (the tenth month of the Muslim calendar) AH 1312 (April 1895), Amadu Bamba moved to Jolof, where he resuscitated the ruins of Mbakke Jolof, the village founded by his great-grandfather Maaram. But the settlement quickly sparked tension with *buurba* (title of the king of Jolof) Samba Laobe Njaay, the French-sponsored king of Jolof. The first authorities of Jolof to meet with Bamba immediately disliked him,[110] and they complained that he was not behaving like their subject but rather like their equal. The chiefs considered him a man of temporal power and a threat to the stability of the kingdom. They claimed that they had never seen a teacher revered by his disciples the way Amadu Bamba was. For them, he was not a religious leader but a chief, and his followers were not disciples but slaves. This reaction should not be surprising; like their counterparts in Kajoor and Bawol, these proud African rulers of noble origin, now reduced to the ranks of civil servants subservient to the French, resented any apparent challenge to their authority, especially when this challenge came from clerics who had been their mere clients in the past.

The continuing influx of Murid disciples in Jolof despite Amadu Bamba's recommendation that they stay in Tuubaa added strain to the already tense relations with the local administration.[111] The move to Jolof did not silence the protestations of the chiefs of Kajoor, who appeared to have been more concerned about the Murids than their colleagues in Bawol. They continued to send alarming reports to the governor's office, accusing the Murids of preparing for war.[112] In addition, Amadu Bamba became entangled in the struggle for power between the king of Jolof and Fara Biram Lo, an African civil servant and his adviser, who also coveted his position.[113] When the governor learned through intelligence sources, which would prove later to be fabrications, that Samba Laobe had become a disciple of Amadu Bamba and that he was conspiring with him to wage jihad, he decided to take radical action. Despite Bamba's denial of any involvement in a conspiracy to fight the French, he was arrested on 10 August 1895, tried, and exiled to Gabon.

CONCLUSION

Amadu Bamba was born to a family of clerics, and like his forebears, he devoted his life to earning the credentials that would make him worthy of his ancestry. He endeavored to master the Quran and the Islamic sciences, which was his primary duty as a member of a family of learned men. However, in contrast to the family tradition that advocated cultural conformism, political neutrality, and accommodation with the rulers, Bamba had a different vision of the role of a cleric in society. This vision was shaped by the social, economic, and political context in which he grew up. He witnessed the violence, famine, and epidemics that had plagued Wolof society in the second half of the nineteenth century. And he also noted the failure of the Muslim establishment to remedy the situation, whether through jihad of the sword or through collaboration with secular rulers.

Bamba believed that to better serve his community, a cleric had to renounce temporal power. But withdrawal from the politics of rulers did not mean seclusion and abandonment of all ambition to influence society's destiny. He was convinced that the best way to heal the society of its sicknesses was to transform the people that made up the society. And for him, the best way to transform the people was with religious and social renewal through education. The centrality of education in Bamba's societal project stemmed from the fact that, for him, the genuine believer was the one who was guided by reason and not emotion. As he wrote in *Massalik,* "Emotion must always be checked and subject to the control of reason."[114] But to be effective, he believed, education should not be limited to the transmission of speculative knowledge; instead, it should aim to transform the whole being. The tool to realize this holistic change was tarbiyya, or the education of the soul, and the Muridiyya was the instrument to dispense this education. Amadu Bamba invested the cultural, symbolic, and spiritual capital he had accumulated through genealogy, learning, and marital alliances to build this instrument. The following chapter discusses his education method and examines the doctrinal underpinnings, practices, and organization of the Muridiyya.

4 ～ The Founding of the Muridiyya

THE MURIDIYYA evolved gradually from a loose network of disciples and sheikhs to an institutionalized Sufi order between the 1880s, when Amadu first adopted *tarbiyya* as a method of education, and 1904, when, in Mauritania, he received the *wird* that consecrated the new *tariqa*. The dominant scholarship on the Murids, however, overlooks this long process of incubation, focusing mainly on the death of King Lat Joor in 1886 and the subsequent French colonial takeover, two events often presented as the turning points in the emergence of the Muridiyya. One consequence of this approach is that it has downplayed the role of the spiritual and cultural in the founding of the tariqa and overemphasized the impact of political and economic structural factors. This chapter aims to correct this imbalance by demonstrating the centrality of religious innovations, beliefs, and motivations in the founding of the Muridiyya. It describes and analyzes the spiritual itinerary of Amadu Bamba and discusses how his thoughts and practices—and people's responses to his ideas and actions—informed the development of the Muridiyya. The chapter offers a thorough analysis of the Murid doctrine, method of education, and organizing principles. It also stresses the crucial role of the disciples and sheikhs as active agents in the founding of the Murid organization. It examines how sheikhs' and disciples' understanding and embodiment of Amadu Bamba's thinking helped to give the Murid tariqa some of its most distinctive features.

AMADU BAMBA'S CONCEPTION OF SUFISM

Amadu Bamba's path to Sufism was paved by his family tradition and his scholarship. In previous chapters, we have seen that his ancestors belonged to the

Qadiriyya and that it was through his family that he was first initiated into this tariqa. Qadiriyya teachings were reflected in Amadu Bamba's writings and practices, but his thought on Islamic mysticism was also influenced by Sufi thinkers and writers outside the *qadiri* order. Bamba was a reader of well-known Sufi masters such as Abu Talib al-Makki (d. AH 386 [996]), Ghazali (d. 1111), Ibn Atta Allah (d. 1309), and al-Yadaali, as well as their local commentators, including the Kunta and Daymani families of the western Sudan. Indeed, his writings are replete with quotations from these scholars. Among the Sufi thinkers, Ghazali had the greatest influence on Bamba, who classified him among the renovators of Islam and the great imams. He often referred to him as his master.[1]

Ghazali, who was both a legist and a Sufi, was known for his effort to reconcile the rigorous and rational interpretation of Islam by the *ulamas*, or learned Muslims, with the spirituality and esotericism of the mystics. He was also a staunch advocate of independence of thought for scholars. Commenting on the relations between rulers and clerics, Ghazali observed that although obedience was owed to the unjust prince, one should not condone his injustice. He noted that the devout Muslim should avoid the court and the company of the unjust ruler and should rebuke him, by words if he can safely do so or by silence if words might encourage rebellion.[2] Similar statements pervade Amadu Bamba's writings. For example, in *Tazawudu Shubaani*, he wrote, "Those who frequent them (the unjust rulers) because of their wealth, share in the corruption which is the source of their power."[3]

Amadu Bamba's conception of Sufism echoed the debates and compromises that have marked the relations between Sufi and anti-Sufi scholars since the twelfth century.[4] In his attitude as well as in his teachings, he was careful to combine the two dimensions of legitimate Sufism outlined by Ibn Khaldun in his commentary on Ghazali: that is, Sufism as a "science of praxis" rooted in the sharia and Sufism as mysticism geared toward the education of the heart. He viewed *tasawwuf*, or mysticism, as a central element of Islam but only second to *tawhid*, the science of the oneness of God, and sharia, which he considered to be the soul and body of the religion.[5] This preoccupation was reaffirmed in his teachings and his scholarly works, in which tawhid and Islam (worship) always came before *ihsaan* (purification). Bamba's idea of Sufism was shaped by a desire to blend mysticism, sharia, and involvement in society.

He distanced himself from extreme asceticism and advocated the participation of the Sufi sheikh in the life of the community. For him, seclusion was acceptable in only two situations—first, when the sheikh was not well prepared to deal with the dangers (to the faith) inherent in an active participation in societal life and, second, when the society was so corrupt that the sheikh was unable to convey his message. Nonetheless, he wrote, "whenever the society needs the sheikh to repair a wrong, then his contribution becomes compulsory."[6]

Amadu Bamba's understanding of Sufism was consistent with what Islamicists term mild asceticism or minimalist Sufism. Minimalist Sufism associates a limited sociability and moderate esotericism with respect for orthodox rituals and forms of worship. In Nimrod Hurvitz's view, "A mild ascetic will participate in various social institutions, such as family and profession, while maintaining independence of mind and a safe distance from corrupting forces such as patronage and the pursuit of riches."[7] This type of Sufism dominated in North Africa and the Western Sudan, where most of the ulamas combined legal scholarship and leadership of a Sufi order, in contrast to the Middle East, where the two groups were often opposed.[8] Because of the mild ascetics' high moral and ethical standards and their willingness to have an impact on society, their practices and discourses can also be perceived as social commentaries.

PHILOSOPHY AND PRACTICES OF EDUCATION

Philosophy of Education

One vital dimension of the transformations that marked the history of Islam in the Western Sudan in the second half of the nineteenth century involved the changes in outlook and orientation of the Muslim leadership. This period saw the emergence of new leaders who were critical of their contemporaries and were committed to promoting Islam through education and institutional Sufism. The appearance of this new leadership in Senegal was made possible by three factors: first, the shifting balance of power between the defeated traditional aristocracy and the populace of Muslim peasants enriched by the grain and peanut trade of the eighteenth and nineteenth centuries; second, easier access to Islamic books, especially Sufi literature that provided an ideology and a method to organize the population; and third, the colonial conquest, which facilitated the circulation of people and ideas.[9]

It is remarkable that the leading figures of this movement—Abdulaay Niass (1845–1922), Amadu Bamba (1853–1927), and Malick Sy (1853 or 1855–1922)—were all born in the 1840s or 1850s, belonged to families with a long tradition of Islamic learning, and were personally affected by the turmoil that shook the Wolof country.[10] They painted a grim image of the society of their time and particularly the Muslim leadership, and they called for reform. Both Amadu

Bamba and Malick Sy criticized local Muslim teachers and scholars for their ethical lapses.[11] Bamba especially deplored the fact that the teaching of the Quran had become a scholastic exercise focused almost exclusively on memorizing the book and also that Islamic knowledge was increasingly dissociated from wisdom.

The decline in the quality of education was blamed on the betrayal of the principles that had traditionally shaped the life of ulamas and teachers and on the influence of *ceddo* values and mores on the Muslim scholarly community. Teachers were accused of placing the quest for prestige and wealth over their duty to dispense knowledge for the sake of God and the good of the community. They competed with each other and became complacent with the aristocracy, whose bad behavior they justified. This attitude led to the corruption of the whole system of education, as exemplified by the adoption of practices such as *wagni* and *lawaan*,[12] wherein masters of the Quran rivaled each other before a crowd of admirers to the sound of drums in order to display their mastery of the holy book. Referring to this situation, the poet Musa Ka lamented that the Quran had become an orphan and that knowledge and wisdom had migrated to the east (Moorish country) because of the turpitudes of the Muslim leadership in the Wolof country.[13]

It is unclear to what extent this criticism reflected actual deviations from positive traditions of Islamic teaching among the Wolof, for it seems that most of what was criticized was deeply ingrained in local educational practices. What was clear, however, was that both Bamba and Malick Sy matured in a crucial period in the history of Islam, a period in which the religion was experiencing rapid expansion and traditional teachers were apparently unable to respond to the new religious demands spurred by the fast-changing sociopolitical and cultural context. These two men were "organic intellectuals," bearers of new ideas about how to better disseminate Islam in Senegal; consequently, their critiques of the "traditional intellectuals" are better understood as commentaries on the ills of Wolof society as a whole.

Amadu Bamba's model of education was a response to the perceived crisis situation. He produced his most important works on education between his installation in Pataar in the 1870s and his settlement in Mbakke Bawol in 1884.[14] In the tradition of Muslim scholars, he formulated his thoughts and ideas on education in the form of books, letters, and sermons presented as responses to questions asked by his disciples and colleagues.

For Amadu Bamba, the primary duty of a human being was to seek an education. However, the ultimate goal of education was to make people into good Muslims who modeled their actions on the teachings of Islam and served their community.[15] For him, knowledge included the esoteric or mystical sciences as well as the exoteric sciences (classical disciplines). In *Massalik al-Jinan*, he wrote, "There is no doubt that a limited time devoted to scientific work is better than a lifetime spent in ignorance."[16] And he added, "It is an obligation for one to accord the same attention to the Quran and the religious sciences as to mystical science."[17] Amadu Bamba also believed that the acquisition of knowledge without practice was a waste of time. He saw science and action as the twin foundations of a virtuous life.[18] Indeed, these two elements underpinned the pedagogy he gradually developed.

The system that Bamba designed was a lifelong education geared toward transforming the character and behavior of the disciple. It comprised three main steps: exoteric education, or *taalim*, which aimed at transmitting knowledge through the study of the Quran and the Islamic sciences; esoteric education, or *tarbiyya*, which targeted the soul; and ascension, *tarqiyya*. This third step, reached by only a small number of especially gifted disciples, allowed the elevation of their souls beyond the futility of material life and put them in a position of leadership in the community. The Sufi concepts of taalim, tarbiyya, and tarqiyya that shaped Bamba's educational system were familiar to learned clerics; what was new was the effort to actually give concrete educational content to these abstract notions.

Amadu Bamba theorized this system of education in his writings and experimented with it from the 1880s until the mid-1890s, when he was exiled to French Equatorial Africa. His emphasis on spiritual education and the efforts he deployed to promote and implement a pedagogy that would expand this form of education were his major innovations. And it is in this insistence on the necessity of educating the spirit that one finds the difference between his approach and that of the cleric reformers of his time. Although they were all critical of past practices, the latter mainly focused their actions on improving the personal ethics of the teacher, whereas Bamba believed that it was equally important to reform pedagogic practices. He seemed more concerned with finding a method that would help translate inner beliefs into outer practices. As he asserted in *Munawir es-Suduur* (The Enlightening of the Heart), "Knowledge, good actions, and good behavior are the root sources of spiritual perfection."[19] Classical education when appropriately dispensed could provide knowledge, but for him, what was missing was a means to teach good actions and instill good behavior in the learners.

However, in contrast to the opinion of Rawane Mbaye, I contend that the emphasis on spiritual education did not mean that Amadu Bamba had abandoned classical instruction.[20] He believed in the necessity of providing different options to respond to the diversity of educational demands expressed by the masses. The first generation of his disciples, using the *daara tarbiyya*, or working school, as a model, played a key role in developing and implementing the system.

For Bamba, the success of education was predicated on the choice of an appropriate teacher for the task at hand. Every type of education required specific skills and competence from the educator in charge. In a response to an anonymous disciple's question about the Sufi conception of education, he described the criteria that should guide the choice of a teacher.[21] In this correspondence, he distinguished between three major types of teachers: the sheikh *taalim* (instruction), who was responsible for the teaching of *ilm es-Zahir* (exoteric sciences): law, the tradition of the Prophet Muhammad, history, the interpretation of the Quran, and worship; the sheikh *tarbiyya* (education), whose aim was to educate the soul and guide the disciple toward spiritual perfection through the use of esoteric sciences (*tasawwuf, baatin* [(hidden)]); and the sheikh *tarqiyya* (ascension). Each of these sheikhs requires a specific profile.

The Sheikh Taalim. The sheikh taalim played the crucial role in Amadu Bamba's educational scheme. Bamba suggested that good knowledge of the sciences, an ability to communicate, and intellectual sagacity and honesty constituted the three criteria that were to guide the choice of this sheikh. He considered that good knowledge for the sheikh taalim was knowledge that, on the one hand, was based on the Quran and the traditions of the Prophet Muhammad and, on the other, was based on the use of rational thinking and comprehension that derived from observation of concrete reality. However, mastery of the appropriate knowledge was not enough; the teacher also needed to be able to communicate effectively with his students. For that reason, Amadu Bamba thought that eloquence was equally important because it allowed the teacher to explain his objectives with clarity and without the use of confusing hypotheses. He believed that the quality of an educator was measured by his communication skills.

For Bamba, the teacher also had to be intellectually fit. That is, he had to be able to research and marshal the knowledge that would help him identify and overcome the shortcomings in his spiritual and material life. The educator's ability to acquire this knowledge was manifested in his willingness to accept the truth without hesitation, to always be on the side of the right, to be able to say "I don't know" if necessary, and to abstain from saying or doing things if he was not sure of their lawfulness.

The sheikh taalim held an important position in society as a producer and disseminator of knowledge. His place was all the more central in the community because without schools and teachers, it would be difficult for people to develop knowledge, and for Amadu Bamba, understanding always had to precede action.[22] But the teacher's duty was not to be limited to disseminating knowledge; his personal life also had to serve as a tool for education, a model for his students to emulate. Bamba observed that access to books did not free one from seeking a guide, and, paraphrasing Ghazali, he reminded us that "[b]ooks are important, but the teacher enlightens and God is the Supreme Knower."[23] Hence, to his mind, venerating an honest and knowledgeable teacher was tantamount to venerating God.[24]

However, Bamba believed that many teachers of his epoch did not deserve this veneration because of their failure to uphold the very principles that were to guide the good scholar. In *Massalik*, he deplored that "some of them [scholars] are abused by their sciences and religious erudition, they do not acknowledge their weaknesses, they are very proud of the number of their disciples, and they are over-confident of their wisdom, whereas their heart is full of such grave sicknesses as pride, hatred, jealousy, etc."[25] For Amadu Bamba, the only way to cure those sicknesses was to educate the soul by submitting to a sheikh tarbiyya for spiritual education.

The Sheikh Tarbiyya. Amadu Bamba listed three qualities required in the sheikh tarbiyya, who specialized in the esoteric sciences. First, he had to understand the nature of the soul in its different states and master the means of curing its defects. He also had to be capable of identifying the sources of sicknesses that could affect the soul and the instruments that could assure its protection. In order to fulfill this task, the sheikh needed to combine scholarly insights and practical knowledge derived from experience with his soul. Second, the sheikh of education needed to comprehend the subtleties of the world and the practical and religious laws that governed the existence of matter and of the soul, so that he could always apply the adequate remedy to the various problems submitted to him. Third, to act in this way, the sheikh had to analyze every problem without passion and prejudice. To do so, he had to fear God and show repentance by shunning all self-glorification and by ridding himself of anything that distanced him from his Lord.

The work of the sheikh tarbiyya was not to transmit formal knowledge per se but to forge character (*defar nit* in Wolof, meaning "to make or repair people"). The techniques he used were geared toward control of the *nafs*, or lower self, which is seen by Sufis as the major obstacle standing between the believer and God.[26] Nafs is the animal instinct found in every human being, and it is the enemy that lures people's minds and bodies to an immoderate search for worldly pleasures. Sufis consider the fight against this formidable enemy to be the greatest jihad. In fact, for the Sufis, God cannot enter the heart of a human being unless the heart is emptied of all trivial and earthly preoccupations.

In *Tazawudu Shubaani*, Amadu Bamba identified seven organs through which the lower self worked, and he described the method to counter its bad effect on the hearts and minds of people.[27] These organs were: the stomach, the tongue, the genitalia, the feet, the eyes, the hands, and the ears. Referring to the stomach and the adverse effect it could have on the faith, Bamba warned against consuming illicitly acquired food and eating too much. He wrote that behaving in such a way only "leads to corruption of the spirit, the drought of the heart and to laziness." As for the tongue, he said that it "should be prevented from lying, slandering or engaging in [futile] controversies." Bamba advised disciples to refrain from seeking unlawful sexual pleasure and recommended chastity before marriage. The feet were to be restrained from walking to do illegal acts or from visiting unjust rulers. Instead, "they should be used to frequent the mosque and to build and strengthen ties between members of the Muslim community." The eyes should be taught not to look at forbidden things, not to threaten, and not to embarrass people. The hands were to respect the bodies and property of Muslims, and they were banned from writing indecencies or anything one would be ashamed of saying in public. As for the ears, Bamba recommended keeping them from listening to idle conversation, such as slander and gossip, or violating people's privacy.

The sheikh tarbiyya was a pivotal figure in Bamba's educational model. If the sheikh taalim cultivated the brain, the sheikh tarbiyya nurtured the spirit as well as the body through his ability to touch the soul. The work of these two sheikhs was complementary. However, lack of spiritual education constituted the greatest danger to disciples. Bamba blamed the deterioration of the mores and character of the people of his generation on the absence of this form of education. He noted that the path to the truth was paved with pitfalls and traps, and only the guidance of those who had already trodden this path could prevent one from being misled by Satan.[28] Thus, as he asserted in *Massalik*, "Anybody who abstains from seeking an education in the hands of a sheikh (*Murshid*) will suffer terrible ordeals (in the hereafter); because those without a [competent] spiritual guide will be guided by Satan, wherever they go, toward perdition."[29]

The Sheikh Tarqiyya. When the sheikh tarbiyya reached a certain level of spiritual purity, he could become a sheikh of ascension, or tarqiyya. At this spiritual juncture, his demeanor and appearance—and simply the fact of interacting with him—became sources of inspiration and an incitement to persevere on the right path. The sheikh of ascension taught by example and led the disciples to spiritual perfection through imitation.

Disciples pursuing the path of tarqiyya lived with their sheikh in his compound, learning from everyday activities. They assisted him in managing the family and ministering to the followers. Sometimes, they were assigned specific tasks in the household or the community. They interacted with the sheikh's guests and traveled with him. They observed him solving problems, arbitrating conflicts, and making decisions about various issues. Only particularly gifted disciples could reach this ultimate stage in the education of the soul. In the quest for spiritual education, the learner also had a major role to play.

Duties of the Student

For Amadu Bamba, four major objectives were to guide the knowledge seeker: first, to combat ignorance; second, to be useful to humanity; third, to enrich the religious sciences; and fourth, to act and live in accordance with the teachings of the sciences.[30] However, he warned that those seeking sciences only for the sake of engaging in polemics or for prestige and honor would earn nothing but punishment from God. Bamba urged the disciples to start seeking an education at a young age, before they were caught in the multiple constraints of adult life. Learning, he argued, was much easier for the young brain than for the mature one. As he wrote in *Nahju*, "Teaching the youth is tantamount to engraving a rock, while educating an old person is comparable to writing on water."[31]

Amadu Bamba also educated the young disciple about the difficulties confronting the student. He affirmed that the sciences were not easy to conquer; they only reluctantly yielded to those who consented to devote their entire lives to pursuing them. Therefore, he advised the learner to accept the necessary sacrifices for the challenging endeavor of mastering the sciences. The student had to learn to tolerate hunger and to be patient and resolute. He had to be passionate in his quest, soft in his manners, chaste, and humble.[32] But above all, the student had to respect the master's rights. Bamba even suggested putting the teacher's rights over the rights of parents because if the former educated the substance of humanity, the spirit, the latter only took care of the body, a perishable envelope. To completely respect the teacher's right was to honor him, to follow his recommendations without hesitation, and to give him material support.[33]

MURID DOCTRINE AND PRACTICES

Hubb, *or Love*

Amadu Bamba provided the most succinct definition of the Murid in his poem *Should They Be Mourned?* in which he stated, "The genuine Murid is the sincere disciple who loves his sheikh, submits to his service and gives *hadiyya* [offering, present, gift]."[34] Love (*hubb*), being at the service of the sheikh (*khidma*), and gift giving (*hadiyya*) are three central principles of Murid doctrine, which define and bestow a tangible substance to the relations between sheikhs and disciples. But of course, one ought to distinguish between the doctrine as theoretically articulated by Bamba and its embodiment through the practices of disciples and sheikhs. The actual practices of Murids represent a compromise between Amadu Bamba's ideal formulation and the concrete aspirations of the disciples, mediated by the sociocultural context and historical circumstances of the founding and development of the Murid tariqa.

Love is an important element of the Sufi way of life. However, the Sufi notion of love differs from the common understanding of this sentiment, which is prosaically defined as "profoundly tender, passionate affection to another person," especially fueled by emotion or sexual urge.[35] The love of the Murid for his sheikh is an absolute and benevolent love, a *"pure amour"* not tainted by the subjective interest of the lover. The best expression of this kind of love is found in this statement of the ascetic Rabia al-Addawwi of Basra: "My Lord, . . . if it is for fear of hell that I serve You, condemn me to burn in its fire, if it is for love of Your paradise, forbid me from entering it; but if it is for Your sake only that I serve You, do not refuse me the contemplation of Your face."[36]

The disciple's love for his sheikh is manifested through an eagerness to obey his recommendations and follow his example on all matters. This need for obedience and imitation of the master was particularly stressed by Sahl al-Tustari (818–96), who likened the relations of the sheikh with his Murid to that of the undertaker and the cadaver who will not object to his washer's actions. This metaphor, often attributed to Amadu Bamba, is widely referred to by Sufi sheikhs in Senegal and elsewhere.[37] However, the language in which this doctrinal principle is couched goes beyond the reality of the relationships between sheikhs and disciples. The emphasis put on love and obedience and the ways it is translated into practices differs from one Sufi order to another and is affected by the nature of local social structures and historical circumstances.

Among the Murids, love for one's sheikh is primarily expressed through the *njebel*, or submission, and through respect for the sheikh's *ndigel*, or recommendations. Murids hold that *jebelu*, or allegiance, to a sheikh is the gate to the Muridiyya. One becomes Murid by submitting to a sheikh. Jebelu is the Murid equivalent of *baya* (*jaayante* in Wolof), the pledge of fealty and support that early Muslims made to the Prophet Muhammad.[38] The ceremony of jebelu is rather simple. The disciple expresses his will to submit to the sheikh, which means to follow his recommendations and to avoid his interdictions on all matters pertaining to this world and to the hereafter. The sheikh then reminds the novice of some prescriptions of Islam and some points of Murid doctrine, after which he prays for him.

The first Murids were the disciples who adhered to tarbiyya in Mbakke Kajoor in 1884. Murid sources explain that Amadu Bamba needed a total commitment from the disciples in order to carry out the enterprise of transforming their bodies and souls. By agreeing to surrender their whole beings to their sheikh, the disciples were bound to follow his recommendations without discussion, and this attitude was the condition for their successful training in the ways of the Sufi.

Jebelu became a central feature of the Muridiyya beyond the strict educational framework in which it was first defined. The Murid sheikh is not solely a spiritual leader but also a temporal guide. His authority transcends the realm of the *daara*. Disciples, particularly those living in the same area as their sheikh, seek his counsel for choosing a wife, naming children, solving family disputes, or before engaging in a business venture; they also wish to be buried near his tomb.

Scholars have characterized the "strict" submission of disciples to their sheikhs as the most distinctive feature of the Muridiyya.[39] All Sufi orders require submission to a sheikh, but the Murids' strong emphasis on this principle sets their organization apart. Murid sheikhs wield much more power and authority over their disciples than other Sufi leaders in Senegal. However, one should be careful to distinguish between the rhetoric of the *tariqa*'s doctrine, the disciples' emphatic claim of blind obedience to their sheikh, and the actual practices. In fact, Murid disciples are often selective when it comes to obeying recommendations, and the sheikhs do not always have it their way; they are careful to make sure that their injunctions do not antagonize the disciples' interests. As observed by Leonardo Villalón, "Sheikh's clout is neither unlimited nor guaranteed," and the maintenance of their status "requires constant attention to legitimizing and reinforcing the bases of that status."[40] This assertion was borne out in the attitude of the Murid sheikhs who partnered with the colonial administration in building a railway connecting Tuubaa to the Dakar-Bamako rail lines: they supplied laborers but refused to negotiate their salaries, fearing that they could be accused of trying to appropriate some of the money.[41]

Students of the Muridiyya propose diverse hypotheses for understanding the roots of the Murids' "extreme" submission to their sheikh. The explanations given emphasize the influence of Wolof social structures and the colonial onslaught on Murid doctrine and practices. Wolof society is stratified and hierarchical, and patron-client relations determine the rapport between dominant and subordinate social groups. It is argued that the slaves who were newly freed from bondage by French rule and did not know what to do with their freedom as well as so-called casted people flocked to the Muridiyya and found in Murid sheikhs the patrons they had lost.[42] The "extreme" submission of Murid disciples to their sheikhs is, then, seen as the reproduction of atavistic behavior brought into the Muridiyya by the masses of low-status Wolof who joined the Murid organization in the late nineteenth and early twentieth centuries.

Octave Depont and Xavier Coppolani used a similar argument to explain the development of Sufi tariqas among the Berbers of North Africa. They noted that by breaking the homogeneity of tribal organization and by destroying the patronage systems, which had been controlled by prestigious families, the French had conferred on subordinate indigenous people a bewildering freedom. Sufi orders, they argued, served as loci for the reproduction of the patronage systems, which were at the heart of Berber societal life.[43]

There is an obvious validity to the assumption that power relations within the Muridiyya are influenced by Wolof social structures. The majority of Murids are, after all, Wolof, but this single factor does not tell the whole story. Other tariqas in Senegal are composed of a majority of Wolof of the same social backgrounds as the Murids, but they are organized differently. The Malikiyya and Niass branches of the Tijaniyya, which developed during the same era and in the same areas as the Muridiyya, recruited the bulk of their followers among the Wolof, but the relations between sheikh and disciples in these organizations differ from those of the Muridiyya. One may argue that the Muslim elite of the Four Communes (Saint-Louis, Rufisque, Gorée, Dakar) and trading posts of Senegal influenced the Tijaniyya Malikiyya, but the majority of its constituency came from the same geographic and socal environments as the Murids.

A closer scrutiny of these arguments reveals a number of problems. First, they give a paramount importance to the sociopolitical context of the formation of the Murid tariqa by narrowly tying the genesis of the organization to colonial conquest and Wolof culture, ignoring the possible influence of Islamic heritage, doctrinal, and spiritual factors. Second, this approach offers a blanket generalization that erases the nuances and differences in the ways in which Murids of different sociocultural and economic backgrounds interacted with their sheikhs. We must be mindful that Amadu Bamba was perceived as both a saint (that is, a man of extraordinary ability) and a sage (a man of extraordinary knowledge), and this double personality appealed to different audiences who related to him in their own ways.[44]

Beyond Wolof social structures, it is the profound mysticism of Amadu Bamba, the great sanctity that the Murids confer on his persona, and the special circumstances of the emergence of the tariqa that constitute the defining elements of the relations between Murid disciples and sheikhs. More than Bu Kunta, Malick Sy, or Abdulaay Niass—all of them renovators and local leaders of the Qadiriyya and Tijaniyya in Senegal—Amadu Bamba benefited from an aura of sainthood that singled him out. This aura was enhanced by the image of a martyr that French persecution bestowed on him. It was this position that partly earned him his spiritual authority and his reputation of exceptional sanctity, which also benefited his descendants and early companions.

Besides the role of sanctity and devotion, one must also keep in mind that the relationships between sheikhs and disciples in the Muridiyya are not homogenous and that the extent of deference and submission varies widely. People become Murid for many different reasons, and they come from all lifestyles. These differing social backgrounds and aspirations are also reflected in their interactions with sheikhs. Murids with a clerical upbringing do not have the same type of relations with their sheikhs as common disciples with only a superficial education. The notion that the religion of the educated is often different from that of the masses also applies to the Muridiyya. Thus, learned clerics embraced the Murid tariqa primarily because of their appreciation of Amadu Bamba's learning and piety. They were more attracted to his image as a sage. Ahmad Dem, a noted tijani cleric, joined the Muridiyya because he was attracted by Bamba's superior spiritual authority.[45] The well-known Kajoorian teacher and writer Ibra Joob Massar tested the founder of the Muridiyya and decided to submit to him because of Bamba's profound mystical knowledge.[46]

For these disciples from learned families, love for the sheikh was expressed in the form of praise-poetry they wrote to magnify their guide's sanctity. They also copied and popularized his works. Ibra Joob Massar, for example, recorded the largest collection of Amadu Bamba's sermons and religious causeries. On a more personal level, sheikhs of clerical origin built marital alliances with Bamba's family. This was the case with Sheikh Amadu Gay, Sheikh Ndaam Abdurahman Lo, Sheikh Mbay Jakhate, and others, who taught Amadu Bamba's sons, offered members of their family to the sheikh for marriage, and also married his daughters. The way that these sheikhs understood and articulated their submission to Bamba was, therefore, different from that of lay disciples.[47]

Murids of aristocratic origin and disciples from the urban and trading elites had distinct relationships with their sheikhs. Some of them joined the Muridiyya as a way of opposing the French; others, mostly the businesspersons, were attracted by the economic power of the Muridiyya. Members of these two groups tended to be less submissive. They respected and venerated their sheikh, but as in the case of Masurang Surang, they acted more like advisers and friends to their spiritual masters and were treated as such.[48]

The commoners, especially disciples living in the working schools or sheikhs' villages, showed greater deference to the leadership and displayed an attitude more congruent with doctrinal stipulations. The image of the saint was more appealing to them. They were critical of their fellow disciples who diverged from the ethical model they offered, and they distinguished between different types of Murids according to their degree of reverence and submission. The Murid *saadikh*, or genuine Murid, is differentiated from those who have "come with the wind," and the *taalibe taakh*, literally meaning "urban disciples" (but characterized more by an attitude than a location) are opposed to the more faithful rural disciples. In many of their Wolofal poems, Mbay Jakhate, Samba Jaara Mbay, and Musa Ka, among the most famous of all Murid poets, condemned the disciples who proclaimed submission but failed to act accordingly. Mbay Jakhate lambasted "those Murids who behave like donkeys [symbol of submission] when they come to Tuubaa but act like goats [symbol of unruliness] when they are away from the village," and he reminded the disciples that "nobody can deceive Amadu Bamba."[49]

Khidma

In addition to the pledge of total submission, Murids also believe in the importance of being at the service of the sheikh. The concept of *khidma* (service) is an important element of Murid doctrine. In fact, the name that Amadu Bamba coined for himself—Khaadim ar Rasul, Servant of the Prophet—was derived from this concept. He also wrote two books, *Muqadimaat al-Khidma* (Prelude to Khidma) and *Bidaayat ul-Khidma* (Initiation into Khidma), in which he described his service to the Prophet.

In the scholarly literature, the word *khidma* is always translated as "work," and as Amadu Bamba wrote, "Science and work are the surest paths to happiness." Two well-known and widely quoted sayings (which are attributed to him but are actually traditions of the Prophet Muhammad) read, "Work is a means of worshipping God" and "Work as if you will never leave this world and pray as if you know that you will die tomorrow."[50] But when referring to work in his writings, Bamba often used the word *khidma*, alongside the words *amal*, which means "labor" or "action," and *kasb*, which means "earning," "gain," or "profit." In the two sayings just quoted, *work* should be understood as khidma, or the performance of service for the sake of godly rewards in the hereafter. The concepts of amal and kasb, in contrast, refer more directly to earthly life. Bamba stated in *Massalik*, "Know that surrender to God (*tawwakul*) should not exclude in any way the performance of *kasb*," that is, labor for the production of wealth.⁵¹ But for him, the quest for wealth was not to be motivated by prestige, by the desire to accumulate power, or by ostentation but only by the will to earn one's own subsistence and avoid dependence on other human beings. As he argued in the *Majmuha*, if the goal of working is to provide the disciple's body with the sustenance it needs to perform sacred duties, then the very act of working becomes a form of worship because if the end is blessed, the means to this end cannot be but equally blessed.⁵² Therefore, amal and kasb are religiously significant only when they serve to generate resources for the accomplishment of pious deeds or for the fulfillment of the biological needs of the physical body, which is the vehicle though which the believer worships; khidma, however, is always performed for the benefit of others and for the sake of otherworldly gains. This distinction, which has not been made by students of the Muridyya, is key to understanding the philosophy that underpins the Murid conception of work. In fact, it mirrors the distinction that Amadu Bamba made between internal action directed toward God and external action directed toward humans or earthly life.

The Muridiyya is known for the prominence it accords to work. Much has been written about the so-called sanctifying virtue of work, seen as the single most important innovation of the Murid tariqa. Looking at the significance of work in the Muridiyya, Jean Copans and the multidisciplinary team of researchers from the Organisation pour la Recherche Scientifique et Technique Outre-Mer, or ORSTOM (now the Institut pour la Recherche et le Développement or IRD), who conducted fieldwork in the Murid heartland in the late 1960s, distinguished between the work habits of disciples in the working schools and those of the ordinary peasants who constituted the majority in the Muridiyya.⁵³ They discovered that much of what was written about the Murid work ethic was only valid for disciples living in the working daara, who were a minority in the Murid order. The research revealed that there were no major differences between the work habits of Murid peasants and non-Murid farmers.

Building on Max Weber, some scholars have found similarities between the Murid conception of work and the Protestant work ethic. Abdoulaye Wade asserted that the Muridiyya is with Protestantism the only religion to believe in the redeeming power of work.⁵⁴ He failed to note, however, that Murids do not believe in the doctrine of predestination, and in contrast to the Calvinists studied by Weber, they encourage the enjoyment of wealth, lavish expenses, redistribution, and generosity. In Amadu Bamba's view, wealth was only valuable when it served the fulfillment of religious duties in this world.

Reviewing Wade and other writers, Philippe Couty criticized materialist interpretations of the Murid conception of work and proposed a new approach that stressed doctrinal elements.⁵⁵ Following Paul Péllissier, he rejected the assumption made by J. Brochier and widely shared by scholars that work is equivalent to prayers for the Murid. This view is based on declarations attributed to Amadu Bamba, such as "Work equals prayer, work for me and I will pray for you." Couty correctly called attention to the contradiction in this assertion, noting that if work can be a valid substitute to prayer, then the worker does not need someone to pray for him.[56] For Couty, what is important for the Murid is not the production of wealth or the trading of labor for paradise, as implied in the preceding quotation, but the fact that work gives an empirical significance to the ideology binding disciples and sheikhs.[57] Work is the instrument through which unsophisticated Murid disciples express the complex Sufi concept of love and submission to one's sheikh. However, Couty only partially understood the Murid perspective.

In reality, work was not an exclusive duty of the disciples, and it was not solely expressed in the form of the physical labor (amal or kasb) of the disciples for the benefit of the sheikh. Sheikhs performed khidma as well. Amadu Bamba recommended that disciples provide khidma to their teachers, to the ulamas, to their elders, to the lone traveler, and to all good Muslims.[58] In the early years of his career, his khidma consisted of writing books and teaching the disciples. After he returned from exile in 1902, writing praise-poems for the Prophet Muhammad became an important part of his khidma.

For the ordinary disciples in the working schools, the cultivation of millet and peanuts and the different menial jobs performed to maintain the schools were forms of khidma. But in the daara, work also had a pedagogic virtue. It was the instrument to shield the disciples' soul against sicknesses such as pride, fear, and attraction to worldly pleasure, and it was a protection from idleness, which Bamba saw as the mother of all sins.[59] It was a means of realizing the Sufi aspiration of keeping the body and the mind perpetually occupied with good actions. Donating to one's sheikh, reading Amadu Bamba's religious poetry, and contributing to the tariqa's projects were all forms of khidma for the disciples living outside the working schools.

Therefore, khidma is not a sanctifying action, nor is it a mere expression of the submission of the disciple to the sheikh; rather, it is a manifestation of the common attachment to the Muridiyya, a way of perpetuating and participating in Amadu Bamba's mission or, as the disciples put it, "ligeey al Serigne Tuubaa," being at the service of Amadu Bamba. For the Murids, prayers, fasting, and other forms of worship are duties common to all Muslims; khidma constitutes their distinctive way of expressing love and fidelity to their sheikh. The economic implication of khidma is important as it results in the accumulation of wealth and prestige within the Murid organization, which primarily benefits the leadership, but this secondary outcome should not blur its ethical and doctrinal dimensions.

Hadiyya

Giving *Hadiyya* (pious gifts) is another of the principal duties of the Murids. Hadiyya is a form of donation, but it differs from *sadaqa* (alms), which are given to the needy and are mandatory for all Muslims. Hadiyya is a voluntary contribution that disciples pay directly to their sheikhs and for which they expect godly rewards. The hadiyya is the Sufi order's principal source of income and an instrument to redistribute resources among disciples and sheikhs.[60] But because hadiyya is presented as a moral and religious obligation, its payment may not be absolutely voluntary.

Sufi doctrine values the disciples' offerings to their sheikhs, but the Murids stand out for their generous donations to their organization and its leaders. It is difficult to put a figure to the amount of money and other goods that Murids donate because these contributions are not recorded. The French estimated that Murid disciples annually gave Amadu Bamba money and various gifts worth hundreds of thousands of francs when he was confined to house arrest between 1907 and 1927.[61] Today, Murids make investments amounting to billions of CFA francs (a dollar is worth about 535 CFAF) in religious or civilian projects in their holy city or their sheikhs' villages.[62]

For the Murid disciple, hadiyya is both an expression of love for the sheikh and a source of baraka. By donating what is dearest to him (his wealth), the Murid gives the ultimate proof of the sincerity of his affection for his spiritual leader. Murids also believe that giving to the tariqa is a way to contribute to the continuing fulfillment of Amadu Bamba's mission.[63] In other words, by helping to realize Bamba's prayers and wishes through their monetary contributions, they are able to prove that his spiritual grace remains operative in this world. And by making this investment, they hope to reap a benefit that will positively affect their lives on earth and in the hereafter.

The first hadiyya is given at the ceremony of jebelu (submission), where the new Murid pledges allegiance to his sheikh. Donations are also made during *ziaras* (pious visits) or during Murid religious celebrations. Hadiyya can be given in cash or in kind, and it has no limitations. Every disciple contributes in accordance with his wealth and generosity, and theoretically, the symbolism of the act of giving and the intention are more important than the amount given. However, rich and generous disciples have come to occupy privileged positions in the Muridiyya. These positions are often sanctioned by marriage in the family of their sheikhs or the attainment of the rank of respected dignitaries. In principle, all disciples are equal in the face of their sheikh, but in reality, those who give more benefit from greater recognition.

Disciples may not receive hadiyya, but contrary to the common wisdom, gift giving is not exclusively their duty. Sheikhs also give hadiyya. They contribute annually to the caliph or head of the Muridiyya, who is the successor of Amadu Bamba, and they are often assigned specific tasks to complete on behalf of the community, such as working in the caliph's farms, building a new village for him, or constructing a mosque. In such a case, the sheikh calls on his disciples to provide the workforce and money needed to complete the tasks assigned. The sheikh's prestige is measured by the contribution he makes to the development of the tariqa.

Besides the regular hadiyya, disciples and sheikhs are sometimes asked to make exceptional donations for specific projects. These contributions are called *sas* (portion) and are mandatory for those who have the resources. This tradition was started by Amadu Bamba in 1926 as a means of raising money for building the mosque of Tuubaa, perhaps the largest mosque in sub-Saharan Africa; it was completed in 1963. Sas has been used recently but on a voluntary basis to collect money for the embellishment and refurbishing of the mosque of Tuubaa. Sas has become a major fund-raising instrument used by the Murid leadership to mobilize resources and labor for special projects.

Hadiyya giving has, for the most part, been analyzed from a utilitarian perspective. Unable to see the material returns of disciples' donations to their tariqa, many scholars concluded that hadiyya was a mere ploy through which clever sheikhs exploited their naive followers. However, more recently, some researchers have called attention to the less apparent but real service that sheikhs also render their disciples. In later works, Cruise O'Brien highlighted the benefit that affiliation to the Muridiyya procured for the adherents, and he downplayed declarations of disciples boasting about the importance of donations they made to their sheikh.[64] Leonardo Villalón demonstrated the significant degree of reciprocity in the exchanges between marabouts and disciples. He observed, "First, the costs to disciples in terms of actual 'sacrifices' made for the *marabout* are rarely, if ever, onerous. And secondly, there is an important degree of reciprocity in exchanges with a *marabout* at least in the sense of the insurance against catastrophe which a relationship with a *marabout* affords a disciple." [65]

As suggested by Christian Coulon, the economic relations between Murid sheikhs and disciples are better understood in the framework of the exchange of gifts that defines patron-clients relations in Wolof society.[66] The prestige of a Murid sheikh is gauged by his generosity; his capacity to meet the material needs of his family, disciples, and clients; and the importance of his contribution to the realization of the tariqa's projects. He is expected to help each of his needy disciples access land, get a wife, secure a good position in the civil service, acquire a bank loan or critical administrative documents, and so forth. Important sheikhs draw substantial wealth from their disciples' offerings, and some of them live a lavish life in glamorous houses and drive expensive American luxury cars. But to maintain their social status and to keep their following's trust, they are also compelled to fulfill their khidma, that is, to share their wealth with the wider Murid community and especially their disciples. For instance, Sheikh Modu Maamun (d. 1968), the son and successor of Sheikh Anta, a prominent leader of the Murids, was known for always running out of money to feed his large family and entourage because he could not say no to those soliciting his help. He was not unique in this regard.[67]

Beyond the idea of reciprocity and patronage, there is also a nonmaterial dimension to Murid conceptions of collecting and sharing resources. Analyzed from this angle, the ethic of gift giving among the Murids bears some similarities to what Marcell Mauss, studying the economic behavior of some Indian communities in British Columbia, called gift economy.[68] For the French sociologist, what drove people in this culture to accumulate resources was not the desire to maximize their pleasures and comforts, as one would assume, but the joy of giving. But for the Murid sheikh, giving is as important as displaying outward signs of wealth. And like the people studied by Mauss, some sheikhs at times engage in ruinous and apparently irrational economic behavior for the sake of maintaining their social status and outdoing other sheikhs in what could be termed a generosity contest. However, from a Murid perspective, the enjoyment of giving should not lead to poverty and total destitution for the giver, as among Mauss's subjects, because this would be perceived as a hindrance to the working of Bamba's baraka in this world.

ORGANIZATION OF THE MURIDIYYA

The Wird

As observed in previous chapters, the wird is the basic distinctive feature of a tariqa. The wird is made of verses of the Quran and prayers that disciples recite individually or collectively, especially after the dawn or evening prayers. It may also contain some prescriptions and proscriptions regulating the religious life of the disciples. According to the Sufi, the wird contains secret names of God and prayers that can lead the disciples to spiritual perfection. Although the use of wird is not a canonical prescription in Islam, it is viewed by Sufis as a prominent part of religious worship. Amadu Bamba defined *wird* as an eminent act of devotion performed during specific times of the day, and he disapproved of its abandonment.[69] Looking at the religious foundations of wird, he wrote that it "originates from prophetic revelations or God's inspiration to a saint" and that it is attested in "the Revealed Book where it is disseminated in fragments, and in the well-preserved Prophetic sayings."⁷⁰ For the Sufi, the wird is a means to purify one's soul and to get closer to God by continuously remembering his name. For Bamba, all wirds were equally good, provided that they emanated from an authentic sheikh.

Amadu Bamba used the three most popular wirds in the Western Sudan. He practiced the *qadiriyya wird*, which he received from a variety of channels. He also used the *wird shaadily* and the *wird tijany*. He was probably introduced to these two last wirds by Moorish sheikhs. This eclecticism is not unusual among Sufi sheikhs, especially those affiliated with the Qadiriyya, who consider the use of multiple wirds as a source of multiplied baraka.⁷¹ The Tijaniyya doctrine, however, forbids disciples from the cumulative use of wirds because the Tijani consider their sheikh to be the seal of sainthood. Sheikh Ahmad Tijani, the founder of this order, claimed to have received his wird directly from the Prophet Muhammad, who assured him that he was the last saint to have direct contact with him.⁷²

While in exile in Gabon (from 1895 to 1902), Amadu Bamba abandoned all the wirds he was practicing except for the Qadiriyya wird, which he declared to have renewed through direct prophetic inspiration.⁷³ He explained this change in a response to a questionnaire about the history of the Muridiyya that was apparently sent to him by the colonial administration in 1917. He wrote, "I [first] received *wirds* (Qadiriyya, Shadiliyya, and Tijaniyya) from sheikhs whom I thought were genuine guides [who had reached ultimate spiritual heights], then I realized that this was not the case. Afterwards, God hid me in the sea (exile in Gabon) where I received the three *wirds* directly from the Prophet without intermediaries. God is witness to what I am saying."⁷⁴

During his second exile in Mauritania, Amadu Bamba stated that the Prophet had authorized him to use his own wird. In a poem he wrote to commemorate the event, Ahmed Ibn Hassan, a Moorish disciple of Bamba, stated that the wird was transmitted to his sheikh in two steps. In the year AH 1321 (1904), Amadu Bamba received the *khalif*, or light, version of the wird, and in the following year during the month of Rabi I (the third month of the Muslim calendar), coinciding with the night of the Prophet's birthday, he was given the *kaamil*, or perfect, version.⁷⁵

Amadu Bamba described the circumstances of the reception of his wird (the kaamil version) in an *ijaaza* (authorization) he wrote for a certain Mustafa Uthman, a native of Aleppo in Syria who was living in Mecca.⁷⁶ In this document, he mentioned that he received the wird directly from the Prophet Muhammad in the month of Ramadan AH 1322 (1905) in a place called Sarsaara in southwestern Mauritania.⁷⁷

The reception of the wird was a turning point in the spiritual development of Amadu Bamba and of Islam in Senegal. For the first time in the history of Islam in sub-Saharan Africa, a black man had parted with Middle Eastern Sufi tariqas to claim the status of a founder. Bamba had evolved from the status of an aspirant seeking baraka from masters to a sheikh deeply engaged in a spiritual quest, and he was now confident that he had reached the level of spiritual perfection and grace achieved by the major founders of tariqas. The composition of the Murid wird marked the summit of his spiritual journey, which had started in Mbakke Kajoor in the 1880s. The wird was the most obvious sign of Amadu Bamba's acknowledgment of his rank as a sheikh and guide for his community.

The Murid wird does not differ markedly from those used by other Sufi orders. It is composed of prayers and excerpts from the Quran that are found in one form or another in other wirds. However, there is some specificity in the conditions of its use. The Murid practicing the wird is required to know the basic religious obligations of a mature Muslim, he must abandon the twenty major sins, he must read each morning and evening a certain number of chapters from the Quran depending on his mastery of the book, and he is encouraged to visit the pious.[78] The Muridiyya differs here from the Tijaniyya, which discourages disciples from frequenting non-Tijaani sheikhs. Another particularity of the Murid wird is that, in practice, it is not a normative prescription. Its use is not mandatory for every disciple. Submission and respect of the sheikhs' recommendations take precedence over wird. Murid sheikhs argue that the objective sought through the use of the wird can be achieved through other educational means.[79]

There are, however, some similarities between the ways the Murid wird is administered and the pedagogic model championed by Amadu Bamba. In both cases, the preoccupation with flexibility and adaptability seems paramount. The sheikh gives the wird only to those who make the request or are deemed qualified. Amadu Bamba gave the wird and even issued an ijaaza to some disciples, mostly those belonging to clerical families and Moorish disciples, but he did not proceed in the same way with commoners.[80] Murid sheikhs continued this tradition. Only a minority of Murids, primarily the learned and old persons, practice the wird on a regular basis. Further, the Murid wird can be used cumulatively with other wirds. M. L. Diop indicated that when Amadu Bamba gave him the Murid wird, he recommended that he keep the wird he was already using if he could combine both; if he could not, he should hold on to the one he had given him.[81] For the Murid, the wird is only one among several means for the purification of the soul. The average Murid disciples consider submission, love for the sheikh, the reading of Amadu

Bamba's religious poems (*dhikr*), and the giving of hadiyya to be more important than the daily recitation of the wird.[82]

The Disciples

Like other tariqas in the Muslim world, the Muridiyya is hierarchical. The structure of power and authority in the order can be described as a pyramid. Amadu Bamba's male descendants in direct line (sons, grandsons, and great-grandsons) occupy the summit of this pyramid. His first companions and their heirs form the second layer of leaders. These leaders also have under their authority leaders of lesser importance, and at the bottom of the pyramid are the disciples, or taalibes, who do not receive submission and do not have the power to distribute the wird. Those in the first two top layers constitute the pyramid's pillars. They represent a chain of allegiance that links the taalibes at the bottom of the pyramid to the paramount caliph, who is the oldest living male descendant of Amadu Bamba.

Besides the Bamba lineage, there are secondary lineages formed by the families of his first disciples. These secondary lineages reproduce, at a lower scale, the pyramidal organization of the order, with a caliph at the summit, lesser leaders at the intermediate position, and taalibes at the bottom.[83] The number of intermediate leaders between the caliph and the taalibes varies because the successful member of a sheikh's family can earn the credentials of a leader and form his own constituency, thus creating a new branch within the lineage with which he is affiliated. All those who occupy a position of authority and receive the submission of disciples are given the title of sheikh. But sheikhs and taalibes are equally disciples of Amadu Bamba, and they submit to the paramount caliph, who is his representative on earth. Therefore, it is more accurate to portray the Muridiyya as a huge pyramid made of many smaller pyramids stacked together.

The disciple often chooses his sheikh among a lineage of sheikhs to whom his family is historically associated. For example, there are Murids who are directly affiliated with Amadu Bamba; some who are linked with the lineages of Ibra Faati or Sheikh Anta, his half brothers; still others affiliated with Ibra Faal or Isa Jenn, two of his first disciples who were not related to him; and so forth. Every disciple, regardless his location on the pyramid, is ultimately connected, directly or indirectly, to the head of the organization through one or more sheikhs. Thus, the family of Ibra Samb was affiliated with al-Hajj Serigne Ja, who was affiliated with Sheikh Anta, and Anta was affiliated with Amadu Bamba. Samb, Ja, and Sheikh Anta were all disciples of Amadu Bamba, but Samb's loyalty was first to Ja, Ja's loyalty was first to Sheikh Anta, and Sheikh Anta's was first to Bamba.

The majority of disciples who first submitted to Amadu Bamba in the 1880s were from Njambur in northern Kajoor, a region where Islam has been well established for more than a century.[84] In his report of 1889, to which I alluded to in the previous chapter, the French administrator Angot noted the existence in northern Kajoor of numerous villages headed by Ibra Saar, Maruba Gey, Amadu Gay, and other lesser-known Murid sheikhs.[85] Apart from Daaru Salaam, no such settlements existed in Bawol at the time. Most of these people were from clerical families, and they were attracted to Bamba because of his piety, superior learning, and mysticism.[86] The first tensions between the Murids and the colonial administration also occurred in northern Kajoor. The early development of the Muridiyya in Njambur contradicts the assumption made by Marty and later adopted by other scholars that the Muridiyya recruited its first followers among newly converted and superficially Islamicized people in Kajoor and Bawol.[87]

Although Amadu Bamba was from Bawol, the Muridiyya did not gain a substantial following in this kingdom until his return from exile in Gabon in 1902. Three major reasons explain the slower development of the Murid order in this area. First, Bamba's reputation as a learned and pious cleric was better established in Kajoor, where he grew up and spent most of his adult life, than in Bawol. Second, the Mbakke family was initially very critical of the Muridiyya.[88] Third, like their counterparts in Kajoor, the African chiefs of Bawol did not welcome the expansion of the Murid organization in the province.

Besides the first batch of disciples from clerical origins, the Muridiyya also recruited people of lower social status. Individuals in these social strata were attracted to the Murid order because its doctrine stressed the Islamic message of equality before God. Amadu Bamba criticized the Wolof tradition of classifying people according to their birth and the purity of their blood. He wrote in *Nahju*, "Whatever nobility one might claim for his ancestors, the truth is that these ancestors originated from water and clay."[89] For him, the only legitimate status of a person in a society was the one conferred on him by his greater faith and his superior learning.

At the ideological level, Murid doctrine requires that all disciples equally submit and humble themselves before their guide, and the sheikh's responsibility is to treat them without discrimination. Amadu Bamba tried to translate these doctrinal stipulations into practice. Murid traditions tell us that he used to assign tasks to disciples regardless of their social status. He ordered Massamba Joob, who was from a noble family of Kajoor, to make leather cases for books, a job that was traditionally given to a leatherworker. To Omar Joob, from a family of weavers, he assigned the reading and teaching of the Quran. He also elevated disciples such as Maruba Gey, Massamba Laam, and Mahmud

The Founding of the Muridiyya ⌒ 99

Mbegere, all of "casted" origins, to the rank of sheikhs. Even some disciples of servile origin, such as Abdulaay Niakhit of Thiès, reached the position of sheikh in the tariqa.

Comparing the theological mysticism of Martin Luther with that of Amadu Bamba, Claude Sanchez highlighted the "social revolution" established in Bamba's criticism of traditional Wolof social hierarchies and his advocacy of equality before God and the sheikh.[90] Cruise O'Brien expressed a similar opinion by stating, "Lower class-groups benefited from a certain relative social promotion, through membership in a community where class and caste were at least informally de-emphasized."[91] One should be careful, however, not to overstate the impact of this social revolution. Even if Murid teachings have contributed to changing the perception of lower-class disciples, that revolution has been unable to undermine the deeply entrenched inequality of Wolof society. Some casted disciples enjoyed the rank of sheikh, but they were less successful in recruiting a following outside their castes. Casted sheikhs mostly recruit followers among their castes. Some noncasted Murid sheikhs marry casted women, but the reverse is not common.

The Sheikh

One becomes a sheikh by the will of the spiritual master. The bestowing of the title of sheikh (or *seekhal* in Wolof) is a discretionary privilege of the founder of a tariqa that is rooted in his baraka. In the Middle East, this power was also accorded to the *sheikh al-turuuq*, a sort of paramount chief of the Sufi orders of a large city, appointed by the government.[92] For the Murids, the power to consecrate a sheikh is God-given. It is a mystical power that belongs in the realm of *baatin* (the hidden, esoteric). Therefore, it is the spiritual grace of Amadu Bamba that makes a sheikh.

The external sign of being a sheikh in the Muridiyya is to have personal disciples, but an individual cannot claim the status of sheikh because he has succeeded in recruiting followers, as certain scholars have inferred. As some of my interviewees put it, it is Amadu Bamba's satisfaction with a disciple and his prayers that creates the magnetism that propels his disciple to the center stage of his community and drives people to submit to him. Consequently, the gathering of people around a sheikh should be seen more as a manifestation of the efficiency of Bamba's baraka than the result of the sheikh's personal merit.[93]

In the Muridiyya, there is not a formal ceremony or symbol marking the elevation of a disciple to the rank of sheikh as in the Qadiriyya and other Sufi orders, in which newly minted sheikhs are given a turban, a *khirqa* (frock), and a cane. Amadu Bamba consecrated the first Murid sheikhs in Daaru Salaam (between 1886 and 1888) as part of the strategy to manage the growing number of people who gathered around him. He chose these sheikhs from among some of his oldest disciples, and they included Ibra Saar, Ibra Faal, Adama Gey, and Massamba Joob. According to Murid traditions, sometime before moving to Tuubaa in 1889, Bamba called these disciples together, expressed his satisfaction and God's satisfaction with them, prayed for them, and then gave them permission to leave Daaru Salaam and return to their families or settle wherever they wished. This practice is called *wacce* (the completion of the study of the Quran by the pupil is known by a similar term, *wacc* (meaning "descend" or "finish one's task"). It relates to the fulfillment of one's duty and the opening of a new phase in the person's life when he can expect to harvest the fruits of his efforts.

The tradition does not mention that Amadu Bamba formally gave the title sheikh to these disciples, but the disciples probably understood that the formal thanks and dismissal by their spiritual leader meant that they had reached a certain stage of spiritual growth. This belief warranted their bearing of the title sheikh in the tradition of the Qadiriyya, from which the Muridiyya originated. It was the allegiance of disciples and the rapid development of the villages and schools they founded that legitimized these new sheikhs' social status. For the newly appointed leaders, the gathering of people around them and the submission of members of their families were proof of the efficacy of Amadu Bamba's baraka and their share in it.

The pace at which sheikhs were consecrated seemed to have quickened after the installation of Amadu Bamba in Tuubaa, as evidenced by the founding of many new Murid villages in Kajoor. The process became more deliberate and formal when Bamba returned from exile in 1902. He stopped commissioning sheikhs in the first years of his house arrest in Diourbel (which began in 1912). This change may have indicated his recognition of the polluting effect that the loss of autonomy and confinement in Diourbel, the heartland of French power, had on him.[94] The task of appointing new sheikhs was continued by his senior disciples. Ibra Faati consecrated more than forty sheikhs, Sheikh Anta and Ahmad Ndumbe each appointed several dozen, and Ibrahima Faal appointed numerous sheikhs as well.[95] The power to consecrate sheikhs was limited to Amadu Bamba and his early followers; after their deaths, attaining the rank of sheikh became a hereditary matter. Today, the Murid leadership is primarily composed of sheikhs who inherited their titles.

Sheikhs played a crucial role in the expansion of the Muridiyya as grassroots leaders. Based on a survey conducted by the colonial administration, Paul Marty estimated the number of Murid sheikhs in 1912 at 164; Lucien Nekkache, who was writing in 1952, put the number at 200.[96] But neither Marty nor Nekkache defined what they meant by a sheikh. They mainly listed the most prominent Murid disciples and leaders they knew or had heard about, and many of the people they mentioned were not sheikhs but rather notables, teachers, and great disciples. They also left out a great number of sheikhs who were among those closest to Amadu Bamba because these sheikhs were not involved in organizing the disciples in the countryside and therefore did not catch the attention of the French administrators who conducted the surveys on which their estimates were based.

In reality, there were three types of sheikhs in the Muridiyya. Certain sheikhs specialized in recruiting and organizing disciples and could be called organizers. Some sheikhs were exclusively devoted to teaching the Quran and religious sciences. And others were involved in both organizing and teaching. This division followed the indications made by Amadu Bamba in a letter he addressed to the senior Murid sheikhs in 1903, where he stated:

> To those who want to study [Quran, religious sciences, and the Arabic language] I recommend that they join my brother Ibra Faati. Those who are only interested in *tarbiyya* I ask to follow my brother Sheikh Anta. Those who would like to combine *tarbiyya* and learning must join Ibra Faati. I have nothing to do with people who are not interested in learning or in *tarbiyya* and they should stay away from me. To the senior disciples, Ibrahima Faal, Ibra Saar, etc., I order you to dismiss those among your followers who misbehave or cause troubles and to keep only the good ones.[97]

The organizers attained their position primarily due to their perceived skills in managing people and their ability to educate and inculcate discipline in the disciples. They may or may not have been known for their learning and piety, but because they were consecrated sheikhs, they shared in Amadu Bamba's baraka. These sheikhs were not directly involved in teaching, although they ran Quranic schools in their compounds and villages. The French survey of 1912 listed the number and locations of schools run by Murid sheikhs.[98] Ibra Faal, Isa Jenn, and Sheikh Anta are perhaps the best representatives of this type of sheikh. It was to these three sheikhs that Amadu Bamba referred the majority of disciples of noble origins who submitted to him.

Bamba clearly appreciated the organizing talent of these sheikhs, but he was less appreciative of their contributions in the domain of education. He was also critical both of their excesses in the pursuit of material wealth and of their rivalries.[99] This ambivalence reflected the tensions between the high ethical standards that Amadu Bamba set for himself and the ethics of some of the sheikhs not interested in asceticism. For example, Bamba's relationship with Sheikh Ibra Faal was not always good. He wrote letters urging the sheikh to be more observant of Islamic prescriptions and not to believe that giving donations was enough. In one of those letters, published by the late caliph Abdu Lahad, he stated:

> In the name of Allah, the Most Merciful, peace be upon the seal of prophets. To the young Murid Ibra Faal, I pray that Allah grant you blessings in this world and the hereafter. As soon as you receive my letter, repent and ask for sincere forgiveness from God, the Most Merciful, "I order you and your family to pray [Muslim canonical five daily prayers] and to persevere in performing it. We do not ask for your material support because Allah is The Giver. Happiness is for those who follow the path of piety."[100]

Bamba also had tense relations with Isa Jenn, who created a stir by contesting Bamba's choice of Balla Coro Mbakke, his brother, as chief of the Murid village founded near the town of Diourbel in 1913. Jenn was among the most powerful and wealthy Murid sheikhs. Dismayed by his disciple's attitude, Amadu Bamba declared that the only thing he regretted in his career was that he had given power to certain people without making sure that they had received the appropriate education to adequately manage that power.[101] He was also critical of his brother Sheikh Anta for his political activism and business-oriented lifestyle.

Those sheikhs who specialized in teaching were closer to Amadu Bamba, and they formed his immediate entourage. Abdu Samat Sylla, a son of one of these sheikh teachers, affirmed that seventy *hafiz ul-Quran* (clerics who knew the holy book by heart) surrounded Amadu Bamba when he moved to his village in Diourbel in 1913.[102] These sheikhs originated from renowned clerical families, and they were not as popular among disciples as the organizers; some of them were not even known outside the small circle of their disciples. M. L. Diop was the personal secretary and barber of Amadu Bamba in Diourbel, and he worked with a team of nine helpers originating from the Niang, Jakhate, Syll, and Siise families of Kajoor, which had reputations for learning and piety. These aides taught the Quran, read and corrected Amadu Bamba's manuscripts, and assisted in the management of his compound and household. In the 1920s, Majemb Sylla was head of the Quranic school in Diourbel, and he directed the reading and writing by a group of disciples chosen by Amadu Bamba.[103] Mbacké Bousso managed the school of Gede and coordinated the teaching in Tuubaa. Abdurahman Lo was sent to Ndaam, where he opened a school and taught Amadu Bamba's sons and the sons of other Murid dignitaries. These schools continue to function to this day, and they are still run by descendants of these sheikhs.

Amadu Bamba was reluctant to let these highly learned disciples engage in the task of recruiting and managing disciples, and he closely monitored their activities by assigning them specific tasks and residences. He preferred to keep them in his compound or to have them open Quranic schools in their traditional villages or in other areas that he chose for them. However, not all teaching sheikhs were happy with their conditions. Some of them resented their position and even requested to be consecrated and commissioned so that they could recruit disciples and benefit from the wealth and prestige that their other colleagues enjoyed. Galo Mbay tells of an instance in Diourbel when his father, a Murid sheikh from the clerical family of Longoor in Njambur, demanded that Amadu Bamba release him and send him away so that he could earn wealth and fame like some of his fellow sheikhs.[104] Apparently, his case was not an isolated one, since in a letter he sent to some of the sheikhs, probably while he was in Diourbel, Amadu Bamba reminded them that he knew better what was good for them and added, "To those sheikhs I have asked to stay with me as to those I have sent away, I say that what I have decided is best for you in this world and the world beyond."[105] Amadu Bamba probably doubted the capacity of these clerics from elite Muslim families to organize and discipline the novices in the way that tarbiyya required. He was also worried about the detrimental consequence on the education of the disciples had these sheikhs been released. He was most preoccupied with maintaining the balance between religious (Quranic) instruction and tarbiyya education.

In addition to the organizers and teachers, there was a third category of sheiks, all of whom occupied a hybrid position. These sheikhs received the allegiance of disciples but at the same time emphasized teaching and spiritual training. Perhaps Ibra Faati and Amadu Bamba's cousin Ahmad Ndumbe were the best examples of this type of sheikh. Maam Cerno was Amadu Bamba's half brother and confidant.[106] He had a reputation for strict orthodoxy and frugality, and it was to him that Amadu referred the disciples who wanted to combine study and work. He offered the model that was most attractive to disciples. Not only was he the oldest among his brothers, he was also the most faithful to his teachings and the closest to the ideal disciple. Similarly, Ahmad Ndumbe is remembered as a tireless worker entirely devoted to Amadu Bamba and his family; he was a sheikh of great piety and asceticism. Like Ibra Faati, he gave much attention to worship and education. Some of his grandsons still run Quranic schools.

The Daara Tarbiyya

The daara tarbiyya, or working school, is an important institution of the Muridiyya and has played a central role in the founding and development of this tariqa. The Wolof word *daara* derives from *dar* (meaning "place" in Arabic), and it has historically designated a Quranic school. Murid sheikhs and disciples manage daaras that are exclusively devoted to Quranic teaching. These Murid daaras do not differ from daaras run by members of other Sufi orders or independent teachers.

However, the daara tarbiyya is a Murid innovation. This school is exclusively reserved for male disciples who voluntarily engage in tarbiyya, or education of the soul. Disciples join the daara tarbiyya at all ages and for a variety of reasons. Some are youths entrusted to a sheikh by their fathers. Others are adults who have already mastered the Quran but wish to spend some years in this institution for their spiritual perfection. Disciples also enrol in the daara tarbiyya at their sheikh's request. During the colonial era, some people entered the working schools to escape military conscription or French control. Daara tarbiyya also welcomed young men who submitted to Murid sheikhs as a way of contesting household authority or traditional land-management practices.[107] Theoretically, the time that a disciple spent in a daara was dependent on the sheikh's will. Since the training was not based on preestablished requirements but on mystical considerations (education of the soul), which belonged in the realm of the baatin, or hidden, the sheikh was the only one qualified to know if the objectives were reached.

Sheikh Ibra Faal has been credited with creating the system of daara tarbiyya.[108] But even though the code of conduct he forged was central in inspiring the functioning of this institution, it seemed that he did not play a direct role in its creation. Murid as well as French sources depict Ibra Faal as a man who loved city life: as early as 1912, he owned many houses in the cities of Dakar, Ndande, Kébémer, Thiès, and Saint-Louis.[109] After his consecration as a sheikh between 1888 and 1889, he settled in Saint-Louis, the former capital of Senegal and French West Africa. He next moved to the neighborhood of Lambinaas in Dakar, the future capital of independent Senegal, and then to the city of Thiès, around 1910. He was primarily involved in trading along the railways between Dakar and Saint-Louis. Murid traditions do not count him among the great Murid sheikh farmers and founders of daaras; rather, it was his sons and first successors, Mustafa, Mortalla, and Hassan, who had reputations as great farmers and heads of daaras.[110]

The daara tarbiyya, in the form it is known today, seemed to have developed gradually as a coping strategy that Amadu Bamba and his first followers adopted to deal with the growing number of adult disciples clustering around them. Daaru Salaam was the first trial ground for the system.[111] Traditionally, Islamic schools in Senegal had a strong educative component geared toward forging the young disciple's character. Referring to this aspect of Quranic education in Senegal, Denis Bouche noted that

> [the French] persistently saw the Quranic school as a poor Arabic equivalent to the French school, but Quranic schools are not meant for the diffusion of knowledge, even religious, they are instruments to forge the character of disciples. . . . Parents confide their children to teachers that have exclusive authority over them for all the duration of their education. They [the pupils] live like Spartans, they are exposed to hunger and the cold, and they wear rugs and must beg for their food. They are assigned chores such as fetching water and firewood. They work their teachers' farms and they are taught only a few hours a day at dawn and after twilight.[112]

Bouche's assessment of the Quranic schools of Senegal is somewhat misleading. In fact, people sent their children to Quranic schools both to mold their character and to give them a religious education. In addition to nightly and dawn lessons, pupils studied during the daytime except on Wednesdays and Sundays, which were reserved for working at the teacher's farm, and Friday afternoons, reserved for worship and leisure. Indeed, if Bouche's description were accurate, Senegal would not have produced the Muslim scholars that have marked its history. However, Bouche was generally accurate in depicting the hardships that the disciples at the Quranic school had to endure, as well as the expectations parents had in regard to seeing their children become mature and well mannered by the end of their training.[113] Training designed to teach youngsters to cope with suffering and hardships and overcome adversity has always been a strong component of traditional African education. These were the goals of the rites of initiation practiced in many African societies, to which young men and women were subjected.

The daara tarbiyya used similar methods but for the sake of purifying the soul. Those who joined Amadu Bamba in the early development of the Muridiyya could not be accommodated through the traditional system of education. Some of them were illiterate adults and could not be sent to a Quranic school with a wooden board to start learning the alphabet. Others had an advanced Quranic education and were seeking spiritual education. Amadu Bamba referred novices to more senior disciples, just as was done in the traditional Quranic schools. It was incumbent on these tutors to educate those entrusted to them. The tutors sheltered the disciples in their houses and put them to work in their farms alongside nephews, sons, and other dependents, in the tradition of the Wolof household. Those students who mastered the Quran and could read Arabic were instructed to study Amadu Bamba's religious poems and to participate in séances of dhikr during the night.

From the late 1880s on, the growing number of sheikhs and their dispersal to other areas led to the transformation that endowed the daara tarbiyya with its salient characteristics. Isolated from their traditional villages, which rarely welcomed their newly earned baraka, and confronted by African chiefs who resented their increasing power, Murid sheikhs often built their daaras in forests or on land away from larger villages. The daara tarbiyya resembled the Sufi *ribat*, where disciples were kept secluded from the rest of the world for the sake of developing their bonds and perfecting their spiritual training. It aided in the conquest of the forests of Bawol, Siin, and Saalum and spearheaded the territorial expansion of the Muridiyya in the post–World War I era.[114]

The daara accommodated single male disciples in teams of ten to fifteen, headed by a *jawrigne* (representative). The word *jawrigne* is a borrowing from the terminology of Wolof political culture. The jawrigne represented the sheikh; he was a married adult who lived with his wife in the daara and tended to the disciples. He was required to provide Quranic education to school-age disciples and to initiate older disciples to Amadu Bamba's religious poems, but his main task was to enforce discipline, distribute work, and watch after the disciples. A sheikh could have many daaras tarbiyya, and he would occasionally pay visits to these schools. The treatment of disciples in the daaras depended on the sheikh's character and wealth. Some sheikhs provided their disciples with food and clothes and forbade begging.[115] Others only fed their disciples during the rainy season, when they were engaged in farmwork, and allowed them to migrate to towns during the dry season to beg or engage in wage labor. Disciples were responsible for the maintenance of their daaras, and they fulfilled this task after harvest when thatch and bamboo were available. As in the ribat, the hardships suffered by the disciples — isolation from loved ones, begging, household chores, hard menial jobs, and so forth — were seen as tools to tame the body and curb negative impulses such as greed and hubris in order to strengthen the spirit, satisfy the sheikh, and thereby earn baraka.

The daara tarbiyya originally grew millet, which was the staple in Senegal before it was superseded by rice, massively imported by the French. Murid sheikhs grew large quantities of millet, and such great sheikhs as Ibra Faati were often solicited by the colonial administration to supply grain in time of food shortages.[116] The abundance of food in Murid villages and the Murids' discipline and solidarity also attracted migrants, who often ended up embracing the order. There was a saying that "a Murid never dies of hunger." With the development of a market economy in Senegal, sheikhs oriented their daaras toward the cultivation of peanuts, and the introduction of this cash crop affected the organization of the daara. C. T. Sy noted that daara specializing in the cultivation of peanuts covered 20 to 30 hectares, as compared to the 10 to 20 hectares of those who grew millet.[117] With the reduction of the cultivation of millet, the sheikh was obliged to shoulder the expenses for feeding his disciples.

After some years of exploitation, the daara generally evolved into a Murid village headed by the sheikh. Disciples who completed their training in the daara tarbiyya often received from their sheikhs a plot of land and help in marrying and starting a family. These disciples often choose to settle near their former daara, where land was more accessible and where they could benefit from the sheikh's support and the solidarity of their peers. The village frequently developed around a well and the house built for the sheikh, and it gradually attracted people because of the security and sociability it offered. The newly built village ultimately absorbed the daara's land. But not all disciples remained in the countryside; some migrated to towns or returned to their villages of origin if they could rely on strong family networks. Others, mostly the youngest, often started apprenticeships or engaged in commerce with the support of their sheikhs, family, and fellow disciples.[118]

THE FOUNDING OF THE MURIDIYYA

Scholars have found a direct correlation between the emergence of the Muridiyya, the death of Lat Joor (the last king of Kajoor) in 1886, and the imposition of colonial rule on the Wolof. This idea was first developed by the colonial writer Paul Marty, and it has since become historical orthodoxy. In his influential work on the Murids, Marty started his narrative of Bamba's life in the year 1886, devoting only two paragraphs to his ancestry and the events that marked the previous thirty-three years of his existence.[119] He viewed everything that Bamba said and did as well as people's responses to his calling as a reaction to the destruction of Wolof traditional rule by the French.

Cruise O'Brien further elaborated this idea of a connection between the demise of the traditional Wolof aristocracy and the development of the Muridiyya by arguing that the "success" of Amadu Bamba was due less to "his personal makeup" then to his social relations with the "courts and the warrior *marabouts*" of the Wolof states.[120] He presented Bamba's ultimate meeting with Lat Joor, just a few days before the latter's death, as a sort of symbolic passing of the torch between the ancient and future leadership of the Wolof people. Cruise O'Brien conceived this meeting as the benchmark in the founding of the Muridiyya.

With the notable exceptions of M. L. Diop and Vincent Monteil, almost all those who have written about the Muridiyya, scholars as well as hagiographers, have mentioned the encounter between Lat Joor and Amadu Bamba. However, there are significant discrepancies between the versions of the story they tell. Amadou Bamba Diop placed the encounter at Mbakke Kajoor; Cheikh T. Sy talked about Daaru Mannaan; Eric Ross proposed Daaru Salaam; Bachir Mbacké and Cruise O'Brien referred to the event but were silent about the date and venue of the meeting.[121] My informants in Mbakke Kajoor affirmed that Amadu Bamba met with Lat Joor in this village just two weeks before the king's death, which occurred in October 1886; yet these same sources maintained that Amadu Bamba left Mbakke Kajoor for good a year after the death of his father in Muharram AH 1300 (1883) and never returned.[122]

In contrast to the conflicting reports surrounding the meeting of 1886, oral and written Murid sources agree that by 1886, Amadu Bamba had been living in Bawol for at least two years.[123] Yet no source refers to a meeting between him and Lat Joor in that kingdom or his trip to Mbakke Kajoor after he left the village in 1883–84. It is even more intriguing to observe that available colonial records made no mention of a meeting between Amadu Bamba and Lat Joor in 1886, although the French and their ceddo allies controlled Kajoor and their influence on the king of Bawol was quite strong. Paul Marty did not refer to this encounter either in his article of 1913 or in his later works on the Murids, yet such an encounter between two high-profile figures of Kajoor in a time of war could not have escaped French intelligence. Had even the French learned of the alleged meeting by 1895, when they tried Amadu Bamba, they would have certainly used this information as evidence in their effort to portray the cleric as a representative of the defeated precolonial aristocracy.[124]

It is likely that the meeting between Lat Joor and Amadu Bamba never actually took place, although it has become a "historical fact" authenticated by oral traditions and scholarly works. I argue that members of the *geej* dynasty (probably Mbakhane Joob, who joined the Muridiyya after losing his position in the colonial administration) invented the story of this encounter. Mbakhane might have started to circulate the story sometime after Amadu Bamba's settlement in Diourbel and after he himself had become a Murid in an attempt to foster closer relations with the hierarchy of the order and to erase the memory of hostility and conflicts that had marred their past relationships.[125] Bachir Mbacké, whose 1935 book has inspired many bearers of Murid oral traditions, popularized the story. A. B. Diop, Mbakhane's son, conveyed the story among the scholarly community through his 1966 article in the *Bulletin de l'Institut Fondemantal d'Afrique Noire*.[126]

The rewriting of the history of the relationship between Lat Joor and Amadu Bamba helped the reconciliation between the geej dynasty, defeated but still prestigious, and the Mbakke family. The mended relations were consolidated by marriages between geej women and Amadu Bamba's heirs and great disciples.[127] Over time, Senegalese nationalist writers lent more credibility to the account of the meeting. They popularized it because it conveniently fit the image they constructed of the cleric as a resister to colonialism. For scholars who conceived the Murid tariqa as an instrument that helped distraught Wolof farmers adapt to colonial rule, the episode of the passing of the torch between the king and the cleric served as a perfect illustration of their theory.

Although some Murid sources evoke the meeting between Amadu Bamba and Lat Joor, they, unlike scholars, do not perceive this event as particularly significant in the history of the tariqa. They instead emphasize events that marked Amadu Bamba's life during his stay in Pataar and Mbakke Kajoor.[128] They see this period, which coincided with the death of his father and the dramatic change in his pedagogy, as the major watershed in the history of the Muridiyya. Murids generally refer to 1884, the year when Amadu Bamba started tarbiyya, as the date of the founding of their order.

I concur that 1884 was an important date in the history of the Muridiyya, but it was just the initial moment of a gradual development that reached its climax in the first decade of the twentieth century, with the formal constitution of the tariqa.[129] In effect, between 1884 and 1903, the Muridiyya appeared more like an informal organization than a tariqa, and Amadu Bamba acted more like a master and a teacher than a Sufi sheikh and leader of a mystical order. As he asserted in a response to a question raised in the questionnaire referenced earlier, he was consumed by his search for a genuine spiritual guide during this formative period, and he knocked on various doors until God revealed to him the right path while he was in exile in Gabon.[130] Before this epiphany, he was engaged in a spiritual journey, perfecting the education of his soul through retreats, dhikr, meditation, and other Sufi exercises. In 1892, he was reaffirming his allegiance to Sheikh Sidiyya Baba in the humble and self-deprecating language that Sufi disciples use when they address their masters. He was also sending questions to his sheikh, inquiring about different points of Sufism and Islamic law.[131]

Like Sufi masters before him, Amadu Bamba was patiently trying to find his way through the uncharted and treacherous path to spiritual perfection. Founders of new tariqa or independent branches of existing tariqa drew their legitimacy from learning, piety, holiness, ancestry, or a combination of some of these qualifications. In the Western Sudan, *sharifan* status, or descent from the Prophet Muhammad, was an important item in the pedigree of tariqa builders. They elaborated saintly genealogies through a laborious construction of family trees that linked their ancestors to the family of the Prophet.[132] In addition to sharifan descent, baraka was another key legitimizing element for the *murshid* (Sufi master and guide).

Amadu Bamba did not claim a saintly genealogy, although some of his hagiographers have made the claim for him.[133] He was certainly an unusually learned and pious person, but he needed recognition of his superior piety and holiness before he could establish himself as a legitimate leader of a tariqa. The events that marked his life between the late nineteenth and early twentieth centuries earned him the legitimacy of a genuine guide and founder of tariqa. In a proclamation he wrote, probably while in exile in Mauritania (from 1903 to 1907), he spelled out what could be viewed as the chart of his spiritual journey from murid (aspirant) to murshid. He wrote, "In AH 1301/1884 God has inspired the author of these words to cling to the Prophet (PBUH). He then devoted himself to his service until AH 1311/1893. In AH 1313/1895, he went for the blessed exile and pursued the efforts to purify his soul, combat Satan and worldly passions (May God the Most High protect us against their influence). This mission lasted until AH 1320/1902. From then on, he continued to honor his Lord and to combat His enemies until 1322 (1904)."[134]

Each one of the five dates singled out in this proclamation could be considered a turning point in the history of the Muridiyya, and it is remarkable that no mention was made of the year 1886, so pivotal to scholarly reconstruction of the Murid order. The year 1884, as noted previously, marked the beginning of tarbiyya and is conceived by the Murids as the date of birth of their organization. The year 1893 corresponded with Amadu Bamba's fortieth birthday, which is a symbolic moment in the life of Muslim saints and clerics engaged in a spiritual quest. It was at age forty that Prophet Muhammad received his first revelations in Mecca. It was also from 1893 that Amadu Bamba started to distance himself from his master in Mauritania and to assert his autonomy and personality. In a poem written in 1893, he stated, "My time is henceforth exclusively devoted to Muhammad until the ultimate day."[135] This statement seems to indicate that Bamba felt that he no longer owed allegiance to a sheikh and that he had chosen the Prophet Muhammad as his guide. This stage is crucial in the spiritual development of a Sufi saint. It constitutes a period of anxiety and expectation, in which the saint is convinced that he has reached a level of spiritual purity that frees him from formal allegiance to a living master but has not yet received the mystical sign of his election to the rank of *wali Allah* (friend of God), *qutb* (pole of the era), or another mystical station that draws him closer to the Prophet Muhammad and God. It is at this juncture that the saint intensifies his prayers, meditations, retreats, and other Sufi exercises, hoping to receive the anticipated sign, which often comes in the form of a dream or a mystical encounter with dead founders of tariqa or the Prophet himself.

The third date highlighted in the proclamation, 1895, coincided with Bamba's mystical encounter with the Prophet in his mosque in Daaru Khudoos (Tuubaa) and his departure in exile to Gabon. These two events are conflated in the oral traditions. We are told that the meeting took place during a spiritual retreat (*khalwa*). Amadu Bamba saw the Prophet accompanied by some of his earliest companions (*sahaba*) and the combatants of Badr, but he could not shake his hand because a veil separated them.[136] When he asked the Prophet why he could not get closer to him, the latter responded that being in contact with him was an honor exclusively reserved to those who fought at Badr, and since Badr could not be repeated, this privilege was no longer accessible.[137] Bamba told the Prophet that he was prepared to pay any cost to earn this privilege. The Prophet warned him that many devout Muslims who had reached his spiritual rank and had the grace of meeting him in this condition had made the same pledge but had failed to carry out their commitment. He added that the honor Amadu Bamba was seeking had a very high price. Amadu Bamba responded that he was ready to foot the bill, that his body and soul were prepared to support any sacrifice as long as a breath of life remained in him.

This story, told by Murid written and oral traditions, served as a mystical explanation of the confrontation between Amadu Bamba and the French.[138] Murids believe that Amadu Bamba's trials at the hands of the French colonial administration were nothing but the fulfillment of the terms of the covenant between their sheikh and the Prophet Muhammad. The suffering that he was to endure was the price he had to pay to access the privileged position of companion of the Prophet. Consequently, the seven-year exile in French Equatorial Africa (from 1895 to 1902) had a critical impact on Amadu Bamba's life and on the development of the tariqa he founded. It was while he was on the way to or in Gabon that he earned the title of *Khadim ar-Rasuul*, or Servant of the Prophet.

The importance of the date 1902, the year of Bamba's return to Senegal, stems from the fact that the year was a testimony to his capacity to survive the ordeal and to defeat French intentions and projects. And this very survival was a powerful sign of divine protection and of election among the Prophet's favorites. The attainment of this new spiritual status was evidenced by the acquisition of the Murid wird in 1904. This occurrence showed a culmination of Amadu Bamba's spiritual quest and marked a new beginning in his career as a sheikh, saint, and founder of tariqa. He clearly assumed this new position by redefining his relationships with his disciples and with fellow sheikhs who belonged to other tariqas. He started to more deliberately address the former, through public proclamations and letters, as his Murids, giving them directions in their material and spiritual lives. He treated the latter as his equals and even sometimes seemed to claim greater holiness and spiritual authority. This transformation was documented through his relationship with Sheikh Sidiyya Baba. Analyzing the cleric's correspondence with his former master, Abdel Wedoud Ould Sheikh observed, "The correspondences indicate a clear evolution in the relationships between Amadu Bamba, Baba and the Ahl Sheikh Sidiyya family. The very deferent disciple of the first letters gradually gave way to a partner, who had become confident in his own legitimacy as founder of *tariqa*, and who—though with courtesy—seemed to distance himself from his former master."[139]

CONCLUSION

The founding and development of the Muridiyya was intimately associated with the spiritual growth of Amadu Bamba and the sociopolitical context in Kajoor and Bawol in the nineteenth and early twentieth centuries. The Muridiyya emerged first as an educational project aimed at renewing and reforming the social order in the increasingly dysfunctional precolonial Wolof kingdoms of Kajoor and Bawol. It was a response both to the contemporary sociopolitical situation that Amadu Bamba judged detestable and to the classical system of education that he blamed for not adequately responding to the challenges of the time. In this regard, his initiative was not original; in Senegambia, Muslim clerics have always spearheaded movements of reform and renewal in times of crisis.

What was new with Amadu Bamba was the method and approach that he advanced for the achievement of societal change. He did not believe in a top-down type of reform, wherein rulers, whether secular or religious, would hold the initiative. He rejected jihad of the sword and collaboration with the court. He proposed education as a central instrument for the transformation of society. But in Bamba's view, not all forms of education suited the task. For him, to achieve enduring impact, the seeds of change had to be sown in peoples' hearts and souls. The type of education he initiated encompassed the body, the mind, and the soul and called for a new pedagogy and teaching techniques that differed from those used in the classical Quranic schools, which primarily focused on the transmission of knowledge.

The educational system that Bamba championed responded to a variety of demands. He tried to put into practice Sufi principles and ideas that circulated as theory and knowledge in Senegal but were not concretely articulated as a basis for developing a method of education. This system of education accommodated atypical disciples, used educators who did not always have the traditional credentials and pedigrees attached to the profession, and employed unconventional teaching practices inspired by Sufi doctrine. It was the breach of traditional ways of teaching that caused the criticism and hostility that confronted the Muridiyya at its founding.

However, in the context of the French encroachment and pressure on Wolof political and social structures, the Muridiyya became a rallying point for the individuals of different social strata who joined the organization. It was the profound mysticism of Amadu Bamba, his distrust of rulers, and, finally, the aura conferred on him by French persecution that attracted people to the Muridiyya. The decentralized structures of the tariqa, organized around individual sheikhs that shared common doctrine but benefited from substantial autonomy of organization, provided an appropriate framework for accommodating disciples of different backgrounds and aspirations.

Sheikhs and disciples played a central role in shaping the Muridiyya. One can safely argue that the ways in which the tarbiyya was practiced in the daara was a compromise between Bamba's ideas, the sheikhs' and disciples' preoccupations, and the constraints of the context. The meaning of such elements of Murid doctrine as hubb, khidma, and hadiyya changed over time to adapt to the shifting context of the relations between sheikh and disciples. Amadu Bamba provided the inspiration through his writings, sermons, and recommendations, and he also had a direct impact on the system through the sheikhs he educated and the guidance he offered. However, because of his numerous arrests and exiles and his confinement to house arrest, it fell on the sheikhs and the disciples to interpret, adapt, and translate his ideas into practice.

5 ↝ Murid Conflict with the French Colonial Administration, 1889–1902

THE CONFLICT between the Murids and the French colonial administration of Senegal, which reached its climax between 1895 and 1907, is the best-documented episode in the history of the Muridiyya. Because of the abundance of relevant archival documents and oral sources, colonial writers, Murid hagiographers, and contemporary scholars have given much attention to this period. However, colonial views and perspectives on the conflict, conveyed through the archives, weigh heavily on scholarly interpretations. In addition, most approaches have taken a narrow view of the confrontation by focusing primarily on the actions initiated by the office of the governor in Saint-Louis. Although information about the rationale and implementation of the administration's policy is readily accessible, we know little about Murid initiatives and responses to this policy beyond what is revealed through (the filtered) archival records. Did Amadu Bamba envision waging jihad of the sword, as argued by French administrators? Was the Muridiyya a real threat to colonial rule, and if so, in what ways? How did Murid disciples and sheikhs explain French hostility, and how did they respond to it? What was the impact of the conflict on the development of the Murid order? In previous chapters, I have provided partial responses to some of these questions. Here, I critically examine Murid and French accounts in order to reconstruct the events that led to the arrest and deportation to Gabon of the founder of the Muridiyya. I also propose a new interpretation of the conflict and examine the crucial role that the personal politics of African and French field administrators, at the provincial and state levels, played in the deterioration of the relationship between the Murids and the colonial administration.

THE FRENCH, THE AFRICAN CHIEFS, AND THE MURIDS

Colonization did not spell the end of the Wolofs' precolonial political structures and their ethic of government. In the late nineteenth century in the aftermath of the conquest, the French maintained a revamped form of traditional chieftainship to compensate for their lack of political legitimacy and for the absence of appropriate administrative personnel. They co-opted segments of the defeated aristocracy in a bureaucratic system that preserved some of chiefs' material privileges but restrained their authority.[1] These chiefs worked under the supervision of French commandants and residents, but despite legal restrictions, they retained a great deal of autonomy and wielded power in their management of the territory under their control. Though they acknowledged the suzerainty of their French overlords, many chiefs claimed for themselves a certain legitimacy stemming from dynastic affiliations and the memory of their social status during the precolonial era.[2] They retained the trappings of the royal courts and gathered entourages of retainers, slaves, and *griots* (bards). They sought to exercise full authority over the population and expected the same level of respect and loyalty that precolonial Wolof rulers had enjoyed from their subjects.

It was during this period when African colonial chiefs were consolidating their power that the Muridiyya started to expand in Kajoor and Bawol. The history of the tense relations between the Murids and the chiefs seems apocryphal to many bearers of oral traditions. Descendants of these chiefs are now respected members of the Murid community, and Murids are loath to retell stories that would open old wounds. They do not want to mention the past mistakes of the ancestors of now devoted Murids, memories that they think would only embarrass the latter without adding anything important to our understanding of the history of their organization.[3] The reluctance of Murid historians to deal with this episode in the history of the order reflects the tensions that, in Pierre Nora's view, characterize the relations between history and memory. For Nora, memory, because of its affective and magical nature, is prone to amnesia and is unwilling to accept contradictions, whereas history, as an intellectual and secular operation, challenges our memory through its ability to reconstruct the past and its tendency to desacralize and critically analyze discourses.[4]

From the start, African chiefs viewed the Muridiyya as a threat to their power. Ibrahima Njaay, head of the province of Njambur in northern Kajoor, was among the earliest and most vociferous critics of the Murid *tariqa*. He was the first chief to denounce the Murids to the colonial administration, complaining that Murid sheikhs had "invaded his province."[5] He accused these sheikhs of exploiting the naive local people, who gave them land and built them houses for free. Njaay also criticized the Murids for their "arrogance." Similar accusations were made by village chiefs across northern Kajoor, particularly in the area of Mbaakol.

Demba Waar Sall, chief of the confederation of Kajoor, echoed these critiques. He had known Amadu Bamba when the latter was living with his father in Kajoor in the last quarter of the nineteenth century. As we have seen in earlier chapters, Sall was the leader of the *ceddo* party that opposed the increasing involvement of Muslim clerics in the government of Kajoor after King Lat Joor returned from exile in Saalum in 1869. He was against the appointment of Momar Anta Sali, Amadu Bamba's father, to the position of *qadi*.[6] Demba Waar was the most powerful Wolof chief, and his advice to the French weighed heavily on the elaboration of their policy in the protectorates.[7] He played a key role as a French ally in the conquest of Kajoor, and the model of indirect rule he inaugurated as head of this former precolonial kingdom from 1886 until his death in 1902 provided a template for the administration of newly conquered territories. He resented the gathering of his enemies in Kajoor behind Amadu Bamba and was instrumental in convincing the colonial administration of the cleric's supposed political ambitions.[8]

It is interesting to note that even though the Murids were facing the hostility of the chiefs of Kajoor, they enjoyed a certain entente with those serving in Bawol. Amadu Bamba had despised Ceyaasin Faal, the king who ruled this kingdom until 1890. He criticized Faal for his drunkenness and his poor administrative skills. But he appreciated the rule of his successor, Tanor Jeng, a Muslim prince who was hostile to the Murids in the beginning but gradually developed a good relationship with them.[9]

The major cause of disagreement between the African chiefs of Kajoor and the Murids was political control of the population. Murid sheikhs engineered the migration of their disciples wherever they faced the hostility of local rulers. The loss of population, particularly in northern Njambur, irritated the African chiefs, who drew a significant portion of their income from the head taxes they collected. The chiefs also resented what they described as the Murid disciples' disrespect of their authority. They were angered by the refusal of Murids to put any authority above their sheikhs', and they complained that Murids responded to their summonses only after they had informed their religious leaders and secured their authorization. Chiefs also protested that their power was undermined by the prestige of Murid sheikhs, who snubbed them and bragged that they recognized only the French commandants and residents as superior authorities.[10] They asserted that the Murids were trying to create a state within the state, an idea that was later endorsed by the French administration. They also denounced the reluctance of Murids to pay taxes even as they lavishly donated to their sheikhs.[11]

The Murids' subversion of traditional Wolof power structures and value systems was another reason for their tense relations with the chiefs. The development of the Muridiyya, especially in the rural areas of the protectorates of Kajoor and Baol, challenged traditional norms of hierarchy and social status. We have observed that the Murid conception of power relations allowed lower-class people to rise in status, and the growing power of these sheikhs of modest origins was particularly upsetting to the colonial chiefs, especially among those who could claim aristocratic descent. It is interesting to note the particular emphasis that chiefs put on the social backgrounds of the Murid sheikhs they complained about. Ibrahima Njaay, for instance, mentioned that Sheikh Maruba Gey was a weaver and that other Murid sheikhs who disrupted the peace in his province were former slaves and bards.[12] Similar remarks were found in letters sent to the French administration by chiefs all over the Wolof kingdoms. The administrators' image of the Muridiyya as an organization regrouping worthless peoples of lower extraction was shaped by these accusations.[13]

The chiefs were conscious of their strategic position as intermediaries between the population of the protectorates and the French administration, and they were aware, as well, of the edge that this position gave them in their conflict with the Murids. Their role was crucial in defining colonial policy because they had some understanding of colonial administration and controlled the sources of information. Chiefs also understood the thinking of the colonial administrators—their fears and expectations. They manipulated the system by presenting their own political agendas under the guise of the colony's interest.[14] And ultimately, they succeeded in swaying the colonial administration to judge the Murids through their own system of values and norms.

Colonial administrators knew very little about Amadu Bamba and the Murids, and this lack of information furthered their apprehension about and prejudices against the Muridiyya. As noted by Lucy Behrman, the French were "separated from the people they governed by language, tradition and thought patterns."[15] They relied primarily on the information provided by their African auxiliaries, and even when the intelligence they collected directly in the field contradicted a chief, they tended to abide by the latter's advice.[16]

The similarity of tone and language between the letters and testimonies of chiefs and the reports on the Muridiyya filed by French colonial administrators, especially between 1889 and 1910, is striking. The reports described the Murids' project to reestablish the ancient kingdoms for themselves, their preparation for jihad, their ambition to create a state within the state, and their hatred of the French. All these allegations were forged by the chiefs and then readily endorsed by the administration. However, French espousal of the chiefs' critiques of the Murids was made easier because it was congruent with their own biases and stereotypes about Islam.

The central role of the African chiefs and field administrators in the production of colonial archives reminds us of the need to treat these sources with the same caution that we apply to oral traditions and hagiographies. The French officers who generated documents relied primarily on local informants, mostly chiefs who were politically active and therefore not neutral observers. French civil servants also distorted and manipulated intelligence to punish their enemies or reward their clients, to substantiate their political views, or to meet their superiors' expectations.[17] Archives are not neutral repositories of documents; they reflect the circumstances of their creation and respond to the economic, political, and social preoccupations of the government they serve. As noted by J. L. Triaud, they speak the language of the victors and the powerful and often fail to accurately convey the visions of the vanquished and powerless.[18] The historian working with archives must therefore be mindful of the assumptions, rationales, and expectations of the state employees and political authorities who generated the information he or she is using.[19]

Although the accusations they leveled against the Murids were often exaggerated, the chiefs were not always wrong in their complaints that Murid sheikhs represented obstacles to the accomplishment of their jobs. Sheikhs sought to control the appointment of chiefs in their areas of influence. In 1896, Amadu Bamba's brothers opposed the choice of Mbakhane Diop, son of Lat Joor, as chief of eastern Bawol, the heartland of the Muridiyya, and when they could not prevent his appointment, they paid him to protect the Mbakke family.[20] Although Murid sheikhs were not invested with any temporal authority, many of them had more influence than the chiefs. In the rural areas where they had many disciples, some sheikhs ostensibly ignored the authority of local African administrators and even competed with them. Some sheikhs harbored the trappings of the defeated Wolof courts and made a great impression on the population. When Sheikh Anta circulated in Bawol and Kajoor on horseback, escorted by a uniformed and well-organized cavalry, he enjoyed as much attention and prestige as a king.[21] Prominent Murid sheikhs were always surrounded by dozens of disciples, and they lived in vast compounds and well-maintained houses that rivaled the chiefs' headquarters. Furthermore, they were much richer than many of the poorly salaried chiefs who resorted to pillage and embezzlement of taxes to sustain their princely lifestyles.

TENSION WITH THE COLONIAL ADMINISTRATION

The tension between the Murids and the African chiefs that started in Kajoor in 1889 was the prelude to a protracted conflict with the colonial administration. The name of Amadu Bamba appeared for the first time in the colonial records in this same year. The cleric was about thirty-six years old at the time and was becoming increasingly popular. It was this growing popularity that drew the French administration's attention to his activities.

From 1889 to 1892, the relationships between the Murids and the French continued to deteriorate. Bachir Mbacké blamed this deterioration on the influence that certain jealous people had on the colonial administration and on biased administrators.[22] Between 1889 and 1891, Amadu Bamba and Governor L. E. Clément-Thomas exchanged letters in an effort to calm the situation.[23] The first letter sent by the cleric is not in the archives, but the governor's response, dating from 27 June 1889, gives us insight into its content.[24] Bamba probably wrote to the governor in early June, three months after Tautain, the head of the Political Affairs Bureau, filed the first report on the Murids and two months after Angot's tour of northern Kajoor and western Bawol.[25] The letter was a reaction to the expulsion of Murid disciples and sheikhs from the provinces of Njambur and Geet. It is clear that Amadu Bamba had informed the governor about the expulsion and pleaded for the return of his disciples and the restitution of the properties that the chiefs had confiscated. In his response, conveyed by the qadi of Kajoor, Clément-Thomas confirmed that he gave the order to expel the Murids from "his country" because of their bad behavior. He also told Amadu Bamba the people he had expelled could not have been his relatives or disciples because they were against everything sacred to Muslims.[26] Bamba responded to the governor's letter in early July, reassuring him about his political stance and reaffirming that he "needed nothing in this futile and transient world."[27]

This exchange of letters was the first in a series of contacts that continued for two to three years. The Murids probably persisted in their complaints, since, according to Bachir Mbacké, the governor finally ordered an inquiry into the conflict. Findings from this probe prompted him to reverse his previous position by allowing the disciples to settle wherever they wanted in the colony, as long as they abided by the rule of law and respected administrative authorities.[28]

By 1892, the tensions between the Muridiyya and the French had subsided. The best illustration of the return to normalcy was the gift of books that Clément-Thomas sent to Amadu Bamba. This likely happened after the cleric paid him a visit. Bamba has been to Saint-Louis before, but this was his first meeting with the chief of the colony. I have not come across administrative reports on the Murids between 1892 and 1895, the date of the resumption of the conflict between the administration and the Muridiyya, and the absence of records on the Murids during this period suggests that the French were not concerned about the organization.²⁹

THE EVENTS OF 1895

After a lull of three years, the relationship between the French and the Murids deteriorated rapidly. The colonial archives deal extensively with the circumstances of this conflict. In a document dated 10 July 1895, M. Leclerc, the administrator of the district of Saint-Louis and the man in charge of investigating Amadu Bamba, outlined a number of grievances against him and the Murids.³⁰ His most serious accusation was that Murids were engaged in intense proselytizing and that the chiefs of the provinces neighboring Jolof, where Bamba was living at the time, had learned that weapons were being transported to his compound. Leclerc mentioned that the cleric could mobilize a thousand followers but stated it was likely that he was not going to act until the end of the rainy season in the month of October. Leclerc added that he was unable to fathom the cleric's intentions despite the fact that spies sent by him and by the African chiefs had been monitoring the sheikh and his disciples' activities for some time. Lecerc indicated that he was not surprised by the failure of his intelligence-gathering efforts because he knew that Bamba was too cautious to betray his secret plans. Leclerc also revisited the events between 1889 and 1892 to explain the continuing threat that the Murids represented to the colony. This report triggered the process that led the interim governor to decide to arrest Amadu Bamba and try him before the Conseil Privé of Senegal. The report that Martial Merlin (1860–1935), director of political affairs for the colony, wrote for the prosecution provided further details about the administration's case against the cleric.³¹

Merlin acknowledged up front that no material evidence of Amadu Bamba's plot to wage jihad could be produced, but he immediately added that there were circumstances that substantiated his guilt and warranted the adoption of preemptive measures. He started his report by reconstructing the cleric's life story, insisting particularly on his historical ties with Lat Joor and the aristocracy of the kingdom of Kajoor. He also described a behavioral pattern that suggested all of Amadu Bamba's activities in Kajoor, Bawol, and Jolof were consciously designed to elude French control.

Merlin also rehashed and reinforced some of Leclerc's accusations by inventing facts to exaggerate the threat that the Murids represented. He put the number of disciples likely to join Amadu Bamba in his imminent revolt at five thousand in Njambur alone, a figure five times higher than Leclerc's estimate.³² In addition, he noted, without naming them, that a number of former chiefs and dignitaries were ready to join the cleric in his planned rebellion. He mentioned that Amadu Bamba's disciples in Tuubaa and Mbakke were buying weapons, donkeys, and horses and that people were hired to pound millet and prepare provisions for the jihad. To support these allegations, Merlin referred to reports from chiefs, but these were neither produced during the trial nor available at the archives.

After making his points about the intentions, connections, and power of Amadu Bamba, Merlin applied to the cleric the label *tijani*.³³ He suggested that Bamba, who was a member of the Qadiriyya, a Muslim order that was friendly to the French, was now professing the Tijaniyya, which in the view of the administration of Senegal epitomized intolerance, fanaticism, and jihad. In the report sent to the minister of colonies, Amadu Bamba was no longer portrayed as a *qadiri* practicing tijani rituals but as a hardcore tijani, implying that he was preparing for a jihad. The accusation that Amadu Bamba was practicing tijani rituals—and therefore preparing for a jihad,—was an obvious case of establishing guilt by association. Since al-Hajj Umar, Maba, Amadu Sheikhu the Madiyanke, and Amadu Lamin Dramé (all clerics who waged jihad in Senegal against the French) belonged to the Tijaniyya, then for Merlin, it was clear that Amadu Bamba, who was initiated into this order, also had to be preparing for a jihad. As already shown, Bamba was, in fact, a qadiri. He was initiated into the Tijaniyya as a step in his spiritual quest, but this initiation did not have practical effects on his political philosophy or the education of his disciples. Very early in his career, he opted for what he called the greater jihad or jihad of the soul.

To cap his charges, Merlin warned the administration about Amadu Bamba's plea for peace and his petition of loyalty by reminding them of the deceitful attitudes of the Muslim jihadists, whose strategy had always consisted of allaying the administration's suspicions before striking treacherously. Following Leclerc's recommendations, he concluded by proposing that Amadu Bamba be deported to Gabon, that his disciples be dispersed, and that his followers from the aristocracy of Kajoor be put under the custody of the trusted chief of Waalo, Yamar Mbooj.

The most intriguing aspect of Leclerc's and Merlin's reports was the silence on the subject of the relationship between the Murids and the colonial administration between 1892 and 1895. They deliberately omitted this episode and jumped back to the events of 1889 to make the case that the Muridiyya had always represented a threat to the stability of the colony. It seems, however, that this last period was marked by peaceful relations between the Murid leadership and colonial authorities. In fact, we learned from a report by Mbacké Bousso that as late as the opening months of 1895, Amadu Bamba was in contact with Governor H. de Lamothe and that he had kept him abreast of his projects. Bousso indicated that he was personally commissioned by the cleric to travel to Saint-Louis to consult with the chief of the colony about his intention to resettle in Jolof in April 1895. Referring to this meeting, he noted: "The Governor of Saint-Louis was very happy about the letter I gave him [on behalf of Amadu Bamba] and the fact that we were consulting with him. He really honored me and he gave me a bundle of fabrics as gift to bring for the Sheikh. This was the state of our relationship with the French until confusion settled in because of the collusion between slanderers and agents of the administration, and the spies' plots."[34]

It is clear that Merlin's report was intended as evidence for the prosecution of Amadu Bamba and that the colonial administration had already made up its mind about the cleric's guilt even before the trial began.[35] One cannot find a single item in the dossier that pleaded for the cleric's exoneration. The decision to try Bamba before the Conseil Privé, which was composed of high-ranking French civil servants likely to approve whatever decision the administration wanted, and not before the Conseil Général, where elected African councils might have challenged Merlin's allegations, betrayed the true intention of the colonial administration. Therefore, one needs to look beyond the evidence presented by Merlin and Leclerc to better understand the motives and circumstances behind the arrest and exile of Amadu Bamba.

Bamba's arrest took place at a time when the colonial administration was becoming increasingly assertive. The end of the nineteenth century marked the final phase of the French conquest of Senegal and the start of the gradual effort for administrative control. The School for the Sons of Chiefs, which trained African administrators and interpreters but was closed in 1872, was reopened in 1892. This decision revealed the French intention to move ahead with the aggressive policy of colonization that began with Louis Faidherbe in 1854 but experienced mixed fortunes with the ebbs and flows of French metropolitan politics. During their tenures as governor, Clément-Thomas (1888–90) and de Lamothe (1890–95) both tried to affirm the administration's authority in Saint-Louis and to reenforce the grip of the administration on the protectorates.[36] After the death of the king of Bawol in 1894, de Lamothe divided the kingdom into two provinces, eastern and western Bawol, and appointed Mbakhane Diop, son of Lat Joor, and Salmon Faal, both alumni of the School of Chiefs in Saint-Louis and graduates from Tunisia, as superior chiefs of eastern Bawol and western Bawol, respectively. These two chiefs took office in 1896.

Although the efforts for greater administrative control might have had a negative effect on the relationship between the Murids and the French in Bawol, it does not fully explain the conflict that led to the arrest and deportation of

Amadu Bamba in 1895. Politically, this kingdom had been part of the French sphere of influence since 1883, when Ceyaasin Faal signed a treaty with Captain Dupré.[37] The Murids were concentrated at the fringes of the kingdom on the eastern side, away from the centers of power located in the western side, and they were not powerful enough to constitute a real security threat.[38]

From an economic standpoint as well, Bawol was not vital to the colony, and there was no urgent need for the kind of tight control that would have warranted a repressive policy against the Murids. The cultivation of peanuts, the principal crop of Senegal, was marginal in the province. It only started to develop after 1907, when the railways linking Senegal to French Sudan reached this area. Even in 1911 when peanut farming became more important, only one-tenth of the arable land of Bawol (about 50,000 hectares) was devoted to it, and as early as 1903 or 1904, peanuts covered 170,000 hectares and 100,000 hectares, respectively, in the neighboring districts of Thiès and Louga.[39] As noted by Péllissier and others, the production of peanuts became significant in Bawol only after the installation of Amadu Bamba in Diourbel in 1912 and the migratory movement that followed that event.[40]

The preceding discussion has shown that in 1895, there were no potent political or economic reasons for the colonial administration of Senegal to arrest Amadu Bamba and dismantle the tariqa he founded. The real causes of his detention and exile must, then, be sought in the internal politics and inner workings of the colonial bureaucracy. It is revealing that the deterioration of the relations between the Murids and the French occurred suddenly after three years of peaceful coexistence in a period when there was a relative power vacuum at the head of the colony. The tenure of Governor de Lamothe—who seemingly had a good relationship with Amadu Bamba and the Murids, to judge by the visits that Murid dignitaries paid him and the exchange of letters and gifts—was terminated in May 1895. His replacement, E. Chaudié (1895–1900), took up his post only after September 1895, when Amadu Bamba had been already arrested, tried, and sentenced to deportation to Gabon. Therefore, the investigation, prosecution, trial, and sentencing of Bamba took place between June and September, a period when the highest administrative position in Senegal was held by an acting governor, M. Mouttet, who relied heavily on field administrators and on the director of political affairs to run the colony. This interlude also coincided with the rainy season, an unhealthy time when powerful colonial authorities in Senegal were usually on leave in France. In fact, six out of the ten administrators who sat in the session of the Conseil Privé that heard Amadu Bamba's case were filling in for colleagues on vacation.[41]

One Murid writer maintains that de Lamothe masterminded the conspiracy against Amadu Bamba before leaving Senegal.[42] This opinion is shared by

Oumar Ba, the archivist and author of an important book on the relationship between the cleric and the colonial administration of Senegal.[43] However, I have not found evidence supporting this assumption. De Lamothe, who took office during the "Jeandet affair" (after A. Jeandet, an administrator, was murdered in Fuuta Tooro), was rather preoccupied with asserting the administration's authority in the Communes by controlling and curbing the growing power of those that David Robinson has called the Saint-Louis opposition. In reality, he was on good terms with Amadu Bamba.[44]

A careful examination of the chronology of events and circumstantial evidence suggests that Merlin and the administrator Leclerc were the masterminds behind the arrest and deportation of Amadu Bamba. They seemed to have acted for reasons that had more to do with their personal political views rather than those of the governor. Merlin and Leclerc were present in Senegal between 1889 and 1892 when the administration first clashed with the Murids, and they were both involved in the incident. In his report of 15 August 1895, which supplied much of the evidence presented to the Conseil Privé, Leclerc regretted his failure to arrest Amadu Bamba in 1892 and wished that this time, the cleric would not dupe the administration and would be dealt with firmly.[45] Merlin may have particularly resented the growing power of the Murids. In his capacity as director of political affairs, he engineered and oversaw the administrative reform of Bawol. He probably perceived the Muridiyya as a potential obstacle to the accomplishment of the task assigned to the young superior chiefs he helped to train.[46]

Merlin and Leclerc, at a time of instability during an interim period when key administrators were absent from the colony, pushed their agenda forward. They used intelligence gathered through chiefs and spies to convince the Conseil Privé to rid the the colony of the man they saw as a threat to its stability and a hindrance to their own authority. The two administrators found a sympathetic reception among their colleagues in the Conseil Privé, who were certainly anxious about the appointment of Chaudié as the first governor-general of the newly created Federation of French West Africa (Afrique Occidentale Française, or AOF, ca. 1895); he was a Paris bureaucrat who had no experience with Africa and the colonies. Convincing the Conseil to strike the Muridiyya during the interim period might have been made easier by the belief that the new and inexperienced head of Senegal would be too preoccupied with the situation in the federation and might be reluctant to act firmly when tensions arose in the protectorates.[47]

It is safe to argue that in 1895, the authorities of Senegal had no compelling political reasons to fear Amadu Bamba and the Murids and that the governor did not perceive them as a threat. There was not a well-thought-out or preconceived plan from the governor's office to destroy the Muridiyya. What happened in August 1895 was the result of the personal politics of subordinate administrators who successfully turned their own political agenda into official colonial policy.

THE ARREST AND TRIAL

Amadu Bamba surrendered to Leclerc, who was sent to arrest him on 18 Safar AH 1313 (10 August 1895) at the locality of Jeewol, in northern Kajoor. He was transported to Louga and then to Saint-Louis, capital of the colony. Available colonial archives are silent about the cleric's conditions and activities between the day of his arrival in Saint-Louis on 12 August and his transportation to Libreville in Gabon on 21 September. I have used oral traditions and Amadu Bamba's written account of these events to reconstruct this important episode in the history of the Muridiyya. The cleric's *rihla* (travel account), titled *Jazaau Shakuur* (Tribute to the Worthy of Recognition), which he composed at the request of a certain Abdul Latif from the Moorish "tribe" of Al-Hajj Mukhtar — probably during his exile in Mauritania (from 1903 to 1907) — is a valuable source on his arrest, trial, and deportation to Gabon.[48]

Bamba wrote that he arrived in Saint-Louis just before the *Maghreb* (prayer of dusk) prayer (between 7 and 8 p.m.) on 12 August and was immediately assigned a residence, where he stayed during the remaining ten days of the month of Safar and the month of Rabbi I, except for the last two days of this month (17 and 18 September), when he was traveling to Dakar.[49] He did not give an account of the trial that took place in the governor's office, and he did not elaborate on the details of his stay in Saint-Louis that lasted over a month and a half. However, we can fill some of the gaps in his narration thanks to information gleaned from the archives and from interviews conducted in Saint-Louis and in the Murid heartland of Bawol and in Kajoor.

Oral sources tell us that Amadu Bamba was first imprisoned in a small cell in the basement of the governor's office in Saint-Louis. He was later removed from this location due to the mediation of some Muslim dignitaries in the city and was relocated to the house of Ahmed Khuri Seen or Ahmed Khuraish.[50] Bamba also resided for some time at a place that now serves as a laboratory, where he was under the custody of a French civil servant. He was then allowed to move around the city.[51] He frequented the botanic garden of Saint-Louis and used to pray in a small mosque in the neighborhood of Balakoss, situated halfway between the garden and his residence.

Amadu Bamba's trial took place on 5 September 1895 and lasted less than two hours. We learn from the proceedings of the Conseil Privé that the cleric was escorted into in the room early in the morning. He listened to the prosecution and was given the opportunity to present his defense. Bearers of Murid traditions offer differing accounts of the trial. They all agree that the cleric's first act on entering the room was to stand for a two-*rakaas* (genuflection) prayer.[52] He then listened to the reading of the charges against him and was interrogated. Here, the sources diverge in their relations of the sheikh's reactions. Some indicate that Amadu Bamba gave the same response to the questions asked by members of the Conseil. He refused to engage in the discussion and kept demanding that they bring forward the informants who accused him of waging jihad so that they prove their allegations.[53] Other sources mention that after listening to the prosecution's charges, Amadu Bamba only recited the Quranic sura *al-Ikhlaas*, which asserts the oneness and might of God, and then remained silent for the rest of the session, ignoring the prosecutors' questions.[54]

The first version of the story seems more probable. It is unlikely that Amadu Bamba would have adopted an attitude that would have been seen by the Conseil as defiant and provocative. Such behavior would have contradicted the stance he had, until then, assumed in his relationship with the colonial administration. In the letters he wrote to the governor between 1889 and 1895 and in his correspondence in general, the cleric always worried about the negative influence that his enemies might have on his relations with the colonial administration, and he asked for the colonial authorities' trust.

Despite Bamba's effort to control his emotions, it seems that his demeanor might have further upset his prosecutors. Bachir Mbacké noted that his father's reluctance to engage in a conversation with his judges, together with the fact that he avoided the gaze of people in the room and silently and calmly pursued his prayers and recitation of the Quran, added to the tension. He explained that this was the cleric's natural behavior, but the French who did not know him mistook it for defiance and disrespect. Mbacké informed us that after listening to Amadu Bamba, the members of the Conseil were split into two factions.[55] Some took offense at the cleric's attitude and recommended that he be executed or eternally banned from Senegal. Others advised restraint, arguing that the sheikh was one of those mystics consumed by their love for God and that he was no threat to anyone. Ultimately, the Conseil decided to seek banishment.[56] This description by Bachir Mbacké might have been inspired by the account that the Quran and *hadiths* (sayings and deeds of Prophet Muhammad) gave of the trial of the Prophet by his Meccan enemies on the eve of his migration to Medina. But in reality, as shown in the archival records, the decision to condemn the cleric to internment in Gabon was quickly and unanimously reached by the Conseil.[57]

THE EXILE

In his rihla, Amadu Bamba provided vital information about the journey that took him to Gabon. He wrote that less than two weeks after the trial, he was sent to Dakar, arriving on the evening of 18 September 1895. He was preparing to rest in the house where he intended to spend the night, but then the governor removed him from there and confined him to a filthy and dark cell.[58] He mentioned that whenever this episode came to his mind, it created the urge to call for jihad of the sword, but the Prophet Muhammad had forbidden him from waging war.[59] Probably at the request of some *Lebu* (indigenous inhabitants of Dakar) dignitaries, he was released from the cell and entrusted to the care of a local African civil servant, who accommodated him until he boarded the ship for Gabon two days later.[60]

Amadu Bamba indicated that the ship stayed in Dakar overnight and did not leave the harbor until Rabi II (the fourth month of the Muslim calendar) AH 1313 (21 September 1895). He stated that while he was waiting in Dakar, a person informed him that a new governor (E. Chaudié) had just arrived in the colony and suggested that he send an official a letter of appeal before Chaudié came in contact with the local administration. Bamba said that he hesitated, but on the insistence of this person, he started drafting the letter and then stopped, regretting his gesture; instead, he began writing a poem reaffirming his trust in God.[61]

Bamba also described his relationship with the ship's crew and his feelings while he was headed to sea. He noted that he was initially lodged in a comfortable cabin, but when the ship's captain read a letter from the governor that was related to Bamba's case, he became very angry and ordered that the cleric and his luggage be taken away from this cabin and sent to another. Bamba said that he spent an indeterminate amount of time in the second cabin, which was not equipped (perhaps he meanst it was without a bathroom or the running water needed to prepare for prayers), and that he was offended because the crew members on whom he had to rely for everything continually mocked him. However, he observed that the fact that he was "unjustly removed from his home and schools, and separated from his family, friends, and disciples was even more painful than the vexations and mistreatments he was subjected to on the ship."[62]

Amadu Bamba mentioned that after he had stayed in the same cabin for days, the ship's captain came to visit him. The captain had been monitoring Bamba's activities for several days and had formed his own opinion of the cleric. He expressed sympathy and compassion for him and agreed that he was the victim of an injustice. Bamba affirmed that like the captain, all the other reasonable passengers on the ship vehemently disapproved of what had been done to him. He particularly appreciated the attitude of the doctor on board, who pledged to provide him with all the assistance he needed; he also commended the attitude of a young Christian (French) crew member who, as he wrote, "behaved with me as if he was one of my Murids."[63] The ship made a stop in Conakry (Guinea), where Amadu Bamba said that he learned for the first time that he was going to Gabon, from a Senegalese of Saalum origin who came to seek his blessings.[64] The ship also stopped in Sierra Leone, Grand Bassam (Côte d'Ivoire), Cotonou (Dahomey), and Douala (Cameroon) before heading to Libreville in Gabon.

Amadu Bamba noted that, on landing, he stayed for a few days in a city (probably Libreville) and then was sent to an island (Mayumba), where he lived for five years before being transported to another island (Lambaréné), where his sojourn lasted for a little less than three years. Referring to his stay in this last location, he wrote, "In this place I endured sufferings that only death surpasses . . . until God Almighty fulfilled my wish."[65]

THE MURIDS WITHOUT BAMBA

The period of Amadu Bamba's exile in Gabon, between 1895 and 1902, is the least documented phase in the history of the Muridiyya. The production of archival records about the tariqa, particularly before the permanent settlement of the cleric in Senegal in 1907, was closely correlated with the highs and lows in the relationship between the Murids and the French. Typically, an absence of information indicates a period of peaceful and stable relations, whereas an abundance of documents often signals a time of heightened tension. The deportation of Amadu Bamba to Gabon brought a lull in the activities of the Muridiyya and consequently a scarcity in relevant archives.

The silence of Murid internal sources about this phase in the history of the organization is, however, more intriguing. Murid sources have been instrumental in collecting and preserving crucial information that complemented, supplemented, and corrected colonial documents. The amnesia regarding the functioning of the tariqa during Amadu Bamba's exile may well have been a symptom of malaise. It might be that the Murids were going through a difficult time, and since the internal history has become, to a large extent, a "history of commemoration," this painful episode has been deleted from the order's collective memory.[66] It also might be that information related to this stage of the development of the Muridiyya existed but had become apocryphal. However, there are fragmented sources that allow one to reconstitute, though only partially, critical information pertaining to this epoch.[67]

In the immediate aftermath of Amadu Bamba's departure for exile, many Murid sheikhs and relatives of the cleric were intimidated by the French administrators and the African chiefs and were reluctant to closely associate themselves with the family he left behind, fearing that they could be targets of repression. When Amadu Bamba left his house in Jolof to comply with Leclerc's ultimatum in August 1895, he entrusted his wives and three sons to his younger brother and confidant Ibra Faati (Maam Cerno). He instructed Ibra Faati to remain in Jolof until after harvest (October to November) and then preferably to relocate to Mbakke Bawol, the Mbakke's traditional village, or to any other place where he could live with the family in peace and security. After leaving Jolof, Maam Cerno moved with Bamba's family to Daaru Salaam, the first village founded by Amadu Bamba but now headed by another of his younger brothers, Sheikh Anta. Sheikh Anta welcomed the family but suggested that it was more appropriate that they settle in Mbakke Bawol, where their older brother Momar Jaara, chief of the village, and the elder members of the Mbakke clan were living. Maam Cerno agreed with the suggestion and moved to Mbakke Bawol. But Momar, who was skeptical about Bamba's calling and was worried about the tense relations between the Murids and the French, was reluctant to accommodate the whole family. He advised Maam Cerno to send Amadu Bamba's wives back to their families and to get rid of those among the people who were following him who were not his own disciples.[68]

Maam Cerno was apparently disturbed by his brother's attitude. He envisaged moving to Kokki to join his maternal uncles, since he felt that he was not getting the help he expected from his paternal lineage. However, Ibra Nguy Mbakke, a cousin of his father, dissuaded him from doing so.[69] Ibra Nguy was descended from Maaram, the founder of Mbakke Bawol. He was also allied through his mother's side to the aristocracy of Bawol that had traditionally commanded the province of Laa, where Mbakke Bawol was located. Ibra gave Cerno the land of Guy Ngoora on the northwestern side of Mbakke, where Cerno built a house.[70]

Cerno lived in Guy Ngoora for about five years, amid many difficulties. The family was beset by illnesses. Eight members died, and two sons of Amadu Bamba suffered serious illnesses; one of them, Baara Mbakke, probably contracted meningitis, which left him with impaired speech.[71] The hardship was compounded by the fact that many Murid sheikhs, concerned about the chiefs' hostility to the tariqa, kept away from the cleric's family. Oral traditions tell us that Ahmad Ndumbe Mbakke, Amadu Bamba's cousin and disciple, was the only major sheikh who continued to support Cerno and the family during the first five years of the exile, and Ndaam Abdrahman Lo, one of the cleric's first disciples, took up the teaching at the school of Daaru Halimul Khabiir (better known as Ndaam).

The absence of Amadu Bamba from Senegal did not end colonial pressure on the Muridiyya. French administrators and African chiefs, especially in northern Kajoor, continued to harass Murid sheikhs and disciples. Tuubaa, the holy city of the order, was evacuated. Some newly built Murid villages in eastern Bawol were dismantled, and the disciples were forced to return to their places of origin.[72] Oral traditions report that the colonial administration used diverse tactics to intimidate and subdue the Murids. Murid sheikhs were declared persona non grata in Njambur, as noted by Murid oral and French sources.[73] The French summoned sheikhs to sign declarations of allegiance.[74] Many sheikhs adopted a low profile. Some migrated to the district of Thiès or to the cities to diffuse suspicion and escape the harassment of the African chiefs who administrated rural areas. Sheikh Ahmad Ndumbe, for example, founded the village of Ker Magey Ndao, near the colonial town of Tivaouane; Mbacké Bousso also moved in Tivaouane, where he settled with Sherif Mulaay, a Moorish cleric of his friend.[75] It was probably at this time that Sheikh Maruba Gey founded in the suburb of the same town the neighborhood that now bears his name. Cheikh Ibra Saar also relocated in the canton of Thiès.[76]

In contrast with standard Murid accounts that emphasize the order's dynamism and the steadfastness of sheikhs when Bamba was away, it seems that during this period many Murid sheikhs actually focused more on their own affairs than on proselytizing or organizing disciples.[77] This was the case with Sheikh Ibra Faal, who was then living in Saint-Louis and Thiès, and Sheikh Anta, who was a skillful businessman. Cerno and Sheikh A. Ndumbe bore the burden of reassuring and maintaining the morale of the disciples, whose commitment was shaken by the dearth of information about their leader. Cerno also continued to cultivate the relationship with Sheikh Sidiyya, the former spiritual master and friend of Amadu Bamba.[78] Overall, as observed by Khadim Mbacké, the Muridiyya did not register any significant growth during the cleric's exile.[79] One may even argue that it experienced some setbacks.

Murid sources tell us that during the first five years of the exile, Amadu Bamba had no contact with his disciples and family. Rumors about his death circulated many times. Stories are told about the time when Maam Cerno and members of the Mbakke family struggled with the idea that Amadu Bamba might never return to Senegal. The fact that the cleric did not give specific instructions with regard to the leadership of the community in his absence and the lack of information about his whereabouts encouraged some Murid sheikhs to claim their autonomy as a way of negotiating peaceful coexistence with the French and with the African colonial chiefs. This situation continued until a certain Abdulaay Nduur, a seaman who met Amadu Bamba in Mayumba (Gabon), brought letters from him, giving proof that he was still alive and well.[80]

We know that when he left Senegal in November 1895, Amadu Bamba was not aware of his destination and therefore was not able to give the information to his family and disciples. I have found in the *Majmuha* some letters he sent to family members and disciples while in Gabon. But unfortunately, they are not dated and therefore cannot give us an indication of when and how frequently he communicated with people in Senegal. But there is evidence that from 1899 on, people had learned that he was interned in Gabon. A letter from that year authorizing his brother Balla Mbakke to visit him is kept at the archives.[81] At least two of his disciples, Amadu Lo Dagana and Sheikh Anta, visited him in Mayumba between 1899 and 1890. Establishing communications between the cleric and the disciples had a bracing effect on the morale of the Murids and may have bolstered their efforts to obtain his release.

THE RETURN TO SENEGAL

Amadu Bamba's return to Senegal in 1902 coincided with the election of François Carpot, a mulatto from Saint-Louis, as deputy of Senegal at the French Parliament. Carpot was elected with the massive support of the indigenous population of the Four Communes, and he also probably benefited from the financial backing of Murid sheikhs such as Ibra Faal and perhaps Sheikh Anta.[82]

Since 1896, the Murid leadership had been encouraging Sheikh Sidiyya to negotiate the release of Amadu Bamba with the colonial administration but to no avail.[83] By 1900, they had started lobbying local politicians. Sheikh Ibra Faal played a central role in this effort. Bachir Mbacké credited him with securing the cleric's freedom and return to Senegal.[84] However, the intervention of Carpot was certainly decisive in achieving this goal. Even though I do not know of any direct evidence of Carpot's role, some indirect evidence linked him to the cleric's return. The administrator Victor Allys, in a letter to Merlin in 1903, accused Carpot of a criminal act in bringing Amadu Bamba back to Senegal; also, Sheikh Ibra Faal, in a letter to the governor in January 1913, referred to Carpot's role in relocating Amadu Bamba to Bawol in 1912.[85]

After leaving Gabon, Bamba arrived in Senegal on 11 November. The scene of his arrival at the Dakar harbor is dramatically captured in a painting by Alpha Waly Diallo. In his brightly colored canvas, Diallo shows the cleric standing alone on top of the ship's stairs, in a spotless white robe and turban, facing the shore with his two arms opened wide in what seems to be a gesture of triumph before a group of French officials and a hysterical crowd of disciples, contained with difficulty by armed guards.[86] It is unclear whether Amadu Bamba's return was actually made public.[87] But the painting is certainly a good expression of the Murid side of the story. Bamba was then conveyed to Saint-Louis, where he met with the governor and stayed for two weeks before being authorized to join his village of Daaru Mannaan in Bawol.

Amadu Bamba told us that it took him two months to complete the journey between Saint-Louis and Daaru Mannaan (his residence) by traveling on horseback and on foot through Kajoor and Bawol (he could have covered the distance in a few days). M. L. Diop offered a detailed account of the journey.[88] He indicated that the cleric made a first stop in Louga, where he stayed with his brother Sheikh Coro for five days, and then he moved to Sanusi to visit his disciple and friend Sire Lo. Sanusi was an important step in the journey to Bawol. Bamba sojourned there for more than three weeks and received the allegiance of a great number of people who came to join the Muridiyya. Most prominent among those people were Ibra Joob Massar and Maniaaw Sylla, two prestigious teachers and scholars. Amadu Bamba then visited some other villages in Kajoor, before stopping in Daaru Salaam (Bawol) where his brother, Sheikh Anta, organized a large reception. The celebration, which lasted ten days, was immortalized by Mor Guèye's reverse glass paintings, and it has become a *maggal* (Murid religious festival), which is still commemorated annually by Murids affiliated with Sheikh Anta's lineage.[89] Amadu Bamba then joined Maam Cerno and his family in Daaru Mannaan by the beginning of the month of Dhul-qida (the eleventh month of the Muslim calendar), corresponding with the end of January 1903.

I am not aware of any existing colonial records related to the conditions of Amadu Bamba's release. Similarly, there seem to be no archival documents pertaining to his two-week stay in Saint-Louis after his return from Gabon. The freedom with which he traveled through Kajoor and Bawol, however, suggests that he was not subject to strict surveillance. The colonial administration might have thought that the cleric was subdued by nearly eight years of exile in the distant and unhealthy land of equatorial Africa and that he might no longer have the will or the ability to revive the organization that had been crippled by harassment and pressure from chiefs and administrators from the time he left Senegal. However, it is clear that Bamba's two-month tour of Kajoor was meant to revive the Muridiyya. He stated that during the exile, he was surrounded by unbelievers in a country where nobody cared about the name of Allah and that what he missed the most was the congregation of his disciples and their love. One of the first things he said he enjoyed after landing in Dakar was sharing food with his disciples.[90]

THE MEANING OF EXILE: THE REWARDS OF SUFFERING

The French conceived of the arrest and deportation of Amadu Bamba as a simple and routine operation for the maintenance of order in the colony, but for the cleric, the events had a profound religious significance. Bamba saw his plight in the hands of the colonial administration as a highly meaningful test of his faith. He likened his condition to that of the Prophet Muhammad in Mecca and drew extensively from Quranic idioms to rationalize his actions and strengthen his resolve. Bamba reported that the first verses he reminded himself of at the beginning of the conflict were excerpts from the sura, "The Spoils of War," in which Allah addresses the Prophet in these terms:[91] "Remember when the infidels contrived to make you a prisoner or to murder or expel you, they plotted, but God planned, and God's plan is the best."[92] Bamba added that when he met Leclerc at Jeewol, the following verse came to his mind: "O! Believers! When you meet unbelievers, in the field of battle, do not turn your backs to them."[93] When he was about to board the ship to Gabon, he said that he recited this verse: "O! Believers! When you meet an army, stand firm and think of God profusely that you may be blessed with success."[94]

By placing the conflict in the broader context of the confrontation between good and evil, Amadu Bamba sought to deny agency to the colonial administration. From the outset, he depicted the French as mere instruments of God, who were acting as they were instructed by a higher power. He wrote in *Jazaau Shakuur*, "I left . . . the house I built in Jolof after receiving the convocation of the governor of Saint-Louis with whom I was in *contention by God's will*."[95] In a poem he started to draft while in custody in Saint-Louis, he mentioned, "I was marching with the pious while God's enemies (the French) thought that I was their prisoner. Indeed, they were wrong. . . . By the grace of the Prophet, I was marching in the company of the honored towards God, the Almighty Possessor of the heavens."[96]

Amadu Bamba understood his deportation and hardships at the hands of the colonial administration as a major step in his jihad of the soul (the greater jihad). In effect, Sufis consider suffering as one of the forms by which humans can become aware of and even get closer to their creator. It is a means by which God disables his friend's *nafs* (carnal soul), purifies his soul, and increases his baraka. In *Massalik*, Bamba observed, "God tests His servant in the proportion of the strength of his faith. If he remains resolute, He increases the suffering but if, on the contrary, he falters and becomes miserable, He leaves him alone or diminishes the suffering. The steadfast servant will not be relieved until he becomes pure, devoid of all sins."[97] Suffering for God's sake was, then, for Bamba a sort of worldly purgatory, more desirable then the otherworldly one. More explicitly, he stated in *Muqaddimaat ul Amdaa,* a panegyric to the Prophet that he composed while in exile, "The hatred of those who believe in trinity (the French), has availed me all that which I desired."[98]

Bamba certainly believed that by the time he left Gabon, he had reached the highest level of spiritual purity and blessedness. He openly made this claim in his writings. In *Jazaau Shakuur,* for example, he declared, "It was while in the Island (Mayumba) that I was shown and cured of all my imperfections."[99] But it was at the level of the intellect and his capacity to please God and the Prophet that the impact of the new *maqaam* (spiritual station) he attained was more clearly perceptible. He mentioned that it was during the exile that he acquired an understanding of the Arab language never achieved by a nonnative speaker.[100] He rewrote many of the poems he composed before the exile after he returned to Senegal in 1902. This was the case, for instance, with *Jazb ul Khuluub, Munawir u siduur,* and many other titles.[101] He also noted, "It was there (in Gabon) where I composed the two preludes to the *khidma* of the Prophet (*Muqaddimaat ul Khidma* and *Bidaayat ul Khidma*) ... which surpass in spiritual power the *Dalail al Khayraat* ... may God bless his author."[102] The *Dalail al Khayraat* is a popular book of prayers on behalf of the Prophet Muhammad written by the well-known fifteenth-century Moroccan Sufi thinker Sulayman al-Jazuli (d. AH 869 [1465]).[103] By comparing his works to that of so accomplished a master, Bamba wanted to highlight the rewards that he had amassed through the exile. He conveyed this feeling of accomplishment to his disciples by drawing a sharp distinction between the spiritual virtues of the writings he completed before and after the exile. In the *Majmuha,* he wrote,

> I want my disciples to understand that my writings while I was in the Sea [exile in Gabon] are composed of [secret] prayers to the Prophet, supplications, praises, and evocations of jihad. For this reason, I have forbidden their diffusion, and I have hidden them. As for what I have produced before the exile, they are not agreeable to God and consequently have not been blessed. Therefore, to those who desire to benefit from my works in this world and the hereafter, I recommend that you persevere in mastering what I have written from the year of grace [probably sometime around 1902], because these writings surpass everything in virtue but the Quran and the traditions of the Prophet.[104]

Amadu Bamba's emphasis on the spiritual virtue of his writings is echoed by the great importance his disciples accord them qualitatively and quantitatively.

Some Murids give his religious poems, or *qasaayid* (plural of the Arab word *qasida*, or poem), the same attention as the Quran. They invest much energy in studying them and in their daily recitation, collectively or alone. In Senegal and among the Murid diaspora, there is a budding industry specializing in editing and distributing his writings. Some hagiographers estimate his works in tons.[105]

THE MEANING OF EXILE: THE POPULAR EPIC

While Amadu Bamba couched his exile experience in the esoteric and convoluted language of Sufi mystics, his disciples gave a more exoteric meaning and belligerent tone to the confrontation with the French. As we have observed, the cleric interpreted many things that happened to him before and during the deportation as the fruit of divine intervention. The miracles he alluded to were, however, more of an epistemological nature. He, for example, claimed an extraordinary intellectual opening that allowed him to penetrate the secret meaning of the Islamic scriptures.[106] The rare occasions on which he referred to an event that happened to him physically, such as a raging bull charging in the ship, he refrained from delving into the details and gave credit to God and the Prophet for the protection they granted him.[107] But this attitude did not preclude the development of stories that attributed numerous extraordinary deeds to him.

Borrowing from the Sufi tradition of *manaaqib* (hagiographic literature in which the glorious spiritual and material feats of a renown Sufi master are told) and the West African griot-style of storytelling, Murid hagiographers and poets have constructed a comprehensive epic of their sheikh's resistance to French oppression.[108] This account parallels and competes with the version of the story told by the colonial administration, and it has, to a large extent, shaped popular views of the conflict.

Fragmented pieces of this epic started to emerge as soon as Amadu Bamba returned from exile in 1902.[109] But it was after the cleric's death in 1927 that the famous Murid poet Musa Ka developed an elaborate master narrative that pieced together the different exile stories. Ka could be construed as the Marty or, better, the anti-Marty of the internal tradition. If Marty's work on the Muridiyya was a good example of what some historians have termed "statist narrative"—that is, an endeavor "to promote the sense of state power and legitimacy and, as a consequence, to silence alternative readings and narratives of the past"—Ka's epic functioned as a counterhegemonic discourse that later became the basis of a different hegemony.[110] Just as Marty wove a persuasive but misleading narrative of the Muridiyya that justified colonial policy and questioned the religious motivations of Amadu Bamba and the orthodoxy of the tariqa he founded, Ka constructed a powerful and coherent epic that placed his sheikh among the most venerable saints of Islam and stressed his suffering and ultimate triumph over the forces of evil represented by the French administration. The enduring influence that Marty's interpretation of the Muridiyya continues to have among many scholars is contrasted with the popularity of Ka's rendering of the odyssey of Amadu Bamba among the Murid faithful.

Musa Ka was born in the 1890s in a village near Mbakke Bawol, and he was placed under the tutelage of Amadu Bamba after his return from exile in Mauritania. He studied with the cleric when he was assigned a residence in Ceyeen between 1907 and 1912, then followed him to Diourbel.[111] It seems that it was at this period that Bamba encouraged Ka to write in Wolofal, in order to spread his message to the majority of Murid disciples who could not read Arabic.[112] It was, however, only after Amadu Bamba's death that Ka started his career in Wolofal. He indicated that since Bamba had praised the Prophet Muhammad, who was an Arab, in Arabic, he was, for his part, going to praise Bamba in Wolof, his mother tongue. Musa Ka is the most prolific and the most renowned Senegalese Wolofal writer.[113]

Ka's most influential work is his reconstruction of Amadu Bamba's confrontation with the French, which he entitled *Jazaau Shakuur (Tribute to the Worthy of Recognition)*, reproducing the title that the cleric gave to his travel narrative. This long poem of 1,344 verses is divided into two cycles, "the cycle of the sea," which describes the trip from Senegal to Gabon and back (764 verses), and "the cycle of the land," which tells of the events that took place between Daaru Mannaan, Mauritania, and Ceyeen (580 verses). In composing this poem, Ka sought inspiration from a wide variety of sources: Amadu Bamba's writings, testimonies from contemporary eyewitnesses, and the hagiography of Prophet Muhammad and other Muslim saints.[114] He did not have access to French archival material, but his reconstruction of the events is quite remarkable.

Perhaps the most fascinating aspect of Ka's epic poetry is his depiction of the mystical and physical battle that Amadu Bamba waged against the French. He drew extensively from the idioms and metaphors of Islamic mysticism and Senegalese heroic tales to construct his narrative. Comparing his sheikh to other saints, he wrote, "Bamba is the only wrestler that deserves the title of champion; he is strong like cable (steel); everybody else is an amateur." He presented the exile as the consequence of Amadu Bamba's covenant with the Prophet "to shoulder the burden destined to the pole of sainthood, and by steadfastly bearing the load, he has surpassed all Muslim saints of his time."[115] Like a playwright, Ka reconstructed imaginary dialogues between his sheikh, God, the Prophet, and many important protagonists of the history of Senegal. Relating the ultimate conversation between Bamba and Amadu Njaay Maabeey, a well-known Saint-Louis cleric, he put these words in his sheikh's mouth, "I am leaving to accomplish a sacred mission and I will return to this land.... I take you as my witness because you will meet me back here in Saint-Louis, you will not die before my return."[116]

Musa Ka asserted that the French had subjected Amadu Bamba to numerous forms of torture, each of which would have taken the life of an ordinary human being.[117] Reminiscent of the biblical figure Daniel, he wrote that in Dakar, the cleric was confronted by a hungry lion, which, in his sight, "behaved like a lamb before its owner." He retold the story of the raging bull, which he situated in a street near the port of Dakar, and added that it was the Archangel Gabriel who came to his sheikh's rescue and broke the dangerous animal's neck. Ka popularized the story that Bamba laid out his mat and prayed on the waves of the Atlantic Ocean when, on the ship transporting him to Gabon, he was prevented from fulfilling his religious duty. He also narrated events that happened in the localities of Mayomba, Lambaréné, and Wiir Wiir in Gabon, where Bamba battled infidel genies, converted some of them to Islam, and foiled numerous attempts by French soldiers to kill him.[118] Ka's works have inspired singers, painters, and artists who have figuratively reproduced the stories he recounted to provide more accessible and vivid images of Amadu Bamba's odyssey to the wider Senegalese and Murids audience that cannot read Wolofal.[119] His epic poetry was also popularized through other media. *Jazaau Shakuur* was turned into a play performed by amateur actors that featured Amadu Bamba, the governor of Saint-Louis, and other French and Africans who were involved in the conflict. This play was very popular in the Murid heartland in the 1970s and 1980s.[120] Today, recordings of Ka's poems chanted by professional Murid singers are sold around the world, following the trails of Murid international migrants.[121] Ka has been instrumental in forging the popular image of Amadu Bamba as a hero who confronted and defeated the French.

The subversive potential of the heroic narratives told by Murid hagiographers such as Ka was not lost on the colonial administration. Administrators were irritated by their capacity to turn setbacks into victories. French officials were apprehensive about the effect that these stories could have on popular imagination and about the possibility of dampening the deterrent power of the coercive measures they took to subdue the cleric and his disciples.[122] Their apprehension was further fueled by the fact that they were unable to counter this form of response to their policy. Sometimes, they would learn about the stories only years after they had begun to circulate.[123] We are presented here with a situation in which it is not history itself that represents a threat to popular memory, as in Pierre Nora's formulation, but the opposite. The Murid popular epic could be seen as a form of what James Scott has termed weapons of the weak.[124] But here, the scene for the confrontation is not the domestic realm but the public sphere. Dissenting discourses are not expressed in the form of a "hidden transcript" masked by polysemy and the ambiguities of its meanings but in the production of a narrative that inflicts a defeat that is imaginary to the powerful but very real to the powerless. The French gradually realized that continuous repression would only enhance Bamba's prestige. They were not aware of the impact their policy was having on the cleric's persona on the spiritual and mystical levels, but they were mindful of the aura of martyrdom and invulnerability that the saga of his exile and return had built.[125] In the face of this situation, the French increasingly felt the need for a different orientation in their relationship with the Murids.

CONCLUSION

The arrest and deportation of Amadu Bamba to Gabon in 1895 was primarily the result of the initiative of individual administrators, who acted based on their own perception of the Muridiyya as a potential obstacle for the functioning of colonial administration. The decision to exile the cleric could be viewed as a preemptive measure aimed at preventing problems rather than the consequence of hostile actions against the colonial administration taken by the Murids or their leader. This decision contradicted the policy of consultation and peaceful management of conflicts that seemed to have guided the relationship between the office of the governor and the Murid leadership since 1892. The triumph of the hardline policy toward the Muridiyya was made possible by a situation in which institutional transformations and changes in administrative personnel conspired to favor the agenda put forward by the advocates of repression. When the bureaucratic machine had been primed for coercion, it developed its own momentum, fed by the memory of the tensions and wars that had marked relations between the French and the Muslim clerics in Senegal and the Western Sudan; by the French tradition of secularism and hostility to religion, which was deeply rooted in the psyche of the colonial administrive corps; and by local African enmities.

Amadu Bamba's seven-year exile was a setback for the Murids, but his return was celebrated as a victory over the all-powerful colonial power and a sign that God was on their side. Ultimately, the removal of the cleric from Senegal did not weaken the Muridiyya as the French had expected but rather bolstered its development. When Bamba left the country in 1895, he was a respected scholar and cleric, a Sufi sheikh whose credentials were based on erudition and piety; on his return, he saw himself and was seen by his disciples and many Muslims in the Senegalo-Mauritanian zone as a *wali Allah* (friend of God), a martyr, and a miracle worker who had overcome the machinations of the French. Drawing on lessons learned from the exile and its political consequences, some sectors of the French colonial administration soon became aware that the policy of repression would not work and that it was necessary to find an alternative approach. The consolidation of colonial power, the increasing demographic weight of the Muridiyya, and the prominent role of Murids in the economy fostered this awareness.

However, the climate of distrust between the Murids and the colonial administration, deriving from more than a decade of tension, rendered the achievement of peace elusive. This distrust was rooted, in part, in the administration's deficit of knowledge about the Muridiyya and its reliance on biased field administrators and African chiefs for the elaboration of its Muslim policy. However, the evaluation of the political consequences of the exile and the responses of Murid disciples to this event created the conditions for the defusing of the tension and paved the way for gradual rapprochement.

Pl. 1. Amadu Bamba's arrival in the port of Dakar on his return from exile in Gabon, November 1902. Painting by Alpha Wali Diallo, commissioned by Oumar Ba to illustrate Oumar Ba, *Ahmadou Bamba face aux autorités coloniales* (Abbeville: Fayard, 1982). Reproduced by permission of Oumar Ba.

Pl. 2. Amadu Bamba teaching disciples in front of his house. Reverse glass painting.

Pl. 3. The trial of Amadu Bamba in the office of the governor-general of West Africa in Saint-Louis. Painting by Alpha Wali Diallo, commissioned by Oumar Ba to illustrate Oumar Ba, *Ahmadou Bamba face aux autorités coloniales* (Abbeville: Fayard, 1982). Reproduced by permission of Oumar Ba.

Pl. 4. Homecoming celebration in Daaru Salaam organized by Amadu Bamba's brother, Sheikh Anta Mbakke, after Bamba's return from Gabon. Reverse glass painting by Mor Guèye from Allen Roberts and Mary N. Roberts, *A Saint in the City: Sufi Arts of Urban Senegal* (Los Angeles: UCLA Fowler Museum of Natural History, 2003). Reproduced with the permission of the Fowler Museum.

Pl. 5. Sokhna Njakhat Sylla, a wife of Amadu Bamba.

Pl. 6. Cell in the basement of the governor-general's palace where Amadu Bamba was kept in custody while awaiting trial.

Pl. 7. Mausoleum of Jaara Buso, Amadu Bamba's mother, in Porokhaan. Site of a popular annual pilgrimage, mostly attended by women. At the time this photograph was taken, a large project to remodel and extend the mausoleum was almost completed.

Pl. 8. Gigis tree in Porokhaan where Amadu Bamba's father, Momar Anta Sali, taught his disciples from 1865 to 1872.

Pl. 9. Mosque of Diourbel.

Pl. 10. Mosque of Tuubaa.

Pl. 11. Murid businesses in "Little Senegal," Harlem, New York City.

Pl. 12. Murids marching during the annual celebration of Amadu Bamba Day (July 28) in New York City.

Pl. 13. The late Cheikh Murtala Mbakke, youngest son of Amadu Bamba, and Mayor David Dinkins at New York City Hall.

Pl. 14. William Ponty, governor-general of French West Africa (1908–15), in full ceremonial dress. Reproduced by permission of the author from Oumar Ba, *Ahmadou Bamba face aux autorités coloniales* (Abbeville: Fayard, 1982).

Pl. 15. Amadu Bamba.

Pl. 16. One of the four small minarets of the great mosque of Tuubaa.

Pl. 17. The well of mercy, dug at the instruction of Amadu Bamba in Tuubaa in the late nineteenth century; a major pilgrimage site for Murid disciples.

Pl. 18. Mihrab, or prayer niche, of the mosque of Tuubaa.

6 ⤳ Slow Path toward Accommodation I

The Time of Rapprochement

HISTORIANS HAVE long analyzed the colonial encounter through the prisms of collaboration and resistance. More recently, some scholars have questioned the heuristic validity of these concepts.[1] They have highlighted the emotional load they carry as they inevitably recall the context of World War II Europe, with some Europeans cooperating with the Nazi regime and others resisting doggedly. Furthermore, looking at colonialism through the lenses of resistance and collaboration leads to conceptual reductionism and oversimplification of the complex field of interactions between colonizers and colonized.

The term *accommodation* is now increasingly used to avoid the rigidity of an artificial binary opposition and to better express the nuances, ambiguities, and complexities in the relationships between European imperialists and their subjects. Accommodation offers the conceptual flexibility to map out the vast arrays of conflicting attitudes deployed by the colonized to adapt to the new *rapport de force* (power relations) imposed by colonial rule.[2] However, accommodation should not be conceived as a one-way process by which the powerless strive to ingratiate themselves with the dominant power. Rather, it should be understood as an evolving dynamic of mutual adjustments, in which the dominator as well as the dominated struggle to minimize conflicts and identify areas of converging interests. The need for accommodation is rooted in the understanding that coercion cannot be an effective tool for administration and that minimal consent from the colonized is necessary for colonial rule to be successful. It originates in the aspirations of colonial administrators to attain their goals at "minimal cost by using available mechanisms of indigenous politics" and in the need for the subjugated facing an alien regime with overwhelming power to develop survival strategies.[3]

This understanding of accommodation is favored in some of the most recent scholarship on Islam under colonial domination in Africa.[4] In a book published in 2000, David Robinson charted the crossing paths taken by four Muslim clerics and the Federation of French West Africa to negotiate relations of accommodation. Amadu Bamba was one of the clerics discussed.[5] In his chapter on relations between the founder of the Muridiyya and the colonial authorities of Senegal, Robinson offered a thorough analysis of what he called the "longest, hardest, most complete, and most enduring" path of accommodation to French rule. In the pages that follow, I explore the converging French and Murid paths of accommodation by focusing on some of the transformations within and outside the Muridiyya that facilitated its adjustment to colonial domination. I argue that the rapprochement between the Murids and the French was an unplanned process. It unfolded gradually, following a twisted trail on which both sides applied and responded to pressure while remaining mindful of the compromises needed to achieve stable relationships.

NEW ORIENTATIONS IN FRENCH COLONIAL POLICY

In 1902, the year of Amadu Bamba's return from exile in Gabon, Ernest Roume (1902–8), a Parisian bureaucrat like Chaudié, was appointed governor-general of the Federation of French West Africa. Roume was a civilian inspector at the Ministry of Colonies, which was created in 1894 and had inherited the prerogatives of the more militarily oriented Ministry of Navy, which had overseen the conquest and "pacification" of France's overseas territories. The founding of this ministry heralded the intensification of colonial rule and subsequently a shift in political approach and administrative practices. Roume arrived in West Africa with an ambitious plan for economic and administrative reform.[6] He was keen to develop a more competent administration capable of peaceful and firm control of the colonies. One of his tools for achieving this goal was better knowledge of the cultures, mores, and leadership of the indigenous people.[7] This knowledge provided the basis for the policy of association, which, in Merlin's view, he favored and which rendered the entente with the Muslims easier.[8] This change in the conduct of colonial business led to a reevaluation of Muslim policy in Senegal. The task of creating a new policy fell on the shoulders of Robert Arnaud, a French Islamicist of Algerian origin who was appointed head of the new Muslim Affairs Service, founded by Roume in 1906. The governor-general also launched the short-lived *Bulletin de la Société de Géographie de l'AOF* and initiated the system of *fiches de renseignements* (intelligence files), which served to monitor the activities of Muslim leaders of different stripes in West Africa.[9]

In this new administrative framework, the perception of the Muridiyya as a threat was changing. In 1895, Merlin and Leclerc feared that the Murids could foment an armed resistance; in 1902, the administration was confident that no such challenge to its rule was likely to happen in Senegal. Officials also realized the futility of trying to roll back the Murid identity of their subjects in Bawol and Kajoor. The Muridiyya was now taking root in rural Senegal. Since Amadu Bamba's return from exile, his prestige, authority, and popularity had increased considerably, and the *tariqa* he founded was experiencing an unprecedented growth in followers.[10] Therefore, short of controlling it, enlisting its support for colonial rule was an imperative for the French.

However, Amadu Bamba's conception of the relations between temporal and spiritual authorities and French misconceptions about his intentions and motivations remained obstacles to building closer relationships. Bamba's political philosophy was shaped by Wolof culture and Sufi ideas. Wolof rulers recognized the man of religion as having the right to dissent or to remain neutral in political matters, and he was granted a measure of autonomy within the boundaries of what was defined as tolerable behavior. The uncooperative cleric was likened to a barren spot in the farmland, which could be circumscribed and ignored as long as it was not too large to spoil the harvest.[11] Sufi ideology urges the sheikh to keep his distance from and be critical of the unjust ruler—but only to the extent that the critiques do not spark or encourage rebellion. It was within this paradigm that Bamba conceived of his relations with the chiefs who represented the colonial administration in the rural areas of Bawol and Kajoor. But Roume's vision of an effective administration made no room for an autonomous or neutral indigenous leadership outside the purview of the colonial regime. As he made clear, one important dimension of his Muslim policy was "to prevent *marabouts* from creating centers for meeting, religious proselytizing, or pilgrimage . . . , to punish those like Amadu Bamba, who tried to found such centers, and to show the populace that the disciplinary actions of the administration were directed at the political activists and not at the sincere Muslims who were free to practice their religion under the protection of the French flag."[12] The second conflict between the French and the Murids should be understood in the context of the increasing centralization of the administration and Amadu Bamba's aspiration for neutrality and autonomy.

THE CIRCUMSTANCES OF THE EXILE TO MAURITANIA (1903–7)

The immediate cause of Amadu Bamba's second exile, to Mauritania, stemmed from the enforcement of Roume's new Muslim policy. As part of the massive information-gathering operation, provincial chiefs were instructed to survey and interview all the influential Muslim clerics under their authority and to create files compiling critical intelligence about them. Mbakhane Diop, the son of Lat Joor and the French-trained chief of eastern Bawol, was charged with collecting information from Amadu Bamba. Incidents sparked by this mission eventually led to the deportation of the cleric. Mbakhane, in a memo to R. du Laurens, the resident of Diourbel, described his encounter with Amadu Bamba. The chief explained the many difficulties he had to confront before he could meet with Bamba.[13] He reported that after making him wait for hours, Bamba finally yielded to his firm resolve and went to Mbakke, where Mbakhane was waiting. But when he entered the meeting room, the cleric laid down his mat and immediately asked about the purpose of the chief's visit. After listening, the cleric gave a disrespectful response, proffered some threats, and ended his speech with these words (between quotation marks in the report):

> Since I returned from Gabon, I no longer want to have anything to do either with the chiefs or with those who are called commandants. I only want to deal with the governor, whom I met in Saint-Louis on my way back to [Bawol]. As for you [Mbakhane] who dare to talk to me, if I did not ruin your life, it is because I have pity for you and I know your father. Also your aunt, whom I met at Ker Mataar, recommended you to me. Beware, something bad could happen to you on your way back. . . . Mbakhane leave me alone and go away, I am not a man of this world, I belong to the hereafter, I only see God and my sight is beyond the mortals.[14]

Mbakhane added that after he finished talking, Amadu Bamba left precipitously, and the cleric's brothers and disciples, who remained behind, scrambled to convince him not to take offense at what the cleric had just said. They argued that he was so absorbed by his relations with God that he did not know how to deal with temporal authorities. In his report, Mbakhane also emphasized the obstacle that the Muridiyya presented to good administration in his province. He deplored the fact that one of his deputies was on the side of the Murids and even tried to convince him to forgo his mission in order to please Amadu Bamba. He complained that many chiefs in Bawol were no longer obeyed and that the province's *qadi* (Muslim judge) had written Sheikh Anta (Amadu Bamba's brother) to warn him about the mission.

These last remarks about the disruption that the Murids were causing in eastern Bawol struck a sensitive chord in the administration. In the account of the incident that he sent to the administrator of Thiès, who oversaw the Bawol administration, the resident, du Laurens, put a special emphasis on the detrimental impact that Amadu Bamba's attitude was going to have in the province if it went unpunished. He wrote, "The Superior Chief's authority has been insolently and publicly challenged and put down by the *marabout*. Our chief's prestige has suffered from this, and also by extension, our administration's prestige from which he received his entitlement. We cannot tolerate this situation and we cannot accept to let grow beside him a power that would counterbalance his influence and hurt the impulsion he receives from us."[15]

Du Laurens particularly stressed the treacherous behavior of the qadi and chiefs who sided with the Murids. He also mentioned the growing power and prestige of Amadu Bamba since his return from exile. However, instead of proposing to send the cleric outside Senegal, as Merlin had done in 1895, he suggested that he be removed from eastern Bawol, which he perceived as a center of proselytism and religious activism, and relocated in another province where he would be closely monitored by the administration.[16]

Du Laurens's letter prompted Vienne, the administrator of the district of Thiès, to demand that Amadu Bamba report to him in eight days. After the cleric failed to bow to his order, Vienne alerted the governor-general. The latter sent two letters and dispatched two negotiators to convince the cleric to go to Saint-Louis. He also asked Sheikh Sidiyya to intervene and talk to Amadu Bamba on his behalf. Bamba's failure to comply with the administration's admonitions led them to believe that he was prepared to resist arrest. Vienne, who seemed to have taken Amadu Bamba's attitude as an insult to his authority, started to send telegram after telegram to Saint-Louis, warning of the gravity of the situation. He proposed that the administration abduct the cleric and send him to a location from which he would never return. Victor Allys, the administrator of the district of Tivaouane, by contrast, proposed a more expedited method. In a personal (nonofficial letter) to Merlin, the general secretary of the colony and interim governor, he suggested that the administration stage a scuffle with Amadu Bamba's disciples on the occasion of his arrest and then kill the cleric amid the confusion.[17]

Between the end of April, when Mbakhane filed his report, and the beginning of June, provincial and cantonal chiefs from Bawol, Kajoor, Siin, and Saalum sent alarming intelligence to the administration, stating that Murids were buying weapons in the Gambia and that more than five thousand disciples were waiting Amadu Bamba's orders to engage in a war against the administration.[18] Spies sent to the cleric's compound did not confirm this information. One of them, Oumar Niang, informed Allys that he had heard Bamba say that he had made a covenant with God to never wage war, that he would not even kill a scorpion or a serpent, and that if the Mahdi had appeared today, he would not join him.[19] The administrators, however, dismissed all information that did not corroborate their beliefs and the chiefs' allegations that Amadu Bamba was preparing to resist.

Among the Murids, tension was also rife. Bamba had been back for only seven months after seven years of exile in Gabon, and many feared that a second arrest would lead to his disappearance once for all. Some disciples were ready to physically oppose his removal from the village of Daaru Mannaan. The Mbakke family was divided. Bamba's senior brother and chief of Mbakke Bawol, Momar Jaara, blamed the cleric for listening to his younger brothers and disciples, and he urged him to obey the governor's order.[20] He also contacted the administration and dissociated himself from what he characterized as a revolt, asking that his village be spared in the case of an armed conflict. Momar invited the French commandant to search the village to make sure that there were no weapons hidden there. The other brothers criticized Sheikh Anta, reproaching him for adding fuel to the fire by confronting Mbakhane instead of appeasing the situation. Facing intense pressure, Bamba had to reassure his disciples by guaranteeing them that nothing detrimental would happen.[21]

Amadu Bamba also engaged the colonial administration to explain his position. He sent his brothers Sheikh Anta and Ibra Faati and his cousin Mbacké Bousso to meet with the governor in Saint-Louis. He responded to the governor's letters in an effort trying to dispel his suspicions and to convince him of his own good intentions. In one of his letters, he wrote:

> I urge you (governor general) not to believe those who come before you to denigrate me for the sake of earning money. The reasons why I did not come to Saint-Louis have to do with my failing health since I returned from Gabon, and nothing with disrespect of your authority. Therefore, I ask you to change your opinion of me. Take a positive view of my actions and understand that I want nothing in this world but piece and tranquility to better follow The Prophet's teachings . . . in the best of my ability. . . . You can tell the person who told you that I am not abiding by the Prophet's recommendations that he did not tell the truth. . . . I assure you that my actions conform to my words.[22]

THE ARREST

Bamba's efforts to mollify the colonial officials were unsuccessful. His refusal to obey their orders was seen as an act of rebellion that had to be repressed.

Merlin, who was the acting governor at the time, certainly understood that the cleric was not a man of violence, but for the sake of preserving the prestige and authority of the colonial state, he believed it was necessary to force the cleric to comply, using lethal force if necessary. In a letter dated 4 June 1903, he instructed the commander in chief of the federation's army to mobilize and head to Daaru Mannaan for the cleric's arrest. Bamba finally surrendered, near Mbakke, to Allys, the commanding officer of the expeditionary force sent to arrest him on 14 June. He was transported to Saint-Louis, where he was sentenced to deportation to Mauritania for an indeterminate length of time.

The similarities between the events that led to Bamba's two exiles—that ending in exile in Gabon and that of 1903, ending in deportation to Mauritania—are striking. In 1895, it was the reports filed by African chiefs that fueled the tension; in 1903, it was also an African chief, Mbakhane Diop, who set in motion the process that ended with the cleric's arrest and deportation. In both conflicts, the threat that the Murids represented to the authority of the African chiefs ultimately led to Bamba's arrest. Finally, the principal actor in the two dramas was the same man—Merlin.

It is interesting to note, however, that despite similar circumstances, the outcomes of the two dramas were markedly different. In 1903, Amadu Bamba was sent to the northern border of Senegal, where contacts with his family and disciples were easier to maintain despite the obstacles put up by some colonial administrators. Beyond that, he was entrusted to his former master and friend Sheikh Sidiyya. Even after his arrest, the administration made sure that he would not seem to be a prisoner.[23] This was a far different situation than the confinement to the filthy cell of November 1895, which Amadu Bamba had deplored in his travel account. Another difference involved the administration's assessment of the cleric's offense. In 1895, Bamba was accused of being at the center of a conspiracy to wage jihad against the French; in 1903, his "rebellious behavior" was blamed on manipulations by his disciples and some troublemakers in Bawol. The accusation that he was a *tijani* that had been leveled in 1895 also disappeared from the administration's rhetoric in 1903. In Saint-Louis, Bamba was not put in jail, and he did not go through a trial. He met with the interim governor, who announced his sentence in the presence of Sheikh Sidiyya's representative.

Merlin gave two reasons to explain why he treated Amadu Bamba with clemency after the second arrest, instead of deporting him back to Gabon as he had threatened. He mentioned that he had a good deal of esteem for Sheikh Sidiyya, who interceded on the cleric's behalf, and that despite his initial rebellion, Bamba had finally surrendered and did not pose a threat of resistance. In reality, Merlin's explanations did not disclose the real motivations behind the administration's attitude. The fact was that in 1895, Sheikh Sidiyya had pleaded for the release of Amadu Bamba,[24] but his intercession was to no avail. With regard to the cleric, his attitude in 1903 should have been judged even more confrontational. In 1895, he was given an ultimatum of less than a week to surrender to Leclerc, and he did so. In 1903, he failed for over a month to comply with the governor's summonses, despite the mediation of at least three negotiators and the exchange of letters.

Merlin's so-called clemency was, in reality, the sign of a gradual but strategic change in the relations between the Murids and the French. This change was underpinned by Roume's political orientation, which Merlin termed association and which called for more diplomacy and less repression when dealing with influential Muslim clerics. In addition, the colonial administrators had begun to realize that their African auxiliaries in the protectorates no longer had much credibility in the eyes of the population. These chiefs of aristocratic origin had been able to maintain order in their jurisdictions only through the use and abuse of coercion.[25] In some areas of rural Bawol and Kajoor, Murid sheikhs were emerging as the legitimate leaders of the population. They wielded great moral authority and enjoyed much respect, despite, or perhaps because of, the hostility of the colonial administration.

It is clear that the shifting rapport de force in the protectorates in favor of the Muridiyya was having an influence on the relations between the French and Amadu Bamba. And it seemed that, as noted by O. Depont and X. Coppolani in the case of Sufi orders in Algeria, coercion would only enhance the Murid sheikhs' prestige and strengthen their disciples' resolve.[26] The alternative was either to adopt an all-out policy of repression to try to destroy the organization—an option that not only was costly but also had uncertain outcomes—or to admit the reality of the new social force and establish a modus vivendi with its leaders. It is my contention that by 1903, although there was not a thought-out policy as to how to deal with the Murids, some sectors within the colonial administration, at the highest level, had started to lean toward the second alternative.[27] They chose to entrust Amadu Bamba to Sheikh Sidiyya, who was seen by the French as the model marabout. This was the first stage of a hesitant and contradictory but pragmatic policy, which gradually led to reconciliation with the Muridiyya.

THE DEPORTATION TO MAURITANIA

Amadu Bamba joined Sheikh Sidiyya's compound in Mauritania in late June 1903. In a letter conveyed by his escort, Merlin urged the Moorish cleric to watch over the banned sheikh and to make sure that he did not communicate with people in Senegal, especially his disciples in Bawol. He added, "He [Amadu Bamba] has strayed from wisdom by not following your advice; because of the services you rendered him and your friendship, your advice should have been sacred to him like a father's recommendations to his son."[28] What Merlin did not articulate clearly but was implicit in his letter was that he hoped that by staying with Sheikh Sidiyya for some years, Amadu Bamba would learn from his exemplary behavior and would be persuaded into engaging in the same cordial and close relationship that tied the French administration to the Sidiyya family.

In Mauritania, Amadu Bamba stayed with Sheikh Sidiyya for the first year but parted from him during the second. We learn from M. L. Diop, one of the Murid disciples who accompanied the cleric in exile, that it was in the locality of Sarsaara (also called Sout-El-Ma by the French and Khomaak by the Wolof), near the northern border of Senegal, where Amadu Bamba decided to separate from his guardian.[29] He disliked the nomadic lifestyle of his host, who was in perpetual movement to search for grazing land and water or to mediate conflicts between feuding Moorish "tribes." Bamba also deplored the fact that many of his disciples from Senegal who came to visit him were assaulted by the bandits that infested southern Mauritania or could not find him because of the frequent traveling. Sheikh Sidiyya opposed Amadu Bamba's decision to go off on his own, arguing that he himself was accountable to the French for Bamba's security and well-being, but he finally consented to let the cleric settle in Sarsaara. He may have convinced the general commissioner of the Civil Territory of Mauritania to accept the arrangement.

Amadu Bamba founded a school in Sarsaara, which specialized in the teaching of religious sciences and *tarbiyya*. He primarily selected disciples who had already mastered the Quran and were strong enough to do menial jobs. Most of these disciples were the elder sons of the first generation of the sheikhs who had joined him when he began his mission in Mbakke Kajoor and Bawol between 1884 and 1895.[30] Since Mauritania was known as a place of knowledge and piety, Bamba wanted to surround himself with disciples who belonged to families with established traditions of Islamic scholarship and who could benefit from the intellectual atmosphere in his country of exile. Perhaps he had also begun thinking about the future of his organization and the need to train the next generation of leaders.

The relationship between Amadu Bamba and his hosts was rocky at times. Bamba had been a disciple of Sheikh Sidiyya in the past, but by 1903, he was confident that he had the credentials of a master. However, for the Moorish clerics, who have historically been the conduits for the transmission of Islamic culture and knowledge to their southern neighbors, it was not easy to acknowledge the intellectual and spiritual authority of a "black" over a "*bidan*," (meaning a "white"); bidan was a name that Moors of Arab and Berber origins coined for themselves.³¹ Murid traditions inform us that when Amadu Bamba decided to settle in Sarsaara despite Sheikh Sidiyya's objections, he was criticized by Mauritanian clerics, who reproached him for violating Sufi teachings by disobeying his spiritual guide.³² Bamba responded that he was not a disciple of Sheikh Sidiyya and that the latter clearly understood that. Sources also refer to instances in which Sheikh Sidiyya displayed the intellectual achievements of his daughters to his host as a way of asserting the profound Islamic tradition of his family. Bamba is said to have later rejoiced before the Moorish cleric, who was paying him a visit (probably in Diourbel), at the accomplishment of his daughter Maymuna Kabiir, who not only successfully completed her education by writing the Quran in its entirety from memory but also prepared on her own the delicious dinner her father shared with his guest.³³ The message he wished to convey was that the daughter was both a learned Muslim and an accomplished wife.

Amadu Bamba was also challenged by Moorish *ulamas* (learned men) who gauged the depth of his knowledge and spiritual power. He engaged in doctrinal debates with Mauritanian scholars and was invited to give his opinions on disputes that involved members of competing Sufi schools. M. L. Diop reported some of those debates and disputes and related Amadu Bamba's positions.³⁴ These positions reveal an effort on the part of the cleric to reconcile divergent point of views and interpretations related to Sufi doctrine and practices. His leitmotif was that Muslims should focus on that which united them instead of emphasizing divisive issues.

The colonial authorities of Senegal did not welcome Amadu Bamba's decision to settle in Sarsaara. They worried about the proximity of his residence to Bawol and Kajoor, where the Muridiyya was continuing to expand. In fact, in contrast with the exile in Gabon, Bamba's deportation to Mauritania did not impede the development of his tariqa. Reports from the districts of Louga, Bawol, Thiès, Tivaouane, and Saalum underlined the mounting popularity of the Muridiyya, illustrated by the significant donations that Murid disciples sent to Mauritania.³⁵ The lieutenant governor of Senegal, in his monthly report to the governor-general, deplored the troubles that Amadu Bamba's stay near the northern border of the colony was creating. He mentioned that Sout-el-Ma had become a place of pilgrimage for large numbers of people crossing the border from Senegal and that Murid disciples were trying to get the cleric involved in the politics of Kajoor. In response to this correspondence, the governor-general suggested that Amadu Bamba be removed from this place and interned in Fort Coppolani, farther north and away from the border.³⁶

Colonial administrators of Mauritania, in contrast, supported Bamba's request to return to Senegal. J. B. Théveniaut, who commanded the canton of Trarza to which Amadu Bamba was deported, backed his demand. He commended the cleric for his correct attitude during his stay in Sout-el-Ma and stressed that his family, especially his brother Sheikh Coro, had pledged to guarantee his loyalty to the administration in the future. Sheikh Sidiyya, who pleaded for the cleric's release, also made the same commitment to the general commissioner of the Civil Territory of Mauritania. The commissioner, who was probably sensitive to the Moorish cleric's request, seconded Théveniaut's proposal.[37] In a letter to the governor, he mentioned that Amadu Bamba was irreproachable during his sojourn in Mauritania and that he had rendered services to the administration whenever he could. He also observed that the cleric had remained neutral during the events in Tagant and Trarza that resulted in the assassination of the administrator Coppolani in 1905. Finally, underlining the poor sanitary conditions in the swampy area where the deportee was living, which had altered his health and character, he strongly recommended that the governor authorize the cleric's return to Senegal. Two months after he made the recommendations, the deportation was ended. Amadu Bamba received a letter approving his return to Senegal, delivered to him by Sheikh Ibra Faal, on the night of Mawhud (the birthday of Prophet Muhammad) of Rabi I AH 1325 (May 1907).

Compared with the rich oral and written literature inspired by the Gabonese exile, the deportation to Mauritania occupies a less prominent place in Murid hagiography. But it nevertheless marked a significant moment in Amadu Bamba's spiritual itinerary. He conceived of the exile to Gabon as a trial and a significant step in the jihad to purify his soul; in contrast, he portrayed the deportation to Mauritania as part of the reward he had garnered. He wrote, "Whoever confounds the meanings of my journey of the year 1321 AH/1903 [year of the departure to Mauritania] with that of my journey of 1313 AH/1895 [year of the departure to Gabon]) is ignorant. The second voyage was indeed an improvement of my [spiritual] life by the Most High; it was a reward from the One Who fulfilled His promise to me."[38]

The special significance that Amadu Bamba ascribed to the Mauritanian exile can be understood by examining the circumstances of his deportation and some of the events that marked his life among the Moors. The change in French Muslim policy and its implication regarding his relations with the colonial administration were not lost on him. Bamba certainly understood that the fact that he was sent not to equatorial Africa but to a Muslim area where he lived among friends with a large measure of autonomy was a strong sign that the French had reevaluated their attitudes toward him. He interpreted this change as an opening that could lead to less contentious relations with the colonial administration. In a sermon he gave in Diourbel, he revealed to his disciples that during his stay in Mauritania (from 1903 to 1907),[39] he was guided in his relations with the French by a Quranic verse from the sura "The Consultation," in which Allah orders Prophet Muhammad to say, "I believe in whatever scripture God has revealed, and I am commanded to act with equivalence among you. God is our Lord and your Lord. To us our actions, to you your deeds. There is no dispute between you and us. God will gather us together, and to Him is our returning."[40] By seeking inspiration from this verse, Bamba seemed to recognize the French as "People of the Book" and no longer as mere miscreants, as he had earlier suggested by the verses he quoted at their first encounter in 1895.[41] He acknowledged that differences existed between them, but this was the result of God's will, and finally, it belonged to God to deliver the ultimate judgment. Therefore, he believed that peaceful coexistence with the colonial administration was possible.

He felt that there were good prospects for improved relations with the French, and he saw this as proof that God was taming his enemies. His positive feeling was compounded by a sense of increased spiritual blessedness. Amadu Bamba was particularly gratified by the recognition of his superior religious status and credentials by Moorish clerics. He wrote, in a popular poem, "My praises and thanks go out to the One with Whom I was perfectly satisfied during my stay in Sarsaara. Most satisfied with Him, I laud Him for bringing me disciples from the Banu Daymaani."[42] The Daymaan is a lineage of prestigious Moorish clerics with a long tradition of Islamic learning and a reputation for *baraka*. A two-volume book of testimonies on Amadu Bamba by some of his Mauritanian disciples and by clerics of other denominations was compiled by the late caliph Abdul Ahad Mbakke.[43] The allegiance and testimonies were all the more significant because, as we saw in previous chapters, Bamba seemed to have suffered in earlier years from the racism and contempt of some of his Moorish colleagues. It is also worth remembering that it was during the stay in Mauritania that the cleric received the inspiration of the *wird* Murid, which capped the founding of the Murid *tariqa*.

HOUSE ARREST IN CEYEEN

The end of the Mauritanian exile and Amadu Bamba's return to Senegal were signs of improving relations between the Murids and the French, but they did not bring freedom to the cleric. Bamba was assigned an obligatory residence in the village of Ceyeen, located in a semidesert area between the borders of the provinces of Jolof and Waalo, where he was granted a territory of 4 square kilometers. The choice of Ceyeen was motivated by the remoteness of the site and the confidence that the governor had in Chief Buna Njaay, son of the former king of Jolof and a graduate of the School of Sons of Chiefs. Ceyeen was sixty kilometers from the nearest train station and thirty-five kilometers from Yang Yang (the chief's headquarters), and it was not connected to any major roads. The colonial administration believed that the distance between this village and the heartland of the Muridiyya in Bawol and Kajoor would dissuade Murid disciples from trying to gather around their spiritual leader.

Amadu Bamba arrived in his new residence by mid-June 1907 after a two-week tour that took him to Dagana, Saint-Louis, Louga, and Kokki, where he visited disciples and friends. It seems that he was not summoned to the office of the governor. Before his arrival in Ceyeen, he had a house built by his disciples, which he named Daaru Rahman (House of the Merciful); a year later, he built another house about a kilometer from the first one, to which he gave the name Daaru Khudoos (House of the Most Holy). He also started a large farm, which he baptized Bustaan ul Aarifiin (Garden of the Savant). By naming and renaming places, Bamba was trying—as he did in Daaru Salaam and Tuubaa in the late nineteenth century and would do later in Diourbel—to confer a new identity to the land of Jolof and domesticate it. Ceyeen also offered him the opportunity to continue *tarbiyya*. The cleric opened a school, where his disciples were engaged in study and agricultural work.[44]

Perhaps one of the most important events during Amadu Bamba's stay in Ceyeen was the affiliation of his senior brother, Momar Jaara, with the Muridiyya.[45] Momar was the chief of Mbakke Bawol, but he had remained a *qadiri* and was critical of his younger brother and his disciples. He was skeptical about the claim of sainthood that Murid disciples made for their sheikh and was worried by their tense relations with the colonial administration. His decision to join the Muridiyya led to the unification of the Mbakke clan behind Amadu Bamba. This development favored an even more rapid expansion of the Muridiyya in eastern Bawol.

For other Murid disciples as for Momar, who frequently visited his brother and spiritual guide, the remoteness of Ceyeen was not an obstacle, for they were eager to pay pious visits to their sheikh. Two months after Amadu Bamba's settlement in the area, the colonial administrators started to express some anxiety about the movement of population that his presence in Ceyeen had provoked. They were even more alarmed by the influx of Murid pilgrims who traveled through Njambur, a Muslim-dominated region that had been a hotbed of resistance to colonization in the near past, and by the rallying of an ever greater number of former chiefs and qadis behind Bamba. As early as October 1907, three months after the cleric moved to Ceyeen, the administrator of Louga proposed to the governor a series of measures aimed at reducing the flow of visitors to his village.[46] These measures included the imposition of a pass that could be obtained only after the would-be pilgrim had fulfilled some mandatory requirements. Those desiring to visit Amadu Bamba were required to report to the headquarters of the commandant of the district of Louga, where they would provide information about the people they were traveling with, the gifts they were taking to the cleric, the approximate time they planned to spend in Ceyeen, the itinerary they wished to follow to get to the village, and a receipt showing that they had paid taxes.

These measures, however, apparently were not helpful in stemming the stream of visitors. The office of the commandant in Louga was swamped daily by a great number of people seeking passes, and because of the shortage of personnel and the poor organization of the tax-collection system, the administration was unable to process the applications it received in a reasonable amount of time. The commandant's inability to deliver the required documents sparked protests among Murids, who ignored administrative procedures and proceeded to Ceyeen without passes.[47]

The colonial officials also realized that despite the fact that the remoteness of Ceyeen was no deterrent to Murid pilgrims, it was a real hindrance to their own capacity to effectively surveil the cleric. Bamba was criticized for violating his promise not to receive pilgrims without passes. In a letter dated March 1909, the administrator of Louga once again trumped up the charge that the Murids were attempting to create a state within the state.[48] To put an end to what appeared a dangerous course of events, the governor imposed new restrictions on the cleric. The Quranic school of Ceyeen was closed, and the disciples were forced to leave the area, the cleric's compound was reduced to twenty huts, and the number of people authorized to stay with him on a permanent basis was limited to fifty men and thirteen women.[49]

Reacting to the mounting tension, Amadu Bamba, in a letter to the administrator of Louga that was probably written in early 1910, reiterated that he was neither a friend nor an enemy to the French.[50] He reaffirmed that he had advised his disciples to avoid taking any actions that could create disturbances in the country. He reminded the administrators that the people in Senegal were their subjects and that they could forbid them from visiting him or bringing him gifts if they wished. He added that he would even be appreciative of such measures because it would spare him the hassle of redistributing the gifts to the numerous people who solicited his help.

Amadu Bamba also continued to demand his transfer to Bawol, his native land. His brothers wrote letters to the governor calling for his return to Mbakke, and they pledged to guarantee his loyalty to the government.[51] From

Saint-Louis, Sheikh Ibra Faal, likely with the support of other less visible Murid sheikhs, was engaged in an intense lobbying effort to secure the cleric's release. He kept up a correspondence with the chief of the colony and enlisted the support of members of the political elite of Saint-Louis, such as François Carpot and Louis J. Descemet. These politicians, who knew the functioning and internal politics of the French bureaucracy, counseled the Murids and conveyed their messages to the administrative hierarchy. They were certainly instrumental in convincing the cleric to make gestures of goodwill that could reassure the French about his loyalty.

In this context, the *fatwa* that Amadu Bamba issued during the jihad of Ma al-Aynin in northern Mauritania and southern Morocco in 1910 bore distinct political significance.[52] It might be that he had decided to make the pronouncement as a response to pressure from the colonial administration or as a reaction to suggestions by Sheikh Sidiyya or Saint-Louisian advisers, but the declaration certainly contributed to the climate of trust that was developing with the colonial authorities. In this fatwa, Amadu Bamba reminded his audience of the historical context and conditions of the jihads waged by Prophet Muhammad, and he noted that, at the present time, he did not see any valid reasons to wage jihad of the sword against the French. He justified his position by underlining the absence of a caliph for the global Muslim community, the weaknesses of the *umma* (community of believers), and the fact that the French did not prevent Muslims from practicing their religion. Referring to the proper attitude for the Muslims under French authority, he urged them to behave toward the French "the same way the Prophet treated the Christians and unbelievers in Mecca," where he was also in a position of inferiority. He supported his recommendations by quoting from the Quran, citing passages in which Allah, addressing the Prophet, said, "Be nobly armed with patience"; "It is not to you to guide them (the unbelievers) in the right path. God guides whom He wishes"; "Do not criticize those who invoke other divinities than Allah"; and "To you your religions, to me mine."[53] Regarding his own attitude, he mentioned that he did not have any hidden agenda or ill intention in regard to the colonial administration and that he remained obedient to it. Comparing colonial rule with the violence of the ancient regime, he praised the peace and order achieved under the French.

This declaration had a strong impact on relations between the Muridiyya and the colonial administration. Its real significance, however, had less to do with its content and more to do with the circumstances of its publication. We know that since beginning his career in the late nineteenth century, Amadu Bamba had opted for the jihad of the soul and that he had opposed the jihad of the sword; we also know that he was critical of the reign of the precolonial Wolof aristocracy. His position regarding wars of religion was not new, and it was congruent with what could be termed the qadiri tradition of the Senegalo-Mauritanian Zone, which he shared with Sheikh Sad Buh and Sheikh Sidiyya and, to some extent, with the Kunta of Timbuktu.[54] What was new with the fatwa was that it signaled a change in the cleric's perception of his stature and role. For the first time, Amadu Bamba openly positioned himself in a conflict that involved neither his organization nor his disciples. More significantly, he chose to do so through a public proclamation that was addressed not only to his own disciples but also to all the Muslims in Senegal, Mauritania, and beyond.

The colonial administration certainly measured the political implications of the fatwa. They appreciated Amadu Bamba's public condemnation of political violence and his call for peace. But they also realized that the cleric was conscious of the power and influence he commanded over a growing segment of the colony's population. The colonial administrators resented the "excessive veneration" that was paid to him, but it was becoming increasingly apparent to them that he could not be kept under house arrest in Ceyeen forever. The need for stable relations with the Muridiyya was made even more urgent by the fact that the Murids were becoming major contributors to the cash crop of peanuts, Senegal's lifeblood.

THE POLITICS OF GOVERNOR-GENERAL PONTY

By 1912, the shift in colonial policy toward the Muridiyya was clearly perceptible. The French started to develop a more pragmatic approach in their relations with Amadu Bamba. The failure of coercion, the increasingly important role of the Murids in the economy of Senegal, and the administration's confidence that it had a better understanding of Senegalese society and the role of Islam dictated this change.

The policy change was initiated by Roume, but it received a major boost under his successor, William Ponty, who became governor-general of French West Africa in 1908. Ponty was a veteran administrator with much experience garnered during previous tours of duty in French Sudan and Madagascar. Like Roume, he was a partisan of the doctrine of association. However, he gave a more concrete content to this policy under the guise of what he called *la politique des races* (race-based policy). The gist of Ponty's view was that African societies were fundamentally "tribal" and that all the large and multiethnic political formations found in the continent were the result of conquests and authoritarian rule imposed primarily by Muslims. He believed that to have an effective administration, the French should reinstate the primordial tribal units.[55] In his memo of 22 September 1909, in which he spelled out the parameters of this policy, he wrote, "It seems possible today to formulate this policy into a body of principles derived from the greater understanding that we now have of the psychology of our subjects, from our constant concern not to offend them in their customs, in their beliefs, and even in their superstitions."[56]

For Islam in Senegal, one important implication of the politique des races was that all of the colony's Muslims were considered members of a single race or ethnic group, as opposed to different strands of the indigenous religions and customs. Ponty did not have much love for Islam, but he did not see it as a threat so long as its development was confined to its secluded ethnic boundaries. His attitude was informed by two central ideas: first, the realization that Islam was profoundly and irreversibly ingrained in the social fabric of the French possessions of the Western Sudan and, second, the belief in a mild and less fanatical "black Islam," which was not prone to advocating social change and was inclined, in the long run, to accept the French civilizing mission.

The idea of black Islam was first theorized in the Service of Muslim Affairs headed by Robert Arnaud, but it was further expounded by Paul Marty, his successor, and the Islamicist P. J. André, in the context of World War I and its aftermath.[57] In the mind of colonial officialdom, this idea was validated by the attitude of France's sub-Saharan Muslim subjects, who remained oblivious to the call of the Ottoman Empire to revolt in the defense of Islam and instead renewed their loyalty to French rule. French trust in their capacity to understand the nature and role of Islam alleviated the fear of the religion and opened opportunities for cooperation with the Muslim leadership. In Triaud's view, black Islam provided the theoretical basis for reconciliation between the colonial administration of Senegal and the Muridiyya.[58] However, it is worth mentioning, as noted by Christopher Harrison, that the French never ceased to consider Islam as a force hostile to their rule.[59] Therefore, at the level of practice, better surveillance was deemed an indispensable condition for normalizing their relationships with the Murids. Surveillance was needed in order to protect the Muridiyya from the contamination of the more radical and politically dangerous Islam of North Africa and the Middle East and to control and contain the increasingly influential but not totally trusted founder of the Murid order.

From 1908 on, a series of administrative restructurings created better conditions for monitoring the development of the Muridiyya. In that same year, the provinces of western Bawol and eastern Bawol were separated from the district of Thiès to form an autonomous district under the authority of a commandant based in the town of Diourbel. The administrator, Jean Baptiste Théveniaut, who had watched over Amadu Bamba when he was in exile in

Mauritania, was appointed commandant of the newly created district. As soon as he assumed his post, he started to request the cleric's transfer to Diourbel, under his guardianship.[60] His proposal was rejected by the lieutenant governor on the ground that Bawol was a center of brewing Islamism and that Amadu Bamba's presence would intensify the atmosphere of Islamic proselytizing.[61] But in 1911, the director of the political bureau added his voice to that of the commandant. He suggested that the relocation of the cleric to his native land was the best solution to counter his popularity and growing influence, which he attributed to his public image as a martyred victim of colonial oppression.[62]

At the same time that they were considering easing the conditions of Amadu Bamba's detention, the colonial administrators were devising measures for tighter control of his organization. In a letter dated 13 April 1911, Governor-General Ponty called the attention of the lieutenant governor of Senegal to the need for strict surveillance of the Muridiyya, and he expressed concerns about the order's expansion in Kajoor and Bawol, especially among the Sereer.[63] For the first time, a section of the annual report on the political situation in Senegal was exclusively devoted to analysis of the evolution of the Murid tariqa. In December, Ponty issued a directive reviving Roume's project of a systematic report on Islamic proselytism in West Africa. Instructions were given to field administrators to create fiche de renseignements about all the prominent Muslim clerics in the colonies.[64]

By the end of 1911, a combination of factors in Senegal and in the metropole favored a reconsideration of Amadu Bamba's situation. Murid sheikhs' vigorous lobbying of local politicians for the transfer of the cleric in Bawol was bearing fruit. Their increasingly important role in the economy as successful traders and farmers was a positive counterbalance to the threat posed by their power over an expanding portion of the population.[65] On the metropolitan scene, Colonel Charles Mangin's idea of recruiting African soldiers for a potential European war was becoming attractive in the face of the mounting tension between France and Germany over Morocco and the deteriorating political climate in Europe. Ponty was an enthusiastic supporter of this idea.[66] And he probably understood that peaceful relations with the Murids could only help if the need arose for the massive conscription of Senegalese soldiers; tense relations with them could be an obstacle.[67]

In January 1912, Amadu Bamba was authorized to relocate to Diourbel. He left Ceyeen on 23 Muharram AH 1330 (13 January 1912) and reached the town on 16 January. He was assigned a residence in the European quarter between the commandant's house and the police headquarters. He was kept under tight security. Only a limited number of persons were authorized to see him.

His brothers and close disciples were required to apply for special permission before they could pay him a visit.

However, spatial proximity between the cleric and the administration created an atmosphere conducive to the pursuit and expansion of the policy of appeasement. In a letter to the head of the political, administrative, and economic affairs services, the lieutenant governor of Senegal, Cor, after a series of meetings with Mbacké Bousso, Sheikh Coro, and Ibra Faati (all well-known Murid sheikhs and relatives of Amadu Bamba), wrote:

> I think that we should take advantage of the situation [Murid concerns about articles attacking them in the newspaper *Le Petit Sénégalais* and the diffusion of so called anti-French poems written by Amadu Bamba] to attempt a *rapprochement* with Amadou Bamba, while maintaining our will to be obeyed by his disciples. . . . It seems to me that we should first create a climate of mutual trust; I think that the nature of our relations with him in the past will make this difficult, but I don't think that it is impossible. In this perspective, I have asked the general commissioner of the territory of Mauritania, who is now on a tour in the Trarza region, to ask Sheikh Sidiyya to send me one of his sons to meet Amadou Bamba in his name and on my behalf.[68]

For the first time, the word *rapprochement* was introduced into the administration's terminology to characterize French relations with Amadu Bamba. Governor-General Ponty gave his blessing to this orientation, stressing that there was no reason to single out the Murids. He gave further proof of his determination to pursue the policy of conciliation by firing Théveniaut, whom he accused of practicing a personal politics of "hatred and harassment" against the Murids, which he deemed detrimental to the goal of establishing peace and calm in the colony.[69] However, Ponty warned that one had to be careful not to rely too much on the support of Murid sheikhs because this would only enhance their prestige and power.[70] The governor-general's attitude showed the ambivalence that typified French policy toward the Muridiyya, especially during Amadu Bamba's lifetime. On the one hand, the French acknowledged the organization's influence and hoped to use the prestige of its leaders to compensate for their own lack of legitimacy; on the other, they feared that using Murid sheikhs as power brokers would add impetus to a social force that was beyond their control and that they could not entirely trust.

Amadu Bamba responded to Ponty's policy by making his pledge to obey the administration more explicit. In two letters to the lieutenant governor, both dated February 1913, he reiterated his commitment to accept the teaching of French to some of his students, to send some of the qualified among them to the high school of Saint-Louis, and to authorize some of his disciples to be trained at the agricultural school.[71] He also requested permission to build a house in Diourbel, where he would live with his family until the administration decided to let him return to his country (Tuubaa). In the second letter, he mentioned that he agreed to follow the commandant of Diourbel's recommendations on all matters, as long as what was required of him did not infringe on the teachings and prescriptions of Islam.

CONCLUSION

By 1912, the relationship between the Muridiyya and the colonial administration had taken a new turn toward peace and stability. Amadu Bamba remained under house arrest and strict surveillance because he was too powerful and inclined to neutrality. However, the French were increasingly convinced that the cleric's collaborators and entourage would be willing to work with them and that Amadu Bamba himself would be cooperative so long as they maintained what Ponty termed a "policy based more on tact and skill than on severity."[72]

This new policy should be seen as the result of lessons learned from the exercise of pressure and responses to pressure initiated by both sides over two decades of tense relations. It is clear that the unanticipated results of the policy of repression, which ultimately led to the strengthening of the tariqa, raised awareness of the need to change tactics. The belief in an imaginary (but politically useful) and innocuous black Islam provided a convenient justification for shifting gears and embracing yesterday's enemies. The increasingly significant Murid contribution to the economy of the colony was another incentive for promoting stable relations.

Finally, the abandonment of coercion allowed the colonial administration a better understanding of the goals and motives of the Murid order, which were not incompatible with French rule. Therefore, the establishment of a climate of entente between the French and the Murids did not mean that the French had succeeded in molding the Murids to their will, as advocated by French colonial writers and some scholars, or that the Murids had successfully resisted the French, as claimed by Murid writers and hagiographers. What was achieved was the creation of a climate of mutual acceptance and tolerance that permitted Murids and French to coexist and pursue their political, economic, and social interests, sometimes in cooperation and at other times separately. The path to accommodation that was blazed by the end of the exile and the relocation of Amadu Bamba to Diourbel was increasingly smoothed by the ability of the Murids to carve out a Muslim space in the land of infidels that Senegal had become after French colonization. In the following chapter, I turn to the process of creating this Murid Muslim space, or *daar al-Islam*, and I examine how the building of a Murid sacred space in Bawol affected the relationship between the Muridiyya and the colonial administration.

7 ⇝ Slow Path toward Accommodation II

Making Murid Space in Colonial Bawol

THE RELOCATION OF Amadu Bamba in the colonial town of Diourbel in 1912 marked an important moment in the relationship between the Muridiyya and the colonial administration. For the first time since 1895, the cleric was allowed to return permanently to his native land of Bawol. He was still under house arrest, but his presence in eastern Bawol was a boost for the morale of Murid sheikhs and disciples. Amadu Bamba also understood that the settlement in Diourbel inaugurated a new era in his relations with the French. For the first time, he requested and obtained the authorization to build a house. The majority of his sons and daughters were born during his stay in Diourbel.[1] However, for him, this town was still part of the *daar al-harb* (also *daar al-kufr*), or house of unbelief, and he would have preferred to return to his beloved village of Tuubaa.

For Amadu Bamba, the constraints imposed by the absence of freedom of movement were mitigated by the realization that the Muridiyya had the capacity to survive French pressure and ostracism and a belief in the possible preservation and continuation of his legacy as a sheikh and guide, founder of a successful *tariqa*. Furthermore, the settlement in eastern Bawol offered good prospects for further ingraining the Murid oder into his native land. The atmosphere of trust that was building with the colonial administration provided the opportunity to gradually transform this area of Senegal into Murid sacred space, or *daar al-Murid*. This process of transformation unfolded in three empirically overlapping but analytically distinguishable steps: first, the Murids' physical occupation of the land; second, the infusion of the landscape with religious and cultural meanings; and third, the containment of

French influence on the Murid sacred space. The Murids' successful cultural appropriation of the landscape of Bawol, in turn, alleviated their fear of French cultural pollution and put them in a position to better adjust to colonial rule. The project of building daar al-Murid, initially suspect in the eyes of French authorities, became more and more acceptable as they continued to push for a policy of conciliation.

COPING WITH THE DAAR AL-KUFR

The preoccupation with creating Murid space in eastern Bawol became particularly pressing when Amadu Bamba was forced, from 1912 on, to cohabit with the French in the *escale* of Diourbel. An escale is a location near a railway station, river, or major roads that functions as a center for economic transactions in semiurban and rural areas. In Bamba's situation, the escale was also a place from which French cultural influence radiated to penetrate surrounding communities. The dilemma that Bamba and his disciples were facing, then, was how they could live the life of virtuous Muslims in a land and environment polluted by the French presence and control. Was it possible to make room for daar al-Islam within the daar al-kufr? Amadu Bamba's predicament was very similar to that of the Sokoto Muslims after the British conquest, as described by Murray Last in the "Colonial Caliphate."[2] The Murid response was also quite similar: maintaining geographic and cultural separateness. The Murids were even more amenable to this solution because the identity of daar al-Islam in the Wolof states had historically been defined by Muslim spatial autonomy rather than Islamic ideological and political control over a territory and its inhabitants, as was the case in northern Nigeria.[3]

Murids initially viewed the confinement to Diourbel as part of a plan aimed at further undermining their organization. For the disciples, Diourbel was the heart of daar al-kufr. It was the headquarters of the newly created district of Bawol and was located within Sereer country that still resisted Islamization.[4] In 1908, the railway linking Dakar to Bamako (in French Sudan) reached the city, and in 1911, the European quarter, or escale, was surveyed to allow for the creation of modernizing infrastructures. Police facilities, a railway station, and a school were built to encourage the expansion of business. With the rail line, the cultivation of peanuts started to develop, and Diourbel soon became one of the major centers of the Senegalese economy. Between 1914 and 1930, the population grew from 2,200 to 11,300.[5] Lebanese, Syrian, and French trading companies monopolized the town's bustling economy, which was fueled by the upsurge in peanut production and a growing population of French and African civil servants.

In Amadu Bamba's view, Diourbel represented a perfect example of daar al-kufr. It stood in stark contrast to the ideal Islamic city, which he described in his book *Matlab ul Fawzayni* and which he tried to build in his village of Tuubaa. His cohabitation with the French promised to be tumultuous. Murid disciples were routinely arrested and put in prison for disturbing the peace with their noisy chanting.[6] The lack of space to teach and accommodate sheikhs and disciples was another constraint. Diourbel might offer happiness in this world, but from the Murids' perspective, those who embraced the city's French materialist culture and lifestyle should not have expected anything but punishment in the hereafter.[7]

For Amadu Bamba, daar al-Islam was primarily defined by the ability of Muslims to shape their social and geographic space—that is, as noted by Eric Ross, the capacity to build a "distinctive spatial configuration which articulates spiritual and social functions."[8] These spiritual and social functions were education, prayer, and farming. As we have seen in previous chapters, Amadu Bamba repeatedly told the colonial administration that he was not interested in ruling people. His life's goal was to secure a land where he could raise his family, educate his disciples, and farm. Commenting on his arrest of 1895, he complained that the French had forced him out of the house he had built for the sole purposes of education and worship.[9] Mbacké Bousso observed that in this regard, Amadu Bamba was following a long-established tradition of his ancestors. He notes that in their dealings with rulers, members of the Mbakke clan had always limited their demands to two things: first, enough land to build a house, a mosque, and a school and to farm and, second, the security needed to carry out their activities.[10] This preoccupation with autonomy and security was at the core of the relationship between Muslim clerics and rulers in Wolof society. The quest for land and security was also, in Lamin Sanneh's view, the driving force behind the dispersal of the Suware scholarly diaspora.[11]

The realization of daar al-Islam, then, required securing a great deal of administrative and cultural autonomy from the state. It was the quest for this autonomy that inspired the founding of Daaru Salaam and Tuubaa. Amadu Bamba mentioned that these two villages were dearest to him because he did not inherit them from an ancestor, and he stated that he had not moved to these villages because of the suitability of the land for agriculture or grazing but for the sole purpose of teaching Islam and worshipping God.[12]

Daar al-kufr, by contrast, was characterized by political and cultural hegemony of the colonial power over the space and the people. In his postexile writings, Bamba frequently referred to Gabon as the heart of daar al-kufr. He deplored the fact that he was surrounded there by unbelievers, in a country where "nobody cared about the name of Allah."[13]

CREATING MURID SPACE IN THE HEART OF DAAR AL-KUFR: AL-MUBARAKA

As soon as Amadu Bamba was assigned a residence in the escale in January 1912, the leading Murid sheikhs (Ibra Faati, Sheikh Anta, and Sheikh Ibra Faal) started to lobby the administration to have him relocated. By mid-February 1913, the colonial authorities decided to grant the cleric a plot of land outside the European quarter, and they gave him permission to build a house. He was authorized to settle on the eastern side of the city on a dune overseeing the dry bed of the Siin River. Murids claim that the French deliberately allocated this site to the cleric because it was haunted and had been left vacant by the local Sereer population.[14]

Amadu Bamba gave his new compound the name al-Buqahat al-Muburakati (Blessed Spot; henceforth al-Mubaraka). The choice of the word *buqahat* (spot) instead of *daar* (house or place) or *medina* (city), names that he used for villages in other contexts, was suggestive.[15] The renaming of the quarter was the first step toward investing the land with a new meaning that liberated it, from an ideological and cultural standpoint, from French control. The word *blessed* reenforced this idea of appropriation of the land by the Murids and reflected the preoccupation with removing the polluting French influence and associating the space with daar al-Islam. But the use of *buqahat* also indicated a sense of insularity and unsettledness. Amadu Bamba viewed himself as an interloper in the daar al-kufr.

The feeling of religious and cultural insularity gradually faded when the Murids were able to "cut out" and appropriate al-Mubaraka as a distinct sacred space. Spatial distinction, in fact, is the main characteristic of the "holy." As a space becomes sacred, it is cut off from the surrounding environment.[16] But the objectification of the religious space is not necessarily expressed in quantitative terms or through physical separation from the profane; it may also be expressed qualitatively through rituals and a specific use of the space. This was the case with al-Mubaraka, which, although located at the margins of the escale, was still contiguous to it. The struggle to carve out al-Maburaka as a sacred space began after Amadu Bamba's settlement there in February 1913.

Bamba moved with a few dozens of his disciples to the new compound, which rapidly blossomed into a village of several hundred people. Before the end of 1913, the number of inhabitants of al-Mubaraka had reached 200; a year later, the commandant of Bawol noted that 576 people lived in Amadu Bamba's quarter on a permanent basis, along with 56 temporary residents; and by the end of 1915, the population amounted to 1,000 people.[17] The way that Amadu Bamba organized his life in al-Mubaraka seemed to indicate that he had accepted the idea of accommodating daar al-Islam within the daar al-kufr. M. L. Diop explained that the only difference between Bamba's private life in Diourbel and life in an Islamic state was that sharia was not applied because of the political context.[18] Diop observed that in al-Mubaraka, Bamba modeled his life on the life of the Prophet Muhammad in Medina: he divided his time between studying, teaching, worshipping, and providing guidance to the community. He had the same number of scribes and servants as the Prophet and had even reproduced the gender division of nine men and one woman found among the Prophet's aides. Diop, like Muslim hagiographers of saints, might have been reading in Amadu Bamba's life archetypal stories replicating the prophetic experience in Medina, but Murid efforts to turn al-Mubaraka into a sacred space was also documented by external sources.[19]

The willingness to re-create daar al-Islam in Diourbel was reflected in the management of space. The women's and men's quarters were separated. A *masjid* (mosque for the five daily prayers) and a library were built in the main square, or *penc*, on the eastern side of the village. Al-Mubaraka gradually became a center of Islamic learning and scholarship, and Moorish and Wolof disciples and teachers flocked to the quarter to work as readers of the Quran and scribes, copying Quranic and other religious books destined for pupils in the new schools that were opened in the area. The French administrator A. Lasselves gave a detailed description of the compound he visited in 1914:

> I had unfettered access to the village. I have seen the organization of the compound and the activities of the different groups living there; here you have disciples that are in close contact with the Sheikh; there you have disciples that teach; farther, you have scribes that copy manuscripts for the cleric and members of his family; and then, you have Amadu Bamba's private quarter surrounded by a tin fence and in which you see a number of wooden and thatched roof huts that are uniformly furnished with iron beds and trunks full of books in Arabic, the largest wooden thatched hut serves as a mosque.[20]

In addition to the use of space, the process of transforming al-Mubaraka into daar al-Islam involved observing Muslim religious festivals, building a communal mosque, and populating the quarter with Murid disciples. Shortly after he moved to his new compound, Amadu Bamba invited his disciples to al-Mubaraka for the celebration of the end of Ramadan, or Eid el Fitr; three thousand disciples from all the districts of the colony responded to the invitation.[21] In January 1914, he appealed to his followers to join him for the celebration the *gammu* (known outside of Senegal as *mawlud*, the birthday of

Prophet Muhammad). French sources estimated that over four thousand disciples joined the cleric in the commemoration.[22] In 1917, twenty thousand Murids converged on al-Mubaraka for the gammu.[23] Bamba also recommended that all Murids commemorate the anniversary of his arrest and exile to Gabon. This commemoration, or *maggal*, has become the most important religious event of the Muridiyya.[24]

It is remarkable that since the founding of the Muridiyya in the 1880s, Amadu Bamba had never before called his disciples to a communal celebration of religious events. The fact that he had decided to do so after 1912, when he was forced to cohabit with the French and when he had understood that he might never again recover his freedom of movement, demonstrated his ambition to inscribe the cultural marks of the Muridiriyya in the French-dominated territory of Bawol. The organization of religious festivals in al-Mubaraka was part of the effort to set this land apart (to cut it off) from the daar al-kufr. As Yi-Fu Tuan mentioned in his exploration of the realm of the sacred, "Where physical boundaries are inconspicuous or absent, processions [one could add religious festivals, pilgrimages, and rituals] serve to establish apartness"— that is, to delimit the domain of the sacred.[25] Scholars of Islam particularly insist on the importance of "ritual and sanctioned practice" in shaping Muslim space.[26] But beyond delimiting the sacred, religious gatherings are also a means of building community consciousness and reinforcing a common religious identity.[27]

The delimitation of Murid sacred space was concomitant with the initiative of physically occupying the quarter. Soon after the founding of the compound, Amadu Bamba ordered some of the senior Murid sheikhs to build secondary residences in al-Mubaraka.[28] Affluent sheikhs constructed brick houses with large courtyards and numerous rooms to host disciples and visitors during pilgrimages and religious festivals. Less wealthy sheikhs built large, squared thatched-roof huts of the type that had become markers of the landscape of the Murid heartland in Bawol and in Kajoor. Some sheikhs would be summoned to al-Mubaraka, sometimes for more than a year, for a specific task such as teaching, consulting, or leading a project.

Al-Mubaraka gradually became the second holy site of the Murids, after Tuubaa. Amadu Bamba's quarter was located at the center of the village, surrounded on the northern, southern, and eastern sides by sheikh's houses. His wives' dwelling was located in the middle of the compound, in a separate fenced place guarded by disciples, and men were forbidden to enter.[29] In 1916, after a good deal of hesitation, the colonial administration gave the Murids authorization to build a Friday mosque for congregational prayers.[30] This large mosque (for the time) constituted the first big project of the Muridiyya, and its completion in two years was an illustration of the growing power of the organization. Bearers of Murid oral traditions note that Amadu Bamba was particularly proud of the mosque. He received words of congratulations and poems magnifying the beauty of the building from as far as Mauritania.[31] Bamba's pride may also be explained by the symbolic significance of the building,[32] for it represented a powerful imprint of the Muridiyya on the landscape of French-dominated Bawol. Physical structures, in fact, often function as externalizations of the intensity and influence of religious beliefs.[33]

Amadu Bamba strived to circumscribe his life within al-Mubaraka and limit his contacts with the daar al-kufr. This attitude spawned conflicts with visiting administrators, who continuously complained about the cleric's reluctance to comply with their convocations and about his tendency to make them wait for long moments at the door of his house when they arrived for a visit.[34] Officials also accused the Murids of abducting and hiding children in the compound. At one point, the administration charged that the 3-meter-high corrugated tin fence that enclosed the compound was a potential danger because it hid the people's activities from French agents.[35] These tensions clearly indicated the administration's discomfort and concern with the increasing spatial autonomy of the Murid quarter.

MURID EXPANSION IN EASTERN BAWOL

Along with the effort to create daar al-Islam within the heart of daar al-kufr, Murids also engaged in a process of territorial expansion throughout eastern Bawol to enlarge the sacred space that al-Mubaraka represented.[36] It is revealing that members of the first generation of Murids who joined the migratory movement to eastern Bawol described their endeavor as *gaddaay*, employing the same Wolof word used to translate the Arab word *hijra* (migration of the Prophet Muhammad to Medina). They insisted on the importance of the Murid identity of the land. Most Murids do not, however, see their migration as a flight from oppression, as is often the case in the Islamic tradition, but rather as a voluntary exile for the sake of acquiring baraka.[37] This migratory process had started earlier, but it was neither provoked nor encouraged by Amadu Bamba in this early phase. In fact, in the early development of the Muridiyya, he actually discouraged the congregation of disciples around him. This attitude is not unusual among Sufi sheikhs who are involved with the quest for spiritual perfection and who are not yet confident that they are adequately equipped to tackle the task of founding and leading a community of disciples. The reluctance to be surrounded by large numbers of people may explain why, before his confinement to house arrest in Diourbel, Bamba had avoided settling in one place for any considerable length of time and why he refrained from inviting his disciples to communal celebrations of Muslim holy days.

However, as observed earlier, after his relocation in Diourbel, Bamba changed his attitude and began to urge Murid sheikhs and disciples to settle in al-Mubaraka and then throughout eastern Bawol. The conjunction of these two events was not mere coincidence. The increasing French influence in his native land called for a reassertion of the Muslim identity of the area, and physical occupation of the space was a means to achieve this goal. The French abandonment of Roume's policy of preventing the formation of centers of Islamic proselytism made the endeavor less contentious. Responding to their leader's appeal, Murid sheikhs founded a string of new villages and re-occupied formerly abandoned ones to provide structure and leadership to the burgeoning number of disciples.[38] Some of these villages were sites of memory associated with important events in Amadu Bamba's life and the founding of the Muridiyya.

Soon after the founding of al-Mubaraka, Bamba commissioned his disciple Mbaye Jakhate to revive the village of Khuru Mbakke, his birthplace. Jakhate moved to the village and opened a Quranic school. Khuru Mbakke also became the burial ground of choice for Amadu Bamba, who refused to bury members of his family in the polluted land of Diourbel. In fact, a dozen of his sons and daughters are buried in the village's cemetery.[39] After the rehabilitation of Khuru Mbakke, Amsatu Jakhate, another renowned Murid sheikh, went to Tuubaa, where Amadu Bamba instructed him to open a school. Sheikh Ahmad Ndumbe founded the village of Saam, 20 kilometers from Diourbel to the east, and Sheikh Ibra Faal founded the village of Daaru Khafoor between Saam and Mbakke Bawol. Both Ahmad Ndumbe and Sheikh Ibra, who were living in Dakar, were expressly asked by Amadu Bamba to move to eastern Bawol.[40] Ibra Faati founded the village of Daaru Muhti on the border of Kajoor and Bawol in 1912.[41]

These initiatives set off a wave of migration that sent Murid sheikhs and disciples to eastern Bawol. By 1926, colonial administrators reported, "The Murids had *conquered* the whole province of Bawol."[42] These migrants were certainly motivated by the availability of land and the security that Murid villages offered, but as they claimed, the search for baraka was also a strong incentive. As evidenced by archival and oral records, Murids from Saalum and other regions of Senegal that did not suffer from land shortages or soil depletion also joined the movement.[43]

Later on, Murid migration expanded to east-central and eastern Senegal and took a new form under the guidance of sheikhs engaged in the cultivation of peanuts. Mamadu Mustafa, Amadu Bamba's elder son and successor, led the effort by founding a number of new villages in the ancient province of Laa in the eastern region of the former precolonial kingdom of Bawol.[44] This migratory movement started what scholars have termed the *front pionier Murid* (Murid migration frontier).[45] It was not initiated by Amadu Bamba, although he gave his blessings for the creation of the new settlements; the sites targeted were on the margins of or outside the Mbakke's original heartland and most of the time close to the railroad. The settlements functioned as *daaras* (working schools) rather than villages; peanut and millet cultivation instead of Quranic education occupied the central place in the life of the communities, which were led by ordinary disciples commissioned by their religious guides, not prestigious and learned sheikhs as during the first phase described earlier.

However, all of these villages and daaras bore typical Murid names and displayed the same architecture and spatial organization that characterized earlier Murid settlements. In Wolof society, villages are traditionally named after their founder or a preeminent person, a physical structure (a tree, well, or topography), or an event (such as a migration). Murid settlements, in contrast, were often named after villages founded by Amadu Bamba in his early career, and as already noted in the case of Daaru Salaam and Tuubaa, these names duplicate some of Allah's attributes, Quranic concepts, or cities associated with Islamic history in the Middle East, such as Medina, Saam (from Arabic *Shaam*, Syria, and Missira (from Arabic *Misr*, Egypt).

Murid villages are built around the penc, a center square delimited by the local sheikh's compound to the west and the mosque to the east.[46] At the center of the square, there is often a large tree, a spacious *mbaar* (a sort of vestibule),[47] and a well or a water reservoir. Artisan shops are also found in this space. The Quranic school is often located in the sheikh's compound. The tree and mbaar are places for social gatherings. The dwellings are aligned along straight, large alleys that depart from the penc and form square angles that delimit blocks of houses.[48] The houses are large, square huts that differ markedly from the round and smaller traditional Wolof huts.[49] The sheikh's quarter is divided into a number of smaller houses called *kees* (box), separated by fences and connected by doors. Each of these smaller houses accommodates a wife and her entourage. Some serve as guesthouses, and the sheikh's private space occupies the center or eastern side of the compound. The whole domain is enclosed by a tin or thatched fence with a single front door that opens into a large empty space that is often occupied by a mbaar that connects the house to the penc.[50] The mbaar seems to function as a bridge between the private sphere, represented here by the different kees, and the penc or public realm.[51] This model differs from the configuration of traditional

Wolof dwellings but belongs to an architectural tradition that is also shared by other West African Muslim communities.[52]

The preceding description suggests that the Murid mode of occupation of space follows a pattern. One important characteristic of this pattern is the use of the square and the straight line, as was observed by French colonial administrators and later scholars.[53] Students of Islamic architecture have noted the important role of geometric forms in endowing space with certain values. As Seyyed H. Nasr observed, "In Islamic architecture space is never divorced from form. . . . Space is qualified by the forms that exist in it."[54] Beyond their architectural functions, square and straight lines have symbolic and spiritual meanings as well. The most sacred object of Islam, the *kaaba* (most sacred Muslim shrine in the mosque of Mecca), is a cube, which, in Muslim belief, is the most perfect geometric shape and also symbolizes the stability and perfection of God's creation.[55] The Kaaba served as model for the building of Prophet Muhammad's house in Medina and as a prototype for all Muslim places of worship.[56] In Islamic medicine and mysticism, the square is believed to be invested with enormous mystical power. In Senegal and many Muslim communities in North and West Africa, this belief is expressed in the *khatem* (seal), or "mystical square," where inscribed numbers and letters are fused to produce an extraordinary force that can be used to heal or to harm.[57] Like the square, the straight line also embodies symbolic meanings. The religion of Islam is often referred to in the Quran as *siraat al-mustaqiim*, the straight path. Muslims in prayer are mandated to rank themselves in straight lines behind the imam and parallel to the wall marking the *qibla* (direction to face for prayer or the kaaba). This sacred geometry of Islam has a profound effect on the built environment in West Africa.[58]

PROTECTING THE DAAR AL-MURID

The project of transforming eastern Bawol into Murid space was not limited to cultural reshaping and physical occupation of the land. It also required keeping the influence of daar al-kufr from spilling over into daar al-Murid. One of the biggest challenges that the Murids faced was keeping French schools out of their sacred space. In 1913, probably as part of the negotiation to move Amadu Bamba out the escale in Diourbel, the Murid leaders reluctantly promised to support the colonial administration's plan to open a French school in Mbakke Bawol. They certainly understood why the French insisted on opening a school in Mbakke and on having them send their children to this institution. They also understood why this initiative was undertaken when Amadu Bamba was back in Bawol and when the Murids where trying to culturally and demographically reshape the landscape. They would not have disagreed with the commandant of the district of Bawol when he observed, in his report of 1915, that "maintaining a [French] school in Mbacke is central to our anti-Mouride propaganda. However, it requires finding a serious, able, discreet, skillful and politically savvy teacher capable of making himself acceptable to all; that person doesn't exist."[59]

The first teacher appointed had to be dismissed a few weeks after his arrival in Mbakke because of objections to his character and behavior. His replacement, a graduate from the School of the Sons of Chiefs of Saint-Louis, joined Mbakke during the 1913 school year, but before the year ended, he had lost half of his pupils. At the end of the 1914–15 school year, he resigned, arguing that his father needed him in Mauritania. For the administration, the resignation was the result of pressure on the teacher; they believed he had converted to the Muridiyya and did not want to offend Amadu Bamba and the dignitaries of Mbakke, who were becoming increasingly vociferous in their opposition to the school.[60] For example, in one of the rare instances when he openly expressed his opposition to the colonial administration, an exasperated Amadu Bamba challenged the commandant of Diourbel to justify his policy of forcing people to study French and asked him how he would have felt if he was compelled to study Wolof.[61] Facing this dogged opposition, the administration finally gave up the project and, with the blessing of Murid notables, transferred the twelve disciples to a school in Diourbel. The willingness of the Murids to accept the transfer of the pupils and to pay for their housing and other needs suggests that they were not totally dismissive of French education but rather were opposed to the presence of the school on the "sacred land" of their organization. The reaction of the people of Mbakke to the school was consistent with the general attitude of the Murids toward the colonial administration. Overall, their attitude was not antagonistic. The people paid their taxes, obeyed administrators, and contributed to military conscription, but they nonetheless strived to maintain cultural hegemony over what they considered to be their sacred space.

The preoccupation with creating and preserving Murid sacred space continued even when colonial rule was consolidated and the tariqa's posterity and legacy were apparently assured. However, after the death of Amadu Bamba, the rapprochement between the colonial administration and Bamba's successor, Mamadu Mustafa Mbakke, reduced the suspicion on both sides in the quest for spatial autonomy. In the 1930s, after the completion of the Diourbel-Tuubaa railroad, Mamadu Mustafa expressed concern about the colonial administration's plan to create an escale in the vicinity of Tuubaa. He insisted that the escale, which was part of a scheme to stimulate the peanut economy of eastern Bawol, be separated from the holy city by a large boulevard or a garden.[62] Previously, in 1928, a year after his father's death, he had secured a deed for the site where the latter was buried and where the Murid envisioned building a great mosque.[63] He feared that the establishment of French local government and the settlement of non-Murid civil servants and businesses would infringe on the sacred nature of the village.[64] The commandant of Bawol finally renounced the creation of the escale and contented himself with upgrading the village of Mbakke Bawol as the administrative and economic center of Eastern Bawol.

Mbakke gradually became a dynamic colonial town administrated by the French but under the moral authority of the Mbakke family. Mustafa's insistence on separating Tuubaa from the escale of Mbakke reflected his misgivings about the blurring of the boundaries between Murid sacred space and secular French space. He wished to establish a sort of haram,[65] which would guarantee the integrity of the holiest site and burial ground of the Muridiyya. The haram was not conceived as a sacred enclave to safeguard the proprieties and bodies of Muslim as in Mecca and Medina but rather as a sanctuary for the preservation and dissemination of Amadu Bamba's baraka.

The colonial administration's acquiescence to Mustafa's request revealed the changing attitude of the French toward the Murids. With the improving relationship between the Muridiyya and the colonial administration and with the Murids' positive contribution to the colonial economy, the development of an autonomous Murid sacred space was no longer seen as a threat to colonial rule. Daar al-Murid could then be well accommodated within the daar al-kufr.

CONCLUSION

The relocation of Amadu Bamba to Diourbel in 1912 created a new type of challenge for the Muridiyya. Since the founding of the tariqa in the 1880s, the life of constant movement that the cleric experienced, whether voluntary or imposed by the colonial administration, and the heightened political tension had prevented him from focusing on strategies to preserve and expand his organization. The assignment of a permanent residence in eastern Bawol heralded the stabilization of relations with the colonial administration, but life in the French escale raised anxieties about the cultural threat that colonization represented. Muslims often perceived European colonization as Christian domination over the land of Islam and a menace to the integrity of their religion. When subjected to colonial rule, some adopted the Shia concept of *taqiyya,* or concealment, and others chose *hijra* (migration). But for the majority who wished to openly practice their faith like Amadu Bamba, the primary challenge was to find a way to reconcile their aspirations to live the life of virtuous Muslims with the need to submit to a non-Muslim power.

The Murid response to this challenge was the creation in eastern Bawol of a culturally autonomous sacred space, or daar al-Murid, in the daar al-kufr that Senegal had become. Spatial and cultural separation from the French, whether physical or symbolic, was crucial in building this Murid space. The establishment of daar al-Murid was a deliberate undertaking spearheaded by Amadu Bamba and carried out by sheikhs and disciples. It had two main goals: to inscribe the tariqa's marks on the land of the founder's forebears and to ensure the perpetuation of its legacy. The process of transforming eastern Bawol into daar al-Murid involved physical occupation of the land by Murid disciples; the cultural reshaping of the landscape through the use of Islamic sacred architecture, geometry, and religious rituals; and the containment of French influence.

Daar al-Murid did not contest French political and administrative domination; rather, it endeavored to achieve symbolic and cultural and, when possible, geographic autonomy from the colonial realm. By stripping daar al-Islam of its political content (that is, the ambition to impose sharia on the land and the people) and by infusing it with cultural meanings (focus on sacred geometry, cultural autonomy, and rituals), the Murids created the conditions needed for its preservation under French colonial rule. The French administrators' hostility to the creation of Murid sacred space in Bawol gradually abated as they increasingly shifted from a policy of coercion to one of control and cooperation with the Muridiyya. They realized that Murid spatial autonomy did not represent a security threat and was instead economically beneficial. They also understood that the cost of opposing the expansion of Murid space far outweighed the benefit. The continuing and successful institutionalization of the Muridiyya as a viable tariqa that had a potential for enduring development within the colonial order also reassured Amadu Bamba and his early companions and made the politics of rapprochement with the French more attractive.

Conclusion

MURID VOICES have been largely muted in the scholarship on the Muridiyya, which has resulted in a lopsided historiography. Thus, works on the political and economic significance of the *tariqa*—the topics that most concerned the producers of the archives that remain the main source of Murid history—far outweigh those on its spiritual, doctrinal, and educational dimensions. One of my aims in writing this book was to bring the Murids back in. Without ignoring the role of the social and economic forces unleashed by the colonial takeover, I have deliberately made the choice to place the Murids on center stage.

I have tried to write a history of the Muridiyya from within. Though based primarily on Murid internal sources, this history has also drawn insights from external voices. Such an approach has mitigated the dominant role ascribed to the influence of macro structural forces and recognized the importance of people's spiritual and psychological needs and their beliefs, knowledge, and concerns. The Muridiyya is not conceived as a coping strategy, a sort of bricolage cobbled together by bewildered Wolof farmers to respond to changes wrought by French colonization, but rather as an integral and vital phase in the development of Islam in Senegal.

Writing a history of the Muridiyya that is centered on Murid disciples and sheikhs' voices required emphasizing two aspects of the order's development that have not received much attention in scholarly literature. First, it was necessary to place the Muridiyya in the broader context of the development of Islam in Senegal and to analyze Amadu Bamba's actions in the light of the ongoing effort by Muslim clerics from the eighteenth century onward to reform the increasingly dysfunctional societies of the Western Sudan. From this perspective, Bamba is no longer viewed as a passive historical actor unwittingly subjected to the social forces that coalesced behind him, as suggested by Marty and subsequent scholars, but as a dynamic agent consciously committed to transforming his society.[1] Second, I have paid serious attention to the beliefs, aspirations, and motivations of the disciples in the founding of the Murid tariqa.

Amadu Bamba's history is foregrounded in the long Islamic tradition of his ancestry, marked by the quest for knowledge, alliance with prestigious Muslim clerical families, and political neutrality, as well as his personal experience growing up in a period of great historical transformations. Like his forebears, he highly valued education, and he devoted his life to acquiring the credentials of a respected Muslim cleric. Following his ancestors' example, he used the cultural and symbolic capital earned from educational accomplishments to marry among prominent Muslim learned families. However, Bamba diverged from his ancestral heritage in three important respects. First, he did not limit his teachings to the transmission of oral and written knowledge within the confines of a school. Instead, he gave a central role to writings for a wider public. Second, he adopted Sufism as both a way of life and an educational tool. Third, he gave a more radical content to the family tradition of distrusting rulers.

Like the clerics who preceded him, Bamba was critical of traditional rule, and also like them, he aspired to transform Wolof society, which was plagued by political violence, slavery, and economic depression. He was equally distrustful of the new colonial order. But if he shared some of the aims of his predecessors and contemporaries, he differed with them on diagnosis and strategy. Bamba blamed the hardships and sufferings that beset the society of his time on people's deviation from the right path—that is, the path paved by the Prophet Muhammad and followed by rightly guided Muslims. He was a proponent of religious and social renewal, but he believed that education was the best instrument to bring about the changes he envisioned. For him, the most effective way to reform society was to change the material of which society was made, the people. Moreover, to have an enduring impact, the seeds of change had to be sown in people's hearts and souls.

However, for Bamba, not every type of education had the desired transforming power. He believed that to have a positive effect on the social order, education had to go beyond the mere transmission of knowledge. It also needed a holistic grasp, the ability to "make" and "remake people" by changing the whole being in its material and spiritual dimensions. In Bamba's view, only the application of Sufi method of teaching could help fulfill this objective. Sufi education, or *tarbiyya*, allows the teacher to mold the soul, the center that controls an individual's feelings and actions, and thereby orient the life of his disciple in the appropriate direction. The Muridiyya was conceived as a vehicle for disseminating tarbiyya education.

Many among those who joined the Murid tariqa were not searching for a teacher, in the narrow sense of the word, but for a guide, somebody who could attend not only to their intellectual well-being but also to their spiritual and existential well-being. In Sufi tradition, this need for guidance was expressed in the form of submission (Arabic *baya* or Wolof *jebelu*), wherein the disciple pledged to follow his sheikh's recommendations on all matters related to this world and the next. Disciples sought in the Muridiyya an instrument for preserving and protecting their faith, but they also aspired to be part of a community bound by mutual trust, fraternity, and solidarity.

People did not join the Muridiyya only because they were traumatized by colonization or because Amadu Bamba was a charismatic figure who, by virtue of his personal magnetism alone, could command their will. The Murid order was attractive to the people of Senegal because it was able to provide adequate responses to their spiritual, psychological, and material needs and to adapt continuously to the changing nature of those needs.

Amadu Bamba's efforts to adapt his calling to his disciples' aspirations were often construed by French colonial writers and later scholars, wedded to an essentialist perception of Islam, as an expression of so-called black Islam—that is, a syncretistic and superficial Islam tainted by traditional African religious beliefs and superstitions and remade to the taste of black Africans. This view was also shared, but for different ideological reasons, by some Senegalese scholars who wanted to see in the Muridiyya a sort of "national Islam" with its own sacred scriptures and philosophy (Amadu Bamba's writings and thought on work), its own holy sites (Tuubaa, Al Mubaraka, and Porokhaan), and its own pilgrimage (the *maggal*).[2] Christian Coulon has correctly demonstrated that sub-Saharan Muslims were never interested in secluding themselves in a cultural peculiarity that would have separated them from "Arab Islam," or the *umma*.[3] In contrast, they continued, like Muslims elsewhere, to look at the heartland of Islam in Arabia as a source for knowledge and spiritual inspiration and as a model to emulate, while remaining mindful of their cultural specificities and values. Amadu Bamba's life exemplified this orientation. He admired the Arabic language, and in many of his writings, he glorified the Arab heroes of Islam and celebrated the intellectual accomplishments and sanctity of Arab Sufi masters. He gave to all of his villages Arab names associated with Islam and the geography of the Middle East. Yet the Muridiyya is one of the rare Sufi orders in sub-Saharan Africa not to acknowledge allegiance (formally or symbolically) to a North African or Middle Eastern tariqa. It has given Senegal its most prolific and recognizable writers in national languages. Although they maintain some measure of cooperation with certain North African countries,[4] especially in the domain of education, Murids take pride in their self-sufficiency and their independence from Arab intellectual and financial sources.

The Murids' determination to maintain autonomy of thought and actions should not, however, be portrayed as the expression of a will to particularize their organization. Amadu Bamba's pedagogy valued adaptable practices over prescriptive norms so as to be flexible enough to respond to changing, and sometimes conflicting, educational demands emanating from people of diverse backgrounds. The integrated system of *taalim*, *tarbiyya*, and *tarqiyya*, which was gradually put in place beginning in the early 1890s in the *zawiya* of Tuubaa, was meant to respond to this challenge.

Likewise, the way in which the Murid *wird* was disseminated reflected the preoccupation with adaptability. Unlike in almost all tariqas daily recitation of the wird was a choice left to the disciple and not a mandatory prescription for the average Murid. Love for the sheikh, work, and gift giving were more important than the performance of formal Sufi ritual practices.

Love for one's spiritual guide was expressed in a variety of ways, depending on the social and cultural backgrounds of the disciples. More than love, the famous "Murid work ethic" gave to the Murid doctrine a concrete content. It also exemplified its versatility. Amadu Bamba distinguished among three different types of work: *khidma* (service), *amal* (labor or activities), and *kasb* (earning or gain). The purpose of khidma was not to produce wealth for the sake of enjoyment but to seek godly rewards in the hereafter. Both amal and kasb were, in contrast, actions directed to earthly life, but they could also be turned into good work, a means to accumulate blessings and win God's satisfaction. Scholars have examined the material implications of the Murid work ethic, but it is equally crucial to understand the religious values and aspirations that underpin this ethic.

A similar observation should be made about *hadiyya* (gift giving), the third most important pillar of Murid doctrine. The motivations behind the Murid disciples' lavish donations to their sheikhs and their generous contributions to their tariqa have long puzzled and fascinated students of the Muridyya. Many see hadiyya as a sort of mask concealing the exploitation that lies at the core of the disciples' and sheikhs' relationships. More recently, other writers have contested this view. They have pointed to the relatively low cost to disciples of their contributions to the tariqa, and they have paid attention to the important degree of reciprocity in the exchange, especially in terms of political and administrative brokerage offered by the Murid leadership. These writers have suggested that the Murid economy needs to be analyzed in the light of Senegalese traditions of patron-client relationships and should not be seen in Marxist terms. Another point is important, though, if we are to understand the meaning of gift giving in the Muridiyya. Most Murids do not expect immediate returns for their gifts; rather, they seek to participate in the manifestation of Amadu Bamba's *baraka* in this world. They believe that Bamba's prayers for the well-being and continuity of his community have already been accepted by God and that now it is their duty to make this acceptance real, by helping his descendants sustain dignified standards of living and by funding the order's most treasured projects. By contributing to the fulfillment of Bamba's continuing mission, they hope to reap rewards in this world and the world beyond.

The gradual transformation of Murid education and doctrinal stipulations into ethical behavior contributed to the development of a Murid counterculture. By counterculture, I mean a set of values, practices, a cultural code, and a worldview that gave structure and meaning to the disciple's life. This counterculture appeared as a viable alternative to the traditional culture of the royal court and French cultural imperialism, and objectively, it represented a threat to colonial rule. The subversive nature of this emerging Murid ethos was already perceptible before the consolidation of French rule over the Wolof states.

The controversies between Amadu Bamba and the clerics in the court of Kajoor and the strained relations with some former Wolof princes co-opted by the French as African chiefs were a prelude to what was to come with the colonial administration. The more the chiefs diverged from the traditional ethic of legitimate rule (descent from legitimized ruling dynasties, the provision of security, the sharing of wealth, patronage of the so-called casted and the weak, respect for men of religion), the more attractive the Murid countermodel became to the masses. The chiefs' loss of credibility primarily benefited the Murid sheikhs, who gradually became the legitimate leaders of the populace in the rural areas of Bawol and Kajoor. Chiefs' complaints about the loss of their authority to Murid sheikhs were echoed by the French denunciation of the fusion of religious and political power in the hands of the Murid leadership, as well as the accusation that Murids tried to create a state within the state. As long as direct rule and cultural hegemony remained important dimensions of colonial thinking and practices, the Murid tariqa remained an obstacle and therefore the enemy.

From 1903 on, important changes in colonial policy and within the Muridiyya gradually helped to diffuse the tension between the Murids and the French colonial administration. One key factor was the critical shift in Muslim policy inaugurated by Governor-General Roume and continued by his successor, Ponty. These two administrators had no affection for Islam, but they adopted a pragmatic and realistic policy toward Muslim clerics. They tried to minimize coercion and instead privileged surveillance and cooperation whenever possible. This policy was different from the Algerian model with which Faidherbe experimented in the mid-1850s and early 1860s, based as it was on a universalistic approach to Islam and the attempt to enlist influential clerics in the French bureaucratic system. Governors Roume and Ponty sought to found their policy on good knowledge of local Islamic culture (which was different, in their views, from Arab, or "pure," Islam), its practitioners, and its inspirers. Unlike Faidherbe, they rejected Islamic jurisprudence as a valid basis for legislation in sub-Saharan Africa, but they recognized relative autonomy and immunity for Islam as a cultural force as long as it did not interfere with or hinder colonial policies. Ponty's *politique des races* further exploited the idea of a different and milder sub-Saharan Islam, which was believed to be politically inoffensive, potentially useful to colonial rule, and therefore tolerable. The image of Islam painted by colonial Islamicists allayed fears of the religion and created a new intellectual mind-set that permitted a better understanding of the motivations and aspirations of Murid sheikhs and disciples, all of which were not necessarily incompatible with colonial rule.

The continuing growth of the Muridiyya and the increasingly important role of Murid disciples in the colony's economy constituted an even greater incentive to find a modus vivendi with the tariqa. Much emphasis has been placed on the correlation between the development of peanuts as a cash crop and the improvement of the relationship between the Murids and the French. Some scholars have even argued that Murid sheikhs, in their capacity as originators of a work ethic that facilitated the supply of massive amounts of cheap labor, were, consciously or subconsciously, important partners of the French administrators in promoting colonial capitalism. I have shown that the changes that led to the rapprochement between the Muridiyya and the French were under way well before peanuts became an important crop in the Murid-dominated areas of Senegal. More important, the reasons why Murids engaged in peanut farming did not differ too much from the reasons why Senegalese of other religious affiliations adopted this crop. Peanuts were conveniently adapted to the soil, climate, rain patterns, and technology available in most areas of Senegal. In addition, they dovetailed well with the food crops grown in the country and did not require a considerable modification of the farmers' work habits. Moreover, like other people in Senegal, Murids needed cash to pay their taxes and for other needs in the market economy imposed by colonization. There is no evidence that Murid identity played a significant role in the peasants' adoption of the crop, nor did the slow death of the Senegalese peanut economy have a negative impact on the development of the Muridiyya.[5]

Another important factor that encouraged French administrators' accommodation to the Muridiyya was their realization that coercion was futile. The confinement of Amadu Bamba to eleven years of exile in Gabon and Mauritania and five years of house arrest in Senegal, along with the continuing pressure on Murid sheikhs, achieved the opposite of the intended outcomes. The Muridiyya became more and more powerful in spite of, and perhaps because of, colonial repression. To the founder's image as a sage and saint was now added that of a martyr and resister who confronted and foiled sinister French plans. Amadu Bamba's ability to survive the ordeal of exile and colonial adversity further convinced people that he had been elected as a *wali Allah* who benefited from divine protection. Similarly, his disciples' faith in his baraka and spiritual power was reinforced. It was apparent that, as in Algeria, coercion would only boost the Murid sheikhs' clout and fortify their disciples' resolve.

The Murids welcomed the French policy of accommodation. From the beginning of his calling, Amadu Bamba had reiterated to colonial authorities his lack of interest in ruling people, his willingness to submit to whatever rulers God chose for him so long as he was guaranteed freedom of worship, and his commitment to limit his actions to guiding his disciples in the right path. He did not see himself as a competitor with the colonial administration for the control of bodies; he was interested in educating the soul and spirit of people. As he wrote in 1910, he was neither a friend nor an enemy of the French. However, though he remained loyal to the colonial administration, Bamba also wanted to limit his contacts with them, just as he had done with Wolof chiefs and other precolonial rulers. In conformity with Sufi tradition, he was willing to act when ordered to do so in domains that did not infringe on Islamic teachings or when he felt that neutrality could be interpreted as a gesture of hostility or rebellion. Improved communication with and proximity to colonial administrators helped him better articulate, adapt, and clarify his positions, and these factors also allowed the colonial administration to better understand his message and weigh its political significance.

Amadu Bamba's permanent settlement in his native land of eastern Bawol in 1912 and the requirement that he live in the European quarter of the town of Diourbel raised new challenges but also opened opportunities for healthier relations with the colonial regime. Like all Muslims under colonial domination, Bamba viewed Christian rule over the land of Islam, despite the French pledge to religious neutrality, as a potential threat to the integrity of his religion. The major question he had to answer was how to reconcile the desire to live the life of a virtuous Muslim with the necessary subjugation to a

Christian power. Bamba had certainly grappled with this question before, but the prospect of spending the rest of his life in geographic proximity to the French made finding a solution more urgent.

His response was to search for spatial and cultural autonomy. This solution was particularly desirable because in the Wolof states, the Islamic identity of a land was historically expressed through Muslim control over geographic space rather than the imposition of sharia rule over a territory and its occupants. Amadu Bamba and his disciples endeavored to create in the *daar al-kufr* (land of unbelief) that Bawol had become because of the pollution of the French presence and rule a *daar al-Islam* (land of Islam) or *daar al-Murid* (land of the Murid). This Murid sacred space was established through physical occupation of the land; the use of Islamic architecture, sacred geometry, and rituals; and the insulation of daar al-Murid against the influence of daar al-kufr. The building of a culturally autonomous Murid space was less contentious in the context of administrative pragmatism, in which assimilation and direct control were no longer priorities. The successful cultural appropriation of the tariqa's heartland assuaged Murid fears of French contamination and proved their organization's ability to survive and prosper under colonial rule. The continuing institutionalization of the Muridiyya made the politics of rapprochement with the French more attractive. Amadu Bamba was still kept under mandatory residence, and as observed by the governor-general after his death in 1927, his loyalty remained "uncertain."[6] There were still frictions, and some powerful sheikhs clashed with authoritarian administrators. Yet there were no longer any doubts among colonial officialdom about the possibility and desirability of working with the tariqa.

Throughout this book, I have tried to tell a history of the Murid tariqa with full attention to Murid voices. This approach is what I have called writing a history of the Muridiyya from within. Meeting this challenge goes beyond a mere incorporation of Murid internal sources and requires of the scholar, as suggested by Frederick Cooper, the willingness to get out of his or her own categories to understand "how people put their thoughts together."[7] The scholar must also recognize that these thoughts could be meaningful bases for actions. The emphasis this study has given to education and religious culture suggests that the history of Muslim institutions in Africa and elsewhere should be reexamined with these dimensions in mind in order to appreciate local initiatives and influences beyond the narrow confines of political collaboration and resistance. The Murid example shows that religious innovations and reforms cannot be viewed as mere forms of social remobilization stimulated by economic or political transformations ushered in through European agency. Religious entrepreneurs were not oblivious to the colonial context—indeed, they strongly felt its influence—but they were deeply motivated by values and aspirations rooted in history, family traditions, and personal ambitions not always reducible to narrow political and materialist aims. Likewise, those who responded to their calling were not merely seeking psychological adjustment, yanked as they were from "peaceful village life" and thrust onto the bewildering world stage by colonizers. They were prompted by deeper spiritual needs and existential anxieties beyond matters of personal survival.

This study has also provided materials to enhance our understanding of how religious authority was built and how this authority affected colonial policy-making. Looking beyond the role played by personal charisma, it has demonstrated the centrality of genealogy, knowledge, and baraka in building the cultural, social, and symbolic capital that are the foundations of religious power. The establishment of power and authority over large segments of the population in turn gave successful Muslim clerics leverage in deciding (consciously or sometimes unconsciously) the ways in which Muslims were to be ruled. Robert Delavignette has convincingly demonstrated that in the colonial context, the most influential were not always those in high positions of power but rather the subalterns (village headmen, African chiefs, district commissioners, and the like) who provided an interface between decisionmakers and the commoners.[8] Although they were not part of the French administrative hierarchy (in contrast to the so-called British indirect rule) influential Muslim clerics exercised similar influence. Through their actions and silences or their mere presence, they exerted strong pressure on those responsible for elaborating Muslim policies. They not only found niches in the colonial system in which to thrive but also sometimes were able to move the system itself in unforeseen directions.[9]

Appendix 1

Ijaaza *Delivered to Momar A. Sali by Samba Tukuloor Ka*

Praise to God alone, peace be upon the seal of prophecy.

May the man of knowledge and wisdom who sees this document understand that *Sidy ad daar* [Master of the house, the nickname that Samba Tukuloor Ka gave himself] has given permission [meaning the ability to use] and authorization [meaning the ability to distribute] to Muhammad son of Habib Allah [Momar Anta Sali Mbakke] his brother in the path of God and of the sheikh [Sheikh Sidiyya al-Kabir], for the use of the *qadiri* wird and the orientations originating from Sheikh Mukhtaar and Sheikh Muhammad, in conformity with the order that the latter has given him face to face, may God be satisfied with them.

[I have given him the permission and authorization] because I know that he is up to the task of using it and giving it to those who are qualified to receive it, and in the hopes that he will be among the pillars of our religion (surely God is the fulfiller of prayers), and because Sheikh Sidiyya's family asked me to write this authorization for him when the time comes.

Appendix 2

Sharifian Genealogy of Amadu Bamba from His Mother's Side

The Prophet Muhammad
Fatimatu bint Rasuul
Al-Hassan
Shafiyatu
Abdulahi
Jalihatu
Musa
Muhammad Dawud
Taysis
Yahya
Abdulahi
Shafih
Musa Buso
Abd al-Qadir Buso
Muhammad Buso
Abdulahi Buso
Ibrahim Buso
Hasan Buso
Sulayman Buso
Zakariyya Buso
Ishmahila Buso
Ibrahima Buso
Uthman Buso
Aliu Buso
Isa Buso
Abubakr Buso
Abdrahman Buso
Buseyri Buso
Abdu Buso

    Sulayman Buso
    Muhammad Hamin Buso
    Abd el-Karim Buso
    Aliun Buso
    Seydi Buso
    Abubakr Buso
    Bukhaari Buso
    Aliu Buso
    Amsatu Buso
    Matabara Buso
Serigne Modu Buso
Sokhna Jaara Buso
Sheikh Amadu Bamba

Appendix 3

Amadu Bamba's Sons and Daughters and Their Mothers

SONS

MOTHERS

Muhamad al-Kabiir — Faati Masamba Joob
Muhamad al-Yadaali — Maryamu Balla
Caliph Muhamad Mustafaa (1888–1945) — Aminata Lo
Caliph Muhamad Falilu (1888–1967) — Awa Buso
Muhamad al-Amin (Baara) (1890–1939) — Aminata Lo
Muhamad al-Bashir (Basiru) (1895–1966) — Faati Madu Maam
Abdul Aziiz (1909–1960) — Faatima Kabiir
Ibrahima I (1911–?) — Faatima Saghiir
Caliph Abdul Ahad (1914–89) — Mariama Jakhate
Caliph Abdul Khaadir (1914–89) — Aminata Buso
Caliph Sheikh Salih (1915–) — Faati Jakhate
Sheikh Shuhaib (1917–1991) — Mariama Jakhate
Abdulahi Samad (1917–?) — Khari Sylla
Abdul Baakhe 1 — Faati Jakhate
Abd al Hamin — Khari Penda Faal
Abdu as Salaam — Kumba Jakhate
Mukhtaar Balla — Khari Penda Faal
Abd al-Mukhtaar — Khari Joob
Abd al-Wahab — Faati Jakhate
Ibrahima II — Aisatu Joob
Abd al-Muhaymin — Faatim Tuuti
Babakar as-Sadiikh — Aminata Joob
Muhamad Murtada (1924–2004) — Faatim Ture
Babakar — Khari Penda Faal
Ahmidun — Faatim Tuuti
Muhamad Abdulahi — Anta Buso
Muhamadu I — Penda Siise

Muhamadu II	Faati Sylla
Abdul Khuduuss	Faati Jakhate
Salihu	Faati Jakhate
Abdul Baakhe II	Faati Jakhate
Al Baawi	Faati Jakhate
Abdulahi	Faati Joob

DAUGHTERS	MOTHERS
Faati jah Mbakke	Sokhna Jah Ture
Umu Kaltum	Mbenda or Penda Ture
Mariam Kunta	Awa Buso
Haasiyatu	Faati Masamba
Faati	Mbenda Buya?
Ruqiyatu	Faatim Tuuti
Njooba	Faatim Tuuti
Muslimatu I	Faatim Tuuti
Faatimatu I	Khadijatu Joob
Ayshatu	Khadijatu Joob
Aminatu I	Mariyama Jakhate
Muslimatu II	Mbeen Jakhate
Mashkuratu	Faati Sylla
Khadijatu I	Faati Madu Maam
Maryamma	Mbeen Jakhate
Zahiratu	Maryama Jakhate
Faatimatu II	Faati Jakhate
Maymuna I	Njakhat Sylla
Faatimatu III	Khari Sylla
Aminatu II	Awa Buso
Maymuna II	Sokhna Buso
Muminatu	Faati Sylla
Salimatu	Aminata Joob
Fatimatu IV	Maryama Jakhate
Khadijatu II	Aminata Buso
Maymuna III	Sokhna Sylla Saghiir

Appendix 4

List of the Transmitters of the Qadiriyya wird *Whom Amadu Praises in His Poem "Silsilat ul Qadiriyya"*

The Prophet Muhammad
Ali (fourth caliph of Islam)
Al-Basri (Hassan al-Basri)
Habib al-Hajami
Dayhud al-Talahi
Mahul karji
Al-Shifti
Al-Hubaydi
Shibli
Ahmad al-Baki
Ashbahi
Abil Wakhayi
Al-Imam Jili (Abd Al-Qadir Al-Jilani)
Ibn Hitah
Abil Najiibi Muhammdin
Al-Hatiimi
Abdi Salaam
Ali
Al-Ghazali
Al-Mushdaari
Al-Tlimsaani
Ibn Arabi
An Ahli al-Kariim
Al Suyuuti
Al-Mahli
Human
Al-Humaami
Muhammada

Al-Maghili
Ali
Ahmada
Nadhbi
Ibn Najib
Al-Mukhataari
Muhammadun
Sheikh Sidiyya al-Kabir
Sidy Muhammad
Sidiyya Baba
Amadu Bamba

Notes

INTRODUCTION

1. See Paul Marty, *Études sur l'Islam au Sénégal*, vol. 1 (Paris: E. Leroux, 1917). Also see his "Les mourides d'Amadou Bamba: Rapport à M. le gouverneur général de l'Afrique Occidentale," *Revue du Monde Musulman* 25 (December 1913): 1–164.

2. Marty was undoubtedly the one French specialist of Islam who had the most influence on colonial Muslim policy in sub-Saharan Africa. For more on the biography of Marty, see Feuillet personnel de Paul Marty, Dossier personnel de l'interprète Lieutenant Colonel Paul Marty, Archives Militaires Françaises, Paris, Château de Vincennes and L. Bercher, "Nécrologie de Paul Marty," *Revue Tunisienne* 33–34 (1938): 15–17.

3. "Islam noir" was conceived of as a corrupt form of Islam characterized by a mixture of traditional African culture and Islamic religious beliefs. It was opposed to the so-called pure or real Islam of the Middle East. For more on this question, see P. J. André, *L'Islam noir* (Paris: Geuthner, 1924); Vincent Monteil, *L'Islam noir* (Paris: Le Seuil, 1980); Mafakha Touré, "Critique historique d'un concept: L'Islam noir" (Mémoire de maîtrise, Université Cheikh Anta Diop de Dakar, 1990–91).

4. The national census of 1988 indicated that 30.1 percent of the Senegalese people living in the country were Murid, which would correspond to 3,311,000 persons today. See Ministère de l'Économie et des Finances, *Direction des Statistiques: Recensement de la population et de l'habitat 1988, rapport national de juin 1993*, "Tableau I-15, Répartition de la population résident selon la religion et la région." Circumstantial evidence, however, suggests that since the census was taken, the percentage of Murids has considerably increased. Tuubaa, the holy city of the Muridiyya, has an estimated population of nearly 1 million, and the number of pilgrims attending the annual Murid religious celebration, or *maggal*, is estimated by journalists at nearly 2 million. The figure of 4 million for 2005 that I am suggesting may, then, not be too far from the exact number, especially if one considers that a large percentage of the nearly 1-million-strong Senegalese diaspora dispersed around the world belongs to the Muridiyya.

5. The maggal (the name is taken from the Wolof word *magg*, meaning "grow," "magnify," or "celebrate") commemorates the date of the first arrest and exile of Amadu Bamba to Gabon, in 1895. It takes place annually in the holy city of Tuubaa around the great mosque, where Bamba and some of his sons are buried.

6. Since at least 2002, the *Times* has published articles on the Murids on the eve of the maggal. See, for example, Norimitsu Onishi, "Industrious Muslims Run a Vatican," *New York Times*, 2 May 2002, A10, and Holland Cotter, "Caught Up in the Aura of a Senegalese Saint," *New York Times*, 16 February 2005, E1. This last piece is an extended review of an exhibit on Murid visual piety at the University of Florida–Gainesville by anthropologists Allen and Mary N. Roberts. For the BBC posting, see www.bbc.co.uk, 29–31 March 2005.

7. *Tariqa* (*turuuq* is the Arabic plural) is often translated as "Muslim brotherhood" or "Muslim order" and sometimes "Dervish" in English. The tariqa is an organization that regroups Sufi disciples around a sheikh. For more on tariqas, see the discussion later in this chapter. In this book, I have refrained as much as possible from using the term *Muslim brotherhood* to avoid the gender connotation that this expression may imply. In reality, tariqas accept women as well as men, and sometimes, women may enjoy prominent positions of power in them.

8. For more on these issues, see Jean Copans, *Les marabouts de l'arachide*, 2nd ed. (Paris: Harmattan, 1988) and his "Mourides des champs, mourides des villes, mourides du téléphone portable et de l'Internet: Les renouvellements de l'économie politique d'une confrérie," *Afrique Contemporaine* 194 (April–June 2000): 24–33; Donal B. Cruise O'Brien and Christian Coulon, eds., *Charisma and Brotherhood in African Islam* (London: Oxford, 1988); and Mamadou Diouf, "Commerce et cosmopolitisme: Le cas des diasporas mourides du Sénégal," *Bulletin du Codesria* 1 (2000): 20–29.

9. The Senegalese sociologist and librarian Momar Coumba Diop offers a survey of this literature. See his "La littérature mouride: Essai d'analyse thématique et critique" (Mémoire présenté sous la direction de Jean François Maurel, École Nationale Supérieure de Bibliothécaires Paris, 1978). Jean Copans estimates four thousand pages of scholarly studies were devoted to the Murids between 1965 and 1980, in addition to four thousand pages authored by colonial administrators specializing in the history of Islam in Senegal. See Copans, *Les marabouts*, 31. It is probable that in the quarter century following the first publication of his book (in 1980), the number of pages dedicated to the Muridiyya in all languages had passed four thousand.

10. Prominent among these scholars are Lucy Behrman, "The Political Significance of Adherence to Muslim Brotherhoods in the 19th Century," *African Historical Studies* 1 (1968): 60–78; "Ahmad Bamba," in John Ralph Willis, ed., *The Cultivators of Islam*, Studies in West African Islamic History 1 (London: Frank Cass, 1979); Irving Leonard Markovitz, "Traditional Social Structure, the Islamic Brotherhoods, and Political Development in Senegal," *Journal of Modern African Studies* 8 (April 1970): 73–96; Donal B. Cruise O'Brien, *The Mourides of Senegal:*

The Political and Economic Organization of an Islamic Brotherhood in Senegal (Oxford: Clarendon Press, 1971); Christian Coulon, *Le marabout et le prince: Islam et pouvoir au Sénégal* (Paris: Pedone, 1981); and Leonardo Vilallòn, "Sufi Rituals as Rallies: Religious Ceremonies in the Politics of Senegalese State-Society Relations," *Comparative Politics* 26 (July 1994): 415–37.

11. Donal B. Cruise O'Brien, *Saints and Politicians* (London: Cambridge University Press, 1975); L. Vilallòn, *Islamic Society and State Power in Senegal: Disciples and Citizens in Fatick* (Cambridge: Cambridge University Press, 1995); and Linda J. Beck "'Patrimonial Democrats' in a Culturally Plural Society: Democratization and Political Accommodation in Patronage Politics of Senegal" (PhD diss., University of Wisconsin–Madison, 1996). For new interpretations of the Senegalese social contracts, see Donal B. Cruise O'Brien, "Le contrat social sénégalais à l'épreuve," *Politique Africaine* 45 (1992): 9–20; Donal B. Cruise O'Brien, M. C. Diop, and M. Diouf, *La construction de l'état au Sénégal* (Paris: Karthala, 2002); and Donal B. Cruise O'Brien, *Symbolic Confrontations: Muslims Imagining the State in Africa* (New York: Palgrave Macmillan, 2003), esp. chap. 9.

12. See Copans, *Les marabouts*; M. C. Diop, "La confrérie mouride: Organisation politique et mode d'implantation urbaine" (Thèse de troisième cycle sous la direction du professeur Jean Girard, UER de Psychology et des Sciences Sociales, Université de Lyon 2, 1980); Gérard Salem, "De la brousse sénégalaise au Boul'Mich: Le système commercial mouride en France," *Cahiers d'Études Africaines* 21 (1981): 267–88, "De Dakar à Paris, des diasporas d'artisans et de commerçants: Étude socio-géographique du commerce sénégalais en France" (Thèse de doctorat de troisième cycle EHESS, Paris, 1983); Donald Carter, "Invisible Cities: From Tuba to Turin—The Senegalese Transnational Migrants in Northern Italy" (PhD diss., University of Chicago, 1992); Victoria Ebin, "Camelots à New York": Les pionniers de l'immigration sénégalaise," *Hommes et Migrations* 1160 (December 1992): 32–37; "À la recherche de nouveaux 'poissons': Stratégies commerciales mourides par temps de crise," *Politique Africaine* (1992): 86–99; "Les commerçants mourides à Marseille et à New York," in *Grands commerçants d'Afrique de l'Ouest*, ed. Emmanuel Grégoire and Pascal Labazée (Paris: ORSTOM, 1993), 101–23; Scott L. Malcolmson, "West of Eden: The Mouride Ethic and the Spirit of Capitalism," *Transition* 71 (1996): 24–43; Sylviane Diouf-Camara, "Senegalese in New York: A Model Minority?" trans. Richard Philcox, *Black Renaissance/Renaissance Noire* 2 (Summer-Fall 1997): 95–115; and Sophie Bava, "De la *baraka* aux affaires: Ethos économico-religieux et transnationalité chez les migrants sénégalais mourides," *Revue Européenne de Migrations Internationales* 19 (2003): 69–84.

13. Vincent Monteil, *Esquisses sénégalaises*, Initiations et Études Africaines 21 (Dakar: IFAN, 1966); Monteil, *L'Islam noir* (Paris: Le Seuil, 1980); Amar Samb, *Essai sur la contribution du Sénégal à la litérature d'expression arabe* (Dakar: IFAN, 1971); Samb, "L'Islam et l'histoire du Sénégal," *BIFAN* ser. B, 33 (1971): 461–507; Fernand Dumont, *La pensée religieuse d'Amadou Bamba* (Dakar:

Nouvelles Éditions Africaines, 1975); and Khadim Mbacké, *Sufism and Religious Brotherhoods in Senegal*, trans. Eric Ross, ed. John Hunwick (Princeton, NJ: Markus Wiener, 2005).

14. Cruise O'Brien, *The Mourides*, 37–38.

15. See, for example, David Robinson, "The Murids: Surveillance and Accommodation," *Journal of African History* (henceforth *JAH*) 40 (1999): 13–21; Robinson, *Paths of Accommodation: Muslim Societies and French Colonial Authorities in Senegal and Mauritania, 1880–1920* (Athens: Ohio University Press, 2000).

16. Richard Eaton, *The Rise of Islam and the Bengal Frontier, 1204–1760* (Berkeley: University of California Press, 1993), 267.

17. Terence Ranger, "Religious Movements and Politics in Sub-Saharan Africa," *African Studies Review* 29 (1986): 2.

18. Louis Brenner's works on Islamic mysticism and education and John Hunwick's research on the role of Muslim *ulama*, literacy, and thought are important exceptions to this trend.

19. Ranger, "Religious Movements," 3.

20. Louis Brenner, "Concepts of Târiqa in West Africa," in *Charisma and Brotherhood in African Islam*, ed. Donal B. Cruise O'Brien and Christian Coulon (Oxford: Clarendon Press, 1988), 35.

21. Amadou Bamba Mbacké, "Munawwiru s-Suduur" [The Enlightening of the Heart], in *Recueil de poèmes en sciences religieuses du serviteur du Prophète, le fondateur du mouridisme*, trans. Serigne Sam Mbaye et al., vol. 2 (Rabat: Dar El Kitab, 1989), 203. Amadu Bamba's view on jihad is shared by Sufis who distinguish between what they call *al jihad al-akbar*, the greater jihad directed against one's carnal soul or lower self, and *al jihad al-asghar*, or the smaller jihad, which is commonly known as jihad of the sword. For an extensive discussion of this question, see Gerhard Böwering, "Règles et rituels soufis," in *Les voies d'Allah*, ed. Alexandre Popovic and Gilles Veinstein (Paris: Fayard, 1996), 139.

22. Richard M. Eaton, *Sufis of Bijapur, 1300–1700: Social Roles of Sufis in Medieval India* (Princeton, NJ: Princeton University Press, 1978). For studies of Uthman dan Fodio and Al-Hajj Umar Tal, see Murray Last, *The Sokoto Caliphate* (New York: Humanities Press, 1967); Mervyn Hiskett, *The Sword of Truth* (New York: Oxford University Press, 1973); David Robinson, *The Holy War of Umar Tal: The Western Sudan in the Mid-nineteenth Century* (Oxford: Clarendon Press, 1985); and Madina Ly Tall, *Un Islam militant en Afrique de l'Ouest au XIXe siècle: La Tijaniyya de Saiku Umar Futiyu contre les pouvoirs tradtionnels et la puissance coloniale* (Paris: Harmattan, 1991).

23. See Annemarie Schimmel, *Mystical Dimensions of Islam* (Chapel Hill: University of North Carolina Press, 1974).

24. J. Spencer Trimingham, *The Sufi Orders in Islam* (Oxford: Clarendon Press, 1971).

25. For more on this important Sufi concept, see discussion later in this chapter.

26. Eaton, *Sufis of Bijapur*, xxi.

27. See Trimingham, *Sufi Orders*, 72.

28. See David Robinson and Jean-Louis Triaud, eds., *Le temps des Marabouts: Itinéraires et stratégies islamiques en Afrique Occidentale Française v. 1880–1960* (Paris: Karthala, 1997).

29. For a survey of this Islamic literature in Africa, see John Hunwick and R. S. O'Fahey, general eds., *Arabic Literature of Africa* (Leiden: E. J. Brill, 1994–).

30. His *Kitab Rimah hizb al-Rahim* (published in the margins of *Kitab Jawahir al-Ma'ani wa Bulugh al-Amani* [The Book of the Pearl of Meaning], by Ali Harazim [Cairo, 1927]) is one of the most important sources on the doctrine and practices of the Tijaniyya tariqa.

31. On the persona of Elhaj Malick Sy and his role in the development of the Tijaniyya in Senegal, see Rawane Mbaye, "L'Islam au Sénégal" (Thèse de doctorat de troisième cycle Université de Dakar, 1975–76); Mbaye, "La pensée et l'action de Elhadji Malick Sy" (Thèse de doctorat d'état Sorbonne Nouvelle, 1992–93) (this doctoral thesis has been published in a three-volume book); El Hadji Malick Fall, "Elhadji Malick Sy au Oualo" (Mémoire de maîtrise, Faculté des Lettres de l'Université de Dakar, Département Arabe, 1994–95); El Hadji Samba Amadou Diallo, "La transmission des statuts et des pouvoirs dans la Tijaniyya sénégalaise: Le cas de la famille Sy de Tivaouane" (Thèse de doctorat de troisième cycle en anthropologie sociale, ethnologie et ethnographie, EHESS, 2005).

32. Vincent Cornell, *Realm of the Saint: Power and Authority in Moroccan Sufism* (Austin: University of Texas Press, 1998), xxv.

33. Marty, *Islam au Sénégal*, 1:3.

34. Cornell, *Realm of the Saint*, xxvi.

35. See Julian Glancy-Smith, "Barakah," in *The Oxford Encyclopedia of the Modern Islamic World*, vol. 1 (New York: Oxford University Press, 1995), 199.

36. Weber's charismatic leader appears in a time of crisis and acts as a revolutionary who breaks with tradition. Charisma, in Weber's view, is typically an antieconomic force, and the charismatic authority repudiates involvement in the everyday routine of life. The charismatic leader's influence is solely based on his followers' belief in his supernatural powers. According to Weber, charisma is unstable and short-lived, and it becomes quickly routinized in the traditional or rational forms of authority after the death of the charismatic leader. See Max Weber, *The Theory of Social and Economic Organization*, ed. Talcott Parsons (New York: Free Press, 1964), 359–64. Scholars who have tried to apply Weber's ideal type of charismatic leader to the baraka-laden Sufi saint of Islam have run into significant empirical problems. Cruise O'Brien and Coulon experienced some of these difficulties when they used the Weberian concept of charisma as a conceptual framework for analyzing different Muslim movements and saints in sub-Saharan Africa; see their *Charisma and Brotherhood in African Islam*, esp. Cruise O'Brien's introduction to the edited volume. They resorted to using the expression *not quite charisma* but still could not overcome the skepticism and doubts of some of the researchers involved in the project about the validity and pertinence of the concept

regarding Muslim sainthood. Their consultant, who specializes in charismatic movements, discouraged the application of the concept to the case studies in hand, and one of the contributors chose not to use the word *charisma* in his chapter. On the difficulties of applying the Weberian concept of charisma to religion and Islam in particular, see also Glen Wade McLaughlin, "Sufi Saint, Sharif Muhammad Fadil Wuld Mamin: His Spiritual Legacy, and the Political Economy of the Sacred in Nineteenth Century Mauritania" (PhD diss., Northwestern University, 1997), 7–11; David M. Anderson and Douglas H. Johnson, *Revealing Prophets: Prophecy in Eastern African History* (Athens: Ohio University Press, 1995), 11–12. For a recent attempt to apply Weberian conceptual categories to Islam in West Africa, see John H. Hanson, *Migration, Jihad, and Muslim Authority in West Africa* (Bloomington: Indiana University Press, 1996).

37. This portrayal owes as much to the traditional Wolof conception of the mother's role and place in the family as to the local Islamic culture. There is a Wolof saying that sums up this conception: "Legee yu ndey agnub doom," which translates as "A child's destiny is determined by his mother's labor [in the household]."

38. For more on Maam Jaara Buso and her image in contemporary Muridiyya, see Eva Evers Rosander, "Mam Diarra Bousso, la bonne mère de Porokhane, Sénégal," *Africa* 58, nos. 3–4 (2003): 296–317. The popular Senegalese female pop star Fatu Gewel Diouf has recently dedicated a song to Jaara Buso, urging women to prepare proudly for porokhaan and celebrating the fact that she is the only woman to deserve a maggal. For more on the use of Muslim religious figures by popular Senegalese musicians, see Fiona McLaughlin, "'In the Name of God I Will Sing Again, Mawdo Malick the Good': Popular Music and Senegalese Sufi Tariqas," *Journal of Religion in Africa* 30, no. 2 (2000): 191–207.

39. The word *karama* (or its plural, *karamat*) is not found in the Quran; it is, however, attested in the *hadiths*, or traditions of Prophet Muhammad. Miracles are such an important part of the political economy of sainthood in Islam that some authors discern what they call a doctrine of miracles. Proponents of this view speak of the taxonomy of miracles based on the nature of the miracle (a gift or a power), its object (the saint or his relations with the outside world), its means (invocations, sermons), and its aims (to teach, reword, or punish). See Denis Gril, "Le miracle en Islam: Critère de la sainteté?" in D. Aigle, ed., *Saints orientaux* (Paris: De Boccard, 1995): 69.

40. Kalabadhi, one of the earliest and most influential theoreticians of Sufism, affirmed that the karamas of saints derive from the *mudjizas* of prophets and constitute evidence of the truthfulness of the prophetic message; quoted in ibid., 72.

41. Amadu Bamba Mbacké, *Massalik Al-Jinan (Les itinéraires du paradis)* (Rabat: Dar El Kitab, 1984), 60.

42. I have conducted extensive interviews with fifty Murid disciples, sheikhs, and Muslims belonging to other tariqas in the Murid heartland of eastern Bawol; in areas of the precolonial kingdom of Kajoor associated with the history of the Mbakke; and in Saint-Louis, Thiès, and Dakar, all major cities of Senegal. I have

worked at the library of Tuubaa and have also consulted private archives and collected audiocassettes produced by popular Murid preachers. I conducted all the interviews in Wolof and made the transcriptions and translations. Although very few interviewees objected to my citing their names regarding specific questions, I have decided, when dealing with sensitive issues, to alter the names of some of my informants to protect their privacy. I have done this on only a very few occasions.

43. See Luise White, Stephan Miescher, and David W. Cohen, eds., *African Words, African Voices: Critical Practices in Oral History* (Bloomington: Indiana University Press, 2001), 19.

44. Jack Goody, *The Power of the Written Tradition* (Washington, DC: Smithsonian Institution Press, 2000), 118.

45. For more on the conflicts and divisions within the Mbakke family, see chapters 2 and 3 of this book.

46. I am particularly indebted to Isa Mbakke in Tuubaa, a great-grandson of Ibra Mbakke Awa Niang, a son of Maaram, Amadu Bamba's great-grandfather; Sheikh Maam Balla Mbakke in Mbakke Bawol, also a great-grandson of one of Maaram's sons; and Serigne Mustafa Njaate Mbakke, who descended from an agnate branch of Amadu Bamba's great-grandfather, for their insightful information on the history of the Mbakke family.

47. Isa Mbakke informed me that he was often summoned by Sheikh Saliu Mbakke, the last living son of Amadu Bamba and the caliph of the Muridiyya, to discuss the history of the family and sort out issues of land tenure; Interview in Tuubaa, 2 July 2000. During my research, I have personally experienced how little most of the descendants of Amadu Bamba know about their history. Of course, many of these people, who are grandsons or great-grandsons of Amadu Bamba, do not need genealogy to prove their blood relations with the founder of the Muridiyya.

48. My awareness of this divide gradually emerged as I noticed discrepancies and silences in versions of stories told by different informants. As I looked at the names and families of these interviewees, I realized that two types of discourses stood out and roughly matched two categories of persons: those bearing the last names Jakhate, Sylla, Syll, Mbay, and Niang, easily identifiable as belonging to old clerical families, and all the rest.

49. In Wolof, the name of the inhabitants of a region is often formed by repeating the name of the place where they live: for example, Bawol-Bawol refers to people living in Bawol, Njambur-Njambur to people living in Njambur; Ajoor, the name given to people living in Kajoor, constitutes an exception. My attention was called to this rift first during an interview with Al-Hajj Sylla, a Quranic teacher in the village of Cilawel near Mbakke Kajoor. When talking about Amadu Bamba's departure from Kajoor and his settlement in Bawol between 1884 and 1885, Sylla noted that among the Mbakke, there were people who liked Kajoor and those who preferred Bawol and that, in the past, members of these two groups did not want to have much to do with each other; Interview, Mbakke Kajoor, 20

July 2000. Later, in interviews with Abdu Samat Sylla in Diourbel and Isa Mbakke in Tuubaa, the terms *penku-penku* and *ajoor* resurfaced again but this time in reference to the sojourn of Amadu Bamba in Diourbel from 1912 and the tensions between Murid sheikhs after his death in 1927.

50. The most dramatic episode of this conflict played out during the settlement of Amadu Bamba's assets after his death. Oral sources tell us that the leading figure of the penku-penku faction, Amadu Bamba's half brother, Sheikh Anta, summoned Mamadu Mustafa, the elder son, either to buy the assets or to let his brothers who had the means do so. As prescribed by Islam, Mamadu Mustafa asked for a forty-day recess to think about the proposal. He took advantage of the time he was given to raise the necessary funds within his maternal clan. Historians of Mamadu Mustafa's lineage tell us that Sheikh Anta, who was very wealthy, was backing Falilu Mbakke (his mother was from eastern Bawol), the second oldest son of Amadu Bamba and ally to the penku-penku, for whom he intended to buy the inheritance. In a letter to Governor Brévié, probably written in 1928 or 1929, Sheikh Mbacké Bousso, who also originated from eastern Bawol, denied the accusation leveled against Sheikh Anta and presented a strong defense of Amadu Bamba's brothers, then under pressure from the French colonial administration to accept the leadership of their nephew. See Serigne Mbacké Bousso, "Deux traités d'un lettré religieux Sénégalais (1864–1945)," translated from the Arabic by Khadim Mbacké (paper, 1994).

51. See Pierre Nora, *Les lieux de mémoire*, vol. 1, *La république* (Paris: Gallimard, 1984), xxxv.

52. *Majmuha* is a compilation of letters, sermons, conversations, and advice to the disciples by Amadu Bamba in Arabic, collected and published by his son and the third caliph of the Muridiyya, Abdul Ahad Mbacké. See A. L. Mbacké, *Majmuha* (Touba: A. A. Mbacké, 1985).

53. For an extensive discussion of Amadu Bamba's writings, see Dumont, *La pensée*, and Samb, *Essai sur la contribution*.

54. Leili Anvar-Chenderoff, "Le genre hagiographique à travers la *tadhkirat al-awliyā* de Farīd al-dīn 'attār," in Aigle, *Saints orientaux*, 41.

55. Michel de Certeau, "Hagiographie," in *Encyclopaedia Universalis*, vol. 11 (Paris, 1992), 161.

56. As quoted in A. Roberts and M. N. Roberts, *A Saint in the City: Sufi Arts of Urban Senegal* (Los Angeles: UCLA Fowler Museum, 2003), 85.

57. Trimingham, *Sufi Orders*, 31. See also John Ralph Willis, *In the Path of Allah: The Passion of Al-Hajj 'Umar* (London: Cass, 1989). Willis observes that the charismatic figure strains the capacity of his iconographers and proves to be a highly unstable figure for biographical treatment (xii).

58. De Certeau, "Hagiographie," 161.

59. Éric Geoffroy, "Hagiographie et typologie spirituelle à l'époque mamelouke," in Aigle, *Saints orientaux*, 89.

60. Eaton, *Sufis of Bijapur*, 11.

61. For a more extensive discussion of this issue, see chapter 5 in this book.

62. As quoted in Cornell, *Realm of the Saint*, 199. J. R. Willis prefers the expression *imitatio nabi*; see *In the Path*, xi.

63. For a broader discussion of this question, see Geoffroy, "Hagiographie et typologie spirituelle."

64. See Hippolyte Delehaye, *Cinq leçons sur la méthode hagiographique* (Brussels: Société des Bollandistes, 1934), esp. chap. 1.

65. See Bachir Mbacké, *Minan El Bakhil al Khadim*, trans. from Arabic to French by Khadim Mbacké as *Les bienfaits de l'éternel* (Dakar, 1995).

66. Cheikh Muhammad Lamine Diop Dagana, *Irwā-unnadim min 'adhbi hubb al khadim*, translated into French and edited by Khadim Mbacké as *L'abreuvement du commensal dans la douce source d'amour du Cheikh al-Khadim* (Dakar: IFAN, Département d'Islamologie, n.d.).

67. Both authors considered their works as pious deeds for which they expected God's blessings. See Mbacké, *Les bienfaits*, 12, and Diop, *Irwā*, 135. Similar motivations were evoked by Muslim authors of biographies and hagiographies of saints. See Chouki El Hamel, *La vie intellectuelle islamique dans le Sahel ouest-africain, XVIe–XIXe siècles* (Paris: Harmattan, 2002), 37–38.

68. Mbacké, *Les bienfaits*, 11.

69. Diop, *Irwā*, 135.

70. Mbacké, *Les bienfaits*, 25.

71. The Murids were clearly aware of what French orientalists and colonial writers thought about their organization. In 1963, at the official inauguration of the Great Mosque of Tuubaa—which, with its 86-meter-high minaret, was the biggest mosque in Africa and one of the largest in the world—the caliph, through his spokesperson, presented the event as a permanent refutation of Paul Marty, who described the Muridiyya as a corrupted Wolof version of Islam. See a copy of the discourse in *Groupe Fallou-Galass-Magazine*, no. 2 (April-May, n.d.), special issue, "La Grande Mosquée de Touba," pt. 2, 1945–1968, 15.

72. The master's thesis that I defended in 1991, which looked at the early history of the Muridiyya, was the first historical work devoted to the organization at UCAD. A revised version of this thesis was published under the title "Autour de la genèse du mouridisme," in *Islam et Sociétés au Sud du Sahara* 11 (1997): 5–38. The shorter DEA thesis ("Touba, genèse et évolution d'une cité musulmane au Sénégal" [Mémoire de DEA Université de Dakar, 1992]) was a brief study of the history and contemporary development of the Murid holy city of Tuubaa.

73. See Marty, *L'Islam au Sénégal*, 261–71.

74. The most recent acknowledgment of the credibility and intellectual authority of Marty's interpretation of the Muridiyya is found in Adriana Piga's *Dakar et les ordres Soufis* (Paris: Harmattan, 2002), where she writes, "'It is the chorus that plays the leading role' this interpretation of Paul Marty has maintained its pertinence, and all the recent studies of the founder of the Muridiyya have confirmed the validity of the French administror's analyses" (75); and in Donal B.

Cruise O'Brien, who credits Marty as the inventor of the so-called Senegalese social contract; see D. B. Cruise O'Brien, M. C. Diop, and M. Diouf, *La construction de l'etat au Sénégal*, 84. Also see Cruise O'Brien, *Symbolic Confrontations*, esp. chap. 9. The enduring popularity of Marty's work on the Murids is even more intriguing in that it was received with much reserve and caution by French scholars of Islam; some even doubted its scientific validity. In fact, when Governor-General William Ponty sent Marty's article to the *Revue du Monde Musulman* (*RMM*), members of the journal's editorial board felt it necessary to write a disclaimer in which they dissociated themselves from Marty's analysis and interpretations. They first warned their readership that the article was, in reality, an administrative report destined for the colonial administration. They then proceeded to expound on their disagreement with Marty's main argument, that the Muridiyya was a new religion. They noted that it was more appropriate to classify the Murid tariqa among the mystic Sufi orders such as those found in South Asia, which are at the extreme fringes of Islam but still part of it. They also observed that Marty's article was not the work of a specialist of Islam but rather the report of a civil servant whose major aim was to help maintain order. The editors added that Marty was dealing with issues that were familiar to scholars of Islam but might be less familiar to functionaries like Marty himself who specialized in other domains. See *RMM* 25 (1913): 1–2. In the late 1960s, Lucy Behrman had called attention to Marty's prejudices against African Muslims and the weakness of his work, but she observed "there is little material to contrast with *Études sur l'Islam au Sénégal*." See Behrman, "The Islamization of the Wolof," in *Western African History*, ed. Daniel F. McCall, Norman R. Bennett, and Jeffrey Butler, Boston University Papers on Africa 4 (New York: Praeger, 1969), 116. More recently, Cruise O'Brien and others have criticized the racist biases in Marty's work, while still agreeing with the substance of his interpretation.

75. See, for example, Eric Ross, "Touba et ses soeurs" (Mémoire de maîtrise, McGill University, 1989); Ross, "Touba, a Spiritual Metropolis in the Modern World," *Canadian Journal of African Studies* 29 (1995): 222–59; Ross, "Tubâ: An African Eschatology in Islam" (PhD diss., McGill University, 1996); Cheikh Guèye, *Touba: La capitale des Mourides* (Paris: Karthala, 2002); and Roberts and Roberts, *A Saint in the City*.

76. James Searing, *God Alone Is King* (Portsmouth, NH: Heinemann, 2001).

77. See Richard Roberts's review of *God Alone Is King*, in *International Journal of African Historical Studies* (henceforth *IJAHS*) 35, no. 1 (2002): 222–24, and David Robinson's review article about the same book, "Islam, Cash Crops, and Emancipation," *JAH* 44 (2003): 139–44.

78. Robinson, "Islam," 144.

79. Victor Turner, *The Ritual Process: Structure and Anti-structure* (Chicago: Aldine, 1969), 2.

80. Paul Ricoeur, *Figuring the Sacred: Religion, Narrative, and Imagination* (Minneapolis, MN: Fortress Press, 1995), 217.

CHAPTER 1

1. For more on the history of the Wolof, see David Gamble, *The Wolof of Senegambia* (London: International African Institute, 1957). Yoro Jaw is a French-trained African chief, member of the aristocracy of Waalo, and important source on the history of the Wolof. Jaw is also the most authoritative source on Wolof culture, and his notebooks on the history and culture of the Wolof, edited and published by the French high school teacher R. Rousseau, are a primary source on the history of the Wolof states. See Rousseau, "Les cahiers de Yoro Dyâo: Étude sur le Walo," *Bulletin du Comité d'Études Historiques et Scientifiques de l'Afrique Occidentale Française* (henceforth BCEHSAOF) 1–2 (1929): 133–211, and "Études sur le Cayor," *BCEHSAOF* 16 (1933): 237–98. See also Amadou Wade, whose work on the kingdom of Waalo was collected and edited by Vincent Monteil in *Esquisses sénégalaises, initiations et études Africaines* (Dakar: IFAN, 1966), 13–71;Victoria Bomba "The Pre-nineteenth Century Political Tradition of the Wolof," *BIFAN* ser. B, 34 (1974): 1–14; and Mamadou Diouf, *Histoire du Sénégal: Le modèle Islamo-Wolof et ses périphéries* (Paris: Maisonneuve and Larose, 2001).

2. See Vincent Monteil, "Al Bakri (Cordoue, 1068), routier de l'Afrique blanche et noire," *BIFAN* ser. B, 1 (1968): 39–116. The historicity of the town and kingdom of Tekrur has been the subject of much debate because of the confusion and contradictions in the information conveyed by Arab geographers and historians. The recent work of Chouki El Hamel on the scholarship of Tekrurian Muslim learned men has, however, shed much light on the history of this area of the Western Sudan; see his *La vie intellectuelle islamique dans le Sahel ouest-africain, XVIe–XIXe siècles* (Paris: Harmattan, 2002), esp. chap. 6 and 7. For a broad but useful review of early literature on the expansion of Islam in Senegal and the Gambia, see Martin Klein, "The Moslem Revolution in Nineteenth Century Senegambia," in *Western African History*, ed. Daniel McCall, Norman R. Bennett, and Jeffrey Butler, Boston University Papers on Africa 4 (New York: Praeger, 1969), 69–131.

3. A. Da Mosto, *Relations des voyages à la côte occidentale d'Afrique*, published by M. Charles Schefer (Paris: Leroux, 1895), 79. There may still be valuable sources about the Islamization of the Wolof in private libraries of old Muslim families in Mauritania and Senegal. Therefore, the narrative I am offering here is not only incomplete but also tentative.

4. Valentim Fernandes, *Description de la côte occidentale d'Afrique*, trans. T. Monod, A. T. Da Mota, and R. Mauny (Bissau, 1951), 7–8.

5. For more on the Jolof Empire, see Jean Boulègue, *Le Grand Jolof, XIIIe–XVIe siècle* (Paris: Karthala, 1987); Boubacar Barry, *Le royaume du Waalo: Le Sénégal avant la conquête* (Paris: Karthala, 1985). See also Oumar Leyti Ndiaye, "Le Djolof et ses Bourbas," *BIFAN* ser. B, 28 (1966): 966–1008, for a reconstruction of the history of Jolof inspired by local oral traditions.

6. For a discussion of the political and social structures of Wolof society, see Felix Brigaud, *Histoire traditionnelle du Sénégal* (Saint-Louis, Senegal: CRDS,

1962); T. L. Irvine, "Castes and Communication in a Wolof Village" (PhD diss., University of Pennsylvania, 1973); and A. B. Diop, *La société Wolof* (Paris: Karthala, 1987). See also Rousseau, "Les cahiers de Yoro Dyâo, and "Études sur le Cayor." For a more extensive discussion of castes in West Africa, see Patrick McNaughton, *The Mande Blacksmiths: Knowledge, Power and Art in West Africa* (Bloomington: Indiana University Press, 1988); Tal Tamari, *Les castes de l'Afrique Occidentale: Artisans et musiciens endogames* (Nanterre, France: Société d'Ethnologie, 1997).

7. See Jean Schmitz, "Un politologue chez les marabouts," *Cahiers d'Études Africaines* 3 (1983): 329–51.

8. Amary Ngoone Sobel was, in reality, the second ruler of Kajoor, but his father, whom he succeeded, ruled only for a couple of days before he died. On the role of Muslims in the founding of Kajoor, see Amar Samb, *Essai sur la contribution du Sénégal à la littérature d'expression arabe* (Dakar: IFAN, 1971), 470.

9. The origin of the much written about "Senegalese social contract," which, according to social scientists, characterized the relationships between the Muslim leadership and the colonial and postcolonial states in Senegal, may well be dated from this period.

10. Quoted in Diop, *La société Wolof*, 218; my translation. All translations into English from French and Wolof sources are mine.

11. See a discussion of these two authors' accounts earlier in this chapter.

12. In Kajoor, for example, Princess Yasin Bubu, who was demoted by the dammeel, allied with the Muslim cleric Njaay Sall and fomented a revolt that toppled the reigning king. For more on the revolt of Njaay Sall in Kajoor, see A. B. Diop, "Lat Dior et le problème musulman," *BIFAN* ser. B, 28 (1966): 493–539, and T. L. Fall, "Recueil sur la vie des Damels," *BIFAN* ser. B, 36, no. 1 (1974): 93–146.

13. Reported by Jean Louis Moreau de Chambonneau, in Carson I. Ritchie, "Deux textes sur le Sénégal (1673–1677)," *BIFAN* ser. B, 30 (1968): 289–354.

14. The jihad of Nasir al-Din, which took place between 1673 and 1677, was described by the French administrator and explorer Chambonneau, then on duty in Saint-Louis, in a manuscript edited and published by Carson Ritchie; see ibid. Chambonneau gave the movement the name Toubenan, from the Wolof word *tuub*, meaning "conversion." Philip Curtin, in "Jihad in West Africa," *JAH* 12 (1971): 11–24, examined the Arabic sources of the jihad, which is called Shur Bubba by the Moors. Wolof oral traditions collected by Fall, "Recueil sur la vie des Damels," and Diop, "Lat Dior," relate the revolt of Njaay Sall in Kajoor but do not associate this episode with the Toubenan movement.

15. Barry, *Le royaume du Waalo*, 136.

16. Curtin, "Jihad in West Africa," 24.

17. James Webb, *Desert Frontier* (Madison: University of Wisconsin Press, 1995).

18. John H. Hanson, *Migration, Jihad, and Muslim Authority in West Africa* (Bloomington: Indiana University Press, 1996), 158.

19. Labat, Chambonneau, and other European writers attributed the failure of the Toubenan to the inability of the movement's leaders to make good on their

promise to end the violence and pillages and eradicate slavery and the slave trade in the Wolof states.

20. Barry, *Le royaume du Waalo*, 135.

21. Lat Sukaabe became king primarily because of his links with the Atlantic Trade, which gave him access to European weaponry. He was a usurper who successfully established his domination in Kajoor and Bawol through the systematic use of firearms. This position of power allowed him to break with the policy of accommodation favored by his predecessors and confront his increasingly powerful Muslim constituency. The Wolof saying "Lat Sukaabe *garmy ngaru fetal*," which translates as "Lat Sukaabe noble by the barrel of the guns," expresses the ability of this king to subvert traditional political norms thanks to the firepower of his army of slave warriors. For more on Lat Sukaabe's rule, see Jean Boulègue, "Lat-Sukaabé Fal ou l'opiniâtreté d'un roi contre les échanges inégaux au Sénégal," in *Les Africains*, vol. 9, ed. Charles A. Julien (Paris: Éditions Jeune Afrique, 1990), 167–96. Mamadou Diouf's *Le Kajoor au XIXe siècle* (Paris: Karthala, 1990) remains the most authoritative interpretation of the history of this Wolof kingdom. See also James Searing, *West African Slavery and Atlantic Commerce* (Cambridge: Cambridge University Press, 1993), 18–26.

22. Diouf, *Le Kajoor*, 9; see also Searing, *West African Slavery*, 18–26.

23. Searing, *West African Slavery*, 22–23.

24. *Fakk taal*, literally meaning "clear and lit," refers to marabouts who specialized in teaching. This name comes from the Quranic school's tradition of studying after dark and at dawn by the light of a bonfire. For an extensive discussion of this issue, see Diop, *La société Wolof*.

25. See J. B. Labat, *Nouvelle relation d'Afrique Occidentale* (Paris, 1728), 13, and Doumet, in C. Becker and V. Martin, "Le Kayor et les pays voisins au cours de la seconde moitié du XVIIIième siècle," *BIFAN* ser. B, 1 (1974): 41.

26. Searing, *West African Slavery*, 89. See also M. Klein, "The Social and Economic Factors in the Muslim Revolution of Senegambia," *JAH* 13(1972): 419–41, 440, and Henry Sène, "Le livre et l'écrit de langue arabe dans la société Sénégalaise, des origines au début du XXième siècle" (Thèse pour un doctorat de troisième cycle en science de l'information et de la communication Bourdeaux, 1982), 138. For Sène, the expansion of Islam in Senegal was intimately linked to the development of Quranic education because the clerics have always based their proselytism on teaching.

27. See Cheikh A. M. Babou, "Le mouridisme des origines à 1912" (Mémoire de maîtrise, Département d'Histoire, Université de Dakar, 1991), 23.

28. The word *ceddo* originally characterized the crown slaves attached to reigning families. But in its broader meaning, it encompasses the rulers and their allies, known for their love of fighting, heavy drinking, pillaging, and hostility to Islam. Here is how Father D. Boilat, a nineteenth-century Senegalese Catholic priest from Saint-Louis, in *Esquisses sénégalaises* (Paris: Karthala, 1984), 301 and 308, described the ceddo as compared to the Muslim cleric: "The marabout is in

principle, a mohamedan priest, but also included in this group is any knowledgeable man that has good mores and obeys the rule of law. Marabouts enlighten the people and promote peace and reconciliation. The *ceddo* is the opposite of the marabout. He is an unbeliever, a frivolous man living off theft and pillage."

29. On the Toroodo Revolution and its impact on the Wolof kingdoms, see Baron Roger, *Kélédor, histoire africaine* (Paris: A. Nepveu, 1828); David Robinson, "The Islamic Revolution in Fuuta Tooro," *IJHS* 2 (1975): 185–221; and Oumar Kane, "Le Fuuta Tooro des Satigis aux Almaamis, 1512–1920" (Thèse de doctorat d'état, Université de Dakar, 1986). Kane's thesis has been published recently in book form, under the title *La première hégémonie peule: Le Fuuta Tooro de Koli Tehella à Almaami Abdul* (Paris: Karthala, 2004); the word *almaamy* is the local rendering of the Arabic word *al imaam*, meaning "religious leader." *Imaam* designates both Muslim ruler and prayer leader.

30. A. Wade, in Monteil, *Esquisses sénégalaises*, 63.

31. Siré-Abbâs-Soh, *Chroniques du Fouta sénégalais*, ed. Maurice Delafosse (Paris: E. Leroux, 1913), 50; Diop, "Lat Dior," 503.

32. Faidherbe quoted in Diouf, *Le Kajoor*, 97. The attribution by Faidherbe of the title Serigne Njambur to Malaamin Saar is intriguing. He was not from this area of Senegal, and the Serigne Njambur did not bear the patronym Saar.

33. I recorded the most complete Muslim version of the story from Mustafa Njaate Mbakke, during our interview in Mbacke Bawol, 30 July 2000.

34. We learn from Roger, *Kélédor*, 17, and oral traditions that Amari Ngoone Ndeela was the first Wolof king to create a standing army. This army, composed of ceddo, was stationed in some strategic areas of the kingdom and was fed by the local population. This information lends more credibility to the oral tradition's version of the circumstances of the death of Malaamin Saar.

35. Many of the clerics who survived the confrontations had migrated out of Kajoor and Bawol or were sold in the Atlantic Trade. See Roger, *Kélédor*, 66, and Diop, "Lat Dior," 504, for descriptions of the king's attitude toward the clerics at the aftermath of the war.

36. For an internal perspective on Lat Joor's rule, see Diop, "Lat Joor." For a scholarly analysis of the circumstances of his reign, see Diouf, *Le Kajoor*, pt. 4, and Searing, *God Alone Is King*, chap. 2.

37. His great-grandfather, Sakhewar Fatma Joob, studied in Kokki, where he was a schoolmate of Maaram Mbakke, Amadu Bamba's great-grandfather. His grandfather was among the Muslims wounded at the battle between the Wolof clerics and Dammeel Amary Ngoone Ndeela in 1795. For an extensive discussion of Lat Joor's lineage and its attitude toward Islam, see Diop, "Lat Dior," 505–23.

38. Sources differ about the circumstances that led to Sakhewar's conversion and migration from Geet. According to some oral traditions, it was after a dream that he decided to convert and join the school of Kokki to study Islam; others report that Sakhewar was removed from his position of chief of Geet by a dammeel from a rival matrilineage and that it was out of dismay that he decided to become a Muslim.

39. For more on the jihad of Amadu Sheikhu the Madiyanke, see Eunice Charles, *Precolonial Senegal: The Jolof Kingdom, 1800–1890* (Boston: African Studies Center, Boston University, 1977), and "Shaikh Amadou Ba and Jihad in Jolof," *IJAHS* 8 (1975): 367–82. Also see David Robinson, *Chiefs and Clerics: Abdul Bokar Kan and Futa Toro, 1853–1891* (Oxford: Clarendon Press, 1975). The word *Madiyanke*, used by Robinson, is formed from *Madiyu*, the Pulaar rendering of *Mahdi*. The Mahdi is a controversial figure of Muslim eschatology who, according to some traditions, will come at the end of time to help Jesus fight Satan and his followers and establish the kingdom of God on earth.

40. See Diouf, *Le Kajoor*, chap. 16, sec. 5 and 6, 238–43, for a thorough analysis of the relations between Lat Joor, Amadu Sheikhu, and Governors Pinet-Laprade and Valière.

41. See *Moniteur du Sénégal*, 7 February 1871.

42. See chapter 3 for an extensive discussion of this issue and the broader question of the relations between Amadu Bamba and the rulers of Kajoor.

43. See "Renseignements sur la situation politique de Cayor en 1879," Archives Nationales du Sénégal (henceforth ANS), 1G 48.

44. Ibid., 10.

45. Ibid., 6.

46. On the conflict between Lat Joor and the French over the railroad, see Diouf, *Le Kajoor*, 265–86, and Claudine Guerresh, "Le livre de métrique du cadi Majakhate Kala," *BIFAN* ser. B, 4 (1974): 714–833.

47. See Valière's 1879 report, ANS, 1G 48; this is also Mamadou Diouf's interpretation.

48. Searing, *West African Slavery*, 22–23. Martin Klein also shares this view of the role of the teachers and local Muslim clerics in the expansion of Islam among the Wolof; see his "Social and Economic Factors." See also Eric Ross, "Marabout Republics Then and Now: Configuring Muslim Towns in Senegal," *Islam et Sociétés au sud du Sahara* 16 (2002): 35–65.

CHAPTER 2

1. *Doomi sokhna*, literally meaning "son of an honorable woman," is a Wolof expression that designates a category of families and people (or a subclass) with a long tradition of Islamic learning and teaching and embodying the most positive Wolof cultural values. However, doomi sokhna are also sometimes criticized for excess pride and a tendency to treat less learned people with contempt.

2. I use *capital* as defined by Pierre Bourdieu. Bourdieu conceives of capital as a social power. He distinguishes between different types of capital based on the accumulation of specific types of resources: "social capital" relates to power acquired through the involvement in social networks beyond the immediate family, "cultural capital" is acquired through the accumulation of information and educational

credentials, and "symbolic capital" is the form taken by any legitimized and recognized type of capital. See Bourdieu, "The Forms of Capital," in *Handbook of Theory and Research for the Sociology of Education*, ed. J. G. Richardson (London: West Port, 1986), 249–58.

3. For the information about the Mbakke family, I rely on my interviews with Sawru Mbay, Mbakke, 1 March 2000, 6 March 2000; Isa Mbakke, Tuubaa, 2 July 2000; Habib Sy, Tuubaa, 26 June 2000; Sheikh Maam Balla Mbakke, Mbakke, 5 May 1991, 29 May 2000; Mustafa Mbakke Njaate, Mbakke, 30 July 2000, 30 June 2000; and Modu Jakhate, Khuru Mbakke, 29 June 2000. All of these interviewees are members of agnate branches of the Mbakke family or members of traditionally learned Wolof families. As I observed in the introduction, these two groups are the best sources for information related to the history of Amadu Bamba's ancestors.

4. Cerno Barakatu Baal, a well-known Muslim cleric and traditional historian of Fuuta in Senegal, said that the Buso compound, also called Galle Cerno (meaning "the cleric's house" in Pulaar), is still standing in Gollera; interview in Parcelles Assainies, Dakar, 27 May 2000. Siré-Abbâs-Soh also alluded to the Busoobe of Gollera in his *Chroniques du Fouta sénégalais*, ed. M. Delafosse (Paris: E. Leroux, 1913), 66. Some years ago, a group of elders from Lao visited the Murid heartland to meet with local historians of the Muridiyya and consult with them about the history of the Mbakke family in Fuuta. One of my interviewees, the late Sawru Mbay, was among the people who met with them; interview in Daaru Salaam, 6 March 2000.

5. Jean Schmitz notes that a *jom* (village) of the Mbakke existed on the northern bank of the Senegal River until the end of the eighteenth century, implying that the Mbakke migration to the south might have taken place at a later date; personal communication, Paris, March 2001. However, it might be that this village was founded by a branch of the Mbakke clan that originally lived on the southern bank but migrated to the north at the same time as the branch led by Usmaan moved toward the south. This hypothesis suggests a dispersal of the Mbakke occurring sometime during the reign of the *deniyankoobe* (sixteenth to eighteenth centuries) through successive waves of migration heading in different directions.

6. Apart from slight differences, my interviewees generally agreed in their rendering of the story of the installation of Usmaan Ba in Jolof. Sheikh Maam Balla Mbakke, Mbakke, 5 May 1991, and Sawru Mbay, Daaru Salaam, 1 March 2000, gave the most complete version.

7. The story goes that Usmaan arrived in Jolof with his family during the rainy season. The day of his arrival, Jolof was hit by a storm, and it rained all night. But when the rain stopped, people were amazed to see that not one drop of water had touched Usmaan or his party. The people who saw the miracle went to the bergel to tell him about it, and the bergel then begged Usmaan to stay with him. Another version relates that Usmaan spent the night outside but that his family and

cattle were protected against the wild animals and the looting ceddo by a ring of fire that burned all night long. Interviews with Sheikh Maam Balla Mbakke, Mbakke, 5 May 1991, and Sawru Mbay, Daaru Salaam, 1 March 2000. A similar story is told about the famous Moroccan Sufi master and founder of the Shadiliyya order Abul Hassan Al Shadili (1196–1258), who, during his journey to Mecca, miraculously made a wall appear every night to protect his disciples against the raiding Bedouins. See Denis Gril, "Le saint fondateur," in *Les voies d'Allah*, ed. Alexandre Popovic and Gilles Veinstein (Paris: Fayard, 1996), 114. The story of Usmaan, probably reconstructed by Murid hagiographers, epitomizes the circularity of Muslim hagiography discussed in the Introduction of this book. According to Sheikh Maam Balla Mbakke, the name of this bergel was Mafinty Niang. For more on the political and social structures of the kingdom of Jolof, see Oumar Leyti Ndiaye, "Le Djolof et ses Bourbas," *BIFAN* 28 (1966): 966–1008, and also Yoro Jaw translated by Gaden in annexes of Siré-Abbâs-Soh, *Chroniques*.

8. Interview with Sheikh Maam Balla Mbakke, Mbakke, 5 May 1991.

9. Bearers of oral traditions of the Mbakke family agree on this date. But Maaram was probably born a decade later. It is unlikely that he would have been able to play the role ascribed to him in events dated from the late eighteenth century if he was born at the beginning of the century. For the conversion of dates from the Muslim calendar to the Gregorian calendar, I rely on G. S. Freeman-Grenville, *The Muslim and Christian Calendars* (London: Oxford University Press, 1963).

10. Many of my sources indicate that he studied until age sixty, but this was certainly a way of emphasizing the importance he attributed to education. He was probably the first member of the Mbakke family to achieve a high level of Islamic education.

11. Isa Mbakke, who is a descendant of Maaram, was my only source to give this information; Isa Mbakke, Tuubaa, 2 May 2000.

12. His first wife originated from a family of Muslim clerics in the village of Tayba Seck in eastern Bawol. He then married his cousin, Awa Niang, from the bergel's family, and then took Aysa Dem as a third spouse. Dem was the mother of Amadu Bamba's grandfather, Balla Aysa Mbakke.

13. Many of my sources stress that Maaram had an unusually large family. The number that is often given in Arabic is *tisha wa tishuun* (ninety-nine) children. There is a certain symbolism in this number, but even if the figure is inaccurate, it gives us an indication of his prominent place in the society of his time and in the Mbakke clan. Interviews with Mustafa Njaate Mbakke, Mbakke, 30 June 2000; Modu Jakhate, Khuru Mbakke, 29 March 2000; and Sawru Mbay, Daaru Salaam, 1 March 2000. At a time when children died at a high rate and when the household economy depended primarily on manual labor, it was understandable that Maaram's abundant male offspring would be perceived as a blessing. But considering the alliances that Maaram was able to build through the marriage of

his daughters and granddaughters, it seemed that women were an even greater asset for the family.

14. For example, Maaram's elder daughter, Sokhna Mbakke Awa Niang, was married to Aymeeru Jakhate of Mbaakol, who belonged to one of the most prestigious Muslim clerical families in Bawol and Kajoor. The sons and daughters from this union married among the maraboutic families of Pir and Kokki. The founders of Ker Makala and Mewndu, two important centers of Islamic education and culture in Senegal, originated from Sokhna Mbakke Awa Niang. Khaali Majakhate Kala, from the Jakhate branch of ker Makala, a central figure in the court of Lat Joor during the second half of the nineteenth century, was a grandson of Sokhna Mbakke. Another granddaughter of Maaram, Mati Mbakke, married into the family of Demba Bunna Sy of Suyuuma in Jolof. The Sy are renowned Muslim clerics of Fuuta origin. Usmaan Sy, the father of Al-Hajj Maalik Sy (the founder of the Malikiyya branch of the Tijaniyya in Senegal), was a product of this marriage. A third granddaughter, Absa Mbakke, married Serigne Njaga Isa Joob, from the famous Muslim clerical lineage of Kokki. Joob was the grandfather of Ibra Faati (Maam Cerno), a brother and close aide of Amadu Bamba.

15. Cheikh Tidiane Sy referred to Maaram's role as adviser and judge in the royal court of Bawol and Kajoor; see his *La confrérie sénégalaise des mourides* (Paris: Présence africaine, 1969), 104. But this information is probably a nineteenth-century reconstruction of Murid hagiographers. All my informants agreed on the fact that Maaram was anxious to maintain his neutrality in the conflict between rulers and clerics in the Wolof states and that he even mediated between the belligerents. Mustafa Njaate particularly emphasized this trait in Maaram's character; interview in Mbakke, 30 June 2000.

16. See chapter 1 for a thorough discussion of this conflict and its aftermath.

17. Interviews with Sawru Mbay, Daaru Salaam, 1 March 2000; Sheikh Maam Balla Mbakke, Mbakke, 5 May 1991; and Isa Mbakke, Tuubaa, 2 July 2000.

18. The name Amadu Farimata was formed from his given name, Amadu, and that of his mother, Farimata. Among the Wolof, the mother's first name was often added to the name of the son or daughter in order to distinguish between many siblings and cousins bearing the same first name. The name of Balla Aysa, Amadu Bamba's grandfather, and that of his father, Momar Anta Sali, follow a similar model. In his writings, Amadu Bamba adopted an arabicized form of his grandfather's and father's names, using their father's first name as a middle name. Balla Aysa became Habib Allah, Momar Anta Sali became Muhammad Ben Habib Allah, and he himself became Muhammad Ben Muhammad Ben Habib Allah, which means Muhammad, son of Muhammad, son of Habib Allah.

19. See Schmitz, "Un politologue chez les marabouts," *Cahiers d'Études Africaines* 3 (1983): 329–51.

20. Interviews with Sheikh Maam Balla Mbakke, Mbakke, 5 May 1991; Isa Mbakke, Tuubaa, 2 July 2000; Mustafa Mbakke Njaate, Mbakke, 30 July 2000; Modu Jakhate, Khuru Mbakke, 29 June 2000; and Sawru Mbay, Daaru Salaam, 1 March 2000.

21. For the conflict between Balla Aysa and members of the Mbakke family, I rely on my interviews with Modu Jakhate, grandson of Majakhate Kala, then the last living son and caliph of the family of Mbay Jakhate, Khuru Mbakke, 29 June 2000, and with Sawru Mbay, Daaru Salaam,1 March 2000. It is interesting to note that my interviewees from the Mbakke family did not refer to this episode. Only Isa Mbakke made some reference to the succession of Ibra Awa Niang and the role of Modu Jee, but he provided a version that is substantially different from those given by the other informants, and he did not mention conflict or tension between the different protagonists.

22. The conflict between agnates in the collateral mode of succession among the clerical families of the Western Sudan was analyzed by Jean Schmitz in "Le souffle de parenté," *L'Homme* 154 (2000): 241–78.

23. Interviews with Isa Mbakke, Tuubaa, 2 July 2000, and Sawru Mbay, Daaru Salaam, 1 March 2000.

24. Interviews with Sheikh Maam Balla Mbakke, Mbakke, 5 May 1991; Modu Jakhate, Khuru Mbakke, 29 June 2000; and Sawru Mbay, Daaru Salaam, 1 March 2000.

25. Sheikh Coro Mbakke, in an interview with Robert Arnaud cited in his "L'Islam et la politique musulmane de la France," *BCAF/RC* 20 (1912): 111, blamed the jihadist Maba Jakhu Ba for the killing of his grandfather. Other sources do not make a connection between the jihad of Maba and the death of Balla Aysa. They only maintain that a Fulbe robber killed Balla Aysa.

26. For an interpretation of Maba based on local oral sources, see the article by his grandson and biographer Tamsir Ousmane Ba, "Essai historique sur le Rip," *BIFAN* ser. B, 19 (1957): 564–91; for a thorough discussion of the jihad based on oral and archival documents, see Martin Klein, *Islam and Imperialism in Senegal* (Stanford: Stanford University Press, 1968), esp. chap. 4.

27. About the presence of Lat Joor and his warriors in Mbakke, see letters from the commandant of the French military post of Nguigis to the governor of Senegal dated November 1864 in ANS, 13 G 271, 20, 23, and 24.

28. See Claudine Guerresh, "Le livre de métrique du cadi Majakhate Kala," *BIFAN* ser. B, 4 (1974): 714–833; see also ANS, 3B 89, 49.

29. For information about the reactions of Muslim clerics to Maba's jihad, see the letters exchanged between the governor and the chief of Pir in ANS, 13 G 257; letter dated 19 September 1866, written by the cleric Abdoulaye, a marabout from Mbaakol, asking for help and informing the governor that some of his constituents had migrated to Saalum against his will and that the village of the Muslim chief of Njambur had been destroyed because he refused to follow the jihad, in ANS, 13 G 318; and Maba's letters to Governor Pinet Laprade, August 1865, in ANS, 13 G 318 and 13 G 257.

30. Mbacké, *Les bienfaits de l'éternel* (Dakar, 1995), 26–27.

31. Ibid., 27.

32. See Amar Samb, *Essai sur la contribution du Sénégal à la litérature d'expression arabe* (Dakar: IFAN, 1971), 264.

33. Moodu Maamun Niang, who reported this story, added that Majakhate Kala buried his pipe while muttering, "Truth stays here with force and power on top of you." Interview in Tuubaa, 8 June 2000.

34. The governor of Senegal at the time, Louis Faidherbe, indicated that Maba destroyed the village of Mbakke in 1864 but denied having done it; see his *Le Sénégal, La France et l'Afrique Occidentale* (Paris: Hachette, 1889), 277–78. Sheikh Tidiane Sy shared this opinion; see his *La confrérie mouride*, 105.

35. Interview with Modu Jakhate, Khuru Mbakke, 29 June 2000.

36. According to Abdou Malal Diop, she died of a sickness that lasted two days. See his "Traduction et commentaire du *Viatique des Jeunes* d'Ahmadou Bamba" (Thèse de doctorat de troisième cycle s/d Professeur Amar Samb Université de Dakar Faculté des Lettres et Sciences Humaines, Département Arabe, 1985), 9. The death was associated with the stress of the migration and the long march from Bawol to Saalum.

37. In his writings as well as in his teachings and sermons, Amadu Bamba was very critical of the rulers of the Wolof states, regardless of their religious obedience. See chapter 3 for an extended discussion of the relations between Bamba and the Wolof rulers. Chapters 6 and 7 treat his relations with the French colonial administration. On the philosophy of nonviolence, see F. Dumont, "Amadou Bamba, apôtre de la non-violence," *Notes Africaines* (January 1969): 121, 20–24. See also Didié Hamoneau, *Vie et enseignement du Cheikh Ahmadou Bamba* (Beirut: Al-Bouraq, 1998), esp. chap. 6.

38. For the biographical information about Momar Anta Sali, I rely on my interviews with Sawru Mbay, Daaru Salaam, 1 March 2000; Sheikh Maam Balla Mbakke, Mbakke, 5 May 91; Isa Mbakke, Tuubaa, 2 July 2000; Mustafaa Njaate Mbakke, Mbakke, 30 July 2000; Modu Jakhate, Khuru Mbakke, 29 June 2000; and Habibu Sy, Tuubaa, 26 June 2000; and also on Mbacké, *Les bienfaits*.

39. In addition to formal education, Momar perfected his training in the science of *tawhid*, or theology, with his friend the qadi Majakhate Kala. Momar Anta also frequented the school of Biraan Siise of Rufisque, where he studied *Tuhfa al Hukkam* (The Most Beautiful [Gift] for the Judge), by Ibn Asim (d. 1425 in Andalusia), a book that was highly valued by qadis and specialists of sharia in the Western Sudan; see Lettre de Théveniaut Administrateur du Cercle du Baol à Monsieur le Lt.Gov. Diourbel le 22 Juillet 1912, ANS, 10D 3, 0035. Momar was also in contact with the Tijaani cleric of Bargny, Cerno Yoro Njaay, with whom two of his sons, Ibra Faati and Sheikh Anta, studied; interview with the late Mustafa Caytu, last caliph of Sheikh Anta's lineage, Mbakke, 8 March 2000. He probably sojourned in other schools to study with specialists of specific books and disciplines.

40. Interview with Modu Jakhate, Khuru Mbakke, 29 June 2000.

41. Modu Jakhate particularly insisted on the hostile attitude of Momar's cousins; interview in Khuru Mbakke, 29 June 2000.

42. Momar Anta Sali's departure was probably made under pressure from the jihadists, contrary to claims by oral traditions that he voluntarily followed the

jihad. In fact, it is difficult to understand why he would have willingly made the long and exhausting trip to Saalum at a time when his two wives, Anta Njaay Mbakke and Faati Joob, were pregnant: Sheikh Anta and Ibra Faati were both born not long after the family arrived in Saalum. If he had the choice, he certainly would have waited until they gave birth before leaving.

43. Aymeru Jakhate, Khaali's grandfather, was married to Princess Asta Joob of the geej reigning dynasty of Kajoor. Khaali himself was married to Princess Debbo Suka, also a geej, and he was known for his Solomonic judgments and controversial role as a judge in the court of Lat Joor. See Guerresh, "Le livre de métrique"; and Samb, *Essai sur la contribution*.

44. For more on Sheikh Sidiyya al-Kabir and the order he founded, see Charles and Elizabeth Stewart, *Islam and Social Order in Mauritania: A Case Study from the Nineteenth Century* (Oxford: Clarendon Press, 1973); Charles Stewart, "A Mauritanian Reformer: Sheikh Sidiyya Baba," *Tarikh* 7 (1971): 65–70, and "Southern Saharan Scholarship and Bilad al Sudan," *JAH* 27 (1976): 73–93. See also David Robinson, *Paths of Accommodation: Muslim Societies and French Colonial Authorities in Senegal and Mauritania, 1880–1920* (Athens: Ohio University Press, 2000), esp. chap. 9.

45. I thank Afia Niang for sharing with me a copy of the certificate that Samba Tukuloor wrote for Momar after the initiation. In the document, Ka stated that he had received an order from Sheikh Sidiyya al-Kabir (d. 1868) and his son Sidi Muhammad (d. 1869) to initiate Momar to the secrets of the Qadiriyya, once he has determined that the latter was well prepared to act on and protect those secrets.

46. Mbacké, *Les bienfaits*, 19.

47. ANS, 13G 264; see also Thierno Ka, "L'enseignement arabe au Sénégal" (Doctorat de troisième cycle, Sorbonne, Paris, 1982), 65.

48. Scholars still debate the motivations of Lat Joor's "conversion." His grandson and biographer Amadou Bamba Diop argues that the conversion to Islam was genuine; Vincent Monteil, building on the abundant correspondence of the dammeel kept in the Senegalese National Archives (where he signed as "Sultan" or "Emir of the Black Muslims"), notes that despite the fact that he violated some prescriptions of Islam, Lat Joor should still be considered a Muslim; see Monteil, "Esquisses sénégalaises," *Initiations et Études Africaines* 21 (Dakar, 1966), 104–5. Mamadou Diouf, by contrast, sees the conversion as politically motivated and part of a strategy to rebuild military power and win back the throne of Kajoor; see his *Le Kajoor au XIXe siècle* (Paris: Karthala, 1990), 232 and 235. In reality, Lat Joor's attitude toward Islam did not differ significantly from that of his predecessors. He followed the tradition of religious pluralism and the selective practice of Islam that had marked the attitude of the rulers of Kajoor since Amary Ngoone Sobel Faal, the kingdom's founder.

49. This is not to be confused with the village of the same name located in eastern Bawol.

50. Interviews with Sawru Mbay, Daaru Salaam, 6 March 2000; Isa Mbakke, Mbakke, 2 July 2000; and Sheikh Mbakke Maam Balla, Mbakke, 29 May 2000.

51. These two cousins were Dame Seynabu Mbakke and Samba Caam Mbakke. See République du Sénégal, *Calendrier historique de la région de Diourbel*, vol. 2, prepared by the Minister of Economy and Finances of Senegal for the general census of 1988 (Dakar: Direction de la prévision et des statistiques, 1988); and interviews with Mustafa Njaate, Mbakke, 30 July 2000, and Isa Mbakke, Tuubaa, 2 July 2000.

52. From the migration to Saalum in 1865 to his death in 1882 or 1883, Momar Anta Sali never lived in Mbakke Bawol on a permanent basis. After his death, he was buried in Kajoor. He clearly did not like Bawol, and the rift among the Mbakke between the penku-penku (people from eastern Bawol) and the Ajoor (people from Kajoor) that I alluded to in the introduction may well have begun with him.

53. See the letter of Mbakhane, son of Lat Joor and chef supérieur du Bawol Oriental, to Résident du Laurens, dated 29 June 1903, in which he explained the nature of the relations between his father and Momar Anta Sali; ANS, 11D 1, 30.

54. Interviews with Sheikh Maam Balla Mbakke, Mbakke, 5 May 1991; Mustafa Njaate Mbakke, Mbakke, 30 June 2000; and Sawru Mbay, Daaru Salaam, 1 March 2000.

55. Marriage with the former wife of a king, especially if this wife had a son by the king, was an honor rarely given to a commoner. However, one should not lose sight of the fact that the marriage between kingly families and marabouts was often the fruit of arrangements that had more to do with politics than respect for the Muslim clerics. Mustafa Njaate mentions that ruling families often resorted to marrying their women to marabouts when these women became mentally ill, bore a handicap, or were thought to carry a curse. He notes that the marriage between Momar A. Sali and Coro Maarooso probably followed this logic. Coro married into many noble families before she was proposed to Momar Anta Sali. The marriage between Momar Anta Sali and Isa Joob also should be understood in this context. Tradition holds that Lat Joor was forced to divorce Joob when a marabout convinced him that keeping this woman in the court would ultimately ruin his power. Isa Joob was the daughter of a renowned cleric of Kokki; she was abducted by Lat Joor during a raid against her father and was married as a concubine. However, the fact that Momar Anta and not another cleric was chosen as a husband for the dammeel's former wife and his niece suggests his prestige in the court.

56. Interview with Cerno Gey, custodian of Momar Anta Sali's mausoleum in Deqele, 20 July 2000.

57. Interviews with Sheikh Maam Balla Mbakke, Mbakke, 5 May 1991 and 29 May 2000.

58. For a comprehensive discussion of the Murid doctrine, see Cheikh Anta Mbacké Babou, "Autour de la genèse du mouridisme," *Islam et Sociétés au Sud du Sahara* 11 (1997): 5–38. Also see chapter 4 in this book.

59. Personal conversation with Professor Khadim Mbacké of IFAN, July 2004. The word *salafist* derives from *salaf*, which means "roots" in Arabic. *Salafist* refers

to a Muslim proponent of a return to pristine Islam as practiced by Prophet Muhammad and his first companions in Medina and Mecca.

60. See notes in annexes of Arnaud, "L'Islam et la politique," 142.

61. Sy, *La confrérie sénégalaise des mourides*, 106.

62. This was the case, for example, with Masamba Joob Saam, who was slightly older than he was but started to follow his teachings in Mbakke Kajoor while Momar was still alive.

63. This story is widely reported by bearers of Murid oral traditions.

CHAPTER 3

1. Vincent Monteil, "Esquisses sénégalaises," *Initiations et Études Africaines* 21 (Dakar, 1966), 159, and Donal B. Cruise O'Brien, *The Mourides of Senegal: The Political and Economic Organization of an Islamic Brotherhood in Senegal* (Oxford: Clarendon Press, 1971), 37, deplored the dearth of information about the persona of Amadu Bamba and called on historians to fill this gap in the historiography of the Muridiyya.

2. The year 1853 is now widely accepted among Murid traditional and academic historians as his date of birth. In the scholarship on the Muridiyya, Mbakke Bawol is cited as the birthplace of Amadu Bamba, as suggested by colonial sources. However, being from Mbakke, I have always been puzzled by the fact that nobody was able to show me the house or place where he was born in Mbakke, whereas there were plenty of sites in the town and its vicinity that were associated with different episodes in his life and that were objects of pious visits. In fact, there is not even a house or site in Mbakke reported to have belonged to his father, Momar Anta Sali. It is more plausible, as told by oral sources, that Amadu Bamba was born in Khuru Mbakke, the first village founded by his father; there, the house where many believe he was born has now become a pilgrimage site for Murid disciples.

3. I recorded this information from the late Modu Jakhate, then the only living son of Mbay Jakhate, in Khuru Mbakke, 22 June 2000. Mbay Jakhate was a son of Khaali Majakhate Kala, a colleague and friend of Amadu Bamba's father.

4. Bachir Mbacké, *Les bienfaits de l'éternel*, trans. and ed. Khadim Mbacké (Dakar, 1995), 15–16. Since biographies of prophets and saints are subject to refashioning and editing to fit the actual fate of the prophecy across space and time, as suggested by David Anderson and Douglas Johnson, it is likely that in the future, we will learn of more miracles performed by the young Amadu Bamba; see Anderson and Johnson, eds., *Revealing Prophets: Prophecy in Eastern African History* (Athens: Ohio University Press, 1995), 11.

5. The different teachers who taught Amadu Bamba are known, but Balla Jatara was not listed among them. I thank Mustafa Ley for sharing with me a letter written by Amadu Bamba in which he acknowledged Jatara as his master.

6. For more on Islamic education in the Western Sudan and Senegal, see Denise Bouche, "L'école française et les Musulmans du Sénégal de 1850 à 1920," *Revue Française d'Histoire d'Outre-Mer* 223 (1974): 218–35; Lamin Sanneh, "The Origins of Clericanism in West African Islam," *JAH* 27 (1976): 49–72, and *The Jakhanke: The History of an Islamic Clerical People of the Senegambia* (London: International African Institute, 1979); Chouki El Hamel, *La vie intellectuelle islamique dans le Sahel ouest-africain, XVIe–XIXe siècles* (Paris: Harmattan, 2002), 37–38; and Rudolph T. Ware III, "Njangaan: The Daily Regime of Qur'anic Students in Twentieth Century Senegal," *International Journal of African Historical Studies* 3 (2004): 515–38.

7. For an examination of the role of memory in the teaching of Quran, see Dale F. Eickelman, "The Art of Memory: Islamic Education and Its Social Reproduction," *Comparative Studies in Society and History* 4 (1978): 485–516.

8. For information about the disciplines taught and the books used in Islamic teaching in Senegal, see Mamadou Ndiaye, "L'enseignement arabo-islamique au Sénégal" (Thèse de doctorat, Université de Dakar, 1975–76); Thierno Ka, "L'enseignement arabe au Sénégal" (Doctorat de troisième cycle, Sorbonne, 1982); and Rawane Mbaye, "La pensée et l'action d'Elhadji Malick Sy" (Thèse pour un doctorat d'état à la Sorbonne, 1992–93). For a reflection on the politics of Islamic education in West Africa, see Louis Brenner, *Controlling Knowledge* (Bloomington: Indiana University Press, 2001).

9. Diop, *Irwā*, 7.

10. Mbacké, *Les bienfaits*, 167.

11. *Lakhas* literally means "to fasten one's waist with a turban or piece of fabric." In the lexicon of Muslim education in Senegal, it means "to migrate or travel far for the sake of studying." It corresponds with the Arabic concept of *rihla li talab al ilm*, or travel for the sake of knowledge. The accomplishment of this migration was an important item on the résumé of a Muslim cleric and a source of baraka.

12. Diop, *Irwā*, 7. The Dayman was a prestigious *zwaya* (clerical) family in Mauritania.

13. For example, when Amadu Bamba discovered *Baqawiyu*, a popular book on Quranic interpretation, in the library of the Muslim chief of Longoor, he was not allowed to take it with him and had to make numerous trips to this village to complete the reading. Interviews with Galo Mbay, whose father, from the Mbay of Longoor, was among the first disciples of Amadu Bamba, Tuubaa, 14 February 2000, and 1 March 2000. Bamba also met opposition from the Lo clerics of Niomre when he first endeavored to marry Aminata Lo, a widow of one of his friends and a member of the Lo clan, on the ground that he did not belong to the right family.

14. See Mbacké, *Les bienfaits*, 17. This information was also reported by Sawru Mbay in an interview in Daaru Salaam, 1 March 2000.

15. See Fernand Dumont, *La pensée religieuse d'Amadou Bamba* (Dakar: Nouvelles éditions africaines, 1975). This book is still the most extensive analysis of Amadu Bamba's writings in any language.

16. We learn from M. L. Diop that Sheikh Coro and Aafe Mbakke, both younger brothers of Amadu Bamba, were initiated into Muslim rituals by their father using *Jawharu Nafiis*, a book on Muslim ritual practices written by Bamba, rather than the more popular précis authored by *Al-Akhdari*. See Diop, *Irwā*, 11–12.

17. Amadu Bamba had a large number of offspring, but many of the children died at an early age. He fathered thirty-three sons and twenty-eight daughters. In the Mbakke clan, he was second to Maaram in terms of family size. See appendix 3 for a list of Amadu Bamba's sons and daughters and their mothers.

18. Mbacké, *Les bienfaits*, 107.

19. Murid sources inform us that Amadu Bamba used to place under his father's pillows anonymous letters with quotations from the Quran that admonished *ulamas* (Muslim scholars) who collaborated with unjust rulers. He also used to remind his father of the Quranic warning that "every judge, even the most righteous among them, will be judged." Interviews with Sawru Mbay, Daaru Salaam, 6 March 2000; Cheikh Mbakke Maam Balla, Mbakke Bawol, 29 May 2000; Mustafa Njaate, Mbakke Bawol, 30 July 2000; and Modu Maamun Niang, Tuubaa, 8 June 2000. Bachir Mbacké recounted that Amadu Bamba told his fellow disciple, Masamba Joob, that he was going to abandon his father if he did not resign from his position of judge in the court of Lat Joor; see Mbacké, *Les bienfaits*, 107. The stories of Amadu Bamba's opposition to the court clerics of Kajoor have become so central to his hagiography that it has become difficult to separate supposed facts from later constructions. It is clear that Bamba was uncomfortable with his father's position in the court of Lat Joor, but it is uncertain whether he went to the lengths described in Murid internal sources in order to antagonize him.

20. Interview with Habibu Sy, Tuuba, 26 June 2000. Sy gave the most complete version of this story, which was also reported by other oral sources.

21. Momar sent Amadu Bamba to consult with his uncles Muhammad Buso and Mapenda Sy of Kumboof in Saalum. Sy was also the brother of Usmaan Sy, the father of Malick Sy, founder of the Malikiyya branch of the Tijaniyya in Senegal. Interviews with Sawru Mbay, Daaru Salaam, 6 March 2000; Mustafa Njaate, Mbakke, 30 July 2000; and Habibu Sy, Tuubaa, 26 June 2000.

22. Interviews with Modu Sey, Massaer Silla, and Bara Mbakke in Mbakke Kajoor, 20 July 2000. *Gigis* is a tree.

23. See Mamadou Lo, "Traduction et commentaire de *Tazawuddu-S-Sigar*, ou Viatique des Jeunes de Cheikh Ahmadou Bamba Mbacké," Travail d'études et de recherches maîtrise d'arabe," Université de Dakar, 1978.

24. The physical and moral portrait of Amadu Bamba sketched here is inspired by my interviews with Galo Mbay, Tuubaa, 14 February 2000; Bamba Jaw, Dakar, 18 April, 13 May, and 18 June 2000; Sawru Mbay, Daaru Salaam, 6 March 2000; and Ibrahima Jaagne Mbay, Dakar, 1 October 1999. I also refer to the book in Wolofal by Modu Maamun Niang entitled *Jaar Jaar I Serigne Tuubaa* (The Itineraries of Amadu Bamba). Colonial officials such as Paul Marty also offered a depiction

of Amadu Bamba. Although a *fiche de renseignement* (intelligence file) describing each of the most important Islamic and Murid leaders of Senegal is kept at the National Archives of Dakar, I was not able to find a fiche for Amadu Bamba.

25. Anthropologists Allen Roberts and Mary Roberts offered an interesting analysis of this picture in their article "The Aura of Amadu Bamba," *Anthropologie et Sociétés* 1 (1998): 15–38. Oumar Ba, a former archivist at the Senegalese National Archives and a researcher, informed me that they were two other pictures of Amadu Bamba taken by a French seaman at the port of Dakar as the cleric was embarking for exile to Gabon. Unfortunately, he could not locate these pictures; interview, Dakar, 15 June 2001.

26. See Abdu Lahad Mbakke, ed., *Majmuha* (Tuubaa: A. A. Mbacké, 1985), 32.

27. The beard issue is an important one. The Prophet Muhammad recommended that Muslims shave their mustaches and sideburns but grow their beards. This hair-grooming style was a means to distinguish Muslims from non-Muslims, who, at the time, liked to shave their beards. Prophet Muhammad took special care of his own beard. With the development of salafist ideas in the Muslim world, the beard had become an important symbol for the expression of one's religious militancy.

28. For information on Bamba's attitude toward material things, see the numerous reports about Amadu Bamba and his Murids in the dossier "Amadou Bamba" at the National Archives of Senegal. See also Paul Marty, *Études sur l'Islam au Sénégal* (Paris: E. Leroux, 1917), 1:230; and Hélène Porcheron, "Les dahiras mourides du marché Sandaga à Dakar," *Plein Sud* 2 (1992): 18–25.

29. I have not seen the written version of this poem, but I have often heard excerpts from the oral version. Interview with Cerno Jaw, Tuubaa Ngelemu, 17 July 2000. Jaw is the son of Modu Jaw Pakha, one of the earliest disciples of Amadu Bamba. He was raised by Falilu, the second successor of Amadu Bamba, and for a long time, he was chief of the village of Tuubaa.

30. In a letter he wrote to the parents of his wife, Fatu Madu Maam Joob, while in exile in Gabon, he urged them to pursue her Islamic education and assured them that he would take care of all material expenses when he returned home; see Mbakké, *Majmuha*, 96. See also another letter published in the same book (160), written while he was in exile in Mauritania, in which he asked his brother Ibra Faati to make sure that his wives performed the regular prayers and did good actions and that his sons continued memorizing the Quran.

31. He rebuked his elder son, Mustafa Mbakke, who failed to groom his hair adequately in imitation of some Murid disciples who wore dreadlocks, reminding him that his rank required that he behave as a well-mannered and decent human being. Interviews with Galo Mbay, Tuubaa, 14 February 2000 and 1 March 2000, and Serigne Mbay, Tuubaa, 1 March 2000. Makhtar Joob also referred to instances when Amadu Bamba admonished Bachir Mbacké for failing to conform to some minor rituals, such as saying the appropriate formulas after sneezing; interviews, Diourbel, 28 June 2000 and 19 July 2000.

32. Mbacké, *Les bienfaits*, 32.

33. Interviews with Sawru Mbay, Mbakke Bawol, 6 March 2000, and Sheikh Maam Balla Mbakke, Mbakke Bawol, 29 May 2000.

34. Mbacké, *Les bienfaits*, 55. This was also the opinion of Elhaj Silla, chief of the village of Cillawell, whose ancestors were the first occupants of Mbakke Kajoor; interview in Cillawell, 20 July 2000.

35. Imam Malik Ibn Anas, whose system of jurisprudence dominates North and sub-Saharan Africa, also made a similar statement when he told the Abbassid caliph, Harun Al Rachid, that he would be ashamed to be seen by the angels standing in front of the door of a king's house for the sake of mere secular businesses.

36. Diop, *Irwā*, 24. Diop mentioned that he received the information from Adama Sall, who took the letter to the court. Sall was one of the first disciples to join Amadu Bamba after his father's death.

37. Ibid., 25. See also Amar Samb, *Essai sur la contribution du Sénégal à la littérature d'expression arabe* (Dakar: IFAN, 1971).

38. Diop, *Irwā*, 9. Bearers of Murid oral traditions tell this story in almost the same words.

39. Ibid., 9–10. This episode in the life of Amadu Bamba is also widely reported in Murid oral traditions. It is curious, however, that Bachir Mbacké did not mention the incident, although he quoted from the poem that Amadu Bamba had written on the occasion of the dispute; see Mbacké, *Les bienfaits*, 426.

40. See Diop, *Irwā*, 9–10, and Mbacké, *Les bienfaits*, 426–27. Many of my informants know by heart some verses of these poems, which they recited during our interviews.

41. Al-Ghazzali articulated this point of view in *Ih'ya 'ouloûm ed-dîn*, where he categorized the relations between the ulama and rulers as follows: "The first, worst of all, is the one in which you [the ulama] go to them [the rulers]. The second, which is less than the first, is the one in which they [the rulers] come to you [the ulama]. The third is the safest: in which you do not see them and they do not see you." See al-Ghazzali, *Ih'ya 'ouloûm ed-dîn; ou, Vivification des sciences de la foi*, ed. G. H. Bousquet (Paris: Besson, 1955), 148.

42. Bachir Mbacké refers to a conversation between Albury Njaay, Buurba Jolof, and Amadu Bamba in which Bamba, responding to a demand for support, said, "Your provocations and those of the so-called jihadists are nothing but useless actions whose tragic consequences you will bear responsibility for [before God]." See Mbacké, *Les bienfaits*, 67.

43. *Zakaat* is an Islamic income tax; when it is given in cash, it amounts to 2.5 percent of the portion of the income that is left after sustenance needs are covered. Zakaat is paid to specific persons identified by the Quran and the traditions of Prophet Muhammad. But in secular Muslim states, zakaat is often given to the imam of the mosque for distribution. In Senegal, adherents to Sufi tariqas generally give their zakaat to their former teachers or their sheikhs.

44. This tour across Senegal and Mauritania is widely reported by bearers of Murid oral traditions. Modu Maamun Niang is the only source to mention the length of the tour, which he puts at eight months. Interview in Tuubaa, 8 June 2000.

45. Amadu Bamba had reportedly given this cane as gift to his brother Sheikh Anta. I have seen the cane displayed in Daaru Salaam, the fief of Sheikh Anta, before and after *eid* prayers. (Eid is the feast marking the end of Ramadan or commemorating the sacrifice of Abraham.) *Muqaddam* means "local representative of Muslim order entitled to disseminate its teachings and initiate new disciples."

46. See Mbacké, *Les bienfaits*, 37; Diop, *Irwā*, 19; Cheikh Tidiane Sy, *La confrérie sénégalaise des mourides* (Paris, 1969); and Khadime Silla, "Immigration et confrérie" (Thèse de DEA Institut National des Langues et Civilisations Orientales, 1992–93), 53.

47. Khadim Mbacké observes that it was during his tour of 1884 that Amadu Bamba acquired Ghazali's *Ihya* (Regeneration of the Religious Sciences), Abu Talib El Makki's *Qut* (Nourishment), Al Qusayry's *Risala* (Epistle), and Sidi Ali Harazim's *Jawar-al-Ma'aani* (The Pearl of Meaning); see Mbacké, *Soufisme et confréries religieuses au Sénégal* (Dakar, 1989), 55, and also his "La tariqua des mourides," *Africa* 53, no. 1 (1998): 102–20, 103. All of these books treat subjects related to Sufism, and they are also found in the library of Sheikh Sidiyya Baba at Butilimit. See Louis Massignon, "Une bibliothèque saharienne: La bibliothèque du Cheikh Sidia au sahara," *Revue du Monde Musulman* 5 (1909): 409–18.

48. Interviews with Afia Niang, Tuubaa, 30 May 2000; Modu Maamun Niang, Tuubaa, 8 June 2000; and Mustafa Ley, Mbakke, 16 May 2000; see also Mbacké, *Les bienfaits*, 111–12.

49. A document found in the archives of Sheikh Sidiyya's family in Mauritania mentioned that Amadu Bamba received an initiation to the Qadiriyya first from his father and then from a certain Muhammad Saar, and he also was initiated by Sheikh Sidiyya Baba in the year of Bu-marâra, which corresponds with AH 1309 (1892–93); see Abdel Wedoud Ould Cheikh, "Espace confrérique, espace étatique," unpublished paper, 2001, 6. This last initiation was probably a renewal and an upgrade and not the first initiation that Amadu Bamba received from Sheikh Sidiyya. There are different levels of initiation to a wird: the level of *izna*, which gives only the right of usage, and the level of *ijaaza*, which involves an authorization to distribute the wird. The 1892–93 initiation may have been that of ijaaza.

50. Appendix 4 provides a list of the names of the transmitters of the Qadiriyya wird whom Amadu Bamba praises in the poem.

51. See Ould Cheikh, "Espace confrérique," 6.

52. Paul Marty, "Cheikh Sidiya et sa voie," *Revue du Monde Musulman* 31 (1915–16): 29–133, 39. It is curious that Marty did not give the reference for this quotation. Marty was prejudiced against black Muslims, and he had a tendency to glorify Muslim leaders who allied themselves with the French, but this quota-

tion expressed the general sentiment that Moorish clerics had toward their black colleagues.

53. I refer here to David Robinson, who was quoting a conversation between Sidiyya and the interpreter, Dudu Seck; see Robinson's *Paths of Accommodation: Muslim Societies and French Colonial Authorities in Senegal and Mauritania, 1880–1920* (Athens: Ohio University Press, 2000), 184.

54. Amadu Bamba Mbacké, *Massalik Al-Jinan* (Rabat: Dar El Kitab, 1984), 28.

55. Mbacké, *Les bienfaits*, 66.

56. Those disciples who stayed with Amadu Bamba were the first sheikhs he consecrated. Included in this group were the disciples Adama Gey; Adama Sall; Ibra Saar; Matar Ture; Masamba Joob; Modu Gay Jemooy; his brothers Cheikh Anta and Ibra Faati; his cousin Ahmad Ndumbe Mbakke; and his first companions, Ndaam Abdurahmaan Lo, Amsatu Jakhate, Amadu Makhtaar Mbay, and Makhuja Uma Mbay.

57. I recorded this story of the encounter between Amadu Bamba and Maniaaw Silla from Sheikh Maam Balla Mbakke during an interview in Mbakke Bawol, 5 May 1991.

58. The number forty should be seen here as more of a symbol than an expression of the reality. Biographers of Muslim saints (and Amadu Bamba is no exception) often see the master's life as a reenactment of Prophet Muhammad's journey to Mecca. Omar, the hero and second caliph of Islam, is ranked fortieth among the Meccan "pagans" who joined Islam. Ibra Faal has come to occupy a similar preeminence in the Muridiyya as the founder of a powerful branch. In my evaluation, the number of Amadu Bamba's followers was much smaller when he was joined by Ibra Faal.

59. This book was entitled *Jazbul Murid* (Attraction of the Aspirant). Interview with Afia Niang, Tuubaa, 30 May 2000. In the personal file of Ibra Faal kept at the colonial archives, it is also mentioned that he was literate in Arabic; see ANS, Dossab.

60. Mbacké, *Les bienfaits*, 121.

61. In Anne Marie Schimmel's words, "the *Majzub*, or 'the enraptured one,' who is under the shock of a mystical vision or any psychological experience, is bereft of his senses and walks around in a fashion prohibited by the law . . . belongs to the darker side of the Sufi world." See Schimmel, *Mystical Dimensions of Islam* (Chapel Hill: University of North Carolina Press, 1975), 19.

62. See chapter 4 for an assessment of the impact of Ibra Faal on the development of the Muridiyya. See also Serigne Babacar Mbow, *La voie Baye-Fall, Maam Cheikh Ibra Fall ou la lumière du dedans* (Geneva: privately printed, 2000); Xavier Audrain, "Baay-Fall du temps mondial: Individus modernes du Sénégal" (Mémoire de DEA d'études africaines, Paris 1, La Sorbonne, UFR 11, de science politique, 2001–2).

63. This was the case with Daaru Asan Njaay of Njare, whose parents even refused to receive Amadu Bamba when he went to the village to visit his former

disciple. Amadu Makhtaru Mbay faced the same hostility when he stayed with Amadu Bamba against his parents' will. He was forbidden to settle in his native village of Longoor when he finished his training and was obliged to move to the neighboring village of New Daaru. Sheikh Ahmad Ndumbe Mbakke, a cousin and early disciple of Amadu Bamba, was ostracized by his family, and some of his older brothers forbade him from eating in their houses. Interviews with Galo Mbay, Tuubaa, 14 February 2000 and 1 March 2000; Mamadu Sall, Tuubaa, 23 March 2000; and Mortalla Mbakke, Gowane, 24 April 2000.

64. Musa Ka, "Marsiyya Maam Cerno Birahim, Ibra Faati," a poem composed as a eulogy after the death of the Maam Cerno in 1943. Audiocassette.

65. I thank Matar Sy for showing me the letter handwritten by Amadu Bamba.

66. Interview with Elhaj Silla, Quranic teacher and head of the village of Cillaawel, Mbakke Kajoor, 20 July 2000.

67. For more on land tenure among the Wolof, see Diop, *La société Wolof*.

68. Cruise O'Brien, *The Mourides*, 165.

69. See Mbaké, *Massalik*, 28.

70. Moor Saaw, one of the imams of Mbakke, was particularly critical of Sheikh Ibra Faal and Amadu Bamba. He used to tell to the former that besides study and worship, there were no other means for a Muslim to get closer to God. Interview with Mustafa Ley, Mbakke Bawol, 16 May 2000.

71. See Mbaké, *Soufisme et confréries religieuses au Sénégal*, 54.

72. This information was almost unanimously reported by interviewees. See particularly my interviews with Sawru Mbay, Daaru Salaam, 1 March 2000, and Mustafa Njaate, Mbakke, 30 July 2000.

73. See letter to Momar Jaara, Mbaké, *Majmuha*, 96.

74. It is common among the Wolof to name their first sons after their fathers or elder brothers, and it is very unusual for someone to reverse a decision taken by a close sibling. Later on, Mamadu Mustafa named his second-oldest son after his uncle Momar Jaara to repair the situation. Interviews with Sheikh Maam Balla Mbakke, Mbakke Bawol, 29 May 2000; Sawru Mbay, Daaru Salaam, 1 March 2000; and Mustafa Njaate, Mbakke, 30 July 2000.

75. See Mbacké, *Massalik al-Jinan*, 104.

76. For more on this topic, see F. De Jong and B. Radtke, eds., *Islamic Mysticism Contested: Thirteen Centuries of Controversies* (Leiden: Brill, 1999).

77. See Diop, *Irwā*, 22, and my interviews with Sawru Mbay, Daaru Salaam, 6 March 2000, and Cheikh Maam Balla, Mbakke Bawol, 29 May 2000.

78. *Daaru Salaam* is also an equivalent of the Wolof expression *Jamm a gen* (peace is best), the name that many dissenters gave to the villages or neighborhoods they found after separating from their communities of origin.

79. According to Ibra Mbay, the threat was to ban those who volunteered to help Bamba and his disciples from marrying with women living in Mbakke. Interview with Ibra Mbay, Daaru Salaam, 13 February 2000. Mbay is a grandson of Amadu Makhtaar Mbay, one of the disciples who followed Amadu Bamba in Daaru

Salaam. The fact that the community of Daaru Salaam was not able to haul a roof without outside help suggests that it was small.

80. Interviews with Ibra Mbay, Daaru Salaam, 13 February 2000, and Sheikh Maam Mame Balla, Mbakke, 5 May 1991.

81. On Khalwa and its spiritual significance, see J. L. Triaud, "*Khalwa* and the Career of Sainthood: An Interpretive Essay," in *Charisma and Brotherhood in African Islam*, ed. Donal B. Cruise O'Brien and Christian Coulon (Oxford: Clarendon Press, 1988), 53–67.

82. See James Searing, *God Alone Is King* (Portsmouth, NH: Heinemann, 2001), for an extensive discussion of the migration of slaves and other commoners in Murid-dominated areas of Kajoor and Bawol.

83. This assumption made by Marty to substantiate his view of the Muridiyya as an attempt to resuscitate the traditional Wolof social and political order is widely endorsed by scholars. See Lucy Behrman, "The Political Significance of Wolof Adherence to Muslim Brotherhoods in the 19th Century," *African Historical Studies* 1 (1968): 60–78; M. Klein, *Islam and Imperialism in Senegal* (Stanford, CA: Stanford University Press, 1968), esp. 225–29; Cruise O'Brien, *The Mourides*; and Momar C. Diop, "La confrérie mouride: Organisation politique et mode d'implantation urbaine" (Thèse de troisième cycle unité d'études et recherches de psychologie et des sciences sociales, Université de Lyon 2), 1980.

84. Interviews with Ibra Mbay, Daaru Salaam, 13 February 2000, and Sawru Mbay, Daaru Salaam, 1 March 2000 and 6 March 2000.

85. For more on the daara tarbiyya and Murid education in general, see chapter 4.

86. This is the number suggested by almost all bearers of Murid tradition.

87. Interviews with Sawru Mbay, Daaru Salaam, 6 March 2000; Ibra Mbay, Daaru Salaam, 13 February 2000; and Sheikh Maam Balla, Mbakke, 5 May 1991.

88. The relationship between Amadu Bamba and Sheikh Ibra Faal was a complex one. Evidence shows that Amadu Bamba in many instances insisted that Faal follow the canonical principles of Islam. A copy of a letter he wrote to him to this end is found in the *Majmuha*. In this letter, quoting from the Quran, Bamba wrote, "As soon as you receive this letter, repent and ask God, the Forgiver and most Merciful for His mercy. Pray and command your family to perform and persist in prayer"; see Mbacké, *Majmuha*, 97. Archival documents as well as Cruise O'Brien also suggest some tension between the two. However, Amadu Bamba never took the initiative to openly break his relations with his famous disciple. They apparently maintained a good relationship until his death in 1927.

89. For the history and contemporary development of Tuubaa and its significance for the Muridiyya, see Eric Ross, "Tuba, a Spiritual Metropolis in the Modern World," *Canadian Journal of African Studies* 29 (1995): 222–59, "Tubâ, an African Eschatology in Islam" (PhD diss., McGill University, 1996), and "Marabout Republics Then and Now: Configuring Muslim Towns in Senegal," *Islam et Sociétés au Sud du Sahara* 16 (2002): 35–65; Abdoulaye Dièye, *Touba: Signes et*

symboles (Paris: Deggel, 1997); Christian Coulon, "Touba, lieu saint de la confrérie mouride," in *Lieux d'Islam: Cultes et cultures de l'Afrique à Java*, ed. Mohammad Ali Amir-Moezzi (Paris: Autrement, 1996), 226–38; and Cheikh Guèye, "L'organisation de l'espace dans une ville religieuse," in *Touba: La capitale des mourides* (Paris: Karthala, 2002). See also Cheikh A. Babou, "Touba, genèse et évolution d'une cité musulmane au Sénégal," Mémoire de DEA, Université de Dakar, 1992.

90. Interview with Sheikh Maam Balla Mbakke, Mbakke, 5 May 1991.

91. In fact, neither Tautain, who was the first colonial administrator to mention the name of Amadu Bamba and his village in a report, nor Angot, who was first to inquire about the Murids, could locate the village. See ANS, 1G 136, in Oumar Ba, *Ahmadou Bamba face aux autorités coloniales* (Abbeville: Fayard, 1982), 26–27.

92. See Hassan Elboudrary, "Quand les saints font les Villes," *Annales ESC* 3 (May-June 1985): 489.

93. Interviews with Sheikh Maam Balla, Mbakke, 5 May 1991, and Sawru Mbay, Daaru Salaam, 6 March 2000. Wolof oral sources report many visits of Al-Hajj Umar Tal in Wolof country, but traditions collected in Fuuta and French sources do not corroborate these reports. See also Serigne Mbacké Bousso, "Deux traités d'un lettré religieux Sénégalais (1864–1945)," translated from the Arabic by Khadim Mbacké (paper, 1994), 3.

94. Interviews with Sheikh Maam Balla Mbakke, Mbakke, 29 May 2000; Isa Mbakke, Tuubaa, 2 July 2000; and Sawru Mbay, Daaru Salaam, 6 March 2000.

95. See Vincent Cornell, *Realm of the Saint: Power and Authority in Moroccan Sufism* (Austin, 1998), 41–42.

96. See Amadu Bamba Mbacké, *Matlabul Fawzayn* (Dakar: Librairie Khadimou Rassoul, n.d.), v. 58 and 112.

97. See Lieutenant Paul Merles Des Isles for a popular legend about the founding of Tuubaa and the different significations of the city's names in his "Contribution à l'étude du Mouridisme" (1949), ANS, 1G 214.

98. This model has inspired the architecture of the new neighborhoods that Caliph Saaliu, the current leader of the Muridiyya, has founded since he became head of the Murid tariqa in 1990.

99. See Diop, *Irwā*, 30–31, and Mbaké, *Les bienfaits*, 44–47.

100. See P. Marty, *L'Islam au Sénégal*, 235.

101. Angot cited three new villages founded by the Murids and the presence of newly appointed Murid sheikhs in the area, ANS, 1G 136, 11–12.

102. These chiefs were mainly from Njambur and northern Kajoor. For further discussion of the relationship between the Murids and the African colonial chiefs, see chapter 5.

103. Tautain, letter of 19 March 1889 to the administrator of Cayor, ANS, 3B/54, fol. 46, in Ba, *Ahmadou Bamba face aux autorités*, 25.

104. Angot, ANS, 1G 132, 12.

105. Ba, *Ahmadou Bamba face aux autorités*, Letter of the Governor to Amadou Bamba, 06/27/1889, 3B/55, fol. 82–83.

106. This trip mentioned by Leclerc is not reported by Murid traditions. However, a letter by Amadu Bamba from Butilimit, dated 22 Ramadan AH 1309 (1891–92), was found in the archives of Harun Ould Sheikh Sidiyya by Abdel Wedoud Ould Cheikh; see Ould Cheikh, "Espace Confrérique," 6. Sheikh Coro, half brother of Amadu Bamba, in his interview with Robert Arnaud, also mentions a trip taken by Amadu Bamba to Mauritania in 1892. One of my interviewees, Alioune Gay, a Tijani notable from Dagana, referred to a trip taken by Amadu Bamba to Mauritania, which was different from his visit of 1884 and the deportation of 1903. He indicated it was during this trip that his father met and submitted to the cleric. Interview in Nietti Kadd, Thiès, 25 June 2000. The trip mentioned in these three sources is probably the same and could be dated in 1892. Amadu Bamba probably traveled to Saint-Louis to meet the governor and then proceeded to Butilimit to visit Sheikh Sidiyya Baba.

107. Sénégal IV 127 Lettres de l'Administrateur du cercle de St. Louis à Monsieur le Directeur des Affaires Politiques, Saint-Louis, le 10 Juillet 1895.

108. Many Senegalese clerical families originated from Jolof. Maba, Amadu Bamba, and Malick Sy's ancestors were from this precolonial kingdom. The cleric Modu Maamun Niang, whose family is also from Jolof, explained this fact by the tolerance and kindness of Jolof rulers toward Muslims; interview, Tuubaa, 8 June 2000.

109. See Mbacké, *Les bienfaits*, 71, and my interview with Afia Niang, Tuubaa, 30 May 2000.

110. On the encounter between Amadu Bamba and the people of Jolof, I rely on my interviews with Sawru Mbay, Daaru Salaam, 6 March 2000; Sheikh Maam Balla Mbakke, Mbakke, 5 May 1991; Mustafa Njaate, Mbakke, 30 July 2000; and Modu Maamun Niang, Tuubaa, 8 June 2000. French sources also provide information about this episode in the life of Amadu Bamba, but their version of the story conflicts with those of Murid internal sources. They tell us that by April or May 1895, Samba Laobe Njaay, the king of Jolof, had become a disciple of Amadu Bamba. This conversion was the main reason for the king's deportation to Gabon in January 1896, a couple of months after Amadu Bamba had been exiled in French Equatorial Africa. The accusation later proved to be a fabrication. See Ba, *Ahmadou Bamba face aux autorités*, 51. Murid oral traditions maintain that there was a rapprochement between Samba Laobe and Amadu Bamba but at a later date. In contrast to French sources, they insist on the hostility of the king toward Amadu Bamba when they first met in 1895. This hostility is epitomized by this statement that Murid historians put in the king's mouth, "The land of Jolof is not vast enough for you and me to cohabit in." The epic of Amadu Bamba's deportation to Gabon, however, put both men in the same places, sometimes sharing the same ordeals.

111. Sometime after he left Tuubaa, a colonial report noted that "Amadu Bamba's popularity has increased since he settled in Jolof"; ANS, 3 E. 55, fol. 253.

112. See the report filed by Leclerc after he arrested Amadu Bamba in August 1895 and the report presented by Merlin to the Conseil Privé during Amadu Bamba's trial, in Ba, *Ahmadou Bamba face aux autorités*, 29, 45.

113. The interpreter Fara Biram Lo was appointed as adviser to the king of Jolof, Samba Laobe, but the two soon fell out, as it was quickly apparent that Lo wanted his boss's job. Lo was later convicted of forging bogus documents presenting the king as a partisan of Amadu Bamba bent on waging jihad. Samba Laobe, who was exiled in Gabon, where he joined Amadu Bamba, was rehabilitated and returned to Senegal. For more about these stories, see Ba, *Ahmadou Bamba face aux autorités*, 81.

114. Mbacké, *Massalik*, 108.

CHAPTER 4

1. See the preamble to Amadou Bamba Mbacké, *Massalik Al-Jinan* (Rabat, 1984), 26, in which he refers to Ghazali as "our spiritual guide, the renovator and great imam."

2. Quoted in Albert Hourani, *Arabic Thought in the Liberal Age, 1798–1939* (Cambridge: Cambridge University Press 1983), 6.

3. See Amadou Bamba Mbacké, "Tazawudu Shubaani" [Viaticum for the Fulfillment of the Youth], in *Recueil de poèmes en sciences religieuses de Cheikh A. Bamba*, vol. 1, trans. Serigne Sam Mbaye et al. (Rabat: Daar El Kitab, 1988), 437.

4. See F. de Jong and B. Radtke, eds., *Islamic Mysticism Contested: Thirteen Centuries of Controversies* (Leiden: Brill, 1999).

5. See Mbacké, *Tazawudu Shubaani*, 263–65.

6. See Mbacké, *Massalik al-Jinan*, 102.

7. Nimrod Hurvitz, *The Formation of Hanbalism: Piety into Power* (London: Routledge, 2002), 10. See also Fernand Dumont, *La pensée religieuse d'Amadou Bamba* (Dakar: Nouvelles Éditions Africaines, 1975), 342–43.

8. See Rahal Boubrik, *Saints et sociétés en Islam* (Paris: CNRS, 1999); Lamine Sanneh, *The Crown and the Turban* (Boulder, CO: Westview Press, 1997), 104; and Vincent Cornell, *Realm of the Saint: Power and Authority in Moroccan Sufism* (Austin: University of Texas Press, 1998).

9. Boubacar Barry, *Senegambia and the Atlantic Slave Trade* (Cambridge: Cambridge University Press, 1998), Martin Klein, *Islam and Imperialism in Senegal* (Stanford, CA: Stanford University Press, 1968), and James Searing, *West African Slavery and the Atlantic Commerce: The Senegal River Valley, 1700–1860* (Cambridge: Cambridge University Press, 1993), discuss this transformation, especially as it related to the end of the Atlantic trade and the development of "legitimate trade." They mostly focus, however, on Muslim access to guns and the role of Islam as an ideology of resistance to the ceddo elite; less emphasis is put on the impact of learning and on the access to religious books, which, in my view, were equally important. For an examination of this dimension, see A. Le Chatelier, *L'Islam dans l'Afrique Occidentale* (Paris: G. Steinheil, 1899), 261; Abdallah Djenidi, "La place du livre dans la formation de l'intelligentsia maraboutique au

Sénégal," *Annales de la Faculté des Lettres et Sciences Humaines* 9 (1979): 221–28; and F. Manchuelle, *Willing Migrants: Soninke Labor Diasporas, 1848–1960* (Athens: Ohio University Press, 1997), esp. chap. 5.

10. Malick Sy's father was murdered before his birth, and one of his uncles died fighting alongside Maba. Abdoulaay Niass's father moved to Saluum during the jihad of Maba, and he was initiated to the Tijaniyya by a follower of the famous jihadist Al-Hajj Umar Tal. A friend of Saer Mati, Maba's son, he was persecuted by the latter's rivals, Mamour Ndari, and the infamous French administrator of Saalum, Paul Broccard. Niass had to flee to Gambia with some of his followers and would return to Senegal thanks to the mediation of Malick Sy, who secured French protection for him. For more on Malick Sy, see Rawane Mbaye, "La pensée et l'action de Elhadji Malick Sy" (Thèse de doctorat d'état, Sorbonne Nouvelle, 1992–93); David Robinson, *Paths of Accommodation: Muslim Societies and French Colonial Authorities in Senegal and Mauritania, 1880–1920* (Athens: Ohio University Press, 2000); and El Hadji Samba Amadou Diallo, "La transmission des statuts et des pouvoirs dans la Tijaniyya sénégalaise: Le cas de la famille Sy de Tivaouane" (Thèse de doctorat de IIIe cycle en anthropologie sociale, ethnologie et ethnographie, EHESS), 2005. On Abdoulaay Niass, see Klein, *Islam and Imperialism*, 223–25, 228, and Daouda Diouf, "Les grandes figures religieuses du Sénégal: L'action éducative dans la stratégie d'Abdoulaye Niasse, face à la colonisation française et à sa politique de laïcisation," *Islam et Développement3* (n.d.): 34–44.

11. See Mbacké, "Massalik al-Jinan," "Tazawudu Sighaari," "Tazawudu Shubaani," and other works; Elhaj Malick Sy, *Kifāyat ar-Rāghibīn* (Enough [Provisions] for the Aspirant), ms. Department of Islamology, Fonds Amar Samb (Dakar: IFAN, n.d.). For further discussions of Amadu Bamba and Malick Sy's views on the Muslim leadership and society of their time, see Elhaj Malick Touré, "Critiques socio-religieuses dans les ouvrages de Cheikh Elhaj Malick Sy et Cheikh Ahmadou Bamba Mbacké," *BIFAN* ser. B, 4 (1978): 887–97; Rawane Mbaye, "Physionomie actuelle de l'Islam au Sénégal, dénonciation des faux marabouts," *AL Qods* 30 (1992): 115–19, and "La pensée et l'action."

12. *Wagne*, literally meaning "to count" in Wolof, was a public contest in which erudites who knew the Quran by heart challenged each other by saying, at the sound of drums, how many times a word appeared in the book; the one who succeeded in getting all his counts right won the contest and was celebrated by his friends and the young girls of the village. *Lawaan* was a ceremony in which young men who finished memorizing the Quran wore dreadlocks and circulated from village to village to celebrate their achievement.

13. See "Kharnubi" (The Century) (audiocassette version), a poem written by Musa Ka, probably during the 1929–30 depression. One must say, however, that reformers often tend to exaggerate the wrongs of their time in order to legitimize their own agendas.

14. See, for example, Amadou Bamba Mbacké, "Nahju Qadaahi al Haaj" [Path to Fulfillment of the Disciple's Needs], in *Recueil de poèmes en sciences religieuses*

de Cheikh A. Bamba, vol. 2, trans. Serigne Sam Mbaye et al. (Rabat: Dar El Kitab, 1989); "Tazawudu Shubaani" [Viaticum for the Fulfillment of the Youth], in Mbaye, trans., *Recueil de poèmes en sciences religieuses de Cheikh A. Bamba*, vol. 1, 437; and *Massalik al-Jinan*. After his return from Gabon in 1902, Amadu Bamba devoted most of his writing to the mystical sciences and praises of the Prophet Muhammad. For more on Amadu Bamba's writings, see Dumont, *La pensée*.

15. See Fernand Dumont, "Amadou Bamba, apôtre de la non-violence," *Notes Africaines* (January 1969): 23.

16. Mbacké, *Massalik al-Jinan*, 36.

17. Ibid., 34.

18. By science, he primarily meant Islamic religious sciences.

19. See Amadu Bamba Mbacké, "Munawwiru s-Suduur" [The Enlightening of the Heart], in *Recueil des poèmes en sciences religieuses de Cheikh A. Bamba*, vol. 2, trans. Serigne Sam Mbaye et al. (Rabat-Dar El-Kitab, 1989), 176.

20. See Rawane Mbaye, "L'Islam au Sénégal" (Thèse de doctorat de troisième cycle, Université de Dakar, 1975–76), 398. In reality, as evidenced by his writings and the different reports filed by the colonial administration, Amadu Bamba had always taught and had created a Quranic school wherever he settled. Mbaye's assumption alludes to the larger debate, partly sparked by colonial stereotypical portrayals of Amadu Bamba and Elhaj Malick Sy as representing, respectively, the mystical and intellectual sides of Senegalese Islam. As shown by Khadim Mbacké, in *Soufisme et confréries religieuses au Sénégal*, Études Islamiques no. 4 (Dakar, 1995); C. A. W. Mbacké and K. Sylla, in *Étude critique et analyse des écrits du Professeur Rawane Mbaye sur le mouridisme et son fondateur* (Edition du Collectif des Mourides de France, 1999); and E. Diallo, in "La transmission des statuts et des pouvoirs dans la Tijaniyya sénégalaise: Le cas de la famille Sy de Tivaouane" (Thèse de doctorat de IIIe cycle en anthropologie sociale, ethnologie et ethnographie, EHESS, 2005), these two clerics had the same pedigree: they pursued the same curriculum, read the same books, and wrote about the same themes, defending similar positions. Their differences related more to their personalities, styles, and political itineraries than to their thinking.

21. See A. A. Mbacké, ed., *Majmuha* (Touba: A. A. Mbacké, 1985), 129–32 (a collection of letters and sermons of Amadu Bamba Mbacké in Arabic). The following discussion of Amadu Bamba's conception of education is based primarily on this document. See also Muhammad Fadl Niang, "Sufism in Senegal: The Example of the Muridiyya" (Master's thesis in sharia, University Qarawiyyin, Morocco, 1999; originally in Arabic).

22. See Mbacké, *Massalik al-Jinan*, 36.

23. Mbacké, *Majmuha*, 131.

24. See Mbacké, *Nahju*, 349.

25. Mbacké, *Massalik al-Jinan*, 128.

26. Later in this chapter I offer a description and analysis of the instruments the Sufi use to control the nafs.

27. See Mbacké, *Tazawudu Shubaani*, 427–43.
28. Mbacké, *Tazawudu Sighaar*, 409.
29. Mbacké, *Massalik*, 62.
30. Mbacké, *Tazawudu Shubaani*, 417.
31. See Mbacké, *Nahju*, 365.
32. Mbacké, *Tazawudu Shubaani*, 421; see also his *Nahju*, 377.
33. See Mbacké, *Nahju*, 391; also his *Tazawudu Shubaani*, 421.

34. The Arabic title of this poem is *Huqqa al Bukau* (Dar El Kitab, 1984), and it was written probably between 1883 and 1884 as a response to Khaali Majakhate Kala, who sent the first verse to Amadu Bamba complaining that his former disciple had abandoned him following the controversy that opposed them (chapter 3). Alluding to the love and respect that the disciple owed to his sheikh, Khaali was asking if one should mourn the dead sheikhs and spiritual guides.

35. See *Random House Webster's College Dictionary*, 2nd ed., s.v. "love."

36. See Attâr, *Le mémorial des saints*, as quoted by Denis Matringe, "La litérature Soufie," in *Les voies d'Allah*, ed. Alexandre Popovic and Gilles Veinstein (Paris: Fayard, 1996), 175.

37. Al-Hajj Umar Tal, for example, wrote, "The disciple needs his sheikh as much as a blind person who wants to cross a river needs a guide," cited by Fernand Dumont, *L'anti-sultan ou Al-Hajj Omar Tal du Fouta, combattant de la foi* (Dakar: Nouvelles éditions africaines, 1974), 71.

38. Serigne Bachir Anta Niang Mbakke, a son of Ibra Faati, Amadu Bamba's half brother and historian of his family, particularly insists on the similarity between *jebelu* and *baya*. Interview in Daaru Muhti, 29 April 1991.

39. See Momar Coumba Diop, "La relation talibé-marabout" (Mémoire de maîtrise, Université de Dakar, 1976), and "La confrérie mouride: Organisation politique et mode d'implantation urbaine" (Thèse de troisième cycle unité d'études et recherches de psychologie et des sciences sociales, Université de Lyon 2, 1980); and Donal Cruise O'Brien, *The Mourides of Senegal: The Political and Economic Organization of an Islamic Brotherhood in Senegal* (Oxford: Clarendon Press, 1971).

40. See Leonardo Vilallòn, *Islamic Society and State Power in Senegal: Disciples and Citizens in Fatik* (Cambridge: Cambridge University Press, 1995), and "Sufi Rituals as Rallies: Religious Ceremonies in the Politics of Senegalese State-Society Relations," *Comparative Politics* 26 (July 1994): 417.

41. See ANS, 2G 30, 19, Cercle de Diourbel, Baol, rapports politiques mensuels, 1930. The document indicates that the director of *travaux publiques* (government projects) was contemplating reducing the salaries of workers from nine to eight francs and wanted the mediation of Murid sheikhs, but the latter were reluctant because they feared that they could be suspected of pocketing the difference.

42. See Cruise O'Brien, *The Mourides*, 83, and "Le talibé mouride," *Cahiers d'Études Africaines* 35 (1969): 502–7; Momar Coumba Diop, "La relation talibé-marabout dans le mouridisme" (Mémoire de maîtrise, Université de Dakar, 1976), 10.

43. Octave Depont and Xavier Coppolani, *Les confréries religieuses musulmanes* (Algiers, 1897), xx–xxi.

44. For a more extensive discussion of the appeal of saints, see Cornell, *Realm of the Saint*, 95.

45. Interview with Abdurahim Dem, son and successor of Ahmed Dem, in Diourbel, 30 July 2000.

46. Interview with Sawru Mbay, Daaru Salaam, 6 March 2000, and Sheikh Maam Balla Mbakke, 29 May 2000.

47. In fact, some of these sheikhs did not spontaneously go to Amadu Bamba; rather, because of their prestigious clerical backgrounds, it was Amadu Bamba who expressly asked that they join him. This was the case, for example, with Amsatu Jakhate, who was entrusted to Amadu Bamba after he made a plea to his father. Similarly, when he was preparing to move to Mauritania during his second exile, Amadu Bamba personally selected those he wanted to follow him there, and he primarily chose disciples belonging to renowned clerical families. Interviews with Elhaj Jakhate, Tuubaa, 10 June 2000, and Modu Maamun Niang, Tuubaa, 8 June 2000.

48. Surang, a successful and politically influential Saint-Louis trader, was an adviser to the Murid leadership and a power broker. He played a central role in solving the conflict that arose among Murid sheikhs after Amadu Bamba's death.

49. For more on Mbay Jakhate's work, see Mamadou Lo, "Un aspect de la poésie 'Wolofal' mouride: Traduction and analyse de quelques titres de Serigne Mbaye Jakhate" (Mémoire de maîtrise, Faculté des Lettres et Sciences Humaines Département de Lettres Modernes, année universitaire, 1992–93).

50. For a comparison of the Murid and Islamic work ethics as expounded in the traditions of Prophet Muhammad, see V. Monteil, "La confrérie musulmane des Mourides au Sénégal," in *Esquisses sénégalaises*, Initiations et Études Africaines 21 (Dakar, 1966), 191.51. Mbacké, *Massalik al-Jinan*, 156.

52. See Mbacké, *Majmuha*, "Advices to the Disciples," 117–18.

53. See Jean Copans' summary of findings from this research in his *Les marabouts de l'arachide* (Paris: Le Sycomore, 1980; Harmattan, 1988); see also P. Couty, *La doctrine du travail chez les mourides*, brochure (Dakar: ORSTOM, 1969), 54.

54. Abdoulaye Wade, *La doctrine économique du mouridisme*, brochure (Dakar: L'Interafricaine d'éditions, 1966).

55. Couty, *La doctrine*.

56. Ibid., 10.

57. Ibid., 16.

58. See C. A. W. Mbacké and Khadime Sylla, *Étude critique et analyse des écrits du professeur Rawane Mbaye sur le mouridisme et son fondateur* (Edition du Collectif des Mourides de France, 1999), 57–59.

59. Mbacké, *Massalik al-Jinan*, 156.

60. The French administrator Maurice Levy estimated the contribution of Algerian disciples to their tariqa in 1895 at 16 million francs against 7.5 million francs

of taxes paid to the French treasury the same year. See Levy, "La guerre sainte est-elle possible?" *Les Grands Faits* (15 August–15 September 1907): 298.

61. In the annual political report of 1926, the lieutenant governor of Senegal referred to 500,000 francs contributed by Amadu Bamba to support the national currency, and he signaled that 200,000 francs were stolen from his house. See ANS, 2G 26, 10 Rapport Politique Annuel, 1926.

62. The latest great Murid project in Tuubaa is a modern hospital built by the daahira Matlab ul Fawzayni for the cost of 5 billion CFA francs ($10 million). Recently (on 2 March 2006), Caliph Saliu Mbakke, leader of the Muridiyya, announced that he had collected a sum of 10 billion CFA francs ($20 million) that he intended to invest to improve the road system in Tuubaa, and he called on Murid disciples to contribute to the project.

63. For an examination of the ethic of wealth production and consumption among contemporary Murids and how it relates to beliefs, see Beth Ann Buggenhagen, "Prophets and Profits: Gendered Generational Visions of Wealth and Value in Senegalese Murid Households," *Journal of Religion in Africa* 31 (2001): 373–401, 374. Also see her "At Home in the Black Atlantic: Circulation, Domesticity, and Value in the Senegalese Murid Trade Diaspora" (PhD diss., University of Chicago, 2003).

64. See Donal Cruise O'Brien,"Don divin, don terrestre: L'économie de la confrérie mouride," *Archives Européennes de Sociologie* 15 (1974): 82–100. In this article, Cruise O'Brien revisits a number of conclusions he made in previous works on the Muridiyya. He blames the misinterpretations made by "colonial writers and development experts," who saw the Muridiyya as a mere form of economic exploitation, on their facile Marxism. Acknowledging his own misinterpretations of the relations between Murid disciples and sheikhs, he notes the difficulty for "profane observers and people not familiar with the Muridiyya" to distinguish between the declarations of Murid disciples and the reality and meanings of their relations with their sheikhs. He underlines the fact that "by asserting his total submission and exploitation by his sheikh, the disciple is not in fact describing the reality, but he is actually boasting." Cruise O'Brien then emphasizes the necessity of looking at the spiritual and religious meanings of the relations between Murid sheikhs and disciples (84–85).

65. Villalón, *Islamic Society and State Power*, 187.

66. See Christian Coulon, *Les musulmans et le pouvoir en Afrique Noire* (Paris: Karthala, 1988), 43.

67. Interviews with Sawru Mbay, Daaru Salaam, 6 March 2000, and Ibra Mbay, Daaru Salaam, 13 February 2000.

68. See Marcel Mauss, *The Gift: The Form and Reason for Exchange in Archaic Societies*, translated from the French by W. D. Halls (London: Routledge, 2002).

69. Mbacké, *Massalik al-Jinan*, 58, 62.

70. Ibid., 58.

71. For further discussion of this tradition of eclecticism in a specific branch of the Qadiriyya, see Glen W. McLaughlin, "Muhammad Fādil Wuld Mamin" (PhD diss., Northwestern University, 1997), 84. In *Al Haq al Mubiin* (The Shining Truth), Cheikh Moussa Camara justified and defended this tradition against Tijani criticism; see Saliou Dramé, "La pensée confrérique de Cheikh Moussa Camara dans la société et l'histoire: Analyse sociocritique de *Al Haq Al Mubîn* (La vérite éclatante)" (Mémoire de DEA, Département Arabe, Université Cheikh Anta Diop, 1998–99).

72. Because of this claim and others, the Tijaniyya has been the object of bitter polemics between scholars and students of Sufism in Mauritania. See Abdel Wedoud Ould Cheikh, "Les perles et le souffre: Une polémique mauritanienne autour de la Tijaniyya (1830–1935)," in *La Tijaniyya*, ed. Jean-Louis Triaud and David Robinson (Paris: Karthala, 2000), 125–63. See also Jamil M. Abun-Nasr, *The Tijaniyya* (London: Oxford University Press, 1965).

73. Ahmad Al Tijani also used the Qadiriyya, Khalwatiyya, and other wirds, but he abandoned them all when he received his own wird through prophetic inspiration. See J. Abu Nasr, *The Tijaniyya*, 37.

74. See Mbacké, *Majmuha*, 30. The key to dating this document is the response to the question about the creation of the Muridiyya, wherein Amadu Bamba stated that the Muridiyya had existed from the date of the prophetic *hijra* (migration) to AH 1335, which coincides with the year 1917. By this response, he meant that there was no difference between the Muridiyya and Islam. It is interesting to note that 1917 was also the year in which Marty published his *Études sur l'Islam au Sénégal*, and it may well be that he was the initiator of this questionnaire. M. L. Diop cites a work authored by the second caliph of the Muridiyya, Falilu Mbakke, wherein he asserted that his father received wirds from many sheikhs prior to the exile. And when he was in Gabon, the Prophet took all those previous initiations away and gave him directly the genuine qadiri wird. See Diop, *Irwā*, 78.

75. See Abdoul Ahad Mbacké, *Cheikh Amadou Bamba: Fondateur de la confrérie des Mourides* (Paris: Éditions d'Art des Heures Claires, 1984), 2:152. This two-volume work is a compilation of testimonies on Amadu Bamba from Moorish sheikhs and disciples, collected by the late caliph of the Murids, Abdul Ahad Mbakke. It contains the testimonies of Sidiyya Baba and Saad Buh, the two major leaders of the Qadiriyya in the Western Sudan.

76. This ijaaza was probably given to Uthman when he visited Mauritania or Senegal or delivered through an intermediary, since Amadu Bamba had never been to Syria or Mecca. See Diop, *Irwā*, 83.

77. Ibid.

78. See Mbacké, *Cheikh Ahmadou Bamba: Fondateur du mouridisme*, 152, and my interview with Mustafa Ley, Mbakke, 7 May 2000.

79. Interviews with Modu Maamun Niang, Tuubaa, 8 June 2000, and Elhaj Jakhate, Tuubaa, 10 June 2000.

80. I have already alluded to the ijaaza that Amadu Bamba issued for Mustafa Uthman. He granted a similar authorization to his brother and disciple Ibra Faati. In a letter he wrote while in Mauritania, he gave his brother permisson to distribute the Murid wird. See Mbacké, *Majmuha*, 147.

81. Diop, *Irwā*, 84.

82. Interviews with Modu Maamun Niang, Tuubaa, 8 June 2000, and Mustafa Ley, Mbakke, 16 May 2000.

83. For example, Sheikh Anta submitted to Amadu Bamba, but as a sheikh, he received the submission of Gora Baakhum, who was linked to Amadu Bamba through him. Gora Baakhum also had Ibra Jonn as a disciple; he was linked to Amadu Bamba through him and Sheikh Anta. Baakhum and Jonn were ultimately both disciples of Amadu Bamba, but their relation with the latter was mediated by their sheikh. At each level, the sheikh managed his own community, and in principle, he received orders from the leaders to whom he directly submitted.

84. Some early disciples, such as Ibra Saar, Ndaam Abdurahman Lo, Amsatu Jakhate, Amadu Makhtaar Mbay, and Serigne Fay, came from well-known Muslim village-schools, such as Njaagne, Ndaam, Mewndu, Lognoor, and Wajja, all located in northern Kajoor.

85. ANS, 1G 136, 11–12, in Oumar Ba, *Ahmadou Bamba face aux autorités coloniales coloniales* (Abbeville: Fayard, 1982), 26–27.

86. Interviews with Sawru Mbay, Daaru Salaam, 1 March 2000, and Galo Mbay, Tuubaa, 14 February 2000.

87. In 1895, the administrators Leclerc and Merlin suggested that Njambur and especially the Muslim village of Kokki were entirely committed to the Muridiyya. Merlin estimated, though with much exaggeration, that five thousand people from Njambur alone were ready to follow Amadu Bamba if he decided to wage a jihad. See Leclerc, "Au sujet du marabout Amadou Bamba," ANFOM, sen. 4/127. The growth of the Muridiyya in Njambur actually intensified after Bamba's return from exile. In a series of reports on the political situation in the colony of Senegal issued by the lieutenant governor in 1904 and 1905, he deplored the growing influence of the Muridiyya in Njambur and the district of Louga; see ANS, 2G 4, 46 and 2G 5, 8. An analysis of the profile of the twenty-nine most prominent Muslim clerics of the district of Louga between 1912 and 1913 reveals that two belonged to the tijani order, two were qadiri initiated by Amadu Bamba, and the rest were Murids. See Paul Marty, "Politique musulmane, activités des marabouts," ANS, 13G 67.

88. Serigne Mustafa Mbakke Beto, grandson and heir to Momar Jaara, stated that his grandfather became Murid in 1907. Interview, Mbakke Bawol, 8 May 2000.

89. See Mbacké, *Nahju*, 367.

90. See Claude Sanchez, "Théologie mystique et action politique chez le réformateur allemand Martin Luther et le marabout sénégalais Cheikh Ahmadou Bamba," *Études Germano Africaines* 1 (1983): 46–56.

91. See Cruise O'Brien, *The Mourides*, 56.

92. The title of Sheikh al-Turuuq was invented by the Ottoman rulers as an instrument to control the powerful but elusive leadership of the Sufi orders in their vast empire. See Pierre-Jean Luizard, "Le Monyen-Orient arabe," in *Les voies d'Allah*, ed. Alexandre Popovic and Gilles Veinstein (Paris: Fayard, 1996), 351.

93. Interviews with Sheikh Maam Balla Mbakke, Mbakke, 29 May 2000; Modu Maamun Niang, Tuubaa, 8 June 2000; and Afia Niang, Tuubaa, 30 May 2000.

94. Besides stopping the commissioning of the sheikh, Amadu Bamba also refused to lead his disciples in Friday prayers and buried members of his direct family outside the city. This attitude may be seen as a form of protest against his internment but also an acknowledgment of a certain deficiency caused by the pollution brought by the French presence. For further discussion of this question, see chapter 7, particularly the section on al-Mubaraka.

95. See the different *marsiyyas*, or eulogies, written by Musa Ka for these prominent Murid sheikhs. The audiocassette version of these poems are sold in the marketplace.

96. Quoted in Cruise O'Brien, *The Mourides*, 101.

97. A French translation of this letter initially written in Arabic is kept in Dossier Amadu Bamba at the Senegalese National Archives. The letter was intercepted by the colonial administration, but some other copies reached the Murid sheikhs, as attested by Mustafa Njaate Mbakke, who told me that he has seen the Arabic version. Interview, Mbakke Bawol, 30 July 2000. He was probably right, since the letter was to be sent to many sheikhs and since many copies were written. In addition, Murids have traditionally copied Amadu Bamba's letters, which they conserve as a relics and sources of baraka. Musa Ka affirmed that he had copied a version of the letter from a copy made by Sheikh Ibra Saar, and he added that Amadu Bamba had given similar instructions in another letter he wrote and entrusted to his disciple Amadu Lo, when he was on his way to exile in Mauritania. See *Jazaau Shakuur*, in Diâo Faye, "L'oeuvre Poétique 'Wolofal' de Moussa Ka ou l'épopée de Cheikh Ahmadou Bamba: L'exemple du 'Jazâ'u šakûr,' le récit d'exils au Gabon et Mauritanie" (Thèse pour un doctorat de troisième cycle Université Cheikh Anta Diop, 1999), 354, 56 and 58.

98. See Paul Marty, *Études sur l'Islam au Sénégal*, 2 vols. (Paris: E. Leroux, 1917), appendices.

99. The rivalry between Murid sheikhs enriched by the cultivation of peanuts, trading, and the donations of disciples was especially intense after Amadu Bamba settled in Diourbel and stable relationships were established with the French. Abdu Samat Sylla recounted that by the time of the construction of the Mosque of Diourbel between 1916 and 1918, there was a *Kadd* (*Acacia albida*) tree in the public place of the Murid quarter facing the mosque, which was called *Kadd uk Junni*, literally meaning "the tree of a thousand francs." This was the place where only wealthy Murid sheikhs would gather. Interview, Diourbel, 28 June 2000.

100. This quotation is an excerpt from the Quran, sura 20 ("Taha"), v. 132. See Mbacké, *Majmuha*, 97.

101. Amadu Bamba reportedly said, referring to Jenn's attitude, "I would never again load a draft bull before assuring first that it was sufficiently tamed." Interviews with Abdu Samat Sylla, Diourbel, 28 June 2000, and Mustafa Njaate Mbakke, Mbakke, 30 June 2000. Alluding to the same incident, he confided to his disciple Ahmad Dem that in his whole life, there was only one instance when he was conscious of having violated God's prescriptions, and that was when he gave power to some ignorant people, which is forbidden by the Quran. Interviews with Abdurahim Dem and Mame Mor Dem, son and grandson of Ahmad Dem, Diourbel, 30 July 2000, and Tuubaa, 29 July 2000.

102. Abdu Samat Sylla, interview, Diourbel, 28 June 2000.

103. See Diop, *Irwā*, 103–9; I also refer to my interviews with Abdu Samat Sylla, son of Majemb Sylla, Diourbel, 28 June 2000, and Makhtar Joob, a grandson of M. L. Joob, Diourbel, 28 June 2000 and 19 July 2000; Makhtar Joob runs the Quranic school founded by his grandfather in Diourbel.

104. Interview with Galo Mbay, Tuubaa, 14 February 2000.

105. A copy of this letter in Arabic was displayed by the Murid archivist and collector Mustafa Cuun at the exhibit at the House of Serigne Tuuba in Harlem on the occasion of Amadu Bamba Day in New York City, 25–28 July 2005.

106. On the relationships between Amadu Bamba and Maam Cerno, see John Glover, "The Hope in This World and the Next: Maam Cerno and the Settlement of Darou Mousty, 1912–1947" (PhD diss., University of Chicago–Illinois, 2000), and "The Mosque Is One Thing, the Administration Is Another: Murid Marabouts and Wolof Aristocrats in Colonial Senegal," *IJAHS* 33 (2000): 351–65. See also James Searing, *God Alone Is King* (Portsmouth, NH: Heinemann, 2001), 242–54.

107. See Guy Rocheteau, *Société Wolof et mobilité*, brochure (Dakar: ORSTOM, 1973).

108. See Cruise O'Brien, *The Mourides*, 165.

109. Marty, *Études sur l'Islam au Sénégal*, 1:246. See also his fiche de renseignement at ANS, 13G 68.

110. Interview with Mustafa Njaate, Mbakke, 30 July 2000.

111. Cheikh T. Sy proposed the return of Amadu Bamba from his first exile in 1902 as the date for the creation of the first daara tarbiyya, but he did not provide evidence to support this assumption; see his *La confrérie sénégalaise des mourides*, 174.

112. Denise Bouche, "L'école française et les Musulmans du Sénégal de 1850 à 1920," *Revue Française d'Histoire d'Outre-Mer* 223 (1974): 218–35.

113. Cheikh Hamidou Kane, in his novel *Ambiguous Adventure* (London: Heinemann, 1972), Amar Samb, in *Matraqué par le destin ou la vie d'un talibé* (Dakar, 1973), and the filmmaker Mahama Johnson Traoré, in *Njangaan*, described and criticized the hardships to which young disciples in the Quranic schools of Senegal are subjected.

114. For more on the ways in which Murid mysticism helped the expansion of peanut cultivation to eastern Senegal, see Paul Pélissier, *Les paysans du Sénégal: Les civilisations agraires du Cayor à la Casamance* (Saint-Yrieix [Haute Vienne]: Fabrègue, 1966).

115. This was, for example, the case with the daara of Sheikh Ahmad Ndumbe. Interview with Mor Talla Mbakke, Gowaan, 24 April 2000.

116. See John Glover on the contribution of Maam Cerno during the periods of famine that beset Kajoor in the early twentieth century, "Maam Cerno," 150–61. I also refer to my interview with the late Sokhna Marema Sey, the last living wife of Ibra Faati, Daaru Muhti, 29 May 1991.

117. Sy, *La confrérie sénégalaise des mourides*, 175.

118. In an article on Murid migrants in New York, I examined how networks of disciples function as sources of social capital for Murid disciples engaged in business ventures. See my "Brotherhood Solidarity, Education, and Migration: The Role of the *Dahiras* among the Murid Muslim Community of New York," *African Affairs* 403 (2002): 151–70.

119. See Marty, *L'Islam au Sénégal*, 223.

120. See Cruise O'Brien, *The Mourides*, 38.

121. See Bachir Mbacké, *Les bienfaits de l'éternel* (Dakar, 1995), 63; Ross, "Touba et ses soeurs," 51; Donal Cruise O'Brien, *The Mourides*, 13 and 40; A. B. Diop, "Lat Dior et le problème musulman," *BIFAN* ser. B, 28 (1966): 493–539; Sy, *La confrérie sénégalaise des mourides*, 109.

122. Interviews in Mbakke Kajoor with Bara Mbakke and Modu Sey, head of the village, 20 May 2000.

123. Cruise O'Brien is the only source that placed Bamba in Kajoor at this date, and by doing so, he established a chronology that conflicts with archival and oral information regarding the dates marking different stages of Amadu Bamba's life in Bawol and Kajoor. For instance, he situated Amadu Bamba in Daaru Salaam in 1891 (see Cruise O'Brien, *The Mourides*, 41), whereas oral sources and French intelligence reports agree that at that date, Amadu Bamba had been living in Tuubaa for more than two years. In fact, as noted earlier, the name of Amadu Bamba appeared for the first time in the archives in 1889, and by then, he was already living in Tuubaa.

124. It is particularly relevant here to observe that most of the evidence gathered by the prosecutors in this trial came from information provided by African chiefs who were also active participants in Kayorian politics during Lat Joor's rule. Therefore, these chiefs certainly would have known of the meeting if it had taken place, and they would have shared the information with the colonial administration.

125. Mbakhane Joob, Dammeel Lat Joor's son, turned out to be one of the worst enemies of the Murids in the early years of his career as chief of eastern Bawol in the late nineteenth century, but later on, he became a disciple of Amadu Bamba and married some of his sisters to Murid sheikhs.

126. See Diop, "Lat Dior et le problème Musulman."

127. Mamadu Mustafa, Amadu Bamba's elder son and first successor, for example, married Fatma Joob, a daughter of Lat Joor's brother. Sheikh Ibra Faal also married two daughters of Lat Joor, Kumba Celemaan and Fama Joob, and two daughters of former kings of Kajoor. For an analysis of the power shift in the Wolof kingdoms in the late nineteenth and early twentieth centuries and how the traditional elite and the emerging Muslim leadership renegotiated the social basis of legitimacy and power, see Catherine Boone, *Political Topographies of the African State: Territorial Authority and Institutional Choice* (Cambridge: Cambridge University Press, 2003), 56.

128. See chapter 3 for a description and analysis of these events.

129. We can speculate that Amadu Bamba might have founded the order earlier had he not been exiled in Gabon between 1895 and 1902. However, as we shall see later in the volume, the exile was a defining moment in the building of his credentials as a Sufi saint and a friend of God. It also enhanced his influence and prestige as a tariqa founder.

130. See Mbacké, *Majmuha*, 30.

131. Abdel Wedoud Ould Cheikh cited a letter that Amadu Bamba wrote to Sheikh Sidiyya in which he was asking questions about legal purification, the use of the *Basmala* (opening verse of the Quran) in prayer, the evaluation of zakaat from ears of millet, the age of circumcision, and food prohibition; see his "Espace confrérique," 6.

132. See Rahal Boubrik, *Saints et société en Islam* (Paris, 1999).

133. See the family trees of Amadu Bamba on his mother's and father's sides in figure 3.1. It is likely that the genealogy that ties Amadu Bamba to the family of the Prophet Muhammad (appendix 2) was built by some of his Moor disciples as a way of justifying their submission to a black African. In effect, Would Muhammad Miska, a Moorish hagiographer of Amadu Bamba, affirmed that the latter owed his baraka to his sharifian origins on his mother's as well as his father's sides and to his love of the *bidan* (white Moors). See Ould Cheikh, "Espace confrérique," 8.

134. See Mbakke, *Majmuha*, 75. This proclamation was circulated by a certain Bashir Ibn Abd Allah Al-Alfaghi, whom Amadu Bamba introduced as a close disciple of his.

135. See Mbacké, *Les bienfaits*, 145.

136. There are different versions of this widely circulated story. The version I give here comes from my interviews with Sheikh Maam Balla Mbakke, Mbakke, 5 May 1991 and 29 May 2000; Sawru Mbay, Daaru Salaam, 1 March 2000 and 6 March 2000; and Elhaj Jakhate, Tuubaa, 10 June 2000. In many of his writings, Amadu Bamba alluded to encounters with Prophet Muhammad, but he did not elaborate on what happened during these encounters. He only indicated recommendations, interdictions, or promises that the Prophet made to him and the commitments he made to the Prophet.

137. In a letter he wrote in 1910 to express his position with regard to the jihad of Mal Aynin in Mauritania, Amadu Bamba (following in this a certain Muslim

tradition) noted that jihad was part of Sunna (prophetic traditions) but that it had been prescribed for specific times and to specific peoples. He explained that jihad could be lawfully performed only in conditions in which Muslims would have weaponry, military forces, and accommodations equal to those of their enemies and in which they could fight under the guidance of a caliph recognized unanimously by the community of believers. See ANS, dossab, 1910.

138. In the following chapter, I offer a thorough discussion of what Murids consider "supernatural" or mystical causes of the conflict with the French.

139. Ould Sheikh, "Espace confrérique," 6.

CHAPTER 5

1. For a discussion of the resilience of traditional power under French rule in Senegal, see Philippe Couty as quoted in Donal Cruise O'Brien, Momar-Coumba Diop, and Mamadou Diof, eds., *La construction de l'état au Sénégal*, 34. See also Catherine Boone, *Political Topographies of the African State: Territorial Authority and Intstitutional Choice* (Cambridge: Cambridge University Press, 2003), 56; and Irving Leonard Markovitz, "Traditional Social Structure, the Islamic Brotherhoods and Political Development in Senegal," *Journal of Modern African Studies* 8 (April 1970): 62–63. In a recent article about Daaru Muhti, the fief of Amadu Bamba's brother Ibra Faati (Maam Cerno), John Glover discussed how African chiefs and rival Murid sheikhs used colonial administrators to further their own economic and political agendas and settle scores; see his "The Mosque Is One Thing, the Administration Is Another," *IJAHS* 33 (2001): 351–65.

2. For more on the relations between the French and the African chiefs in colonial Senegal, see Kalidou Diallo, "Les chefs de canton du Fouta, 1860–1960 (Mémoire de maîtrise, Département d'Histoire, Université de Dakar, 1985). See also François Zucarelli, "De la chefferie traditionnelle au canton: Évolution du canton colonial au Sénégal, 1855–1960," *Cahiers d'Études Africaines* 50 (1973): 213–38.

3. On many occasions, I have tried, unsuccessfully, to convince my interviewees to provide specific information about chiefs who denounced Murids to the colonial administration. Bachir Mbacké and Musa Ka blasted the African chiefs for their role in fueling the tension between the French and Amadu Bamba, but they generally avoided citing names or referring to specific events.

4. See Pierre Nora, *Les lieux de mémoire*, vol. 1, *La République* (Paris, 1984), xix–xx.

5. Angot, "Mission Angot dans le Diambour et le Baol 1889," ANS, 1G 136, 11.

6. See James Searing, "Accommodation and Resistance: Chiefs, Muslim Leaders and Politicians in Colonial Senegal, 1890–1934" (PhD diss., Princeton University, 1985), 53.

7. It was, for example, to Demba Waar Sall and not to the governor that the notables of Bawol appealed in 1889 for the abolition of the monarchy in this king-

dom. See ANS, 2D 7 Baol, correspondence 1889, letter from "Diambours to Demba War."

8. See Rapport de Monsieur le Directeur des Affaires Politiques au Conseil Privé, séance du 5 Septembre 1895, in Oumar Ba, *Ahmadou Bamba face aux autorités* (Abbeville: Fayard, 1982), 62. Ba was an archivist at the Senegalese National Archives in Dakar. His book is an important collection of archival documents pertaining to the relationships between Amadu Bamba and the colonial administration. It is an indispensable source for the reconstruction of the history of the Muridiyya.

9. See "Rapport sur Amadou Bamba et ses Mourites," by Lasselves, commandant of the Cercle of Diourbel, 22 Octobre, 1915, ANS, dossab, 4.

10. Mbakhane Diop, chief of Eastern Bawol, accused Amadu Bamba of undermining his authority because he ignored his summons and claimed that he would only respond to the governor's directives; see ANS, dossab, April 1903; Paul Marty, *Études sur l'Islam au Sénégal* (Paris: E. Leroux, 1917), 1:278, also notes this attitude of the Murids.

11. See numerous complaints by Coumba Ndofène Diouf, superior chief of Siin; Ibrahima Ndaw, chief of Ndukumaan; Ibra Dior in Salum; and Mbakhane Diop, chief of eastern Bawol, ANS, dossab, 1903.

12. See the Angot report, ANS, 1G 136, 11–12.

13. As early as June 1889, rehashing the complaints of Ibrahima Njaay and the local chiefs of the province of Njambur, Governor Clément-Thomas was accusing Amadu Bamba of gathering around him people of low social background and of emptying and perverting "his villages." See letter of governor-general to Amadu Bamba, in Ba, *Ahmadou Bamba face aux autorités*, 28.

14. The chiefs' attitude toward the abolition of slavery constitutes a good illustration of this assumption. Knowing the economic importance of peanuts to the colonial administration, chiefs in Kajoor convinced the French that an aggressive antislavery policy in the protectorates would lead to the massive migration of slave-owning agriculturalists and to the ruin of the colony's economy. The French bought into this argument and not only turned a blind eye to the use of slave labor but also deannexed territories formerly under their direct rule to make it easier for slave owners to continue their practice. It must be added, however, that the system of forced labor practiced by the colonial administration was nothing but a disguised form of slavery. In other words, both the chiefs and the French administration had an interest in impeding the application of French liberal laws to people living in the protectorates.

15. Lucy Behrman, "French Muslim Policy and Senegalese Brotherhoods," in *Aspects of West African Islam*, ed. Daniel McCall and Norman R. Bennett, Boston University Papers on Africa 5 (Boston: African Studies Center, Boston University, 1971), 201.

16. This was the case in 1903 when intelligence gathered by spies clearly showed that Amadu Bamba was not preparing for war to resist arrest, but the administration

nevertheless continued to mobilize troops to attack the cleric following the alarming reports and advice they received from African chiefs. For more on these events, see chapter 6.

17. In chapter 3, I referred to the case of the interpreter Fara Biram Lo. Lo forged letters to substantiate an alleged alliance between King Samba Laobé of Jolof and Amadu Bamba in order to discredit the former, whose job he coveted. In chapter 7, I discuss the case of Théveniaut, the commandant of Diourbel, whose thirst for power and will to subdue the Murids finally led to his dismissal.

18. See J.-L. Triaud, introduction to *Le temps des Marabouts: Itinéraires et stratégie islamiques en Afrique Occidentale Française v. 1880–1960*, ed. David Robinson and Jean-Louis Triaud (Paris: Karthala, 1997), 13.

19. On the pitfalls of archival documents, see M. N. Mack, "The AOF Archives and the Study of African History," *BIFAN* ser. B, 42 (1980): 277–98; see also David Edwards, *Heroes of the Age* (Berkeley: University of California Press, 1996), 10.

20. See "Plainte des frères d'Amadou Bamba" in lettre de Prempain, administrateur du cercle de Thiès au Gouverneur Général, 26 mai 1903, ANS, 11D 1, 30; also Allys, administrateur de Tivavouane, rapport politique, 24 June 1903, in ANS, dossab.

21. See lettre de l'administrateur René Massetche, Résident du Baol au Commandant du Cercle de Thiès, 25 Octobre 1905, ANS, 10D 3, 35.

22. See Bachir Mbacké, *Les bienfaits de l'éternel*, translated and edited by Khadim Mbacké (Dakar, 1995), 49–50.

23. Bachir Mbacké, in ibid., as well as Paul Marty, in *L'Islam au Sénégal*, 225, referred to these letters.

24. See Ba, *Ahmadou Bamba face aux autorités*, 28; Bachir Mbacké also mentionsed this letter in *Les bienfaits*, 65.

25. See my analysis of these two reports later in this chapter.

26. Ba, *Ahmadou Bamba face aux autorités*, 28.

27. See Marty, *Études sur l'Islam*, 1:225.

28. Mbacké, *Les bienfaits*, 66.

29. This was also the opinion of David Robinson, who, when referring to the events of 1889, observed, "Saint Louis did not become alarmed about Bamba at this time"; see his *Paths of Accommodation: Muslim Societies and French Colonial Authorities in Senegal and Mauritania, 1880–1920* (Athens: Ohio University Press, 2000), 214.

30. See Leclerc, "Au sujet du marabout Amadou Bamba," ANFOM, sen. 4/127. This document summed up the findings of the inquiry into the Muridiyya ordered by the interim governor, Mouttet.

31. See "Au sujet du marabout Amadou Bamba," ANS, 3E 55, fol. 253.

32. This was indeed a large overestimation. In fact, Marty estimated the number of Murids in Njambur in 1913 at 450; see his *Études sur l'Islam*, 1:320.

33. On the significance of the label *tijani* in the French colonial discourse on Islam in Senegal, see David Robinson, "French 'Islamic' Policy and Practice in

Late Nineteenth Century Senegal," *JAH* 2 (1988): 415–35, and "Ethnography and Customary Law in Senegal," *CEA* 126 (1992): 185–221.

34. As reported by Mbacké, in *Les bienfaits*, 72. Bousso's statement is in quotation marks in the text. It is intriguing that this letter, which might have been an important piece for the defense of Amadu Bamba, is nowhere to be found in the archives.

35. See James Searing, *God Alone Is King* (Portsmouth, NH: Heinemann, 2001), 78.

36. On the policy of these two governors, see Robinson, *Paths of Accommodation*, 69.

37. See Monographie du cercle de Diourbel, ANS, 10D 5, 8.

38. According to colonial estimates, Muslims were a minority in Bawol, and the Muslim population was composed of a majority of Tijaani and Qadiri. The Murids formed a minority but a fast-growing one. See ibid.

39. Ibid.

40. See Paul Pélissier, *Les paysans du Sénégal: Les civilisations agraires du Cayor à la Casamance* (Saint-Yrieix [Haute Vienne]: Fabrègue, 1966), 337–38.

41. The councils who sat in the trial of Amadu Bamba were: M. M. Mouttet, interim governor; de Kersaint-Gilly, commissioner for the colonies, head of the administrative services; Boyer, lieutenant colonel, interim superior commander of the colonial army; Jurquet, interim director of internal affairs; Cnapelynck, interim attorney general; Clarac, physician, interim chief of health services; Nogaret, navy lieutenant and representative of the commander of the naval forces; J. Beziat, private council; Sambain, deputy private council; and M. Superville, interim secretary archivist. See Ba, *Ahmadou Bamba face aux autorités*, 62.

42. Cheikh Abdoulaye Dièye, *L'exil au Gabon, 1895–1902: Sur les traces de Cheikh Ahmadou Bamba* (Dakar: Ndigel, 1985).

43. See Ba, *Ahmadou Bamba face aux autorités*, 67.

44. On the "Jeandet affair" and the involvement of the Saint-Louis "opposition," see Robinson, *Paths of Accommodation*, 64–69.

45. Leclerc report of 15 July, ANFOM, sen. 4/127, 5.

46. In fact, both Mbakhane Diop and Salmon Fall were teenagers when they were appointed chiefs of eastern and western Bawol, respectively, in 1896. Mbakane was sixteen, and both young men, after graduating from the School of Sons of Chiefs in Saint-Louis, were escorted by Merlin to Tunis, where they completed their training.

47. The governor-general, who was headquartered in Saint-Louis, was also the head of the administration of the colony of Senegal. The two positions were separated in 1904 with the appointment of lieutenant governors who were responsible for the direct administration of the individual territories of the federation.

48. Amadou Bamba Mbacké, *Jazaau Shakuur* [Tribute to the Worthy of Recognition], translated into French and edited by the Association of Murid Students of University Cheikh Anta Diop of Dakar (UCAD) (Dakar, n.d.). There are

probably other versions of this work. M. L. Diop, in his biography of Amadu Bamba, quotes extensively from what seems to be a different version that provides details missing in the one translated by the students.

49. See Mbacké, *Jazaau Shakuur*, 7.

50. M. L. Diop mentions the initiatives of Muslims in Saint-Louis and Njambur who proposed to intervene on behalf of Amadu Bamba, but the latter declined, telling them to leave everything in God's hands. See Diop, *Irwā*, 47. It was also reported that Ahmad Njaay Mabeey, a Muslim notable in Saint-Louis, initiated a petition and collected signatures from the Muslim dignitaries of the city to plead for the release of Amadu Bamba. Interview with Madické Wade, Saint-Louis, 6 July 2001.

51. Amadu Bamba's depiction of his stay in Saint-Louis did not corroborate some of the information disseminated by oral traditions. Bamba spoke of hardships he suffered in Saint-Louis but did not mention imprisonment in a cell or change of venues of detention. He seemed to indicate that he inhabited the same location during his sojourn in the city. See Mbacké, *Jazaau Shakuur*, 11.

52. The symbolism of two rakaas is important. Muslims perform this abridged prayer in a situation of emergency and adversity. Sheikh Hamallah, founder of a dissident branch of the Tijaniyya in French Sudan (present-day Mali), adopted this practice when he confronted the hostility of the colonial administration. See Louis Brenner, *West African Sufi* (Berkeley: University of California Press, 1984), and Alioune Traoré, *Cheikh Hamahoullah, homme de foi et résistant: Islam et colonization en Afrique* (Paris: Maisonneuve et Larose, 1983). Therefore, the prayer that Amadu Bamba is said to have performed during his trial can be seen as a statement against the colonial administration, and that is how it is understood by contemporary Murid disciples, who gather every year in Saint-Louis to commemorate this event. For a discussion of the religious and political significance of this event, see Cheikh Anta Babou, "Urbanizing Mystical Islam: Making Murid Space in the Cities of Senegal," *International Journal of African Historical Studies* (forthcoming).

53. See Mbacké, *Les bienfaits*, 51, and also Diop, *Irwā*, 47.

54. This is the standard version of Murid oral traditions.

55. Mbacké, *Les bienfaits*, 51.

56. Murid oral tradition considers that Amadu Bamba's stay in Saint-Louis was extended because members of the Conseil could not agree about a sentence. But it seems that the delay between the condemnation and the execution of the sentence was instead due to transportation arrangements; the ship transporting Bamba to equatorial Africa was scheduled to arrive in Dakar from South America on 20 September.

57. See Délibération du Conseil Privé séance du 5 février 1895, in Ba, *Ahmadou Bamba face aux autorités*, 62. "Internment" was a provision of the decree of 30 September 1887 (also known as the Indigenat Law) that defined the disciplinary powers vested in the colonial administration. It was a form of punishment

meted out to those convicted of grave political offenses. The provision was the remnant of a wartime law designed to give the authorities a free hand to deal with any offense that was not expressly described by the law but was considered dangerous for public security and colonial rule. See Mbaye Guèye, "Les éxils de Cheikh Ahmadou Bamba au Gabon et en Mauritanie," *Annales de la Faculté des Lettres et Sciences Humaines de l'Université de Dakar* 25 (1995): 49.

58. See Mbacké, *Jazaau Shakuur*, 35.

59. Ibid.

60. Interview with Ibrahima Jaagne Mbay, Dakar, 1 October 1999; Mbay is a grandson of Ibra Binta Gey, the civil servant who hosted Amadu Bamba in Dakar on his way to Gabon after he was released from the cell. Jaagne Mbay later studied with the cleric in Diourbel.

61. According to Musa Ka, it was a lieutenant (it could have been a much lower-ranked soldier) in the colonial army named Yoro who suggested that Amadu Bamba write the letter of appeal; see Mbacké, *Jazaau Shakuur*, 110. The name of Lieutenant Yoro, which seems to function as a metaphor, comes up in other stories related to the interactions between Bamba and the colonial administration. M. L. Diop related the same story but did not mention the name of the person who advised Bamba to write the letter; see his *Irwā*, 49.

62. Mbacké, *Jazaau Shakuur*, 53–55.

63. Ibid., 57.

64. See Diop, *Irwā*, 50.

65. See Mbacké, *Jazaau Shakuur*, 31.

66. On Murid oral tradition as a history of commemoration, see Searing, *God Alone Is King*, 93.

67. On the situation of the Muridiyya after the departure of Amadu Bamba in exile, I rely primarily on my interviews with Isa Mbakke, a cousin of Amadu Bamba and great-grandson of Balla Mbakke, Tuubaa, 2 July 2000. He provided the most detailed narrative of this episode in the development of the Muridiyya, and I supplement the data from this interview with information I collected from interviews with Sawru Mbay, Mbakke, 6 March 2000, and Mustafa Njaate, Mbakke, 30 July 2000. M .L. Diop's biography of Amadu Bamba also offers useful information.

68. Interview with Isa Mbakke, Tuubaa, 2 July 2000.

69. Isa Mbakke is a grandson of Ibra Nguy, and it might be that he was giving credit to his ancestor for an initiative that could have been a collective decision of the family of Modu Jee Mbakke, which ruled this area of Mbakke Bawol.

70. Interview with Isa Mbakke, Tuubaa, 2 July 2000.

71. A traditional healer later convinced Cerno to abandon the house on the ground that it was haunted. See ibid.

72. See ANS, III-2G 1/106, Rapports politiques, commerciaux et agricoles mensuels, cercle de Dakar-Thiès; rapport mensuel, Septembre 1895 par l'administrateur du cercle, Thiès le 7 Octobre 1895.

73. Interview with Galo Mbay, Tuubaa, 14 February 2000. Also see Marty, *L'Islam au Sénégal*, who stated that the chief of Njambur had forbidden Murid disciples to enter the territory under his authority (225).

74. It is even alleged that written records of these declarations exist and that the third caliph of the Murids, Abdul Ahad Mbakke, after difficult negotiations with the French government through the government of Senegal and the late Murid billionaire Njuga Kebe, was able to see them, but they are kept secret because of the subversive nature of the information they contain. Interview with Bachir Mbakke A. Niang, who claims to have read excerpts concerning his father, Maam Cerno, Daaru Muhti, 18 July 2000. Maam Moor Dem also claimed to know some of the people who helped the caliph translate the documents into Arabic; interview in Tuubaa, 29 July 2000. Whether this document exists is uncertain, but I am aware that Arabic translations of Amadu Bamba's file at the Senegalese National Archives and some of the letters he exchanged with the French are kept at the library Maktabatul Cheikh ul Khadime of Tuubaa.

75. Interviews with Makhtar Buso, a son of Mbacké Bousso, Tuubaa, 11 June 2000, and Mortalla Mbakke, a grandson of Sheikh A. Ndumbe, Gowaan, 29 April 2000.

76. See Marty, *Islam au Sénégal*, 256.

77. Interview with Bachir Mbakke A. Niang, Daaru Muhti, 18 July 2000. It is interesting to note that though some bearers of Murid oral traditions are reluctant to talk about these events, disciples and descendants of Maam Cerno Ibra Faati, who bore the burden of watching over Amadu Bamba's family during the exile, are quite open to this question.

78. Abdel Wedoud Ould Cheikh has found letters he sent to Sheikh Sidiyya while Amadu Bamba was away in Gabon; see his "Espace confrérique, espace étatique," unpublished paper, 2001, 7.

79. See Khadim Mbacké, *Soufisme et confréries religieuses musulmanes au Sénégal*, 69.

80. Interviews with Mustafa Njaate Mbakke, Mbakke, 30 July 2000; Sawru Mbay, Daaru Salaam, 1 March 2000; and Sheikh Maam Balla Mbakke, Mbakke, May 1991 and 29 May 2000.

81. ANS, 3B/72, fol. 297, letter no. 72. See a copy of this document in Ba, *Ahmadou Bamba face aux autorités*, 91.

82. For more on the political significance of Carpot's election and his involvement with French subjects in the protectorates, see Wesley Johnson, *The Emergence of Black Politics in Senegal: The Struggle for Power in the Four Communes* (Stanford, CA: Stanford University Press, 1971).

83. See excerpts from the letter that Maam Cerno wrote to Sheikh Sidiyya to this end in Ould Cheikh, *"Espace confrérique,"* 7.

84. See Mbacké, *Les bienfaits*, 77.

85. See ANS, dossab, 1903 and 1913.

86. See the painting in Ba, *Ahmadou Bamba face aux autorités*; insert between pp. 106 and 107. Diallo is a painter who specializes in the reproduction of historical scenes. He has done extensive works on colonialism and resistance in Senegal.

87. Neither oral traditions nor the French archives make reference to the announcement of the cleric's return or a public reception. Bachir Mbacké, though, notes that a group of disciples went to welcome Amadu Bamba at the harbor, in *Les bienfaits*, 77–78.

88. See Diop, *Irwā*, 68–70.

89. See a reproduction of Mor Guèye's glass paintings of the Daaru Salaam reception in Allen and Mary Roberts, *A Saint in the City: Sufi Arts of Urban Senegal* (Los Angeles: UCLA Fowler Museum of Natural History, 2003), 101.

90. Interviews with Galo Mbay, Tuubaa, 14 February 2000 and 1 March 2000.

91. Amadu Bamba made this statement in a sermon he delivered while under house arrest in Diourbel, probably in the 1920s, since he made reference to events that happened in 1918. For a complete transcription of this sermon, see Mbacké, *Majmuha*, 20.

92. Quran, sura 8, v. 30. See Ahmed Ali, *Al Quran: A Contemporary Translation* (Princeton, NJ: Princeton University Press, 1988), 156.

93. Quran, sura 8, v. 15, in ibid., 155.

94. Quran, sura 8, v. 45, in ibid., 158.

95. See Mbacké, *Jazaau Shakuur*, 7 (emphasis added).

96. See *Assiiru Maha al Ibraari* [I March with the Honored], French translation in Amar Samb, *Essai sur la contribution du Sénégal à la littérature d'expression arabe* (Dakar: IFAN, 1972), 445, and also the version in Amadou Bamba Mbacké, *Assiiru Maha al Ibraari*, trans. and ed. Pape K. Seck (Dakar: Impression Édition Islamique, n.d.), 6. Excerpts from this poem are also found in Diop, *Irwā*, 45.

97. See Amadou Bamba Mbacké, *Massalik Al-Jinan* (Rabat, 1984), 188.

98. Amadou Bamba Mbacké, *Muqaddimaat ul amda fii mazzayaal miftaah* [*Les prémices des éloges sur les mérites de celui qui est la clef*] (Dakar: Impression Édition Islamique, n.d.), 63.

99. Mbacké, *Jazaau Shakuur*, 19.

100. Ibid., 23.

101. Interviews with Elhaj Jakhate, Tuubaa, 10 June 2000, and Afia Niang, Tuubaa, 30 May 2000.

102. Mbacké, *Jazaau Shakuur*, 15.

103. For more on Al Jazuli, see Vincent Cornell, *Realm of the Saint: Power and Authority in Moroccan Sufism* (Austin: University of Texas Press, 1998), esp. chap. 6 and 7.

104. See "Confidences to the Disciples," Mbacké, *Majmuha*, 21. Amadu Bamba made the same statement with slight variations in a letter he wrote to Ibra Faati, probably while he was in Mauritania (from 1903 to 1907), giving him instructions as how to teach his writings, in ibid., 147.

105. The number that is often given is seven tons, and there is much emphasis on works that Amadu Bamba had allegedly thrown in the sea or buried in Tuubaa. Of course, here also, one should be reminded of the symbolism of the number seven, which is the number of years that Bamba spent in Gabon. The number seven is also recurrent in the Quran, where Allah, for example, refers to seven skies.

Fernand Dumont has estimated the writings of Amadu Bamba at forty-one poems or thirty thousand verses. But since he published his work in 1974, more poems have been discovered; see Samb, *Essai sur la contribution*, 435. Abdou Malal Diop cited forty-nine pieces of work; see his "Traductions et commentaire du *Viatique des Jeunes* d'Ahmadou Bamba" (Thèse de doctorat de troisième cycle s/d Professeur Amar Samb Université de Dakar Faculté des Lettres et Sciences Humaines, Département Arabe, 1985), appendices. The printing of Amadu Bamba's works was started in the 1930s by entrepreneurial Murid disciples who had connections in Tunisia, where an Arabic printing press was available. In the 1940s and 1950s, M. L. Diop convinced the second caliph of the Murids to collect and edit some of the cleric's writings. However, it was in the 1970s, with the building of a library and printing press in Tuubaa, that the publication and diffusion of Amadu Bamba's writings experienced an unprecedented expansion.

106. See Mbacké, *Muqaddimaat al amda*, 40 and 48.

107. See Mbacké, *Jazaau Shakuur*, 55.

108. For more on the griot, its status, and its role in West African societies, see Isabelle LeyMarie, "The Role and Functions of Griots among the Wolof of Senegal" (PhD diss., Columbia University, 1979); Sory Camara, *Gens de la parole: Essai sur la condition et le rôle des griots dans la société Malinké* (Paris: Karthala, 1992); Thomas A. Hale, *Griots and Griottes: Masters of Words and Music* (Bloomington: Indiana University Press, 1998); and Mamadou Diawara, *L'empire du verbe et l'éloquence du silence: Vers une anthropologie du discours dans les groupes dit dominés du Sahel* (Cologne: Köppe, 2003).

109. For example, from 1903 on, administrators started to express their frustration and dismay at the fact that Murids were claiming Bamba had returned to Senegal voluntarily after he had completed the mission God assigned him and that he could have come through the air had he wanted to do so. See Vienne, administrateur du cercle de Thiès, rapports annuels et semestriels sur le bas Sénégal, 2G 3, 7, ANS, dossab, May 1903; Allys, Administrateur de Tivavouane, 1905 rapport 1ier trim, ANS, dossab, 1903.

110. For more on the role of memory and the state in the writing of history, see the special issue of the *International Journal of African Historical Studies* devoted to these questions, especially the introductory comments of Richard Roberts, "History and Memory: The Power of Statist Narratives," *IJAHS*, 33, no. 3 (2000): esp. 513–33. Marty's works on Islam in Africa, particularly his writings on the Muridiyya, seem to offer a good model of the "statist narrative." Marty was an expert Islamist who worked for an administration keen on basing its policy on knowledge of the local people's cultures; most of his sources came from colonial archives. Further, his findings served as the basis for the formulation of official policy, and his scholarship was prominent in the colonial library. The lieutenant governor of Senegal commended Marty's works for dissipating the mystery that surrounded Amadu Bamba and for providing clear guidance for French Muslim policy in Senegal; see ANS, 2G 13, 7, "Rapport polique d'ensemble sur le Sénégal, 1913." In

1917, his office issued a directive mandating the purchase of two copies of Marty's book *L'Islam au Sénégal* for each district of the colony of Senegal for the education of the administrators. Four copies were also bought for the office of the governor-general and the public library. See ANS, 13G 67.

111. On the events between 1902, Amadou Bamba's return to Senegal, and 1913, the date of the installation in Diourbel, see chapter 6.

112. See Diâo Faye, "L'oeuvre poétique wolofal de Moussa Ka" (Thèse pour un doctorat de troisième cycle, Université Cheikh Anta Diop de Dakar, 1999), 66.

113. See Amar Samb, "Jaaraama," BIFAN ser. B, 36 (1974): 592–612.

114. During my field research, I came across some of Musa Ka's informants.

115. See *Jazaau Shakuur* (the Wolofal version) in Faye, "L'oeuvre poétique," 94.

116. Ibid., 111–12.

117. Some Murid sources estimate the number of tortures at 285. Numbers have a great symbolism among the Sufis. Each letter of the Arabic alphabet has a numerical value, and mystics claim that by combining some of these letters (numbers), they can learn a good deal about the present and the future and have an impact on peoples' lives. This belief gave birth to the science of numerology, which is mostly practiced by followers of Sufism. For more on this science, see Brenner, *West African Sufi*; see also Cheikh A. Tall, *Niche des secrets: Recueils d'arcanes mystiques dans la tradition soufie (Islamique)* (Dakar: Librairie islamique, 1995). In this case, 285 refers to the number of verses that are contained in the Quranic sura "The Cow," which is the second sura of the Quran and one of the longest and most important.

118. Mbacké, *Jazaau Shakuur* (Wolofal version), in Faye, "L'oeuvre poétique," 118, 128, 152.

119. Allen and Mary Roberts, in an interesting analysis of the unique picture of Amadu Bamba, explored some of the themes associated with the exiles and the popular imagery that grew from these events. See "The Aura of Amadu Bamba," *Anthropologie et Sociétés* 1 (1998): 15–38.

120. This play, entitled *Bamba mos xam* (Bamba, You Have to Taste Him to Know Him), was created by amateur artists in Kaolack, the largest city in midwest Senegal; these artists toured the Murid heartland of Bawol and Kajoor and inspired the creation of local groups, who developed their own version of the play.

121. See Cheikh Anta Babou, "Brotherhood Solidarity, Education and Migration: The Role of the *Dahiras* among the Murid Muslim Community of New York," *African Affairs* 403 (2002): 151–70; Sophie Bava, "De la baraka aux affaires: Ethos économico-religieux et transnationalité chez les migrants sénégalais mourides," *Revue Européenne de Migrations Internationales* 19 (2003): 69–84.

122. In a letter to Governor Merlin, dated 3 June 1903, an administrator blamed the miraculous stories told about Amadu Bamba for the aura of sainthood that now surrounded the cleric and induced many Muslim clerics to submit to him. He wrote, "This *marabout*'s [(Amadu Bamba's)] prestige has not ceased to augment since he returned from Congo [(French Equatorial Africa)]. His followers

like to recount everywhere they go that he returned from his own volition when he terminated his mission, because like Mohamet, he wanted to isolate himself in order to better worship and harvest God's blessing. They add that he returned at the moment of his choice despite the opposition of the 'toubabs' [(white people in Wolof, here meaning the French)]." ANS, dossab, juin 1903, piece no. 3.

123. For example, in May 1942, the general secretary of the Second Bureau was alarmed by the discovery of a xenophobic (read anti-French) poem in Wolofal authored by Musa Ka. And they only afterward learned that this poem was written between 1930 and 1935, in the context of Sheikh Anta's deportation to Mali. ANS, 11D 1, 0049.

124. James C. Scott, *Weapons of the Weak: Everyday Forms of Peasant Resistance* (New Haven, CT: Yale University Press, 1985) and *Domination and the Arts of Resistance: Hidden Transcripts:* (New Haven, CT: Yale University Press, 1990).

125. In 1913, in a letter to the governor-general, the director of political, administrative, and economic affairs wondered about what the colonial administration should do with Amadu Bamba. The dilemma was that by keeping him under house arrest, they would only add to his aura as a martyr, but if they released him, the Murids would see this as evidence of their sheikh's superior spiritual power and invulnerability and not as an expression of clemency. See ANS, dossab, janvier 1913, piece no. 2.

CHAPTER 6

1. See Jean-Louis Triaud, introduction to *Le temps des Marabouts: Itinéraires et stratégies islamiques en Afrique Occidentale Française v. 1880–1960*, ed. David Robinson and Jean-Louis Triaud (Paris: Karthala, 1997), 13–14, and Jürgen Osterhammel, *Colonialism: A Theoretical Overview* (Princeton, NJ: Markus Wiener, 1999), 63–67.

2. Shula Marks, in *The Ambiguities of Dependence in South Africa: Class, Nationalism, and the State in Twentieth Century Natal* (Baltimore: Johns Hopkins University Press, 1986), offers an interesting analysis of the complexities and contradictions in peoples' responses to domination.

3. Osterhammel, *Colonialism*, 65.

4. In the context of Muslim politics in Africa, the use of accommodation should not be restricted to the colonial era; Nehemia Letvzion has demonstrated that ulamas in sixteenth-century Songhay also resorted to this strategy in their relations with the Sony and Askia dynasties. See Letvzion, "Islam in West African Politics: Accommodation and Tension between the 'Ulamâ' and the Political Authorities," *Cahiers d'Études Africaines* 71, no. 3 (1978): 333–45. I have also discussed, in the first two chapters of this book, how Wolof Muslim clerics negotiated a modus vivendi with their often "pagan," or nominally Muslim, kings.

5. David Robinson, *Paths of Accommodation: Muslim Societies and French Colonial Authorities in Senegal and Mauritania, 1880–1920* (Athens: Ohio University Press, 2000), esp. chap. 11.

6. For more on Roume's policy and how it was shaped by republican idealism, see Alice Conklin, *A Mission to Civilize: The Republican Idea of Empire in France and West Africa, 1895–1930* (Stanford, CA: Stanford University Press, 1997).

7. Robinson, *Paths of Accommodation*, 39.

8. See discours de M. Merlin assurant l'intérime du GG Roume devant le Conseil du Gouvernement durant la session ordinaire de Décembre 1906, ANS, 5E 13, 8. Scholars have shown that the conceptual differentiation between the doctrines of association and assimilation does not have much relevance at the level of practice. However, Merlin's statement indicates that in the colonial mind, the personal sensibilities of an administrator could have an important impact on the ways policies were conducted. In the administration of the protectorates, for example, Roume was eager to return to values and practices associated with the precolonial political order to find legitimate chiefs with traditional credentials. After the death of Demba Waar Sall, a slave of the crown and military ally of the French-appointed chief of the confederation of Kajoor, he rejected the candidacy of his son, Meissa Mbay Sall, and picked Mayacine Jeng, who had stronger credentials because he was descended from both Bawol and Kajoor ruling dynasties.

9. On 27 November 1902, Roume dispatched an important memo outlining the rationale and guidelines for the surveillance of Islam in the federation. He insisted on the need to monitor the activities of all Muslims who had or were likely to have some influence on the population. This surveillance would be done by collecting and centralizing information regarding their names, social backgrounds, family lineages and allies, the Muslim orders to which they belonged, the Sufi masters who initiated them, the number of disciples they had in their schools, and the names and social status of the parents of these disciples; see ANS, 3G 7. It was also under Roume, in 1906, that the subseries 19G, exclusively devoted to Muslim affairs, was created as a subdivision of the G series of the colonial archives. See D. Robinson, "France as a Muslim Power,"*Africa Today* 46 (1999): 105–27, endnote 13, 124.

10. On the growing influence of the Muridiyya after the return of Amadu Bamba from exile in 1902, see the reports of R. du Laurens, résident of Bawol, Vienne, administrator of Thiès and Victor Allys, in ANS dossab, 1902–3. Oral traditions also report that the Muridiyya was gaining increasing influence in Bawol.

11. It was this tradition that Majakhate Kala called on to convince Lat Joor to leave Amadu Bamba alone, when the latter was engaged in a polemic with the court regarding the enslavement of Muslims captured at the battle of Bundu. See chapter 3 for an extensive discussion of these issues.

12. See ANS, 3G7, Roume's memo of 27 November 1902 to the administrators.

13. See Mbakhane's report to du Laurens, résident of the province of Bawol in ANS, dossab, letter no. 3, Chef Supérieur au Résident, 25 April.

14. Ibid.

15. See ANS, dossab, letter no. 74, Résident à l'administrateur de Thiès, 1903.

16. Ibid.

17. See letter in Oumar Ba, *Ahmadou Bamba face aux autorités* (Abbeville, 1982), 104.

18. See some of these letters in ibid., 96–110.

19. See Oumar Niang's report in ibid., 112.

20. See letter of du Laurens, résident of Diourbel to the administrator of the district of Thiès, in ibid., 100.

21. M. L. Diop, for example, notes that all those around Amadu Bamba, except the disciples he had personally trained, were panicked, and some criticized Bamba harshly. He mentioned that, in contrast, the cleric was calm and that he continued to reassure the people that nothing bad would happen to them. According to Diop, Bamba even wrote a prayer and asked one of his Moorish disciples, Muhammad b. Ali Yaqub, to recite it out loud three times at the arrival of the soldiers, to assuage their anger and hostility. See Diop, *Irwā*, 73.

22. See the French translation of this letter, originally in Arabic, in ANS, dossab no. 14, 1903.

23. See Allys's instructions to the team in charge of conveying Amadu Bamba to Saint-Louis, 14 June 1903, in Ba, *Ahmadou Bamba face aux autorités*, 116–17. In these instructions, Allys recommended that Amadu Bamba be escorted only by an interpreter, a guard, and Sheikh Sidiyya's envoy to avoid being seen as a prisoner.

24. A copy of the letter he sent to the administration on behalf of Amadu Bamba in 1896 was found in the archives of the Sheikh Sidiyya family by Ould Cheikh; see A. W. Ould Cheikh, "Espace confrérique, espace étatique: Le mouridisme, le confrérisme et la frontière Mauritano-sénégalaise," paper (2001), 7. In this letter addressed to Merlin, Sheikh Sidiyya demanded that the administration pardon Amadu Bamba and return him to Senegal or send him to his compound in Mauritania.

25. In a letter to the governor-general, dated July 1903, the lieutenant governor of Senegal, Camille Guy, noted, "It is precisely because we have been respectful of the local customs [of the people in the protectorates] that we are accepting the perpetuation of abuses of power and excesses against which the population has been slow to react, to the detriment of the economic development of the country and the expansion of our ideas and civilization. ... Our authority seems sufficiently established in Senegal for us to need any longer the maintenance of the great provinces led by African chiefs." Quoted in Kalidou Diallo, "Les chefs de canton du Fouta, 1860–1960" (Mémoire de maîtrise, Département d'histoire, Université de Dakar, 1985), 73. By 1907, all the provinces were dismantled and the African chiefs fired.

26. See O. Depont and X. Coppolani, *Les confréries religieuses musulmanes* (Algiers, 1897).

27. See, for example, ANS, 2G 3, 7, Rapports semestriels et annuels, cercles du Bas Sénégal, Rapport sur la situation politique et économique des cerles du Bas

Sénégal pendant le premier semestre de 1903. In this document, Roume noted that he believed that "accommodation with the Muslim leadership was possible and that it had already started with Moorish clerics (Sidiyya Baba and Sheikh Saad Buh)."

28. See Lettre de Merlin à Sheikh Sidiyya, 23 June 1903, in Ba, *Ahmadou Bamba face aux autorités*, 119.

29. See Diop, *Irwā*, 75.

30. Interviews with Afia Niang, Tuubaa, 30 May 2000 and 31 May 2000; A. S. Sylla, Diourbel, 28 June 2000; and Makhtaar Joob, Diourbel, 28 June 2000 and 19 July 2000.

31. M. L Diop mentions an instance when Al-Hajj Ibrahim al Baghadadi, an Arab cleric who joined the Muridiyya in Mauritania, faced the criticism of Moors, who reproached him for submitting to a black; see Diop, *Irwā*, 126–27. More recently, there has been a reversal of this tendency. The Tijaniyya branch of Ibrahima Niass in Senegal has been very successful in recruiting *bidan* (Mauritanians who call themselves whites) disciples. On this question, see Diana Stone, "The Inversion of a Historical Tendency? The Tijaniyya Niass Movement in Mauritania," paper presented at the Conference on the Tijaniyya at the University of Illinois—Urbana/Champaign, 1–5 April 1996.

32. Interviews with Modu Maamun Niang, Tuubaa, 8 June 2000, and Afia Niang, Tuubaa, 30 May 2000–31 May 2000.

33. Interviews with Modu Maamun Niang, Tuubaa, 8 June 2000, and Sawru Mbay, Daaru Salaam, 1 March 2000. Anta Baabu and Soxna Buso Njaay, who were both aides to Maymuna El Kabir, told the same story in my interviews with them in Mbakke, 20 January 2002.

34. See Diop, *Irwā*, 93–95.

35. See ANS, 2G 5, 7, Sénégal rapports politiques 1–2–3–4ième trimestre, AOF à Paris; ANS, 2G5, 8, Sénégal rapports politiques mensuels.

36. See letter of 22 March of the governor-general to the lieutenant governor in Ba, *Ahmadou Bamba face aux autorités*, 126.

37. Ibid., 127.

38. Cited by Diop, in *Irwā*, 74.

39. See chapter 5, note 92.

40. Ahmed Ali, *Al Qur'an: A Contemporary Translation* (Princeton, NJ: Princeton University Press, 1988), sura 42, v. 15, 413. This verse relates to the relationships that, from the perspective of the sharia, or Islamic law, should exist between Muslims, Christians, and Jews.

41. In the Muslim state, Christians and Jews are recognized as "Peoples of the Book," who have the right to live, profess their faith, and manage their business as protected people, or *dhimmi*, subjected to a tax, or *jizya*. See chapter 5, especially the section titled "Rewards of Sufferings," for a discussion of Bamba's mystical interpretation of the arrest and exile to Gabon.

42. See Diop, *Irwā*, 76.

43. See Abdoul Ahad Mbacké, ed., *Cheikh Amadou Bamba: Fondateur de la confrérie des Mourides*, 2 vols. (Paris: Editions d'Art des Heures Clires, 1984). Ould Cheikh also referred to some of those Moorish disciples of Amadu Bamba and the hagiographic litterature they have produced to celebrate their sheikh's accomplishements; see his "Espace confrérique."

44. Interview with Afia Niang, Tuubaa, 30 June 2000.

45. According to Momar's grandson Sheikh Mbakke Beto, his grandfather became Murid in 1907; interview, Mbakke, 8 May 2000. This statement is corroborated by colonial sources, which reported a spectacular visit of Momar Jaara to Amadu Bamba while the latter was kept under house arrest in Ceyeen. This first visit seemed to coincide with his formal submission to his brother. Momar traveled to Ceyeen on 12 September 1907 with thirty-one followers, twenty of whom were on horseback. See ANS, dossab, 12 September 1907.

46. See lettre de l'administrateur de Louga au lieutenant gouverneur du Sénégal, à Saint-Louis, dated 3 October 1907, in Ba, *Ahmadou Bamba face aux autorités*, 131.

47. See Paul Marty, *Études sur l'Islam au Sénégal* (Paris: E. Leroux, 1917), 1:229.

48. See note in ANS, dossab, 1909.

49. See Lettre no. 455 du chef du bureau politique du 14 avril 1909, ANS, dossab, 1909. See also Cheikh A. Mb. Babou, "Le Mouridisme des origines a 1912" (Mémoire de maîtrise, Université de Dakar, 1991), 97.

50. See Arabic version and translation of this letter in ANS, dossab, 1910.

51. See letter written by the brothers of Amadu Bamba—Momar Jaara, Ibra Faati, and Sheikh Anta, ANS, dossab, 1909.

52. See ANS, dossab, piece no. 3, 19 December 1910. Several French translations of this proclamation are kept at the National Archives of Senegal in the dossier Amadu Bamba. There is no available Arab version of the document, which has led some Murid writers to deny the authenticity of the document. However, the ideas expressed in this fatwa with regard to jihad of the sword and the attitude toward the French colonial administration are consistent with some of the views that Amadu Bamba expressed elsewhere.

53. These verses are excerpts from the sura "The Consultation," v. 48, and the sura "The Infidels," v. 6.

54. Cheikh Moussa Camara provided a good articulation of this qadiri antijihad tradition. See Amar Samb, ed. and trans., "La condamnation de la guerre sainte de Cheikh Moussa Kamara," *BIFAN* ser. B, 38, no. 1 (1976): 158–99. On the attitude of the Kunta toward jihad, see their polemic with the jihadist Al-Hajj Umar in Mohamed Mahibou and J. L Triaud, *Voilà ce qui est arrivé: Bayân mâ waqa`a d'al-Hâgg 'Umar al-Fûtî: Plaidoyer pour une guerre sainte en Afrique de l'Ouest au XIXe siècle* (Paris: Centre national de la recherche scientifique, 1983).

55. On the influence of Ponty's politique des races on the administration of Senegal, see François Zucarelli, "De la chefferie traditionnelle au canton: Évolu-

tion du canton colonial au Sénégal, 1855–1960," *Cahiers d'Études Africaines* 13 (1973): 213–38.

56. See Wesley Johnson, "William Ponty and Republican Paternalism in West Africa, 1908–1915," in L. H. Gann and Peter Duignan, eds., *African Proconsuls* (New York: Free Press, 1978), 127–57.

57. The adoption of the idea of black Islam marked a departure from the Algerian model promoted by Governor Faidherbe and the Islamicist Coppolani, which advocated a universal approach to Islam and the use of the Sufi leadership in a sort of system of indirect rule. For more on France's changing perceptions of Islam in West Africa, see Christopher Harrison, *France and Islam in West Africa, 1860–1960* (Cambridge: Cambridge University Press, 1988).

58. See Jean L. Triaud, "Islam in Africa under French Colonial Rule," in *The History of Islam in Africa*, ed. Nehemia Levtzion and Randall Pouwels (Athens: Ohio University Press, 2000), 175.

59. Harrison, *France and Islam*, 109.

60. See Letter to the lieutenant governor dated 1 July 1908, in Ba, *Ahmadou Bamba face aux autorités*, 139.

61. See Sénégal, rapports politiques trimestriels: deuxième trimestre, Sénégal à AOF, AOF à Paris, ANS, 2G 8, 10.

62. See rapport d'ensemble sur les territoires de protectorat, 1911, ANS, 2G 11, 6, 11.

63. See correspondance no. 566 du 13 Avril 1911 au sujet du rapport politique du quatrième trimestre pour l'année 1910 addressée par le cabinet du G.G. au Lt. Gov. du Sen. ANS, 2G 5. The growing influence of the Muridiyya among the non-Muslim Sereer of Bawol and Thiès was particularly upsetting to Ponty because it undermined the very foundations of the politiques des races by blurring the ethnic boundaries it artificially drew between the people of West Africa.

64. Circulaire du lt. gov. à tous les administrateurs portant sur la transmission de la circulaire no 117 du 24 Dec. 1911 relative à la surveillance de l'Islam et à la réactivation du répertoire du prosélytisme musulman en Afrique Occidentale Française, ANS, 10D 3, 25. Files about all the major Murid sheikhs were opened between 1912 and 1913. Most of these files are available at the Senegalese National Archives in Dakar in the series 13G 67.

65. Sheikh Anta, for example, won Lieutenant Governor Peuvergne's praises for building a 19-kilometer-long and 10-meter-wide road linking his village of Gawaan to the popular market of Dappa and the town of Diourbel. See letter of Commandant Théveniaut to the lieutenant governor, 20 June 1908, and the lieutenant governor's response dated 2 July 1908, in ANS, 10D 3. Administrators also stressed the increasingly important role of Murid-dominated Bawol in the production of peanuts, especially after the Thiès-Kayes-Niger railway reached this district in 1911. See Monographie du cercle de Diourbel, ANS, 10D 5, 9. For more on the influence of economic considerations on the rapprochement between the Murids and the colonial administration, see Lucy Behrman, *Muslim*

Brotherhoods and Politics in Senegal (Cambridge, MA: Harvard University Press, 1970), 48.

66. Marc Michel notes that the "Plan Ponty," which proposed the recruitment and incorporation of two divisions of African soldiers in the French army, was a major boost to Mangin's project; see Michel, *L'appel à l'Afrique: Contributions et réactions à l'effort de guerre en AOF, 1914–1919* (Paris: Sorbonne, 1982), 4 and 7.

67. In fact, the Murids, with the approval of Amadu Bamba, helped the colonial administration recruit at least four hundred soldiers, despite the fact that some Murid sheikhs were suspected of hiding people fleeing conscription. For more on colonial conscription in Senegal, see Myron Echenberg, *Colonial Conscripts: The Tirailleurs Sénégalais in French West Africa, 1867–1960* (Portsmouth, NH: Heinemann, 1991).

68. See letter of Lieutenant Governor Cor to directeur des services politiques, économiques et administratives, dated 21 October 1912, in ANS, dossab, 1912 (emphasis added).

69. See telegram of Ponty to the lieutenant governor, 8 August 1912, in ANS, dossab, 1912.

70. See letter of Governor General Ponty to Lt. Gov. Cor, ANS, dossab, 8 November 1912.

71. See letters in ANS, dossab, 6 février 1913.

72. Rapport d'ensemble sur les territoires, 1911, ANS, 2G 11.

CHAPTER 7

1. It is interesting to know, however, that only a minority of his children were actually born in the city of Diourbel. Amadu Bamba preferred to send his pregnant wives to the village of Daaru Halim al Khabiir or Ndaam, near Tuubaa, to deliver and nurture the babies there.

2. Murray Last, "The Colonial Caliphate," in *Le temps des Marabouts: Itinéraires et stratégies islamiques en Afrique Occidentale Française v. 1880–1960*, ed. David Robinson and Jean-Louis Triaud (Paris: Karthala, 1997), 67–85. For a more extensive discussion of strategies of adaptation and doctrinal debates sparked by the European conquest of Muslim territories, see Muhammad Sani Umar, "Muslim Intellectuals' Responses to British Colonialism in Northern Nigeria, 1903–1945" (PhD diss., Northwestern University, 1997). See also Umar, *Islam and Colonialism: Intellectual Responses of Muslims of Northern Nigeria to British Colonial Rule* (Leiden: E. J. Brill, 2005).

3. On the failure of jihad in the precolonial Wolof kingdoms, see Lucy Colvin, "Islam and the State of Kajoor: A Case of a Successful Resistance to Jihad," *JAH* 15 (1974): 587–607. On the relationship between Muslim clerics and rulers in the precolonial Wolof states, see Boubacar Barry, *Le royaume du Waalo: le Sénégal avant la conquête* (Paris: Karthala, 1985); Mamadou Diouf, *Le Kajoor au XIXe siè-*

cle (Paris: Karthala, 1990). For northern Nigeria, by contrast, see the proclamation of Uthman dan Fodio as translated in A. D. H Bivar, "A Manifesto of the Fulani Jihād," *JAH* 2 (1961): 235–43, esp. principle no. 11, where Uthman wrote: "And that by assent the status of a town is of its ruler: if he be Muslim, the town belongs to Islam; but if he be heathen the town is a town of heathendom from which flight is obligatory."

4. On the Islamization of the Sereer, see James Searing, "Conversion to Islam: Military Recruitment and Generational Conflict in a *Sereer*-Safèn Village (Bandia), 1920–1938," *JAH* 44 (2003): 73–94.

5. E. Ross, "Touba et ses soeurs" (Mémoire de maîtrise, McGill University, 1989), 66; Ross, "Tubâ: An African Eschatology in Islam" (PhD diss., McGill University, 1996); Ross, "Touba: a Spiritual Metropolis in the Modern World," *Canadian Journal of African Studies* 29 (1995): 222–59; Ross, *Sufi City: Urban Design and Archetypes in Touba* (Rochester, NY: Rochester University Press, 2006). See also ANS, 10D 5, 8, "Monographie du cercle de Diourbel, " février 1911.

6. Interviews with Galo Mbay, Tuubaa, 14 February 2000, and Abdu Samat Sylla, Diourbel, 28 June 2000.

7. Sufis are critical of city life, which they associate with the nafs. See chapter 4 for a discussion of Amadu Bamba's conception of Sufism.

8. Eric Ross, "Marabout Republics Then and Now: Configuring Muslim Towns in Senegal." *Islam et Sociétés au Sud du Sahara* 16 (2002): 38.

9. See Amadou Bamba Mbacké, *Jazaau Shakuur* [Tribute to the Worthy of Recognition], translated into French and edited by the Association of Murid Students of University Cheikh Anta Diop of Dakar (UCAD) (Dakar, n.d.).

10. See "Lettre à monsieur Brévié," in "Deux traités d'un lettré religieux Sénégalais (1864–1945)," by Serigne Mbacké Bousso, translated from the Arabic by Khadim Mbacké (paper, 1994).

11. See Lamine O. Sanneh, *The Jakhanke: The History of an Islamic Clerical People of the Senegambia* (London: International African Institute, 1979).

12. As reported by Bachir Mbacké, *Les bienfaits de l'éternel*, translated and edited by Khadim Mbacké (Dakar, 1995), 44–45.

13. See Mbacké, *Jazaau Shakuur*, 31. In one of his poems, he depicted Gabon as a "city of sin" and prayed that God would deliver him from its captivity. Quoted in Diop, *Irwā*, 58.

14. Interview with Makhtaar Diop, grandson of M. L. Diop, the biographer of Amadu Bamba, Diourbel, 28 June 2000.

15. See Hans Wehr, *A Dictionary of Modern Written Arabic*, 4th ed., ed. J. M. Cowan (Ithaca, NY: Spoken Language Services, 1994), 84. "Al Buqahat al Mubarakati" is a Quranic expression that refers to the story of Moses's flight from Egypt and the idea of the Promised Land. Amadu Bamba, who often drew from Quranic idioms to describe his experience with the French, certainly found some similarities between his exile and aspiration to live in daar al Islam and this story. See Quran, "The Story," sura, 28, v. 30, which reads: "When he [Moses] drew near,

a voice called out to him from the tree on the *blessed spot* on the right side of the valley: O Moses! I am verily God, the Lord of all of the worlds," in *Al Quran: A Contemporary Translation*, ed. Ahmed Ali (Princeton, NJ: Princeton University Press, 1988), 331 (emphasis added).

16. Yi-Fu Tuan, "Sacred Space: Exploration of an Idea," in *Dimensions of Human Geography: Essays on Some Familiar and Neglected Themes*, ed. Karl W. Butzer, Department of Geography Research Paper 186 (Chicago: University of Chicago, 1978), 84–85. Tuan notes that the Latin word *sacer*, from which the English word *sacred* is derived, as well as the Hebrew root k-d-sh, which means "holy," and the Greek word *templos* that gave the Latin word *templum* and the word *temple*, are all associated with the idea of "cutting out" and "setting apart."

17. ANS, dossab, Rapport sur les mourides d'Amadou Bamba dans le cercle du Bawol, Mars, Avril, Mai et Juin 191 See also Paul Marty, *Études sur l'Islam et les tribus Maures: Les Brakna* (Paris: E. Leroux, 1921), 234.

18. Diop, *Irwā*, 110.

19. In his biography of Amadu Bamba, Diop included a poem he wrote to honor these aides. See Diop, *Irwā*, 102–10.

20. ANS, dossab, Rapports sur les mourides, Mars, Avril, Mai, Juin 1914.

21. ANS, 2G 13, 54, Rapport sur les mourides, mois de septembre 1913.

22. ANS, dossab, Rapport de l'administrateur, février 1914.

23. ANS, 2G 17, 5 Rapport politique d'ensemble sur le Sénégal, année 1917.

24. According to Murid oral traditions, the *ndigel*, or recommendation to commemorate the maggal, was given by Amadu Bamba in 1912 in Diourbel. He annually commemorated the event during his stay in Diourbel, and after his death, his son and successor, Mamadu Mustafa, moved the maggal to Tuubaa as a collective annual celebration of the Muridiyya. For more on the maggal, see Christian Coulon, "The Grand Magal in Touba," *African Affairs* 391 (1999): 195–210. See also Sophie Bava and Cheikh Guèye, "Le grand magal de Touba: Exil prophétique, migration et pélerinage au sein du Mouridisme," *Social Compass* 48 (2001): 421–38.

25. See Yi-Fu Tuan, "Sacred Space," 85.

26. See Barbara Metcalf, ed., *Making Muslim Space in North America and Europe* (Berkeley: University of California Press, 1996), 3.

27. Victor Turner particularly emphasizes the role of pilgrimage as "communitas," that is, a means of building social bonds between believers. See *Dramas, Fields and Metaphors: Symbolic Action in Human Society* (Ithaca, NY: Cornell University Press, 1974), 169.

28. Many of these houses are still visible in Al Mubaraka, better known now as Ker Gu Mag (literally, the senior or first house), where they are occupied by descendants of the Murid sheikhs who built them.

29. The seclusion of a holy man's wife is common in Islam. Amadu Bamba strictly forbade men from entering the women's quarter of his house. Disciples even refused to accompany colonial administrators who sometimes arrived to in-

spect the compound without notice. I was told a story about an epidemic of smallpox in Diourbel in 1919, when Bamba, informed that a male nurse named Lam was trying to access the women's quarter, grabbed a cane and chased the person away. Interview with Galo Mbay, Tuubaa, 14 January 2000.

30. ANS, 2G 18, Sénégal, situation politique, rapports trimestriels, 1–2–3; Sénégal, rapport politique premier trimestre 1918.

31. On the building of the congregational mosque of Al Mubaraka, see ANS, 2G 18, Cercle de Diourbel, Rapports mensuels d'ensemble, 1918; see also Diop, Irwā, 99–100, and Abdoul Ahad Mbacké, ed., *Cheikh Ahmadou Bamba: Fondateur de la confrérie des Mourides*, 2 vols. (Paris: Editions d'Art des Heures Claires, 1984).

32. The architecture of the mosque followed the Ottoman style, which is characterized by a large central dome over a square prayer hall with a minaret in each of the four corners. This design was uncommon in West Africa, where the Maghrebi architectural tradition of columned hall and single minaret without a central dome was more common (this is also the style of the central mosque of Tuubaa). The decision to adopt an Ottoman-style mosque at a time when the French were at war with the Ottoman Empire may also be seen as a form of symbolic expression of dissent. I thank Eric Ross for calling my attention to the typical Ottoman style of the mosque of Diourbel and its possible political significance; personal conversation, 22 March 2005.

33. Jonathan Bloom, for example, associates the addition of the minaret to the mosque and the sophistication of mosque architecture with the growing influence and power of Islam: Bloom, *Minaret: Symbol of Islam* (Oxford: Oxford University Press, 1989), 19.

34. See ANS, dossab, the reports of Lasselves, the administrator of the district of Diourbel, on the Murids for the month of November 1913.

35. ANS, dossab, Rapport sur Amadou Bamba et ses mourides, Diourbel, 22 Octobre 1915.

36. Interviews with Sheikh Maam Balla, Mbakke, 5 May 91 and 29 May 2000, and Mor Talla Mbakke, Gowaan, 24 April 2000. In his many poems celebrating the accomplishments of Amadu Bamba and leading Murid sheikhs, Musa Ka told, in superlative terms, the heroic stories of Murid conquest of the wilderness of Kajoor and Bawol. It is also interesting to observe that in the 1980s when the caliph of the Murids banned the consumption of alcohol and tobacco and the playing of drums in Tuubaa, Murid sheikhs in Mbakke, Diourbel, and some of the villages in eastern Bawol followed suit.

37. My interviewees described the move to join Amadu Bamba in the early years of the Muridiyya in eastern Bawol as *gaddaay* (migration, flight). Murid disciples, however, may have joined the migratory movement for a variety of reasons, although many may have been driven primarily by a religious motivation.

38. Lucien Nekkache, Le Mouridisme depuis 1912, Rapport au gouvernement du Sénégal, Saint-Louis, Sénégal, 1952; also Cheikh Tidiane Sy, *La confrérie sénégalaise des mourides* (Paris: Présence africaine, 1969), 152.

39. Interview with Sadiikh Kan and Modu Jakhate, Khuru Mbakke, 29 June 2000. By the time I visited Khuru Mbakke in 2000, a new building was being constructed on the site where Amadu Bamba's mother's hut is believed to have stood. The Mbakke compound in Khuru Mbakke has recently become a pilgrimage site for Murid disciples.

40. Mor Talla Mbakke, a grandson of Sheikh Ahmad Ndumbe and historian of his family, stated that after his settlement in Diourbel, Amadu Bamba asked both Sheikh Ahmad Ndumbe and Sheikh Ibra Faal to leave the West (Dakar) for the East (or Bawol). Interview in Gowaan, 24 April 2000. In the Murid heartland, the west, or *sowwu* (that is, the Atlantic coast where the major colonial cities were located), functions as a metaphor for French and European cultural domination. It is opposed to the east, or *penku*, which is the *qibla* (direction for prayer) and also the location of Mecca and Medina, the holy sites of Islam. In Senegal, the expression *to travel to the East* also means to perform the pilgrimage to Mecca.

41. On the founding of Daaru Muhti and colonial reactions to the initiative, see Musa Ka, *Marsiyya Maam Cerno Birahim*, a eulogy in Wolofal written after the latter's death in 1943, audiocassette; see also John Glover, "The Hope in This World and the Next: Maam Cerno and the Settlement of Darou Mousty, 1912–1947" (PhD diss., University of Chicago, 2000); James Searing, *God Alone Is King* (Portsmouth, NH: Heinemann, 2001).

42. ANS, 2G 26, 10, Sénégal, "Rapport politique annuel," 1926.

43. Examples include M. L. Diop, who originated from Dagana in the Senegal River valley; the Dem of Kajoor; and the Thiam family of Kell in the region of Thiès. For more on the origins of Murids who migrated to eastern Bawol, see Lucien Nekkache, "Le mouridisme depuis 1912," Rapport au Gouvernement du Sénégal (Saint-Louis, Sénégal, 1952).

44. See Paul Pélissier, *Les paysans du Sénégal: Les civilisations agraires du Cayor à la Casamance* (Saint-Yrieix [Haute Vienne]: Fabrègue, 1966), 304.

45. For a study of this episode in the development of the Muridiyya, see R. Portères, "Aménagement de l'économie agricole et rurale au Sénégal," brochure 1 and 2 (March-April 1952); Pélissier, *Les paysans*, esp. chap. 6; Donal Cruise O'Brien, *The Mourides of Senegal: The Political and Economic Organization of an Islamic Brotherhood in Senegal* (Oxford, 1971); Jean Copans, *Les marabouts de l'arachide* (Paris: Le Sycomore, 1980; Harmattan, 1988). See also Nekkache, "Le mouridisme depuis 1912."

46. Non-Murid Wolof villages also have a penc, but it is often smaller and oriented differently, and it plays a different role in the life of the community. Since the penc is the public sphere where the power of the village's leader is exerted, its functions very much reflects the nature of this power. The importance of the penc in the Murid village reflects, to a large extent, the greater religious and political authority that Murid sheikhs enjoy over their disciples.

47. The mbaar consists of a sort of vestibule with a roof made of tin or thatch (and now more of concrete) that is supported by pillars and open on four sides.

48. ANS, dossab, Rapport sur Amadou Bamba et les mourides à Diourbel, 29 Octobre 1913, and also Rapport sur Amadou Bamba et ses mourides, 1915.

49. Michel Villeneuve, for example, observes, "Murid quarters are recognizable by the square huts that always signal the presence of Murid disciples in an area, all other people, regardless of their ethnic affiliation, live in round huts"; see "Une société musulmane d'Afrique noire: La confrérie des mourides," *Institut des Belles Lettres Arabes* (Tunis) 110 (1965): 127–67, 137. Square huts were also found in non-Murid villages, but they were more typical of Murid dwellings.

50. This architecture draws inspiration from both the Islamic tradition of space making and traditional Wolof court culture. The division of the sheikh's compound into smaller houses connected by doors reflects a social reality that can be associated with the Muslim conception of space. See, for example, Alexandre Guérin, "Some Features of a Village: Architecture in Transition from Antiquity to Islam," *Al-'Usur al-Wusta* 2 (1999): 51. The large space left open at the entrance of the house reminds one of the *bulo*, a sort of vestibule found in traditional Mandingo and Wolof royal compounds. See Abbé David Boilat, *Esquisses sénégalaises* (Paris, 1984); Ross, "Marabout Republics," 57–62; also Adama Guèye, "The Impact of the Slave Trade in Kayor and Baol: Mutations in Habitat and Land Occupancy," in *Fighting the Slave Trade*, ed. Sylviane Diouf (Athens: Ohio University Press, 2003), 50–61.

51. In Guérin's study of the architecture of a Muslim village in Syria, the *mastaba* (a platform made of cut stone raised half a meter from the ground) serves as a bridge between the private and public domains; see his "Some Features," 49.

52. Ross, "Marabout Republics," 43.

53. Lasselves, the head of the district of Bawol, repeatedly marveled at the cleanliness of the Murid quarter and the Murid use of the straight line, two things he considered difficult to teach the "Blacks." See ANS, dossab, Rapport sur Amadou Bamba et les mourides à Diourbel, 29 Octobre 1913, and also Rapport sur Amadou Bamba et ses mourides, 1915. One must note, however, that people in Senegal were using the square and the straight line in their built environment for centuries before the emergence of the Muridiyya. See, for example, Michel Adanson's description of the African quarter of Saint-Louis and the village of Sor in *Histoire naturelle du Sénégal: Coquillages; avec la relation abrégée d'un voyage fait en ce pays, pendant les années 1749, 50, 51, 52 et 53* (Paris, 1757), 21. Adanson attributed the use of symmetry in the Wolof built environment to the positive influence the French of Saint-Louis exerted on the local population. The use of these forms certainly predated the arrival of the French and may have been influenced by Islam, which reached this area in the ninth century, as argued by Labelle Prussin in *Hatumere: Islamic Design in West Africa* (Berkeley: University of California Press, 1986), 53. Most of the objects associated with African traditional religions in Senegal (the shrine enclosure, calabash, pestle, and mortar) tend to be round, whereas objects associated with Islam (the prayer enclosure, prayer mat, reading and writing board, charms) tend to be square or rectangular. What set the

Murids apart in the twentieth century was, perhaps, their more systematic and conscious use of sacred geometry to shape their space.

54. See Seyyed Hossein Nasr, foreword to *The Sense of Unity: The Sufi Tradition in Persian Architecture*, ed. Nader Ardalan and Laleh Bakhtiar (Chicago: University of Chicago Press, 1973), xii.

55. Ibid., xiii.

56. Alexandre Papadopoulos, *Islam and Muslim Art*, translated by Robert Erich Wolf (New York: H. N. Abrams, 1976), 195.

57. On the role of Khatem in West African Islamic eschatology, see Prussin, *Hatumere*, 74–76, and Allen Roberts and Mary N. Roberts, *A Saint in the City: Sufi Arts of Urban Senegal* (Los Angeles: UCLA Fowler Museum of Natural History, 2003), 174–77.

58. Prussin, *Hatumere*, 53.

59. ANS, dossab, Rapport sur Amadou Bamba et ses mourides, 1915.

60. Ibid.

61. ANS, dossab, Rapport confidentiel sur les mourides d'Amadou Bamba, Janvier 1914.

62. ANS, 11D 1, 0049, Affaires politiques et religieuses.

63. On the legal status of the land surrounding the mausoleum of Amadu Bamba and the great mosque and penc of Tuubaa, see Guèye, *Touba*, 102. It is worth noting that the land granted to the Murids was, in the words of the colonial administration, "a *perfect square* of 400 hectares" (emphasis added); see ibid.

64. Tuubaa is today a city of nearly 1 million people, but it is administratively considered a village privately owned and managed by the caliph of the Murids, who is the last living son of Amadu Bamba. The city benefits de facto from a status of quasi- extraterritoriality, similar to that of the Vatican; the government of Senegal does not have much say in its administration.

65. As an adjective, *haram* means "what is forbidden, unlawful in Islam." As a noun, it refers to the inviolable and sacred space surrounding the Kaaba in Mecca, where only Muslims are allowed access (it is used in that last sense here). See Wehr, *Dictionary of Modern Written Arabic*, 201.

CONCLUSION

1. Adriana Piga is the latest among a long list of writers to reaffirm the validity of this assumption made by Paul Marty in 1913; see her *Dakar et les ordres soufis* (Paris: Harmattan, 2002), 75.

2. The best representatives of this tendency are L. S. Senghor, who saw the Muridiyya as a form of expression of his idea of "African socialism," and his intellectual and political rival Cheikh Anta Diop, who conceived of the Murid tariqa as a sort of Senegalese national Islam. In his speech at the inauguration of the mosque of Tuubaa in 1963, Senghor stated: "What Amadu Bamba wanted, once

again, what he wished to accomplish was to implant Islam in the land of the Blacks, by Africanizing Islam, let me dare say, by *negrifying* it. He wanted to adapt Islam to our situation of a developing country of negro-African peasants. This is what explains his enlightening conception of work, particularly farm work, as a functional dimension of prayer"; see L. S. Senghor, *Liberté I* (Paris: Le Seuil, 1964), 423–24. Diop emphasizes, somewhat mistakenly, that for the Murids, Diourbel and Tuubaa replaced Mecca; see Diop, *L'Afrique noire précoloniale* (Paris: Présence africaine, 1987), 164.

3. See Christian Coulon, "Islam africain ou Islam arabe: Autonomie ou indépendance," *Année Africaine* (1976): 250–75, 254.

4. The Al Ahzar school networks founded by Amadu Bamba's youngest son, the late Sheikh Murtalla Mbakke, count among their staff teachers provided by the Egyptian government.

5. Jean Copans, who more than any other researcher has emphasized the connection between the Muridiyya and peanuts, notes in the most recent edition of his book *Les marabouts de l'arachide* (1988) that the death of peanut economy did not weaken the Muridiyya; he suggested that scholars explore other avenues to explain the historical development of the order. In a recent article, he called for a reflection on the values that underpin the Muridiyya, referring to the organization's capacity to innovate and adapt to changing contexts and environments in Senegal and the rest of the world. See his "Mourides des champs, mourides des villes, mourides du téléphone portable et de l'Internet: Les renouvellements de l'économie politique d'une confrérie," *Afrique Contemporaine* 194 (April-June 2000): 26.

6. See Governor General of French West Africa, "Rapport politique d'ensemble AOF 1927," ANS 2G 26, 8.

7. For Frederick Cooper, "Understanding indigenous categories—be they those of French colonial minister, an African trade unionist, or Islamic religious leader—requires asking how people put their thoughts together; in other words, scholars must make an effort to get out of their own categories." See Cooper, *Colonialism in Question: Theory, Knowledge, History* (Berkeley: University of California Press, 2005), 11.

8. See Robert Delavignette, *Les vrais chefs de l'empire* (Paris: Gallimard, 1939), translated as *Freedom and Authority in French West Africa* (London: Frank Cass, 1969).

9. Cooper, *Colonialism*, 242.

Bibliography

INTERVIEWS

Cheikh Anta Babou Interviews in Senegal, 1991–2002

Oumar Ba, Dakar, 15 June 2001
Anta Kumba Baabu, Mbakke, 12 February 2000; Mbakke, 20 January 2002
Barakatu Baal, Dakar, 27 May 2000
Makhtaar Buso, Tuubaa, 11 June 2000
Elhaj Sheikh Caam, Mbakke, 22 April 2000
Maamun Caam, Mbakke, 3 January 2000, 26 April 2000, 9 May 2000
Ngagne Caam, Dakar, 12 September 1999
Abdurahim Dem, Diourbel, 30 July 2000
Maam Moor Dem, Tuubaa, 29 July 2000
Alioune Gay, Nietti Kadd, Thiès, 25 June 2000
Cerno Gey, Deqele, 20 July 2000
Elhaj Jakhate, Tuubaa, 10 June 2000
Modu Jakhate, Khuru Mbakke, 29 June 2000
Bamba Jaw, Dakar, 8 April 2000, 13 May 2000
Cerno Jaw, Tuubaa, 17 July 2000
Mbay Jimbeng, Tuubaa, 21 April 2000, 22 April 2000
Hajja Faatu Joob, Saint-Louis, 11 July 2001
Makhtaar Joob, Diourbel, 28 June 2000, 19 July 2000
Muhammad Joob, Mbakke, 7 May 2000, 16 May 2000
SerigneTako Joob, Daaru Salaam, 13 February 2000
Mamadu Juuf, Bargny, 4 June 2000
Mustafa Ley, Mbakke, 7 May 2000, 16 May 2000
Sheikhuna Lo, Daaru Manaan, 30 April 2000
Ababakar Mbakke, Mbakke, 30 June 2001
Baara Mbakke, Mbakke Kajoor, 20 May 2000
Basiru Mbakke A. Niang, Daaru Muhti, 29 May 1991, 18 July 2000
Isa Mbakke, Tuubaa, 2 July 2000

Mor Talla Mbakke, Gowaan, 29 April 2000
Mustafa Aafe Mbakke, Tuubaa, 5 June 2000, 6 June 2000
Mustafa Mbakke Beto, Mbakke, 8 May 2000
Mustafa Njaate Mbakke, Mbakke, 30 July 2000, 30 June 2001
Serigne Mustafa Caytu Mbakke, Gawaan Mbakke, 9 February 2000, 8 March 2000, 16 May 2000, 31 May 2000, 16 June 2000
Shaikh Maam Balla Mbakke, Mbakke, 5 May 1991, 29 May 2000, 7 June 2000
Galo Mbay, Tuubaa, 14 February 2000, 1 March 2000
Ibrahima Jaagne Mbay, Dakar, 1 October 1999
Ibra Mbay, Daaru Salaam, 13 February 2000
Sawru Mbay, Daaru Salaam, 1 March 2000, 6 March 2000
Afia Niang, Tuubaa, 30 May 2000, 31 May 2000, 20 January 2002, 22 January 2002
Modu Maamun Niang, Tuubaa, 8 June 2000
Sokhna Buso Njaay, Mbakke, 20 January 2002
Mamadu Sall, Tuubaa, 23 March 2000
Modu Sey, Mbakke Kajoor, 20 July 2000
Sokhna Marema Sey, Daaru Muhti, 29 May 1991
Musa Siise, Saint-Louis, 7 May 2001
Habibu Sy, Tuubaa, 26 June 2000
Abdu Samat Sylla, Diourbel, 28 June 2000
Elhaj Sylla, Mbakke Kajoor, 20 July 2000
Massaer Sylla, Mbakke Kajoor, 20 July 2000
Madicke Wade, Saint-Louis, 6 July 2001

ARCHIVAL MATERIALS

Archives Nationales du Sénégal (ANS)

Dossier Amadou Bamba (This is a folder containing most of the archival materials related to the relations between Amadu Bamba and the colonial administration of Senegal. It is kept in the Office of the Director of the National Archives.)
3B 55, fol. 82–83, Lettre du Gouverneur à Amadou Bamba, 06/27/1889
3B 89, 49
3B 94
1D 27
10D 3/25, Circulaire BP, 67, 22–09–1912, Le Lt. Gouverneur aux Administrateurs de Cercle
10D 3-0035, Lettre de l'Administrateur René Massetche, Résident du Baol au Commandant du Cercle de Thiès, 25 octobre 1905
10D 5-8, Monographie du Cercle de Diourbel
11D 1-30, Plainte des Frères d'Amadou Bamba; Lettre de Prempain, Administrateur du cercle de Thiès au Gouverneur Général, 26 mai 1903; Rapport politique d'Allys, Administrateur de Tivavouane, 24–06–1903

11D 1/0049, Affaires politiques et religieuses, Partis, syndicats, Mouridisme, Marabouts, Tidjanites
2D 7-1, Baol: Correspondence 1889
1G 48, Renseignements sur la situation politique de Cayor en 1879
1G 136 Angot, "Mission Angot dans le Diambour et le Baol 1889"
1G 214, Paul Merles Des Isles, "Contribution à l'Étude du Mouridisme," 1949
Lucien Nekkache, "Le Mouridisme depuis 1912," Rapport au gouvernement du Sénégal, Saint-Louis, Sénégal, 1952
2G 3-7, Allys, Rapport 1er trim., 1905
2G 6-4, Sénégal, Rapport mensuel, January, February, March 1906
2G 10-5, Correspondence no. 566, du 13–4–1910: Gouv. Général W. Ponty au Lieutenant Governeur du Sénégal
2G 11-6, Chef du Bureau Politique, Sénégal, Rapports d'ensemble, 1911
2G 27–28
2G 117, Sénégal, Rapport politique May? 1911?
13G 257
13G 264
13G 318
13G 271–318
13G 271 (20) (23) and (24)
J 86, "Rapport à Monsieur le Gouverneur Général de l'Afrique Occidentale Française sur les écoles coraniques," par Paul Marty, 20 novembre 1913?

Centre d'Archives d'Outre-Mer (France)

ANFOM, Senegal IV 127, Lettres de l'Administrateur du cercle de St. Louis à Monsieur le Directeur des Affaires Politiques, Saint-Louis, le 10 Juillet 1895
ANFOM, Sénégal IV 127, Lettre de l'Administrateur du cercle de St. Louis à Monsieur le Governeur du Sénégal et Dependances

UNPUBLISHED MATERIALS

Audrain, Xavier. "Baay-Fall du temps mondial: Individus modernes du Sénégal, des dynamiques de construction de sujets individuels et d'invention d'une modernité vehiculée par l'originale communauté islamique des Baay-fall." Mémoire de DEA d'études africaines, Paris 1 La Sorbonne, UFR 11, de science politique, 2001–2.
Babou, Cheikh Anta Mb. "Amadu Bamba and the Founding of the Muridiyya: The History of a Muslim Brotherhood in Senegal, 1853–1913." PhD diss., Michigan State University, 2002.
———. "Le Mouridisme des origines à 1912." Mémoire de maîtrise, Université de Dakar, 1991.
———. "Touba, genèse et évolution d'une cité musulmane au Sénégal." Mémoire de DEA, Université de Dakar, 1992.

Beck, Linda J. "'Patrimonial Democrats" in a Culturally Plural Society: Democratization and Political Accommodation in Patronage Politics of Senegal.'" PhD diss., University of Wisconsin—Madison, 1996.
Bousso, Serigne Mbacké. "Deux traités d'un lettré religieux Sénégalais (1864–1945)." Translated from the Arabic by Khadim Mbacké. Paper, 1994.
Buggenhagen, Beth Ann. "At Home in the Black Atlantic: Circulation, Domesticity, and Value in the Senegalese Murid Trade Diaspora." PhD diss., University of Chicago, 2003.
Carter, Donald. "Invisible Cities: From Tuba to Turin—The Senegalese Transnational Migrants in Northern Italy." PhD diss., University of Chicago, 1992.
Charles, Eunice. "French West African Policy and Muslim Resistance in Senegal." Presentation at the Sixteenth Annual Meeting of the African Studies Association, Syracuse, NY, 31 October–3 November 1973.
Colvin, Lucy. "Kajoor and Its Diplomatic Relations with Saint-Louis du Sénégal, 1763–1861." PhD diss., Columbia University, 1972.
Diallo, El Hadji Samba Amadou. "La transmission des statuts et des pouvoirs dans la Tijaniyya sénégalaise: Le cas de la famille Sy de Tivaouane." Thèse de doctorat de IIIe cycle en anthropologie sociale, ethnologie et ethnographie, EHESS, 2005.
Diagne, Mody. "La religion, celle de votre famille, la vôtre." Devoir de vacances, IFAN Cahiers de l'École William Ponty, 1940–41.
Diallo, Kalidou. "Les chefs de Canton du Fouta, 1860–1960." Mémoire de maîtrise, Département d'histoire, Université de Dakar, 1985.
Diop, Abdou Malal. "Traduction et commentaire du *Viatique des Jeunes* d'Ahmadou Bamba." Thèse de doctorat de troisième cycle s/d Professeur Amar Samb Université de Dakar Faculté des Lettres et Sciences Humaines, Département Arabe, 1985.
Diop, Cheikh Muhammad Lamine Dagana. *Irwā-unnadim min 'adhbi hubb al khadim*. Translated and edited by Khadim Mbacké as *L'abreuvement du commensal dans la douce source d'amour du Cheikh al-Khadim, ou la biographie de Cheikh Ahmadou Bamba*. Dakar: IFAN, Département d'Islamologie, n.d.
Diop, Momar Coumba. "La confrérie mouride: Organisation politique et mode d'implantation urbaine." Thèse de troisième cycle unité d'études et recherches de psychologie et des sciences sociales, Université de Lyon 2, 1980.
———. "La littérature mouride, essai d'analyse thématique et critique." Mémoire pérsenté sous la direction de Jean François Maurel, École Nationale Supérieure de Bibliothécaires, Paris, 1978.
———. "La relation talibé-marabout." Mémoire de maîtrise, Université de Dakar, 1976.
Dramé, Saliou. "La pensée confrérique de Cheikh Moussa Camara dans la société et l'histoire: Analyse sociocritique de *Al Haq Al Mubîn* (La vérite éclatante)." Mémoire de DEA, Département Arabe, Université Cheikh Anta Diop, 1998–99.

Fall, El Hadji Malick. "Elhadji Malick Sy au Oualo." Mémoire de maîtrise, Faculté des Lettres de l'Université de Dakar, Département Arabe, 1994–95.

Faye, Diâo. "L'œuvre poétique wolofal de Moussa Ka ou l'épopée de Cheikh Ahmadou Bamba." Thèse pour un doctorat de Troisième Cycle, Université Cheikh Anta Diop de Dakar, 1999.

Glover, John. "The Hope in This World and the Next: Maam Cerno and the Settlement of Darou Mousty, 1912–1947." PhD diss., University of Chicago, 2000.

Guèye, Cheikh. "L'organisation de l'espace dans une ville religieuse: Touba (Sénégal)." Thèse pour l'obtention du titre de Docteur de l'Université Louis Pasteur en Géographie, Strasbourg, Germany, 1999.

Irvine, T. L. "Castes and Communication in a Wolof village." PhD diss., University of Pennsylvania, 1973.

Ka, Musa. *Jazaau Shakuur*. Audiocassette sung by Mama Njaay.

———. "*Marsiyya*, Maam Cerno Birahim Ibra Faty." Audiocassette sung by Mama Njaay.

Ka, Thierno. "L'enseignement arabe au Sénégal." Doctorat de troisième cycle, Sorbonne, Paris, 1982.

Kane, Oumar. "Le Fuuta Tooro des Satigis aux Almamis, 1512–1920." Thèse de doctorat d'état, Université de Dakar, 1986.

LeyMarie, Isabelle. "The Role and Functions of Griots among the Wolof of Senegal." PhD diss., Columbia University, 1979.

Lo, Mamadou. "Un aspect de la poésie 'Wolofal' mouride: Traduction and analyse de quelques titres de Serigne Mbay Jaxate." Faculté des Lettres et Sciences Humaines, Département de Lettres Modernes, Mémoire de maîtrise, Université de Dakar, 1992–93.

Lo, Mamadou. "Traduction et commentaire de *Tazawuddu-S-Sigar*, ou 'Viatique des Jeunes' de Cheikh Ahmadou Bamba Mbacké travail d'études et de recherches maîtrise d'arabe." Université de Dakar, July 1978.

Lydon, Ghislaine. "On Trans-Saharan Trails: Long-Distance Trading Networks and Cross-Cultural Exchange in Western Africa, 1840s–1950s." PhD diss., Michigan State University, 1999.

Mbacké, Amadou Bamba. *Jazaau Shakuur* [Tribute to the Worthy of Recognition]. Translated into French and edited by the Association of Murid Students of University Cheikh Anta Diop of Dakar (UCAD). Dakar, n.d.

———. *Nahj Qada Alhaaj* (*La voie vers la satisfaction des besoins des disciples en matière de règles de conduite*). Translated from the Arabic by Khadim Mbacké, 1982.

Mbacké, Khadim. "Deux traités d'un lettré religieux sénégalais, Serigne Mbacké Bousso (1864–1945)." Traduit par Khadime Mbacké (1994), 3.

Mbaye, Rawane. "L'Islam au Sénégal." Thèse de doctorat de troisième cycle, Université de Dakar, 1975–76.

———. "La pensée et l'action de Elhadji Malick Sy." Thèse de doctorat d'état, Sorbonne Nouvelle, 1992–93.

McLaughlin, Glen W. "Muhammad Fādil Wuld Mamin." PhD diss., Northwestern University, June 1997.

Ndiaye, Baba. "L'Islam au Sénégal, l'école coranique." Cahiers de l'École William Ponty, IFAN, n.d.

Ndiaye, Mamadou. "L'enseignement arabo-islamique au Sénégal." Thèse de doctorat de troisième cycle, Université de Dakar, 1975–76.

Niang, Modu Maamun. *Jaar jaari Serigne Tuubaa* [The Itineraries of Amadu Bamba]. Brochure in Wolofal, n.d.

Niang, Muhamad Fadl. "Sufism in Senegal: The Example of the Muridiyya." Thesis for a master's in sharia, University Qarawiyyin, Morocco, 1999. [Originally in Arabic.]

Ould Cheikh, Abdel Wedoud. "Espace confrérique, espace étatique: Le mouridisme, le confrérisme et la frontière Mauritano-sénégalaise." Paper, 2001.

Portères, R. "Aménagement de l'économie agricole et rurale au Sénégal." Fascicule I et II, Mars-Avril, 1952.

Ross, Eric. "Touba et ses sœurs." Mémoire de maîtrise, McGill University, 1989.

——. "Tubâ an African Eschatology in Islam." PhD diss., McGill University, 1996.

Sakho, Youssoufa. "Les croyances religieuses au Sénégal." Cahiers de l'École William Ponty, IFAN, n.d.

Salem, Gérard. "De Dakar à Paris, des diasporas d'artisans et de commerçants: Étude socio-géographique du commerce sénégalais en France." Thèse de doctorat de troisième cycle, EHESS, Paris, 1983.

Searing, James. "Accommodation and Resistance: Chiefs, Muslim Leaders and Politicians in Colonial Senegal, 1890–1934." PhD diss., Princeton University, 1985.

Sène, Henri. 'Le livre et l'écrit de langue arabe dans la société sénégalaise, des origines au début du XXième siècle." Thèse pour le doctorat de troisième cycle en science de l'information et de la communication, Bourdeaux, France, 1982.

Stone, Diana. "The Inversion of a Historical Tendency? The Tijaniyya Niass Movement in Mauritania." Paper presented at the conference on the Tijaniyya at the University of Illinois–Urbana-Champaign, 1–5 April 1996.

Sylla, Khadime. "Immigration et confrérie." Mémoire de DEA, Institut National des Langues et Civilisations Orientales, Paris, 1992–93.

Touré, Mafakha. "Critique historique d'un concept: L'Islam noir." Mémoire de maîtrise, Université Cheikh Anta Diop de Dakar, 1990–91.

Umar, Muhammad Sani. "'Muslim Intellectuals' Responses to British Colonialism in Northern Nigeria, 1903–1945." PhD diss., Northwestern University, June 1997.

PUBLISHED SOURCES

Abun-Nasr, Jamil M. *The Tijaniyya*. London: Oxford University Press, 1965.

Adanson, Michel. *Histoire naturelle du Sénégal: Coquillages; avec la relation abrégée d'un voyage fait en ce pays, pendant les années 1749, 50, 51, 52 et 53.* Paris, 1757.

Aigle, D., ed. *Saints orientaux.* Paris: De Boccard, 1995.

Al-Ghazzali. *Ih'ya 'ouloûm ed-dîn; ou, Vivification des sciences de la foi*, edited by G. H. Bousquet. Paris: M. Besson, 1955.

Ali, Ahmed. *Al Quran: A Contemporary Translation.* Princeton, NJ: Princeton University Press, 1988.

Anderson, David M., and Douglas H. Johnson. *Revealing Prophets: Prophecy in Eastern African History.* Athens: Ohio University Press, 1995.

André, P. J. *L'Islam Noir.* Paris: P. Geuthner, 1924.

Anvar-Chenderoff, Leili. "Le genre hagiographique à travers la *tadhkirat al-awliyā* de Farīd al-dīn 'attār." In Aigle, ed., *Saints orientaux.*

Arnaud, Robert. "L'Islam et la politique musulmane de la France." *BCAF/RC* ser. 3, 20 (1912): 115–27, 141–54.

Ba, Oumar. *Ahmadou Bamba face aux autorités coloniales.* Abbeville: Fayard, 1982.

Ba, Tamsir Ousmane. "Essai historique sur le Rip." *BIFAN* ser. B, 19 (1957): 564–91.

Babou, Cheikh A. Mb. "Autour de la genèse du Mouridisme." *Islam et Société au Sud du Sahara* 11 (1997): 5–38.

Babou, Cheikh Anta. "Brotherhood Solidarity, Education and Migration: The Role of the *Dahiras* among the Murid Muslim Community of New York." *African Affairs* 403 (2002): 151–70.

———. "Contesting Space, Shaping Places: Making Room for the Muridiyya in Colonial Senegal." *Journal of African History* 46 (2005): 405–26.

———. "Educating the Murid: Theory and Practices of Education in Amadu Bamba's Thought." *Journal of Religion in Africa* 33 (2003): 309–27.

———. "Education, généalogie, et *baraka*: Une exploration de quelques sources de l'autorité spirituelle d'Ahmadou Bamba." *Afrique et Histoire*, forthcoming.

———. "Urbanizing Mystical Islam: Making Murid Space in the Cities of Senegal." *International Journal of African Historical Studies*, forthcoming.

Barry, Boubacar, Le Waalo. "Mémoire inédit de Monsérat sur l'histoire du nord du Sénégal de 1818 à 1839," édité et publié par Boubacar Barry. *BIFAN* ser. B, 1 (1970): 1–43.

———. *Le royaume du Waalo: Le Sénégal avant la conquête.* Paris: Karthala, 1985.

———. *Senegambia and the Atlantic Slave Trade.* Cambridge: Cambridge University Press, 1998.

Bava, Sophie. "De la baraka aux affaires: Ethos économico-religieux et transnationalité chez les migrants sénégalais mourides." *Revue Européenne de Migrations Internationales* 19 (2003): 69–84.

Becker, Charles, and V. Martin. "Kayor et Baol: Royaumes sénégalais et traite des esclaves au XVII ième siècle." *Revue Française d'Histoire d'Outremer* 62 (1975): 270–300.

―――. "Le mémoire inédit de Doumet (1769) sur le Kayor et les pays voisins au cours de la seconde moitié du XVIIIe siècle." *BIFAN* ser. B, 1 (1974): 25–92.
Behrman, Lucy. "French Muslim Policy and Senegalese Brotherhoods." In *Aspects of West African Islam*, edited by Daniel F. McCall and Norman R. Bennett, 185–208. Boston University Papers on Africa 5. Boston: African Studies Center, Boston University, 1971.
―――. "The Islamization of the Wolof." In McCall, Bennett, and Butler, eds., *Western African History*, 102–31.
―――. *Muslim Brotherhoods and Politics in Senegal*. Cambridge, MA: Harvard University Press, 1970.
Bercher, L. "Nécrologie de Paul Marty." *Revue Tunisienne* 33–34 (1938): 15–17.
Berger, Peter L. *The Sacred Canopy: Elements for a Sociological Theory of Religion*. Garden City, NY: Doubleday, 1969.
Bivar, A. D. H. "A Manifesto of the Fulani Jihād." *Journal of African History* 2 (1961): 235–43.
Bloom, Jonathan. *Minaret: Symbol of Islam*. Oxford: Oxford University Press, 1989.
Boilat, Abbé David. *Esquisses sénégalaises*. Paris: Karthala, 1984.
Bomba, Victoria. "The Pre-nineteenth Century Political Tradition of the Wolof." *BIFAN* ser. B, 34 (1974): 1–14.
Boone, Catherine. *Political Topographies of the African State: Territorial Authority and Institutional Choice*. Cambridge: Cambridge University Press, 2003.
Boubrik, Rahal. *Saints et société en Islam*. Paris: CNRS, 1999.
Bouche, Denise. "L'école française et les musulmans du Sénégal de 1850 à 1920." *Revue Française d'Histoire d'Outre-Mer* 223 (1974): 218-35
Boulègue, Jean. *Le Grand Jolof, XIIIe–XVIe siècle*. Paris: Karthala, 1987.
―――. "Lat-Sukaabé Fal ou l'opiniâtreté d'un roi contre les échanges inégaux au Sénégal." In *Les Africains*, edited by Charles A. Julien, vol. 9, 167–96. Paris: Éditions Jeune Afrique, 1990.
―――. "La participation possible des centres de Pir et Ndogal à la révolution islamique Sénégambienne de 1763." In *Contributions à l'Histoire du Sénégal*, 119–25. Cahiers du CRA. Paris: AFERA, 1987.
Bourdieu, P. "The Forms of Capital." In *Handbook of Theory and Research for the Sociology of Education*, edited by J. G. Richardson, 249–58. New York: Greenwood Press, 1986.
Bourlon, Abel. "Mourides et mouridisme." In *Notes et études sur l'Islam en Afrique*, edited by CHEAM, 53–74. Paris: Peyronet, 1962.
Boutillier, J. L. "Les captifs en AOF, 1903–1905." *BIFAN* ser. B, 30 (1968): 513–36.
Böwering, Gerhard. "Règles et rituels soufis." In Alexandre Popovic and Gilles Veinstein, eds., *Les voies d'Allah*, 139–56. Paris: Fayard, 1996.
Brenner, L. "Concepts of Tarīqa in West Africa: The Case of the Qādiriyya." In *Charisma and Brotherhood in African Islam*, edited by Donal B. Cruise O'Brien and Christian Coulon, 33–52. Oxford: Clarendon Press, 1988.

———. *Controlling Knowledge*. Bloomington: Indiana University Press, 2001.
———. *Réflexions sur le savoir islamique en Afrique de l'Ouest*. Bordeaux, France: Centre d'étude d'Afrique noire, Institut d'études politiques, 1985.
———. *West African Sufi: The Religious Heritage and Spiritual Search of Cerno Bokar Saalif Taal*. Berkeley: University of California Press, 1984.
Brigaud, Felix. *Histoire traditionnelle du Sénégal*. Saint-Louis: C.R.D.S.-Sénégal, 1962.
Brochier, J. *La diffusion du progrés technique en milieu rural sénégalais*. 2 vols. Dakar, 1964.
Brooks, George E. *Western Africa to c. 1860 A.D.: A Provisional Historical Schema Based on Climate Periods*. Bloomington: African Studies Program, Indiana University, 1985.
Buggenhagen, Beth Ann. "Prophets and Profits: Gendered Generational Visions of Wealth and Value in Senegalese Murid Households." *Journal of Religion in Africa* 31 (2001): 373–401.
Camara, Sory. *Gens de la parole: Essai sur la condition et le rôle des griots dans la société Malinké*. Paris: Karthala, 1992.
Carrère, Fréderic, and Paul Holle. *De la Sénégambie française*. Paris, 1855.
Certeau, Michel de. "Hagiographie." In *Encyclopaedia Universalis*, vol. 11. Paris, 1992.
Charles, Eunice. *Precolonial Senegal: The Jolof Kingdom, 1800–1890*. Boston: African Studies Center, Boston University, 1977.
———. "Shaikh Amadou Ba and Jihad in Jolof." *International Journal of African Historical Studies* 8 (1975): 367–82.
Chatelier, Alfred le. *L'Islam dans l'Afrique occidentale*. Paris: G. Steinheil, 1899.
Clarke, Peter B. *West Africa and Islam*. London: E. Arnold, 1982.
Colvin, L. A. G. "Islam and the State of Kajoor: A Case of Successful Resistance to Jihad." *JAH* 4 (1974): 587–607.
Conklin, Alice. *A Mission to Civilize: The Republican Idea of Empire in France and West Africa, 1895–1930*. Stanford, CA: Stanford University Press, 1997.
Cooper, Frederick. *Colonialism in Question: Theory, Knowledge, History*. Berkeley: University of California Press, 2005.
Copans, Jean. *Les marabouts de l'arachide*. Paris: Le Sycomore, 1980; Harmattan, 1988.
———. "Mourides des champs, mourides des villes, mourides du téléphone portable et de l'Internet: Les renouvellements de l'économie politique d'une confrérie." *Afrique Contemporaine* 194 (April–June 2000): 24–33.
Cornell, Vincent. *Realm of the Saint: Power and Authority in Moroccan Sufism*. Austin: University of Texas Press, 1998.
Coulon, Christian. "The Grand Magal in Touba." *African Affairs* 391 (1999): 195–210.
———. "Islam Africain ou islam Arabe: Autonomie ou indépendance." *Année Africaine* (1976): 250–75.
———. *Le marabout et le prince: Islam et pouvoir au Sénégal*. Paris: Pedone, 1981.

——. *Les musulmans et le pouvoir en Afrique Noire.* Paris: Karthala, 1988.

——. "Prophets of God or of History? Muslim Messsianic Movements and Anti-colonialism in Senegal." In *Explorations in African Religion,* edited by Wim Van Binsbergen and Matthew Schoffeleers, 346–66. London: KPI, 1985.

——. "Touba, lieu saint de la confrérie mouride." In *Lieux d'Islam: Cultes et cultures de l'Afrique à Java,* edited by Mohammad Ali Amir-Moez, 226–38. Paris: Autrement, 1996.

Couty, Philipe. *La doctrine du travail chez les mourides.* Brochure. Dakar: ORSTOM, 1969.

Creevey, Lucy. "Ahmad Bamba." In Willis, ed., *The Cultivators of Islam.*

——. "The Political Significance of Wolof Adherence to Muslim Brotherhoods in the 19th Century." *African Historical Studies* 1 (1968): 60–78.

Cruise O'Brien, Donal B. "Le contrat social sénégalais à l'épreuve." *Politique Africaine* 45 (1992): 9–20.

——. "Don divin, don terrestre: L'économie de la confrérie mouride." *Archives Européennes de Sociologie* 15 (1974): 82–100.

——. *The Mourides of Senegal: The Political and Economic Organization of an Islamic Brotherhood in Senegal.* Oxford: Clarendon Press, 1971.

——. *Saints and Politicians.* London: Cambridge University Press, 1975.

——. *Symbolic Confrontations: Muslims Imagining the State in Africa.* New York: Palgrave Macmillan, 2003.

——. "Le talibé mouride." *CEA* 35 (1969): 502–7.

——. "Towards an 'Islamic Policy' in French West Africa." *JAH* 8 (1967): 303–16.

Cruise O'Brien, Donal, and Christian Coulon, eds. *Charisma and Brotherhood in African Islam.* Oxford: Clarendon Press, 1988.

Cruise O'Brien, Donal, M. C. Diop, and M. Diouf, eds. *La construction de l'état au Sénégal.* Paris: Karthala, 2002.

Cultru, P. *Premier voyage du sieur de la Courbe, fait à la coste d'Afrique, 1685.* Paris: E. Champion, 1913.

Curtin, Philip. *Economic Change in Precolonial Africa: Senegambia in the Era of the Slave Trade.* Madison: University of Wisconsin Press, 1975.

——. "Jihad in West Africa, Early Phases and Interrelations in Mauritania and Senegal." *JAH* 12 (1971): 11–24.

De Jong, F., and B. Radtke, eds. *Islamic Mysticism Contested: Thirteen Centuries of Controversies.* Leiden: Brill, 1999.

Delafosse, Maurice. "L'état actuel de l'Islam dans l'AOF." *RMM* 11 (1910): 32–54.

——. *Haut-Sénégal-Niger.* Paris: E. Larose, 1972.

Delavignette, Robert. *Les vrais chefs de l'empire.* Paris: Gallimard, 1939. Translated as *Freedom and Authority in French West Africa.* London: Frank Cass, 1969.

Delehaye, Hippolyte. *Cinq leçons sur la méthode hagiographique.* Brussels: Société des Bollandistes, 1934.

Depont, O., and X. Coppolani. *Les confréries religieuses musulmanes.* Algiers, 1897.

De Rochefort, Claude Jannequin. *Voyage de Lybie au royaume de Sénéga, le long du Niger*. Paris, 1643.

Deschamps, Hubert. *L'Afrique Occidentale en 1818*. Paris: Calmann-Lévy, 1967.

Diagne, Pathé. *Pouvoir politique traditionnel en Afrique Occidentale*. Paris: Présence africaine, 1967.

Diawara, Mamadou. *L'empire du verbe et l'éloquence du silence: Vers une anthropologie du discours dans les groupes dit dominés du Sahel*. Cologne: Köppe, 2003.

Dièye, Abdoulaye. *L'exil au Gabon, 1895–1902: Sur les traces de Cheikh Ahmadou Bamba*. Dakar: Ndigel, 1985.

———. *Touba: Signes et symboles*. Paris: Deggel, 1997.

Diop, A. Bamba. "Lat Dior et le problème musulman." *BIFAN* ser. B, 28 (1966): 493–539.

Diop, A. Bara. *La sociéte Wolof: Tradition et changement—Les systèmes d'inégalité et de domination*. Paris: Karthala, 1981.

Diop, Cheikh Anta. *L'Afrique noire précoloniale: Étude comparée des systèmes politiques et sociaux de l'Europe et de l'Afrique noire, de l'antiquité à la formation des états modernes*. Paris: Présence africaine, 1987.

Diouf, Daouda. "Les grandes figures religieuses du Sénégal: L'action éducative dans la stratégie d'Abdoulaye Niasse, face à la colonisation française et à sa politique de laïcisation." *Islam et Développement* 3 (n.d.): 34–44.

Diouf, Mamadou. "Commerce et cosmopolitisme: Le cas des diasporas mourides du Sénégal. *Bulletin du Codesria* 1 (2000): 20–29.

———. *Histoire du Sénégal: Le modèle islamo-Wolof et ses périphéries*. Paris: Maisonneuve and Larose, 2001.

———. *Le Kajoor au XIXe siècle*. Paris: Karthala, 1990.

Diouf, Sylviane. *Fighting the Slave Trade*. Athens: Ohio University Press, 2003.

Diouf-Camara, Sylviane. "Senegalese in New York: A Model Minority?" Translated by Richard Philcox. *Black Renaissance/Renaissance Noire* 2 (Summer-Fall 1997): 95–115.

Djinnedi, Abdalla. "La place du livre dans la formation de l'intelligentsia maraboutique au Sénégal." *Annales de la Faculté des Lettres et Sciences Humaines* 9 (1979): 221–28.

Dumont, Fernand. "Amadou Bamba, apôtre de la non-violence." *Notes Africaines* (January 1969): 20–24.

———. *L'anti-sultan; ou, Al-Hajj Omar Tal du Fouta, combattant de la foi*. Dakar: Nouvelles éditions africaines, 1974.

———. *La pensée religieuse d'Amadou Bamba*. Dakar: Nouvelles éditions africaines, 1975.

Dumont, Louis. *Homo hierarchicus: The Caste System and Its Implications*. Chicago: University of Chicago Press, 1974.

Eaton, R. M. *The Rise of Islam and the Bengal Frontier, 1204–1760*. Berkeley: University of California Press, 1993.

———. *Sufis of Bijapur, 1300–1700: Social Roles of Sufis in Medieval India.* Princeton, NJ: Princeton University Press, 1978.
Ebin, V. "Camelots à New York, les pionniers de l'immigration sénégalaise." *Hommes et Migrations* 1160 (December 1992): 32–37.
———. "Les commerçants mourides à Marseille et à New York." In *Grands commerçants d'Afrique de l'Ouest,* edited by Emmanuel Grégoire and Pascal Labazée. Paris: ORSTOM, 1993.
Echenberg, Myron. *Colonial Conscripts: The Tirailleurs Sénégalais in French West Africa, 1867–1960.* Portsmouth, NH: Heinemann, 1991.
Eickelman, D. F. "The Art of Memory: Islamic Education and Its Social Reproduction." *Comparative Studies in Society and History* 20, no. 4 (1978): 485–516.
Elboudrary, Hassan. "Quand les saints font les villes." *Annales ESC* 3 (1985): 489–508.
El Hamel, Chouki. *La vie intellectuelle islamique dans le Sahel ouest-africain, XVIe–XIXe siècles.* Paris: Harmattan, 2002.
Evers Rosander, Eva. "Mam Diarra Bousso la bonne mère de Porokhane, Sénégal." *Africa* 58, nos. 3–4 (2003): 296–317.
Faidherbe, Louis. *Le Sénégal et la France dans l'Afrique Occidentale.* Paris, 1889.
Fall, R. "Teeñ Ce Ndeela et la consolidation de l'autorité politique des Faal." In *Contributions à l'histoire du Sénégal,* edited by Jean Boulègue, 109–19. Paris: AFERA, 1987.
Fall, T. L. "Recueil sur la vie des damels." *BIFAN* ser. B, 1 (1974): 93–146.
Fernandes, Valentim. *Description de la côte occidentale d'Afrique.* Translated by T. Monod, A. T. Da Mota, and R. Mauny. Bissau, 1951.
Fisher, Humphrey. "Conversion Reconsidered." *Africa* 43 (1973): 27–40.
Freeman-Grenville, G. S. *The Muslim and Christian Calendars.* London: Oxford University Press, 1963.
Froelich, J. C. *Les musulmans en Afrique Noire.* Paris: Orante, 1962.
Gaden, Henri. "Légendes et coutumes Sénégalaises, Cahiers de Yoro Dyâo." *Revue d'Ethnographie et de Sociologie* 3 (1912): 1–31.
Gamble, David. *The Wolof of Senegambia.* London: International African Institute, 1957.
Geoffroy, Éric. "Hagiographie et typologie spirituelle à l'époque mamelouke." In Aigle, ed., *Saints orientaux,* 83–98.
Glancy-Smith, Julian. "'Barakah.'" In *The Oxford Encyclopedia of the Modern Islamic World,* vol. 1. New York: Oxford University Press, 1995.
Glover, John. "The Mosque Is One Thing, the Administration Is Another: Murid Marabouts and Wolof Aristocrats in Colonial Senegal." *IJAHS* 33 (2000): 351–65.
Goody, Jack. *Literacy in Tradititional Societies.* Cambridge: Cambridge University Press, 1975.
———. *The Power of the Written Tradition.* Washington, DC: Smithsonian Institution Press, 2000.
Gouilly, Aphonse. *L'Islam dans l'Afrique occidentale française.* Paris: Larose, 1952.

Gril, Denis. "Le Miracle en Islam: Critère de la sainteté?" In Aigle, ed., *Saints orientaux*, 69–81.
——. "Le saint fondateur." In Popovic and Veinstein, eds., *Les voies d'Allah*, 104–20.
Groupe Fallou-Galass-Magazine. Fallou Diop, founder and publisher.
Guérin, Alexandre. "Some Features of a Village: Architecture in Transition from Antiquity to Islam." *Al-'Usur al-Wusta* 2 (1999).
Guerresh, Claudine. "Le livre de métrique du Cadi Majaxate Kala." *BIFAN* ser. B, 4 (1974): 714–833.
Guèye, Adama. "The Impact of the Slave Trade in Kayor and Baol: Mutations in Habitat and Land Occupancy." In Diouf, ed., *Fighting the Slave Trade*, 50–61.
Guèye, Cheikh. *Touba: La capitale des mourides.* Paris: Karthala, 2002.
Guèye, Mbaye. "Les exils de Cheikh Bamba au Gabon et Mauritanie, 1895–1907." *Annales de la Faculté des Lettres et Sciences Humaines de l'Université de Dakar*, no. 25 (1995): 41–57.
Hale, Thomas A. *Griots and Griottes: Masters of Words and Music.* Bloomington: Indiana University Press, 1998.
Hamoneau, Didié. *Vie et enseignement du Cheikh Ahmadou Bamba.* Beirut: Al-Bouraq, 1998.
Hanson, John H. *Migration, Jihad, and Muslim Authority in West Africa: The Futanke Colonies of Karta.* Bloomington: Indiana University Press, 1996.
Harrison, Christopher. *France and Islam in West Africa, 1860–1960.* Cambridge: Cambridge University Press, 1988.
Hiskett, Mervyn. *The Sword of Truth.* New York: Oxford University Press, 1973.
——. *The Development of Islam in West Africa.* New York: Longman, 1984.
Houdas, O., trans. and ed. *Tarikh es-Soudan.* Paris: E. Leroux, 1900.
——. *Tarikh el-Fettach.* Paris: E. Leroux, 1913.
Hourani, Albert. *Arabic Thought in the Liberal Age, 1798–1939.* Cambridge: Cambridge University Press, 1983.
Hunwick, John, and R. S. O'Fahey, general eds. *Arabic Literature of Africa.* Leiden: E. J. Brill, 1994– .
Hunwick, John, and Eve T. Powell. *The African Diaspora in the Mediterranean Lands of Islam.* Princeton, NJ: Markus Wiener, 2002.
Hurvitz, Nimrod. *The Formation of Hanbalism: Piety into Power.* London: Routledge, 2002.
Johnson, Wesley. *The Emergence of Black Politics in Senegal: The Struggle for Power in the Four Communes.* Stanford, CA: Stanford University Press, 1971.
——. "William Ponty and Republican Paternalism in French West Africa, 1908–1915." In *African Proconsuls*, edited by L. H. Gann and Peter Duignan, 127–57. New York: Free Press, 1978.
Journal of the History of Sufism. Special issue, "The Qadiriyya Order," 1–2 (2000).
Ka, Musa. "Jaaraama." Translated into French by Amar Samb. *BIFAN* ser. B, 36 (1974): 592–612.

Kane, Cheikh Hamidou. *Ambiguous Adventure*. London: Heinemann, 1972.
Kane, Oumar. *La première hégémonie peule: Le Fuuta Tooro de Koli Tehella à Almaami Abdul*. Paris: Karthala, 2004.
Klein, Martin. *Islam and Imperialism in Senegal*. Stanford, CA: Stanford University Press, 1968.
———. "The Moslem Revolution in Nineteenth Century Senegambia." In McCall, Bennett, and Butler, eds., *West African History*, 69–101.
———. "The Social and Economic Factors in the Muslim Revolution of Senegambia." *JAH* 13 (1972): 419–41.
Labat, J. B. *Nouvelle relation d'Afrique Occidentale*. Paris, 1728.
Laborde, Cécile. *La confrérie Layenne et les Lébous du Sénégal: Islam et culture traditionnelle en Afrique*. Talence: Centre d'études d'Afrique Noire, 1995.
Laitin, David D. *Hegemony and Culture: Politics and Religious Change among the Yoruba*. Chicago: University of Chicago Press, 1986.
Last, Murray. "'The Colonial Caliphate' of Northern Nigeria." In Robinson and Triaud, eds., *Le temps des Marabouts*, 67–82.
———. *The Sokoto Caliphate*. New York: Humanities Press, 1967.
Levtzion, Nehemia. "Islam in West African Politics: Accommodation and Tension between the 'Ulamâ' and the Political Authorities." *Cahiers d'Études Africaines* 71, no. 3 (1978): 333–45.
Levy, Maurice. "La guerre sainte est-elle possible?" *Les Grands Faits* (15 August–15 September 1907): 291–302.
Lonsdale, J. "The Prayers of Waiyaki." In Anderson and Johnson, eds., *Revealing Prophets*, 240–92.
Lovejoy, Paul. *Transformations in Slavery: A History of Slavery in Africa*. Cambridge: Cambridge University Press, 1995.
Lovejoy, Paul, and A. S. Kanya-Forstner, eds. *Slavery and Its Abolition in French Africa: The Official Reports of G. Poulet, E. Roume, and G. Deherme*. Madison: African Studies Program, University of Wisconsin–Madison, 1994.
Luizard, Pierre-Jean. "Le Moyen-Orient arabe." In Popovic and Veinstein, eds., *Les voies d'Allah*, 343–71.
Mack, M. N. "The AOF Archives and the Study of African History." *BIFAN* ser. B, 42 (1980): 277–98.
Mage, Eugène. *Voyage au Soudan occidental (1862–1866)*. Paris: Karthala, 1980.
Mahibou, Mohamed, and J. L Triaud. *Voilà ce qui est arrivé: Bayân mâ waqa`a d'al-Hâgg 'Umar al-Fûtî: Plaidoyer pour une guerre sainte en Afrique de l'Ouest au XIXe siècle*. Paris: Centre National de la Recherche Scientifique, 1983.
Malcolmson, Scott L. "West of Eden: The Mouride Ethic and the Spirit of Capitalism." *Transition* 71 (1996): 24–43.
Markovitz, Irving Leonard. "Traditional Social Structure, the Islamic Brotherhoods, and Political Development in Senegal." *Journal of Modern African Studies* 8 (April 1970): 73–96.

Marks, Shula. *The Ambiguities of Dependence in South Africa: Class, Nationalism and State in Twentieth-Century Natal*. Baltimore: Johns Hopkins University Press, 1986.
Martin, B. G. *Muslim Brotherhoods in Nineteenth-Century Africa*. Cambridge: Cambridge University Press, 1976.
Marty, Paul. "Cheikh Sidiyya et sa 'voie.'" *RMM* 31 (1915–16): 29–134.
——. *Études sur l'Islam au Sénégal*. 2 vols. Paris: E. Leroux, 1917.
——. *Études sur l'Islam et les tribus Maures: Les Brakna*. Paris: E. Leroux, 1921.
——. "Les mourides d'Amadou Bamba: Rapport à M. Le Gouverneur Général de l'Afrique Occidentale." *RMM* 25 (1913): 3–164.
——. "La politique indigène du Gouverneur Ponty." *RMM* 31 (1915): 1–22.
Massignon, Louis. "Une bibliothèque saharienne: La bibliothèque du Cheikh Sidia au sahara." *RMM* 5 (1909): 409–18.
Matringe, Denis. "La litérature soufie." In Popovic and Veinstein, eds., *Les voies d'Allah*, 173–94.
Mauny, Raymond. *Tableau géographique de l'ouest africain au Moyen Age*. Dakar: IFAN, 1961.
Mbacké, Abdoul Ahad, ed. *Cheikh Amadou Bamba: Fondateur de la confrérie des Mourides*. 2 vols. Paris: Editions d'Art des Heures Claires, 1984.
——. *Majmuha*. Touba: A. A. Mbacké, 1985.
Mbacké, Amadou Bamba. *Assiiru Maha al Ibraari*. Translated into French and edited by Pape K. Seck. Dakar: Impression Édition Islamique, n.d.
——. *Huqqa al Bukau*. Rabat, 1984.
——. *Massalik Al-Jinan*. Rabat, 1984.
——. *Matlabul Fawzayni*. Dakar, n.d.
——. "Munawwiru s-Suduur" [The Enlightening of the Heart]. In *Recueil de poèmes en sciences religieuses de Cheikh A. Bamba*, translated by Serigne Sam Mbaye et al., vol. 2, 176 (Rabat: Dar El Kitab, 1989).
——. *Muqaddimaat ul Amdaa, Fii Mazzayaal Miftaah* [Les prémices des éloges sur les mérites de celui qui est la clef]. Dakar, n.d.
——. "Nahju Qadaahi al Haaj" [Path to Fulfillment of the Disciple's Needs]. In Mbaye et al., trans., *Recueil de poèmes en sciences religieuses de Cheikh A. Bamba*, vol. 2.
——. "Tazawudu Shubaani" [Viaticum for the Fulfillment of the Youth]. In Mbaye et al., trans., *Recueil de poèmes en sciences religieuses de Cheikh A. Bamba*, vol. 1.
——. "Tazawudu Sighaari" [Viaticum for Adolescents]. In Mbaye et al., trans., *Recueil de poèmes en sciences religieuses de Cheikh A. Bamba*, vol. 1.
Mbacké, Cheikh Bachir. *Les bienfaits de l'éternel, ou, la biographie de Cheikh Amadou Bamba Mbacké*. Translated and edited by Khadim Mbacké. Dakar, 1995.
Mbacké, Cheikhouna Abdou Wadoud, and Khadime Sylla. *Étude critique et analyse des écrits du professeur Rawane Mbaye sur le mouridisme et son fondateur*. Edition du Collectif des Mourides de France, 1999.

Mbacké, Khadim. *Soufisme et confréries religieuses au Sénégal*. Études Islamiques no. 4. Dakar, 1995.

——. *Sufism and Religious Brotherhoods in Senegal*. Translated by Eric Ross. Edited by John Hunwick. Princeton, NJ: Markus Wiener, 2005. Translation of *Soufisme et confréries religieuses au Sénégal*.

——. "La tariqua des mourides." *Africa* 53, no. 1 (1998): 102–20.

Mbaye, Rawane. "Physionomie actuelle de l'Islam au Sénégal, dénonciation des faux marabouts." *AL Qods* 30 (1992): 115–19.

Mbaye, Sam. "Tasawuuf wa Cheikh Amadou Bamba." In *Les grandes conferences islamiques de Serigne Sam Mbaye*, ed. Pape Sall, vol. 2. 1998.

Mbow, Serigne Babacar. *La voie Baye-Fall, Maam Cheikh Ibra Fall ou la lumière du dedans*. Geneva: privately printed, 2000.

McCall, Daniel F., Norman R. Bennett, and Jeffrey Butler, eds. *Western African History*. Boston University Papers on Africa 4. New York: Praeger, 1969.

McLaughlin, Fiona. "'In the Name of God I Will Sing Again, Mawdo Malick the Good': Popular Music and Senegalese Sufi Tariqas." *Journal of Religion in Africa* 30, no. 2 (2000): 191–207.

McNaughton, Patrick. *The Mande Blacksmiths: Knowledge, Power and Art in West Africa*. Bloomington: Indiana University Press, 1988.

Michel, Marc. *L'appel à l'Afrique: Contributions et réactions à l'effort de guerre en AOF, 1914–1919*. Paris: Sorbonne, 1982.

Miské, A. B. "Al Wasiit (1911) Tableau de la Mauritanie à la fin du dix-neuvième siècle." *BIFAN* ser. B, 30 (1968): 117–65.

Mollien, Gaspard. *L'Afrique Occidentale en 1818, vue par un explorateur français, Théodore Mollien*. Introduction by Hubert Deschamps. Paris: Calmann-Lévy, 1967.

Monteil, Vincent. "Al Bakri (Cordoue, 1068), routier de l'Afrique blanche et noire." *BIFAN* ser. B, 1 (1968): 39–116.

——. *Esquisses sénégalaises*. Initiations et Études Africaines 21. Dakar, 1966.

——. *L'Islam noir*. Paris: Le Seuil, 1980.

Mosto, A da. *Relation des voyages à la côte occidentale d'Afrique*. Published by Charles Schefer. Paris: E. Leroux, 1895.

Nasr, Seyyed Hossein. Foreword to *The Sense of Unity: The Sufi Tradition in Persian Architecture*, edited by Nader Ardalan and Laleh Bakhtiar. Chicago: University of Chicago Press, 1973.

Ndiaye, Leyti. "Le Djolof et Ses Bourbas." *BIFAN* ser. B, 28 (1966): 966–1008.

Nora, Pierre. *Les lieux de mémoire*. Vol. 1, *La République*. Paris: Gallimard, 1984.

Osterhammel, Jürgen. *Colonialism: A Theoretical Overview*. Princeton, NJ: Markus Wiener, 1999.

Ould Cheikh, Abdel Wedoud. "Les perles et le souffre: Une polémique mauritanienne autour de la Tijaniyya (1830–1935)." In *La Tijaniyya: Une Confrérie musulmane à la conquête de l'Afrique*, 125–63. Paris: Karthala, 2000.

Papadopoulos, Alexandre. *Islam and Muslim Art*. Translated by Robert Erich Wolf. New York: H. N. Abrams, 1976.
Pélissier, Paul. *Les paysans du Sénégal: Les civilisations agraires du Cayor à la Casamance*. Saint-Yrieix (Haute Vienne): Fabrègue, 1966.
Person, Yves. *Samori: Une révolution Dioula*. 3 vols. Paris: Presses universitaires de France, 1975.
Piga, Adriana. *Dakar et les ordres soufis*. Paris: Harmattan, 2002.
Popovic, Alexandre, and G. Veinstein, eds. *Les voies d'Allah*. Paris: Fayard, 1996.
Porcheron, Hélène. "Les *dahiras* mourides du marché Sandaga à Dakar." *Plein Sud* 2 (1992): 18–25.
Prussin, Labelle. *Hatumere: Islamic Design in West Africa*. Berkeley: University of California Press, 1986.
Quesnot, F. "Les cadres maraboutiques sénégalais." In *Notes et études sur l'Islam en Afrique*, edited by CHEAM, 127–95. Paris: Peyronet, 1962.
———. "Influences du mouridisme sur le tidjanisme." In *Notes et études sur l'Islam en afrique*, edited by CHEAM, 115–27.
Ranger, Terence. "Religious Movements and Politics in Sub-Saharan Africa." *African Studies Review* 29 (1986): 1–69.
Ricoeur, Paul. *Figuring the Sacred: Religion, Narrative, and Imagination*. Minneapolis, MN: Fortress Press, 1995.
Ritchie, Carson I. "Deux textes sur le Sénégal, 1673–1677." *BIFAN* ser. B, 30 (1968): 289–354.
Roberts, Allen, and Mary N. Roberts. "The Aura of Amadu Bamba." *Anthropologie et Sociétés* 22 (1998): 15–38.
———. *A Saint in the City: Sufi Arts of Urban Senegal*. Los Angeles: UCLA Fowler Museum of Natural History, 2003.
Roberts, Richard. "History and Memory: The Power of Statist Narratives." *IJAHS* 33 (2000): 513–33.
———. Review of *God Alone Is King*. *IJAHS* 35, no. 1 (2002): 222–24.
Robinson, David. *Chiefs and Clerics: Abdul Bokar Kan and Futa Toro, 1853–1891*. Oxford: Clarendon Press, 1975.
———. "Ethnography and Customary Law in Senegal." *CEA* 126 (1992): 185–221.
———. "France as a Muslim Power." *Africa Today* 46 (1999): 105–27.
———. "French 'Islamic' Policy and Practice in Late Nineteenth Century Senegal." *JAH* 29 (1988): 415–35.
———. *The Holy War of Umar Tal: The Western Sudan in the Mid-nineteenth Century*. Oxford: Clarendon Press, 1985.
———. "Islam, Cash Crops, and Emancipation." Review of *God Alone Is King*. *Journal of African History* 44 (2003): 139–44.
———. "The Islamic Revolution in Fuuta Tooro." *IJAHS* 8 (1975): 185–221.
———. "The Murids: Surveillance and Accommodation." *JAH* 40 (1999): 13–21.
———. *Paths of Accommodation: Muslim Societies and French Colonial Authorities in Senegal and Mauritania, 1880–1920*. Athens: Ohio University Press, 2000.

Robinson, David, and Jean-Louis Triaud, eds. *Le temps des Marabouts: Itinéraires et stratégies islamiques en Afrique Occidentale Française v.1880–1960.* Paris: Karthala, 1997.
Rochefort, Claude Jannequin de. *Voyage de Lybie au royaume de Sénéga, le Long du Niger.* Paris, 1643.
Rocheteau, Guy. *Société Wolof et mobilité.* Dakar: ORSTOM, 1973.
Roger, Baron Jacques François. *Kélédor, histoire africaine.* Paris, 1828.
Ross, Eric. "Marabout Republics Then and Now: Configuring Muslim Towns in Senegal." *Islam et Sociétés au Sud du Sahara* 16 (2002): 35–65.
———. *Sufi City: Urban Design and Archetypes in Touba.* Rochester, NY: Rochester University Press, 2006.
———. "Touba: A Spiritual Metropolis in the Modern World." *Canadian Journal of African Studies* 29 (1995): 222–59.
Rousseau, R. "Les cahiers de Yoro Dyâo: Études sur le Waalo." *BCEHSAOF* 1–2 (1929): 133–211.
———. "Études sur le Cayor." *BCEHSAOF* 16 (1933): 237–98.
———. "Le Sénégal d'autrefois: Étude sur le Toubé (Les papiers de Rawane Booy). *BCEHSAOF* 14 (1931): 334–64.
Saint-Martin, Yves. *L'empire toucouleur et la France.* Dakar, 1966.
Salem, Gérard. "De la brousse sénégalaise au Boul'Mich: Le système commercial mouride en France." *CEA* 21 (1981): 267–88.
Samb, Amar, ed. and trans. "La condamnation de la guerre sainte de Cheikh Moussa Kamara." *BIFAN* ser. B, 38, no. 1 (1976): 158–99.
———. *Essai sur la contribution du Sénégal à la littérature d'expression arabe.* Dakar: IFAN, 1972.
———. "L'Islam et l'histoire du Sénégal." *BIFAN* ser. B, 33 (1971): 461–507.
———. *Matraqué par le destin ou la vie d'un talibé.* Dakar: Nouvelles éditions africaines, 1973.
Sanchez, Claude. "Théologie mystique et action politique chez le réformateur allemand Martin Luther et le marabout sénégalais Cheikh Ahmadou Bamba." *Études Germano Africaines* 1 (1983): 46–56.
Sanneh, Lamine. *The Crown and the Turban.* Boulder, CO: Westview Press, 1997.
———. *The Jakhanke: The History of an Islamic Clerical People of the Senegambia.* London: International African Institute, 1979.
———. "The Origins of Clericanism in West African Islam." *JAH* 27 (1976): 49–72.
Schimmel, Anne Marie. *Mystical Dimensions of Islam.* Chapel Hill: University of North Carolina Press, 1975.
Schmitz, J. "Le souffle de la parenté: Mariage et transmission de la *baraka* chez les clercs musulmans de la vallée du fleuve Sénégal." *L'Homme* 154 (2000): 241–78.
———. "Un politologue chez les marabouts." *Cahiers d'Études Africaines* 91 vol. 23, 3 (1983): 329–51.
Scott, J. C. *Domination and the Arts of Resistance: Hidden Transcripts.* New Haven, CT: Yale University Press, 1990.

———. *Weapons of the Weak: Everyday Forms of Peasant Resistance*. New Haven, CT: Yale University Press, 1985.
Searing, James. "Conversion to Islam: Military Recruitment and Generational Conflict in a *Sereer*-Safèn Village (Bandia)' 1920–1938." *JAH* 44 (2003): 73–94.
———. *God Alone Is King*. Portsmouth, NH: Heinemann, 2001.
———. *West African Slavery and Atlantic Commerce: The Senegal River Valley, 1700–1860*. Cambridge: Cambridge University Press, 1993.
Sénégal, République du. *Calendrier historique de la région de Diourbel*. Prepared by the Minister of Economy and Finances of Senegal for the general census of 1988. Dakar: Direction de la prévision et des statistiques, 1988.
———. *Recensement de la population et de l'habitat 1988, Rapport National de Juin 1993*.
Senghor, L. S. *Liberté I*. Paris: Le Seuil, 1964.
Siré-Abbâs-Soh. *Chroniques du Foûta Sénégalais*. Edited by Maurice Delafosse. Paris: E. Leroux, 1913.
Stewart, Charles. "A Mauritanian Reformer: Shaikh Sidiyya Baba." *Tarikh* 7, no. 25 (1971): 65–70.
———. "Southern Saharan Scholarship and Bilad al Sudan." *JAH* 27 (1976): 73–93.
Stewart, Charles, and Elizabeth Stewart. *Islam and Social Order in Mauritania: A Case Study from the Nineteenth Century*. Oxford: Clarendon Press, 1973.
Sy, Cheikh Tidiane. "Ahmadou Bamba et l'Islamisation des Wolof." *BIFAN* ser. B, 32 (1970): 414–33.
———. *La confrérie sénégalaise des mourides*. Paris: Présence africaine, 1969.
Sy, Elhaj Malick. *Kifāyat ar-Rāghibīn* [Enough (Provisions) for the Aspirant]. Ms. Department of Islamology, Fonds Amar Samb. Dakar: IFAN, n.d.
Tal, Umar. *Kitab Rimah hizb al-Rahim*. Published in the margins of *Kitab Jawahir al-Ma'ani wa Bulugh al-Amani* [The Book of the Pearl of Meaning], by Ali Harazim. Cairo, 1927.
Tall, Cheikh A. *Niche des secrets: Recueils d'arcanes mystiques dans la tradition Soufie Islamique*. Dakar: Librairie islamique, 1995.
Tall, Madina Ly. *Un Islam militant en Afrique de l'Ouest au XIXe Siècle: La tijaniyya de Saiku Umar Futiyu contre les pouvoirs tradtionnels et la puissance coloniale*. Paris: Harmattan, 1991.
Tamari, Tal. *Les castes de l'Afrique Occidentale: Artisans et musiciens endogames*. Nanterre, France: Société d'Ethnologie, 1997.
Thilmans, Guy, and N. Isabel de Moraes. "Dencha Four, souverain du Bawol." *BIFAN* ser. B, 36 (1974): 691–714.
Tidjani. "Le mouritisme au sénégal." *Le petit Sénégalais*, 29 August 1912, 1.
Touré, Elhaj Malick. "Critiques socio-religieuses dans les ouvrages de Cheikh Elhaj Malick Sy et Cheikh Ahmadou Bamba Mbacké." *BIFAN* ser. B, 4 (1978): 887–97.
Traoré, Alioune. *Cheikh Hamahoullah, homme de foi et résistant: Islam et colonization en Afrique*. Paris: Maisonneuve et Larose, 1983.

Triaud, Jean L. "Islam in Africa under French Colonial Rule." In *The History of Islam in Africa*, edited by Nehemia Levtzion and Randall Pouwels, 169–89. Athens: Ohio University Press, 2000.

———. "*Khalwa* and the Career of Sainthood: An Interpretive Essay." In *Charisma and Brotherhood in African Islam*, edited by Donal B. Cruise O'Brien and Christian Coulon, 53–67. Oxford: Clarendon Press, 1988.

———. *La légende noire de la Sanûsiyya: Une confrérie musulmane saharienne sous le regard français, 1840–1930*. Paris: Editions de la Maison des sciences de l'homme, 1995.

———. "Le renversement du souverain injuste." *Annales ESC* 3 (1985): 509–19.

Triaud, Jean-Louis, and David Robinson, eds. *La Tijâniyya:Une confrérie musulmane à la conquête de l'Afrique*. Paris: Karthala, 2000.

Trimingham, John Spencer. *A History of Islam in West Africa*. London: Oxford University Press, 1962.

———. *The Sufi Orders in Islam*. Oxford: Clarendon Press, 1971.

Tuan, Yi-Fu. "Sacred Space: Exploration of an Idea." In *Dimensions of Human Geography: Essays on Some Familiar and Neglected Themes*, edited by Karl W. Butzer, 84–85. University of Chicago: Department of Geography, Research Paper 186, 1978.

Turner, Victor. *Dramas, Fields and Metaphors: Symbolic Action in Human Society*. Ithaca, NY: Cornell University Press, 1974.

———. *The Ritual Process: Structure and Anti-structure*. Chicago: Aldine, 1969.

Umar, Muhammad Sani. *Islam and Colonialism: Intellectual Responses of Muslims in Northern Nigeria to British Colonial Rule*. Leiden: E. J. Brill, 2005.

Van Hoven, Ed. "The Nation Turbaned: The Construction of Nationalist Muslim Identities in Senegal." *Journal of Religion in Africa* 30, no. 2 (2000): 225–48.

Vansina, Jan. *Oral Tradition as History*. Madison: University of Wisconsin Press, 1985.

Vilallòn, Leonardo. *Islamic Society and State Power in Senegal: Disciples and Citizens in Fatick*. Cambridge: Cambridge University Press, 1995.

———. "Sufi Rituals as Rallies: Religious Ceremonies in the Politics of Senegalese State-Society Relations." *Comparative Politics* 26 (July 1994): 415–37.

Villeneuve, Michelle. "Une société musulmane d'Afrique noire: La confrérie des mourides." *Institut des Belles Lettres Arabes* (Tunis) 110 (1965): 127–63.

Wade, Abdoulaye. *La doctrine économique du mouridisme*. Dakar: L'Interafricaine d'éditions, 1970.

Wade, Amadou. "Chroniques du Waalo Sénégalais." In Monteil, ed., *Esquisses Sénégalaises*, 13–71.

Ware, Rudolph T. III. "Njangaan: The Daily Regime of Qur'ânic Students in Twentieth Century Senegal." *International Journal of African Historical Studies* 3 (2004): 515–38.

Webb, James. *Desert Frontier*. Madison: University of Wisconsin Press, 1995.

Weber, Max. *The Theory of Social and Economic Organization*. Edited by Talcott Parsons. New York: Free Press, 1964.

Wehr, Hans. *A Dictionary of Modern Written Arabic*. 4th ed. Edited by J. M. Cowan. Ithaca, NY: Spoken Language Services, 1994.

White, Luise, Stephan Miescher, and David W. Cohen, eds. *African Words, African Voices: Critical Practices in Oral History*. Bloomington: Indiana University Press, 2001.

Willis, John Ralph, ed. *The Cultivators of Islam*. Studies in West African Islamic History 1. London: Frank Cass, 1979.

———. *In the Path of Allah: The Passion of Al-Hajj 'Umar*. London: Cass, 1989.

Zucarelli, François. "De la chefferie traditionnelle au canton: Évolution du canton colonial au Sénégal, 1855–1960." *Cahiers d'études africaines* 50 (1973): 213–38.

Index

Abderrahman al-Akhdari (al-Akhdari), 55; *Jawharu Nafiis* (versification by Bamba), 55
accommodation, 141–61, 181, 248n4
Addawwi, Rabia al-, 86
African colonial chiefs, 99; French-Bamba relations and role of, 238n3; French colonial administration and, 116–19; Muridiyya and, 116–17; wealth of, 119
Al-Hajj Mukhtar, 126
Allys, Victor, 132, 145
Almada, André de, 22
amal (labor/activities), 90–92, 178
André, P. J., 157
Angot, 73, 99, 224n91, 224n101
Arnaud, Robert, 48, 142, 157
arrest of Bamba, 248n125; and deportation, 115; of 1895, 75, 121–27, 164, 194; house, 93, 101, 114, 152–56, 160, 168, 181; motives behind, 123; of 1903, 145–47. *See also* internment, in Gabon
assets of Bamba, 200n50

Ba, Almaamy Maba Jakhu, 29, 41–42, 48, 122, 211n25, 211n29
Ba, Amadu Sheikhu, 29, 58–59, 122
Ba, Mamour Ndari, 227n10
Ba, Oumar, 125, 218n25
Ba, Saer Mati, 44, 227n10
Ba, Usmaan, 34–35, 208n6
Baakhum, Gora, 233n83
Baal, Cerno Barakatu, 208n4
baatin (the hidden), 13, 82, 100, 105
Baba, Sidiyya (Sheikh), 28, 44, 48, 74, 110, 113, 131, 132, 145, 147–48, 148, 151, 155, 156, 220n49, 221n53, 225n106; Bamba and, 61, 148–52; Bamba entrusted to, by French, 148; Bamba hosted by, 61; Bamba's exile to Mauritania and, 148–52; Bamba's leaving opposed by, 149–50; on blacks, 62
Bakri, Abu Abdallah al-, 21

Balla, Maam Sheikh, 2. *See also* Mbakke, Maam Balla (Sheikh)
baraka (spiritual power), 7–9, 61, 93, 179, 183; search for, as incentive for Murid migration, 169
Barry, Boubacar, 23, 24
Bawol: African chiefs of, and Murid expansion, 99; Bamba's demand of transfer to, 154–55, 158; Bamba's return to, 143, 162–63; Bamba's transfer to, 66–70, 158; daar al-kufr, 163–64; Faal, Lat Sukaabe, reform in, 21–24; Islam in, 21–24, 158; making Murid space in colonial, 162–74; Mbakke, Maaram, trip to, 38; Mbakke, Momar Anta Sali, dislike of, 214n52; Murid expansion in, 166–71; as sacred space, 162–63; Thiès separated from, 157. *See also* Daaru Salaam; Mbakke Bawol
beards, distinguishing Muslims from non-Muslims, 218n27
Behrman, Lucy, 118, 202n74
Bel, Alfred, 8
bepp tree, 72
Berber, Sanhaja, 72
Berbers, 8, 88
Bidaayat ul-Khidma (Initiation into Khidma) (Bamba), 90, 135
bidan, 149
Bidaya al-Hidaya (al-Ghazzali, al-Ghazali or Ghazali, Abu Hamid), 55
Bidaya al-Hidaya commentary (Bamba), 55
birthplace of Bamba, 215n2
black Islam, 157, 160, 177, 253n57
Boilat, D., 205n28
Bouche, Denis, 106
Boudrari, Hassan El, 71
Bourdieu, Pierre, 207n2
Bousso, Mbacké (Sheikh), 103, 122–23, 131, 146, 164, 200n50; Cor meeting with, 159
Brenner, Louis, 4–5
Brévié (Governor), 200n50

285

Broccard, Paul, 227n10
Brochier, J., 92
Bubu, Yasin (Princess), 204n12
Buh, Sad (Sheikh), 28, 156
Bulletin de la Société de Géographie de l'AOF, 142
Bulletin de l'Institut fondemantal d'Afrique Noire, 110
Buqahat al-Muburakati, al- (Blessed Spot). *See* Mubaraka, al-
Buso, Awa, 74, 75
Buso, Maam Jaara, 9, 34, 42, 43, 52
Buso, Muhammad, 52, 54, 61, 66, 67, 217n21
Bustaan ul Aarifiin (Garden of the Savant), 153

Calvinism, 91
Camara, Moussa (Cheikh), 252n54
capital, 207n2
Carpot, François, 132, 155
caste system, 100
ceddo (slave warriors), 26, 29–30, 47, 204n28. *See also* Sall, Demba Waar
celebrations instigated by Bamba, 166–67
Celemaan, Kumba, 237n127
Certeau, Michel de, 13
Ceyaasin, 117
Ceyeen, 152–56
Chambonneau, Jean Louis, 23
charisma, 197n36
Chaudié, E., 124, 125, 128, 142
childhood of Bamba, 52–54
children of Bamba, 57–58, 67, 189–90, 254n1
Christians, 4, 15; Bamba refers to French as, 60; Bamba's view of, 181–82; Muslim view of domination by, 173; Ricoeur on, 19; Sufi compared to, 14; treatment of, 155
Clément-Thomas, L. E., 120, 123
coercion, for colonial rule, 141
colonial archives, 116–19
"Colonial Caliphate" (Last), 163
Conseil Privé, 124, 125, 127
Cooper, Frederick, 182
Copans, Jean, 91, 261n5; *Les marabouts de l'arachide* (Marabouts of Peanuts), 3
Coppolani, Xavier, 88, 148, 151
Cor (lieutenant governor of Senegal), 159
Cornell, Vincent, 8
Coulon, Christian, 94, 177
Couty, Philippe, 91–92
Cruise O'Brien, Donal B., 3, 66, 94, 100, 108, 109, 231n64, 236n123
cults, 13–14
Curtin, Philip, 24

daara tarbiyya, 73, 81, 105–8
daar al-harb, 162

daar al-Islam (land of Islam), 161–65, 182; al-Mubaraka, transformation to, 166
daar al-kufr (land of unbelief), 163–68, 171, 173, 174, 182; Bawol, 163–64; Diourbel as example of, 164; Gabon as heart of, 164
daar al-Murid (Murid sacred space), 162–63, 171, 173, 174, 182
Daaru Halimul Khabiir, 73, 131
Daaru Khafoor, 169
Daaru Khudoos (House of the Most Holy), 73, 112, 153
Daaru Mannaan, 73, 109, 133
Daaru Muhti, 18, 169
Daaru Naar, 73
Daaru Rahman (House of the Merciful), 73, 153
Daaru Salaam (peace is best), 73, 109, 222n78; Bamba leaves, 75; Bamba leaves family in, 73; Bamba stops in, 164; daara tarbiyya and, 105–6, 130; development of, 66–67; founding of, 68–69; Mbakke, Anta (Sheikh), given, 70; naming of, 170
Dalail al Khayraat, 135
dammeel-teigne (title of king with dual crowns), 26
da Mosto, Alvise, 21
Daniel (biblical), 138
daughters of Bamba, 35, 189, 190; Momar Anta Sali Mbakke, abduction of, 42. *See also* Mbakke, Faati Jah
daughters of Sidiyya (Sheikh), 150
Daymaan, 152
Delavignette, Robert, 183
Delehaye, Hippolyte, 15
Dem, Ahmad, 89
Depont, Octave, 88, 148
Descemet, Louis J., 155
Des Isles, Paul Merles, 224n97
dhikr (remembrance of God's names), 6, 98, 107, 110
Diallo, Alpha Waly, 132
diet, of Bamba, 57
Din, Nasir al-, 23, 24, 204n14
Diop, Amadou Bamba, 109, 110, 213n48
Diop, Anta (Cheikh), 260n2
Diop, Mbakhane, 109, 119, 123, 147, 214n53, 236n125, 241n46; Bamba encounter with, 144; Bamba's brothers oppose, 119
Diop, Momar Coumba, 194n9
Diop, Muhammad Lamine, 12, 15, 61, 97, 103, 109, 133, 149, 150, 166, 217n16, 243n61, 250n21
Diourbel, 166; Bamba house request in, 160; Bamba relocation to, 158–63, 173; as daar al-kufr example, 164

286 ⇔ *Bibliography*

disciples of Bamba, 86, 90, 98–100, 100, 107, 221n56, 231n64; Bamba giving orders to, 70; growth of, 69; slaves and, 75. *See also* specific disciples
divine intervention, 136–39
doomi sokhna (son of honorable woman), 207n1
Dramé, Ahmadou, 61, 122
Dupré (Captain), 124

Eaton, Richard, 4, 5, 14
eclecticism, 232n71
education, 212n39, 228n20; of Bamba, 4–5, 52–54; Bamba's emphasis on, 4, 62–66, 79–85, 114, 176; exoteric, 81, 82, 178; hadiyya, 93–95; Islamic, 79, 216n6, 216n8; khidma, 90–92; of Maaram Mbakke, 36; Muridiyya philosophy of, 79–85; Quranic, 106; sheikh-disciple relationship, 86; student duties, 85; Malick Sy's emphasis on, 79–80; teacher choice, 82. *See also* tarbiyya
escale, 163
exile, 112, 128–29, 181, 243n67, 255n15; of Bamba by French colonial administration, 128–29, 139; of Bamba to Mauritania, 61, 143–46, 148–52; epic of, 136–39; rewards of suffering, 134–36

Faal, Amari Ngoone Ndeela (King), 37–39, 206n34, 206n37; Muslim clerics and, 26–28
Faal, Amary Ngoone Sobel, 22, 23, 25, 204n8, 213n48
Faal, Ceyaasin, 117, 124
Faal, Debbo Suka (Princess), 213n43
Faal, Ibra (Sheikh), 66, 98, 101, 102, 103, 105, 132, 151, 155, 165, 169, 221n58, 222n70, 223n88, 237n127, 258n40; Bamba's relationship with, 64–65, 103, 223n88; orders received by, 70
Faal, Ibrahima. *See* Faal, Ibra (Sheikh)
Faal, Lat Sukaabe (King), 21–26, 33, 205n21
Faal, Makodu, 41
Faidherbe, Louis, 27–28, 123, 180, 212n34
faith, 134–36
Fall, Salmon. *See* Mbakke, Ibra Faati
father of Bamba. *See* Mbakke, Momar Anta Sali
Fati, Muhammad, 56
fatwas (legal opinions), 55, 155
Federation of French West Africa, 125, 142, 241n47
Fernandes, Valentim, 21, 23
fiches de renseignements (intelligence files), 142
Fodio, Uthman dan, 5, 7
Four Communes, 88, 132

Four Rightly Guided Caliphs, 5
French colonial administration, 114, 179–80, 183; accommodation and, 141–61, 181, 248n4; African chiefs, Murids and, 116–19; Bamba fatwa and, 155–56; Bamba granted land by, 165; Bamba in closer proximity to, 159; Bamba misunderstood by, 143; Bamba's arrest and trial, 126–27, 146–48; Bamba's exile to Mauritania and, 143–46; on Bamba's move to Ceyeen, 152–56; Bamba praises, 155; Bamba's relations improving with, 147–48; Bamba's return to Bawol influences, 162–63; Bamba's return to Senegal and, 132–33, 151; Bamba's arrest as routine for, 134–36; Bamba's behavior misunderstood by, 127; Bamba's exile by, 128–29, 139; on Bamba's settlement in Sarsaara, 150; cohabitation of cultures and, 164; 1895 events, 121–26; on heroic narratives, 138; in Kajoor and Bawol, 22–24, 74–75; mosque building authorized by, 167–68; Murid conflicts with, 115–40; Muridiyya surveillance continuing, 157–58; Murid mixed feelings by, 159; Murid recruiting soldiers for, 254n67; Murid spatial autonomy concerns of, 168; Murid tension with, 99; Murid without Bamba, 129–32; policy changes of, 142–43, 249n8; Ponty's politics, 156–60; rapprochement with Murids, 141–74; schools of, in Murid space, 171; Sidiyya (Sheikh) trusted by, 148; tension with, 120–21; tighter control of Bamba organization by, 158; tribal unit reinstatement by, 156–57
French study policy, 172
front pionier Murid (Murid migration frontier), 170
fund-raising, 94

Gabon: Bamba's internment in, 16, 51, 64, 75, 96, 99, 110, 112, 115, 122, 124, 126–29, 132–47, 150–51, 164, 181, 225n110; as heart of daar al-kufr, 164
Gabriel (Archangel), 138
gaddaay (migration of Prophet Muhammad to Medina), 168, 257n37
Gay, Alioune, 225n106
Gay, Modu Jemooy (Sheikh), 89, 99, 221n56
geej, 25–28, 109–10, 213n43
Geet, 29, 120, 206n38
genealogy, of Bamba, 111
Geoffroy, Eric, 13
Gey, Adama, 64, 70, 101, 221n56
Gey, Maruba (Sheikh), 99, 118, 131
Ghazali, Abu Hamid. *See* Ghazzali, Abu Hamid al-

Bibliography ⌐ 287

Ghazzali, Abu Hamid al-, 59, 83; Bamba influenced by, 78, 220n47; *Bidaya al-Hidaya*, 55
gigis bamba, 56
good, and evil, 134
Goody, Jack, 10
Great Mosque of Tuubaa, 201n71
Guèye, Mor, 133
Guy, Camille, 250n25

hadiths, 127, 198
hadiyya (gift giving), 86, 93–95, 98, 114, 178, 179
hagiography, 12–13, 136; Bamba's life depicted by, 14–15; methodologies of, 14–19
hair-grooming, 218n27, 218n30
Hajj, Muhammad al-, 61
Hanson, John, 24
haram, 173, 260n65
Harrison, Christopher, 157
Hassan, Sheriful, 65, 105
heroic narratives, 136–39
hijra (migration of Prophet Muhammad to Medina), 168, 173
houses, of Bamba, 73
hubb (love), 85–90, 114
Huqqa al Bukau, 229n34

Ibn Anas, Imam Malik, 219n35
Ibn Atta Allah, 78
Ibn Hassan, Ahmed, 96
Ibn Khaldun, 78
Ibn Maslama Muhammad, 59
idleness, 92
ijaaza, 185
ilm es-Zahir (exoteric science), 82
imitatio Muhammadi model, 15
Institut pour la Recherche et le Développement (IRD), 91
internment of Bamba in Gabon, 16, 51, 64, 75, 96, 99, 110, 112, 115, 122, 124, 126–29, 132–47, 150–51, 164, 181
IRD. *See* Institut pour la Recherche et le Développement
Islam, 21–24; among Wolofs, 21–22, 28–31; architecture of, 171; in Bawol, 158; in Bengal, 4; education promoting, 79; mysticism of, and Bamba, 42, 228n20; mysticism of, in Africa, 5–9; Ponty's feelings on, 157, 158; science, 53–54; after sixteenth century, 21–22; slaves resisting, 26; surveillance of, 249n9; wives seclusion in, 167, 256n29. *See also* black Islam; Muridiyya; zakaat
Islam noir, 1, 193n3
Ismail, Abu Ibrahim, 71

Ja, al-Hajj Serigne, 98
Jaabi, Waar, 21
Jakhate, Absa, 46
Jakhate, Amsatu, 169, 221n56, 230n47, 233n84
Jakhate, Aymeeru, 210n14, 213n43
Jakhate, Khaali Majakhate Kala, 30, 42, 46, 58–59, 210n14, 211n21, 212n33, 215n3, 229n34, 249n11; Bamba taught poetry by, 54; Momar Anta Sali Mbakke, relationship with, 44
Jakhate, Mbay (Sheikh), 89, 90, 211n21, 215n3
Jakhate, Modu, 208n3, 211n21, 212n41, 215n3
Jakhate family, 37, 199n48
Jatara, Balla, 215n5
Jaw, Yoro, 203n1
Jawharu Nafiis (The Precious Jewels) (Bamba), 55, 217n16
Jazaau Shakuur (Tribute to the Worthy of Recognition) (Bamba), 126, 134, 135
Jazaau Shakuur (Tribute to the Worthy of Recognition) (Musa Ka), 137
Jazuli, Sulayman al-, 135
Jeandet, A., 125
jebelu (submission, allegiance), 86, 87, 93, 177, 229n33
Jeey, Moor Maam, 47
Jeng, Mayacine, 249n8
Jenn, Isa, 98, 102; Bamba on, 235n101; Bamba's relationship with, 103
jihad: Bamba's opposition to, 60; fatwa issued during, in Mauritania, 155; influencing Mbakke family, 41–42; of nafs, 5; pressure on Mbakke, Momar Anta Sali (father), 212–13n42; of the soul, 5, 122, 155
jihad al-akbar (greater jihad/jihad of the soul), 5, 122, 155
Jilani, Abd al-Qadir al- (Sheikh), 6, 44, 62
Johnson, Douglas, 215n4
Jolof, 21–22, 27, 29, 33–38, 41, 43, 52, 54, 69, 71, 121, 123, 130, 134, 153; Bamba and people of, 225n110; Bamba's move to, 74–76
Joob, Asta (princess), 213n43
Joob, Coro Maarooso, 44, 214n55
Joob, Faati, 43, 213n42
Joob, Fama, 237n127
Joob, Fatu Madu Maam, 74, 218n30
Joob, Ibrahim Makodu, 58–59
Joob, Ibra Massar, 89, 133
Joob, Isa, 46
Joob, Lat Joor, 29–31, 41, 48, 54, 56, 59, 77, 117, 119, 123, 144, 206n36, 211n27, 214n53, 217n6, 236n124, 237n127, 249n11; Bamba's relationship with, 108–10; conversion of, 213n48; defeat of, 69; Momar Anta Sali Mbakke's encounter with, 44–45; outcast, 46

Joob, Makhtar, 218n31
Joob, Massamba, 70, 99, 101
Joob, Mbakhane. *See* Diop, Mbakhane
Joob, Omar, 99
Joob, Sakhewar Fatma, 206nn37–38

Ka, Musa, 65–66, 80, 90, 136–37, 138, 238n3; *Jazaau Shakuur* (Tribute to the Worthy of Recognition), 137
Ka, Samba Tukuloor, 44, 54, 185–86, 213n45
kaaba (sacred shrine of Mecca), 171
Kabir, Sidiyya al- (Sheikh), 44, 61, 186, 213n44, 213n45
Kajoor: Bamba's departure from, 66–70, 199n49; Bamba's move to, 56; Bamba's relationship with court clerics of, 58–60, 63; Lat Sukaabe Faal's reforms in, 21–24; French colonial administration concern of, 74–75; Islam in, 21–24; Momar Anta Sali Mbakke in, 42–47
Kalabadhi, 198n40
Kamara, al-Hajj, 61
Kan, Almaamy Abdul Kader, 27, 37
Kan, Gammu, 43
karamas (miracles), 9, 14, 15, 136, 198n39, 215n4
Karim, Muhammad Ibn Muhammad al-, 54
kasb (earning/gain), 90–92, 178
Kebe, Njuga, 244n74
Ker Amadu Yala, 29, 30
Ker Gu Mag. *See* Mubaraka, al-
Khadim ar-Rasuul (Servant of the Prophet), 112
Khalifa, Sid Muhammad (Sheikh), 44
khanaqah (place for Sufi teaching), 5–6
Khatimaq-ul tasawwuf (al-Yadaali), 61
khidma (service), 86, 90–95, 114, 135, 178
Khuraish, Ahmed, 126
Khuru Mbakke, 43, 52, 169
Kunta, Bu, 28, 89
Kunta of Timbuktu, 7, 156
Kunti, Sidi Mokhtar al- (Sheikh), 44

Laam, Massamba, 99
Labat, Jean B., 23
Lamothe, H. de, 123–25
land granted to Bamba, 165
Lasselves, A., 166
Last, Murray, "Colonial Caliphate," 163
Latif, Abdul, 126
Laurens, R. du, 144, 145
lawaan ceremony, 227n12
Leclerc, M., 125, 134, 143, 148; on Bamba, 233n87; Bamba's arrest regretted by, 125; Bamba investigated by, 121; Bamba surrenders to, 126; ultimatum of, 130

letters of Bamba, 154, 217n19, 234n97, 237n131, 243n61
Ley, Mustafa, 215n5
life's goal of Bamba, 164
lineage of Bamba, 98–100
Lo, Ale, 56
Lo, Aminata, 216n13
Lo, Fara Biram, 226n113, 240n17; Njaay, Samba Laobe, and, 75
Lo, Ndaam Abdurahman (Sheikh), 73, 89, 103, 130–31, 221n56; Muslim village school of, 233n84
Lo, Sire, 133
Lo family village, 69
love, in Sufi, 85–90, 178
Luther, Martin, 100

madness, Bamba accused of, 60
maggal (annual pilgrimage), 1, 133, 167, 177, 194n5, 256n24
Majmuha (Bamba), 12, 91, 135, 223n88
Mal Aynin, 237n137
Mangin, Charles, 158
marabouts, 7–8, 94, 143, 205–6n28, 214n55
Marabouts de l'arachide, Les (Marabouts of Peanuts) (Copans), 3
marriages: of Bamba, 55, 74, 110; between kingly families and marabouts, 214n55; of Maaram Mbakke, 36; of Momar Anta Sali Mbakke, 214n55
Marty, Paul, 2, 7–8, 108, 109, 136–37, 193n2, 201n74, 202n74; Bamba depicted by, 217n24; black Islam and, 157; on blacks, 62; Muridiyya assessment of, 1, 17; on Murid sheikhs, 101–2; prejudice of, 220n52; Tuubaa described by, 73
Massalik Al-Jinan (Paths to Paradise) (Bamba), 9, 61, 62, 66–68, 76, 81, 83, 84, 90–91
materialism, 218n28
maternal lineages, 53
Matlab ul Fawzayn (Quest for Happiness in the Two Worlds) (Bamba), 72, 164
maturation of Bamba, 55–58
Mauritania: Bamba's exile to, 61, 143–46, 148–52; fatwa issued during jihad in, 155
Mauss, Marcell, 95
mbaar (sort of vestibule), 170, 258n47
Mbacké, Bachir, 12, 15, 16, 18, 41, 44, 52, 58, 61, 62, 64, 109, 127, 132, 217n6, 218n31, 219n42, 238n3; Bamba biography by, 13; on Murid/French relationship, 120
Mbacké, Khadim, 67, 131
Mbakke, Aafe, 217n16
Mbakke, Abdul Ahad, 12, 103, 152, 244n74
Mbakke, Abdul Khaadir, 40, 42

Mbakke, Ahmad Ndumbe (Sheikh), 101, 104, 130, 131, 169, 222n63, 258n40
Mbakke, Amadu Bamba, 242n51; *Abderrahman al-Akhdari al-Akhdari* versification, 55; allegiance to, 49; appearance of, 57; *Bidaayat ul-Khidma* (Initiation into Khidma), 90, 135; *Bidaya al-Hidaya* commentary, 55; on classification of people, 99; defining elements of life of, 50; *Jawharu Nafiis* (The Precious Jewels), 55, 217n16; *Jazaau Shakuur* (Tribute to the Worthy of Recognition), 126, 134, 135; on lower self, 84; *Majmuha*, 12, 91, 135, 223n88; *Massalik Al-Jinan* (Paths to Paradise), 9, 61, 62, 66, 67, 68, 76, 81, 83, 84, 90–91; *Matlab ul Fawzayn* (Quest for Happiness in the Two Worlds), 72, 164; *Mullayinu Suduur* (The Enlightener of the Heart), 55; *Munawir Es Sudur* (The Enlightening of the Heart), 81; *Muqaddimaa ul Amda*, 135; *Muqadimaat ul Khidma* prelude to khidma, 90, 135; *Muwayibul Quduuss* (Gift from the Holiest), 55; *Nahju*, 61, 85, 99; prestige, rise of, 74; prestigious families, ties with, 54; *Should They Be Mourned?* 85–86; *Silsilat ul Qadiriyya*, 61; *Silsilat ul Qadiriyya* transmitters, 191–92; *Tazawudu Shubaani*, 78, 84; *A Viaticum for the Children*, 56. *See also specific topics*
Mbakke, Amadu Farimata, 38, 210n18
Mbakke, Anta Njaay, 43, 213n42
Mbakke, Anta (Sheikh), 17, 44, 49, 68, 95, 98, 102, 130, 131, 132, 144, 146, 165, 200n50, 213n42, 221n56, 253n65; cane given by Bamba, 220n45; Gora Baakhum and, 233n83; orders received by, 70; sheikhs of, 101
Mbakke, Astu, 43
Mbakke, Baara, 130
Mbakke, Balla Aysa, 39–40, 42, 44, 209n12, 210n18, 211n25; Mbakke family, conflict with, 211n21
Mbakke, Caliph Saliu. *See* Mbakke, Saliu (Sheikh)
Mbakke, Coro (Sheikh), 44, 48, 133, 151, 159, 211n25, 217n16; Maba Jakhu Ba and, 211n25
Mbakke, Dame Seynabu, 214n51
Mbakke, Faati, 42
Mbakke, Faati Jah, 55, 66; Mbakke, Falilu, 48, 58, 69, 200n50
Mbakke, Ibra Awa Niang, 39, 199n46, 211n21. *See also* Mbakke, Awa Niang
Mbakke, Ibra Faati, 18, 49, 98, 104, 107, 123, 130, 131, 133, 146, 165, 210n14, 213n42, 218n30, 221n56, 241n46; Bamba and, 235n106; Cor, meeting with, 159; sheikhs of, 101

Mbakke, Ibra Nguy, 130
Mbakke, Isa, 199n46, 200n49, 208n3, 209n11, 211n21
Mbakke, Maam Balla (Sheikh), 2, 47, 48, 208n3, 208n5
Mbakke, Maam Cerno. *See* Mbakke, Ibra Faati
Mbakke, Maaram, 27, 33, 34, 43; Bawol trip of, 38; marriages of, 36; social status of, 36–37; sons and daughters of, 35
Mbakke, Mamadu Mustafa, 67, 69, 105, 172, 200n50, 218n31, 222n74, 237n127
Mbakke, Mati, 210n14
Mbakke, Maymuna Kabiir, 150
Mbakke, Modu Jee, 40, 211n21
Mbakke, Modu Maamun (Sheikh), 95
Mbakke, Momar Anta Sali (father of Bamba), 30, 40, 49, 52, 56, 59, 117, 185, 186, 210n18, 212n38, 215n2; Bamba, conversation with, 48–50; Bamba criticizes, 45; Bamba influenced by death of, 47–49, 60–62; Bamba reverses journey of, 66; Bamba teaches with, 46; Bawol, dislikes, 214n52; daughter's abduction, 42; death of, 47–49; jihad pressure on, 212–13n42; Coro Maarooso Joob, marriage to, 214n55; Lat Joor Joob, encounter with, 44–45; Mbakke Bawol, return of, 43; Pataar, move to, 45; reputation of, 44; in Saalum and Kajoor, 42–47; sons of, and their mothers, 46
Mbakke, Momar Jaara, 49, 66, 67, 130, 146, 153, 222n74, 233n88
Mbakke, Mor Talla, 105, 258n40
Mbakke, Mustafa Njaate, 206n33, 208n3, 210n15
Mbakke, Saliu (Sheikh), 199n47, 224n98, 231n61
Mbakke, Samba Caam, 214n5
Mbakke, Serigne Bachir Anta Niang, 229n38
Mbakke, Serigne Mustafa Beto, 233n88, 252n45; Mbakke, Sokhna Awa Niang, 210n14
Mbakke Bawol, 16, 36, 38–45, 52, 66–69, 80, 130, 137, 146, 153, 169, 171, 173, 199
Mbakke family, 33–50; Balla Aysa, conflict with, 211n21; Bamba absence influences, 131; Bamba and marriage to women of, 222n79; Bamba opposed by, 10–11, 67; Bamba's tensions with, 67, 68; from Fuuta to Jolof, 34–39; Jakhate family and, 38; jihad influences, 41–42; Muridiyya, criticism by, 99; purpose guiding, 33–34; rulers dealings with, 164; Saalum, migration of, 41–42; Sy family and, 37; traditions of, 33–50 *See also specific family members*

Mbay, Amadu Makhtaar, 221n56, 222n63
Mbay, Galo, 104
Mbay, Ibra, 222n79
Mbay, Makhuja Uma, 221n56
Mbay, Samba Jaara, 90
Mbay, Sawru, 208n4, 209n13, 211n21
Mbaye, Rawane, 81
Mbay family, 199n48
Mbegere, Mahmud, 100–101
memory, 116, 216n7
Merlin, Martial, 125, 142, 143; Allys letter to, 132, 145; on Bamba, 233n87; Bamba arrest ordered by, 147, 247n122; Bamba granted clemency by, 147–48; Bamba, relationship with, 121–22; Bamba's exile to Mauritania and, 149; Murids' growing power resented by, 125
millet, 107, 170
Ministry of Colonies, 142
Ministry of Navy, 142
miracles, 9, 14, 15, 136, 198n39; of Bamba, 14, 15, 215n4
Miska, Muhammad, 237n133
Monteil, Vincent, 109
Moorish ulamas, 150
mosques, 68
mothers of Bamba's children, 189–90. *See also specific names*
Mouttet, M., 124, 241n41
Mubaraka, al-, 165–68, 169
Muhammad (Prophet), 215n59, 219n43, 221n58, 237n136; Bamba chooses as guide, 111–12; Bamba depicted as replicating life of, 15; Bamba guided by, 152, 155, 166; Bamba's genealogy and, 189, 237n133; Bamba relates to, 134; Bamba's life modeled after, 166; Bamba's mystical encounter with, 112; Bamba studies, 53; Bamba writes on behalf of, 135; baraka and, 8; descent from, 111; deviation from path of, 176; kaaba as model for house of, 171; law of, 82; Medina, migration to, 72, 176; praise-poems to, 92; Qadiriyya wird from, 61–62, 96; Sufism and rule of, 5–6, 68; traditions of, 86, 90; war forbidden by, 128. *See also* hadiths; hijra
Muhammad, Sidi, 213n45
Mukhtaar (Sheikh), 186
Mulaay, Sherif, 131
Mullayinu Suduur (The Enlightener of the Heart) (Bamba), 55
Munawir Es Sudur (The Enlightening of the Heart) (Bamba), 81
Muqaddimaat ul Kidma prelude (Bamba), 90, 135
Muqaddimaa ul Amda (Bamba), 135

Muridiyya, 153, 223n83; African colonial chiefs and, 116–17; as African socialism, 260n2; autonomy, quest for, 164; Bamba brings to Bawol, 166–67; Bamba's return to Bawol influences, 143, 162–63; Bamba's revival of, 133; census of, 193n4; daara tarbiyya, 105–8; disciples of, 98–100; doctrines and practices of, 85–95; duties of student, 85; education philosophy of, 79–85; food of, 107–8; founding of, 108–13, 232n74; hadiyya, 93–95; hagiography and, 12–14; hubb (love), 85–90, 114; Joob, Lat Joor, death correlated with, 108; khidma, 90–92; literature of, 2–3; Marty's assessment of, 1; organization of, 95–108; Ponty's politics and, 156–60; relevance of, 2; religious dimension of, 3; salafists' influence on, 48; in Senegal, 143; sheikhs of, 100–104, 114, 203n47; sheikh taalim and, 82–83; sheikh tarbiyya and, 83–84; sheikh tarqiyya and, 84–85; surveillance of, 157–58; turning points of, 111; wird, 95–98; work of, 90–91
Murid, tariqas, 10, 47, 93–94, 110–14, 116, 152, 160, 172–80, 182
Murids, 158, 254n67; accommodation and, 141–61, 181, 248n4; African chiefs, disagreement with, 117–18; African chiefs, French colonial administration and, 116–19; of aristocratic origin, 89–90; without Bamba, 129–32; Bamba's exile influencing, 136–40; Bamba's return to Senegal and, 132–33; on Diourbel confinement, 163–64; Eastern Bawol expansion of, 168–71; French colonial administration, conflicts with, 115–40; French colonial administration, mixed feelings of, 159; French colonial administration, rapprochement with, 141–74; French colonial administration, soldiers recruited by, 254n67; French colonial administration, tension with, 99; lineage of sheikhs, 11–12; Merlin resents power growth of, 125; migration frontier of, 170; mysticism of, 236n114; naming of villages of, 170; Ibrahima Njaay and, 117; oral sources, 14–16; oral tradition and history of, 9–12; political function of, 3; Ponty supporting peaceful relations with, 158; sheikh prestige, 94–95; sheikhs in Njambur, 131; socialism, 260n2; space and architecture of, 171; spatial autonomy of, 167–68; submission of, 87; subversion of Wolof power structures, 118; Tuubaa and, 71; written sources of, 16–19
Murid saadikh (genuine Murid), 90
Muslim Affairs Service, 142, 157
Muslim Brotherhood, 194n7

Bibliography ↩ 291

Muslims, 233n84; Bamba on enslaving, 59; clerics and politics, 22–24, 26–28; as single race, 157. See also tariqas
Muwayibul Quduuss (Gift from the Holiest) (Bamba), 55
mysticism, 53, 78; in Africa, 5–9; of Bamba, 42, 88–89, 228n20; Murid, 236n114; of square, 171. See also tariqas

nafs (animal instincts), 83, 134, 228n26
Nahju (Bamba), 61, 85, 99
Nasr, Seyyed H., 171
ndigel (recommendations), 86, 256n24
Ndumbe, Ahmad (Sheikh), 236n115
Nekkache, Lucien, 101–2
New York Times, 1, 194n6
Niakhit, Abdulaay, 100
Niang, Afia, 213n45, 244n74
Niang, Awa, 209n11
Niang, Mafinty, 209n7
Niang, Modu Maamun, 212n33, 220n44
Niang, Oumar, 145
Niang family, 199n48
Niass, Abdulaay, 28, 79, 89, 227n10
Niass, Ibrahima, 36, 251n21
Njaay, Albury, 219n42
Njaay, Amadu Maabeey, 138
Njaay, Buna, 153
Njaay, Daaru Asan, 221n63
Njaay, Ibrahima, 116–17, 118, 239n13
Njaay, Samba Laobe, 225n110, 226n113; Bamba tension with, 75; Fara Biram Lo and, 75
Njaay family village, 69
Nora, Pierre, 12, 116, 139

obedience, 78
Omar (second caliph of Islam), 221n58
oral tradition, 9–14, 242n56
Oral Tradition (Vansina), 10
Organisation pour la Recherche Scientifique et Technique Outre-Mer (ORSTOM), 91
ORSTOM. See Organisation pour la Recherche Scientifique et Technique Outre-Mer
Ottoman Empire, 157, 257n32
Ould Sheikh, Abdel Wedoud, 113

paintings, of Bamba, 132–33
paternal lineages, 53
peanut cultivation, 3, 30, 69, 107, 124, 156, 169–70, 180, 234n99, 239n14, 261n5
Péllissier, Paul, 91–92, 124
personality of Bamba, 57
Petit Sénégalais (newspaper), 159
Peuvergne (Lieutenant Governor), 253n65
Piga, Adriana, 201n74

politics: of Bamba, 30; of Murids, 3; Muslim clerics and, 22–24, 26–28; of Ponty, 156–60
politique des races, la (race-based policy), 156, 157
Ponty, William, 1, 180, 202n74, 252n55, 253n63; conciliation policy supported by, 159; Islam, feelings toward, 157; Islamic proselytism, reports on, 158; peaceful relations with Murids supported by, 158; politics of, 156–60; Roume compared to, 156
portrait of Bamba, 217n24
power. See also baraka; rapport de force; Bamba's, growth of, 145; Murid, 125; mystical, 171; struggle of Bamba, 75; Wolof, 118

Qadiriyya, 6, 44, 54, 61, 62, 78, 89, 96, 100, 101, 122; Bamba's initiation, 220n49; Bamba's third initiation, 61; eclecticism in, 232n71
Qadiriyya wird, 95–96; Bamba embraces, 95–96; transmitters of, 191–92
qibla (direction to face for prayer), 171
Quran, Bamba studies, 52–53. See also wird

Rachid, Harun Al, 219n35
Ranger, Terrence, 4
rapport de force (power relations), 141
rapprochement: Cor's letter of, 159; French colonial administration with Murids, 141–74; Ponty's politics and, 156–60
Revealed Book, 96
ribat, 107
Ricoeur, Paul, 19
Roberts, Allen, 218n25, 247n119
Roberts, Mary, 218n25, 247n119
Roberts, Richard, 18
Robinson, David, 17, 18, 125, 142, 221n53, 240n29
Ross, Eric, 109, 164
Roume, Ernest, 142, 148, 156, 180, 249n9; Bamba letter to, 146; Bamba's exile to Mauritania and, 143–46

Saalum: Bamba's move to, 52–53; Mbakke family's move to, 41–42; Momar Anta Sali Mbakke in, 42–47
Saar, Ibra (Sheikh), 99, 101, 131, 221n56; expulsion of followers from Kajoor and Njambur, 74; Muslim village school of, 233n84; orders received by, 70
Saar, Ibra Fatim, 30
Saar, Malaamin, 36, 37, 206n34; killing of, 27
Saar, Muhammad, 220n49
Saar, Njamme, 66
Saaw, Moor, 222n70
sacred space, 162–63, 174, 182

sainthood, 7–8, 12–13, 90; of Bamba, 9–10, 11, 88, 89. *See also* wilaaya
salafists, 48
Saliu, Caliph, 224n98
Sall, Adama, 43, 221n56
Sall, Demba Waar, 30, 31, 69, 117, 238n7, 249n8
Sall, Meissa Mbay, 249n8
Sall, Njaay, 204n12
Samb, Ibra, 98
Sanchez, Claude, 100
Sanneh, Lamin, 164
Sanusi, al-, *Umul Barahim*, 55
Sarsaara school founding, 149
Schimmel, Annemarie, 15, 221n61
Schmitz, Jean, 22, 208n5
School for the Sons of Chiefs, 123
Scott, James, 136
Searing, James, 17–18, 19, 26, 31
Seck, Dudu, 221n53
seclusion, 78
Seen, Ahmed Khuri. *See* Khuraish, Ahmed
Senegal, Bamba's return to, 112, 132–33, 246n109
Senegalese social contract, 204n9
Senegalo-Mauritanian Zone, 156
Senghor, L. S., 26on2
sentencing of Bamba, 124, 147, 242n56
Sereer dynasty, 22, 158, 163, 165
serigne fakk taal, 25–26
service, 86, 90–95, 114, 135, 178
Service of Muslim Affairs, 142, 157
seven, symbolism of, 245n105
Shadili, Abul Hassan Al, 6, 22, 209n7
Shadiliyya, 6
sharia, 78, 166
Sharifan genealogy mother's side, 187–88
Sheikh al-Turuuq (title of), 234n92
sheikhs: of Bamba, 100–104; Bamba invites, 230n47; commissioning stopped by Bamba, 234n94; of Muridiyya, 100–104, 203n47; Murid prestige of, 94–95; in Njambur, 131; Sufi ideology regarding, 143; tariqas and, 100; wealth of, 119. *See also specific sheikhs*
sheikh taalim, 82–83
sheikh tarbiyya, 83–84
sheikh tarqiyya, 84–85
Should They Be Mourned? (Bamba), 85–86
Siddiyya Baba (Sheikh). *See* Baba, Sidiyya (Sheikh)
Sill, Mandumbe Mar, 59
Silla, Khadime, 61
Silla, Maniaaw, 64, 221n57
Silsila (saintly lineages, chain of transmission of wird), 6

Silsilat ul Qadiriyya (Bamba), 61
Silsilat ul Qadiriyya transmitters (Bamba), 191–92
siraat al-mustaqiim (straight path), 171
slavery, 69, 118; African chiefs and, 116; Bamba and, 176, 205n19, 205n21, 205n28, 239n14, 249n11; Faati Mbakke abducted by slave raiders, 42; rulers and, 23. *See also* ceddo
slaves: classes of, 22; disputes over, 58; Islam resisted by, 26; Abdul Khaadir Mbakke killed by, 40; Muslim, 58–59; newly freed, 88; resistance of, 28; Demba Waar Sall leads, 30–31
social capital, 207n2
space, 165, 259n50, 259n53. *See also* sacred space
spies, in Bamba compound, 145–46, 239n16
spiritual quest, 60–62
square, mystical power of, 171
storytelling, 136
suffering, 134–36; Bamba on rewards of, 134–36
The Sufi Orders in Islam (Trimingham), 5
Sufism, 176–77; in Africa, 5–9; of Bamba, 56, 77–79; Bamba's conception of, 56, 77–79; development of institutional, 68; on God entering heart of human, 83–84; love in, 85–90, 178; Muridiyya, founding of, 77–114; nafs controlled by, 228n26; ribat resembling daara tarbiyya, 107; on sheikhs and unjust rulers, 143; tarbiyya of, 62–66
Surang, Masurang, 90, 227n48
Sy, Al-Hajj Maalik, 7, 28, 89, 197n31, 210n14, 217n21, 227n10, 228n20; education, emphasis on, 79–80; father of, 227n10
Sy, Demba Bunna, 210n14
Sy, Elhaj Malick. *See* Sy, Al-Hajj Maalik
Sy, Habib, 208n3
Sy, Malick. *See* Sy, Al-Hajj Maalik
Sy, Mapenda, 217n21
Sy, Matar, 222n65
Sy, Tidiane (Sheikh), 48, 61, 108, 109, 210n15, 235n111
Sy, Usmaan, 210n1
Sy family, 37, 69
Sylla, Abdu Samat, 200n59
Sylla, Al-Hajj, 199n49
Sylla, Majemb, 103
Sylla, Maniaaw, 14, 133
Sylla family, 199n48
Syll family, 199n484

taalibe taakh (urban disciples), 90
taalim (exoteric, classical education), 81, 82, 178. *See also* sheikh taalim
taifa, of Sufism, 5–6, 65

Bibliography ⸺ 293

Tal, Al-Hajj Umar, 5, 7, 71, 122
tarbiyya (esoteric education, education of soul), 73, 74; of Bamba, 62–66, 81–82, 102, 149; centers of, 70–77; Islamic values instilled by, 5; Muridiyya and, 177, 178; requirements of, 104; sheikh, 83–84; as vocation, 62–66
tariqas (Muslim mystical orders), 116, 194n7; of Bamba, 14, 51, 77, 86–89, 92, 124, 129, 137, 143, 150, 162; Bamba's separation from, 97–98; daara tarbiyya's role in, 105; founding of, 111; history of, 10; Murid, 10, 47, 93–94, 110–14, 116, 152, 160, 172–80, 182; Muridiyya founding and, 91–95, 98; organization of, 2–7; Qadiriyya, 44, 78; of Senegal, 16–18; sheikhs and, 100; studying, 16–18; wird and, 95. *See also* daara tarbiyya
tarqiyya, 81–85, 178
tasawwuf, 68, 78
Tautain, 224n91; Bamba's report on, 73
tawhid (science of oneness of God), 78
Tazawudu Shubaani (Bamba), 78, 84
teaching methods, 67
Théveniaut, Jean Baptiste, 151, 157–58, 159
Thiès, 157
Tijani, Muhammad al-, 6
Tijani/Tijaniyya, 6, 7, 36, 88, 89, 96, 97, 122, 147; Bamba accused of practicing, 122
tobacco, 42
Tooroodo Revolution, 27
tortures, 138, 247n117
Toubenan movement, 23
trial of Bamba, 241n41
Triaud, J. L., 119, 157
Trimingham, J. S., 6, 65; on hagiography, 13; *The Sufi Orders in Islam*, 5
truth, 212n33
Ture, Matar, 221n56
Turner, Victor, 19
Tustari, Sahl al-, 7, 86
Tuubaa, 164, 167, 201n71, 231n62, 260n64; founding and settling of, 70–74; naming of, 72
two-rakaas (genuflection) prayer, 127, 242n52

ulamas (learned men), 150
Umarian movement, 24
Umul Barahim (al-Sanusi), 55
unjust rulers, 143
Uthman, Mustafa, 96, 233n80

Valière, François X., 29, 30
Vansina, Jan, *Oral Tradition*, 10
Viaticum for the Children, A (Bamba), 56
Vienne, 145
Villalón, Leonardo, 87, 94

Wade, Abdoulaye, 91
wagni (to count), 227n12
wali Allah (friend of God), 5, 71, 112, 140, 181
war opposition, 145–46, 156
wealth, of Bamba, 91
Webb, James, 24
Weber, Max, 91
wilaaya (sainthood), 7–8, 9, 11, 12–13, 88, 89, 90
wird, 95–98. *See also* Qadiriyya wird
wives, of Bamba, 57–58, 130, 256n29. *See also* specific names
Wolofs, 20–32, 56, 116, 212n37; Bamba critical of, 212n37; Bamba resented by, 56; conduct of, 59; Islam and Lat Joor Joob, 28–31; Islamic presence among, 21–22; Lat Sukaabe reform in, 24–26; Murid subversion to power structures of, 118; Muslim clerics and Amari Ngoone Ndeela, 26–28; naming of children, 222n74; naming of villages, 170; non-Murid villages of, 258n46; Demba Waar Sall as chief, 117
writings of Bamba, 3, 55, 135–36, 250n21. *See also* letters of Bamba; *specific works*
Wyschogrod, Edith, 13

Yadaali, Muhammad al-, 54, 61, 78. *See also* al-Karim, Muhammad Ibn Muhammad
Yaqub, Muhammad b. Ali, 250n21
Yoro (Lieutenant), 243n61

zakaat (Islamic income tax), 39, 60, 219n43
zawiya (lodge), 44, 48, 178